Pain and Prosperity

Reconsidering Twentieth-Century
German History

EDITED BY PAUL BETTS

AND GREG EGHIGIAN

Stanford University Press, Stanford, California 2003

Stanford University Press
Stanford, California

© 2003 by the Board of Trustees of the
Leland Stanford Junior University.
All rights reserved.

Printed in the United States of America
on acid-free, archival-quality paper

Library of Congress Cataloging-in-Publication Data
Pain and prosperity : reconsidering twentieth-century German history/
edited by Paul Betts and Greg Eghigian.
    p. cm.
Includes bibliographical references and index.
  ISBN 0-8047-3937-4 (alk. paper) —
  ISBN 0-8047-3938-2 (pbk. : alk. paper)
    1. Germany—History—20th century. 2. Germany—History—
Philosophy. 3. Political culture—Germany. 4. National socialism—Moral
and ethical aspects. 5. Germany (East)—Social conditions. I. Betts, Paul.
II. Eghigian, Greg.
  DD232 .P34 2003
  943.087—dc21   2002012265

Original Printing 2003
Last figure below indicates year of this printing:

12 11 10 09 08 07 06 05 04 03

Designed by Eleanor Mennick
Typeset by Alan Noyes in 10/12 Sabon

Contents

Contributors

PAUL BETTS is lecturer in German history at the University of Sussex in Brighton, England. He is the author of *The Pathos of Everyday Objects: A Cultural History of West German Industrial Design, 1945–1965* (Berkeley: University of California Press, 2003) as well as several articles on West and East German modernism, including most recently "The Twilight of the Idols: East German Memory and Material Culture," *Journal of Modern History* (September 2000). He is currently working on a history of East German material culture.

GREG EGHIGIAN is associate professor of Modern European history at Penn State University. He is the author of *Making Security Social: Insurance, Disability, and the Birth of the Social Entitlement State in Germany* (University of Michigan Press, 2000) and coeditor with Matthew Berg of *Sacrifice and National Belonging in Twentieth-Century Germany* (Texas A&M University Press, 2002). He is presently working on a cultural history of forensic psychology in East and West Germany.

SABINE BEHRENBECK is currently program director of the Deutsche Forschungsgemeinschaft in Bonn, which serves as Germany's main granting agency for scholarly research. She is the author of *Der Kult um die toten Helden: Nationalsozialistische Mythen, Riten und Symbole 1923 bis 1945* (Vierow: SH-Verlag, 1996) and coeditor of *Inszenierungen des Nationalstaats: Politische Feier in Italien und Deutschland seit 1860/71* (Cologne: SH-Verlag, 2000). She has written numerous articles on twentieth-century political iconography, the culture of memory, and the history of mentalities. Among her most recent are "Heil," in *Deutsche Erinnerungsorte*, ed. Etienne François and Hagen Schulze (C. H.. Beck Verlag, 2001); "Versailles and Vietnam: Coming to Terms with War," in *America's War and the World: Vietnam in International and Comparative Perspectives*, ed. Andreas Daum and Wilfried Mausbach (Cambridge: Cambridge University Press, 2001); and "Between Pain and Silence: Remembering the Victims of Violence in East and West Germany after 1949," in *Violence and Normality: Approaches to a Cultural and Social History of Europe during the 1940s and 1950s*, ed. Richard Bessel and Dirk Schumann (Cambridge: Cambridge University Press, 2001).

GEOFFREY COCKS is Royal G. Hall Professor of History at Albion College in Michigan. He is the author of *Psychotherapy in the Third Reich: The Goering Institute* (Oxford University Press, 1985; Transaction, 1997) and *Treating Mind and Body: Essays in the History of Science, Professions, and Society Under Extreme Conditions* (Transaction, 1998). He is presently working on two books, *The Wolf at the Door: Stanley Kubrick and the Holocaust* and *Sick Heil: A Social History of Illness in Nazi Germany*.

PETER FRITZSCHE is professor of history at the University of Illinois at Urbana-Champaign. He is the author of numerous books, including *Reading Berlin 1900* (Harvard University Press, 1996) and *Germans into Nazis* (Harvard University Press, 1998). A Guggenheim fellow, he is currently completing a study of nostalgia in nineteenth-century Europe.

KATHERINE PENCE is assistant professor of European history at Baruch College, City College of New York. She is the author of several articles on gender and consumer culture in postwar East and West Germany and is currently revising her book manuscript, *From Rations to Fashions: The Gendered Politics of East and West German Consumption, 1945–1961*.

INGRID M. SCHENK is an independent scholar and freelance writer based out of Atlanta, Georgia. She received a Ph.D. from the University of Pennsylvania in 1996 for a dissertation entitled "From Calories to Kidney-Shaped Tables: Consumerism and the Constitution of West German National Identity, 1945–1965." Among her current projects is an examination of the impact of Joint Export Import Agency initiatives on manufacturing and agriculture in the southeastern United States and West Germany during the late 1940s and early 1950s.

PATRICIA R. STOKES is completing her dissertation, entitled "Contested Conceptions: Experiences of Pregnancy and Childbirth in Germany, 1913–1933," at Cornell University. She is the author of the 1998 Social History of Medicine prize essay, "Pathology, Danger, and Power: Women's and Physicians' Views of Pregnancy and Childbirth in Weimar Germany," *Social History of Medicine* 13 (December 2000): 359–80.

PAIN AND PROSPERITY

Introduction: Pain and Prosperity
in Twentieth-Century Germany

UPON German president Richard von Weizsäcker's visit to Prague several months after the fall of the Berlin Wall, Czech president Vaclav Havel gave a speech in which he sought to make sense of a Germany in the process of reunification. Like many observers at the time, Havel found himself unable and unwilling to divert his attention away from Germany's nefarious recent past. At the same time, however, he was drawn to the promise of a new Germany, one that potentially had the power to bridge the gulfs separating Western and Eastern Europe, as well as a violent past and peaceable future:

I have spoken of the historic duties facing Germany today. I should also say what we should do. Here too after all that has happened there is still much fear of Germans and a big Germany. People are still alive who have experienced the war, lost loved ones, suffered in concentration camps, and hidden from the Gestapo. Their suspicion is understandable, and it is natural that others share it. From this comes our task of overcoming this fear. . . . Suffering obliges us to be just, not unjust. Those who have really suffered usually know this. In addition forgiveness—and with it one's own freedom from anger—can only come from justice. Today seems to be important for another reason. I do not know whether in the future multipolar world Germany will be called a great power or not. But she has long been a potential great power: as a pillar of European spirituality that, if she wishes, can help us all to defy the dangerous pressure of technological civilization with the stupefying dictatorship of consumerism and a ubiquitous commercialization, leading to precisely that alienation analyzed by German philosophers.[1]

Whatever else one makes of Havel's "neo-Heideggerian" musings,[2] he successfully invoked a familiar set of themes in modern German history: loss, death, suffering, suspicion, justice, forgiveness, consumerism, dominion, spirituality. To be sure, such issues are hardly unique to Germany; yet they have assumed—and still do—a special intensity there. This is partly the result of the fact that Germany alone played host to the full spectrum of political forms over the course of the last century, including monarchy, republican socialism, fascism, Cold War liberalism, and Soviet socialism. That Germany served as one of the century's busiest construction sites of political experimentation and utopian ventures has left in its wake a distinctive legacy of fear and loathing, hope and promise. A good deal of this of course is closely connected to Nazism and the Holocaust, whose unparalleled record of mass death and destruction tends to function like a black hole absorbing so much German history both before and after the "German Catastrophe." Not that this legacy is somehow confined to Germany and Germans; on the contrary, it is arguably the real specter that haunts the "dark continent" of twentieth-century Europe.[3] The unsettled account of complicity, compliance, "fellow traveling," and "shattered humanity" left deep scars across the face of postwar Europe.[4] All European countries have suffered from their own traumas and myth-making about Nazi occupation, developing national and local variants of what Henry Rousso has famously diagnosed the "Vichy Syndrome."[5] Still, it is precisely the constellation and perceived magnitude of these traumas (including their relative suppression in the former German Democratic Republic, or GDR) that not only distinguishes modern German history from the others, but makes it emblematic of Europe's twentieth century more generally. After all, the nation whose ideological conflicts, economic crises, and catastrophic policies epitomized the first part of what Eric Hobsbawm calls the "Short Twentieth Century" is the same one whose division into consumerist wonderland and socialist experiment stood as a microcosm for the second half of the century.[6] In a very tangible sense, the history of the twentieth century is the history of Germany.[7]

Little wonder that recent years have witnessed a lively transatlantic discussion about the scope and significance of twentieth-century German history and identity. While it is in part inspired by the new post–Cold War effort to assess Germany's changed role within both Europe and the world, the debate is also fueled by a pronounced uncertainty about how to interpret Germany's historical place within the larger narratives of the century. Even if one may detect a shared assumption among specialists that German history is somehow coterminous with the century's more general "crisis of classical modernity," the creation of new post–Cold War histories of modern Germany has been bedeviled from the outset. To the extent that the events of 1989 have destroyed the stable and stabilizing narratives of German–German Cold War history, debate has inevitably pivoted upon the possibility and desirability (especially given the Nazi legacy) of raising the long-buried ghosts of national identity as the fulcrum of modern German history. How one integrates the Third Reich, the Holocaust, and even the GDR within a new post-Reunification framework effectively dramatizes the high political stakes of this historiographical shell game. Complicating the situation even further is the fact that the conventional sites of German memory production—namely the state, universities, and the world of high *Kultur*—no longer enjoy their former virtual monopoly on determining what counted as the collective past; so much so that German history has increasingly become the stuff of mass-media fascination and pop-culture makeovers over the last twenty years. But however one evaluates this mass production of history, it is undeniable that the German past—much like its capital—is under radical reconstruction.

Even before the erection of the Berlin Wall, there were two sets of images of modern Germany. On the one hand, we have visions of trench warfare, poison gas, hyperinflation, unemployment, anti-Semitism, concentration camps, genocide, and rubble; and on the other, medical, scientific, and technological innovation, market prowess, modern urban living, precision tools, premier beers and cars, film, radio, tourism, and rich intellectual life. This peculiar array of attributes, symbols, and stereotypes has proven powerful and enduring, informing the ways in which those both inside and outside twentieth-century Germany have understood it. What does it mean for a society to be so closely identified with inflicting and withstanding enormous suffering as well as with promoting and enjoying unprecedented affluence? What did experiences of misery and abundance, fear and security, destruction and reconstruction, trauma and rehabilitation have to do with one another over the course of the century? How has Germany been imagined and inhabited as a country uniquely stamped by pain and prosperity?

Our volume is an attempt to reconsider the twentieth-century history of Germany in terms of this leitmotif of pain and prosperity. Particularly in the years since Reunification, observers such as Havel have wondered which of the two terms represents the "true" Germany. By no means do we wish to arbitrate the conflict, but aim instead to explore the opposition itself: its sources, manifestations, and consequences. The question for us is not whether Germany is or should be a land identified exclusively with either Auschwitz or the Autobahn, but rather how the ideals and values of pain and prosperity reciprocally informed one another in Germany's recent past. How have they framed German perceptions of belonging and belief, health and history, frustration and future, self and society?

In treating the themes of pain and prosperity in tandem, we believe that the histories of German violence and normality are best explored relationally. For one thing, this helps avoid the pitfalls of static one-dimensional models, for example, the warfare state vs. welfare state, terror vs. the "civilizing process," or aggression vs. affluence. For another, we wish to expand the meaning of pain and prosperity beyond their conventional usages as respective physiological and/or economic concepts. It is our hope that the thematic coupling will fruitfully challenge disciplinary provincialism by incorporating the insights of those methodologies (for example, cultural anthropology and the history of everyday life) that might sharpen analysis and broaden discussion of twentieth-century Germany. Any earnest historical inquiry into the relationship of pain and prosperity as cultural topics cannot help but touch upon numerous fields and themes, including military history and the history of violence, racism and the ideology of exclusion, sex relations and gender studies, medicine and the history of trauma, the economics of misery and the sociology of plenty, social history and the history of sociability, as well as material culture and narratives of entitlement. We make no pretense to being exhaustive. Rather, we hazard to present some possibilities for exploring the dynamic interplay between pain and prosperity insomuch as it gave form to the perceptions, memories, and actions of twentieth-century Germans.

The scope of the volume roughly spans from the turn of the century to the present. World War I, however, serves as our general departure point, because it not only radically reorganized Germany's social and cultural order, but because it also gave rise to this distinctly modern dialectic of pain and prosperity. It unleashed formidable new narratives of loss and suffering that shaped German political fortunes and destinies for the subsequent two generations. As Omer Bartov has noted, it was precisely such sentimental narratives (specifically stories of the stab-in-the-back legends and the spiritual birth of the nation amid the trenches and the "storms of steel") that helped redeem a lost war effort and anticipate another one.[8] Of course this is not to suggest that collective experiences of German pain and imagined prosperity somehow first emerged in 1914. As Greg Eghigian shows, the mass politicization of suffering and entitlement was an integral and integrating element of Wilhelmian political culture. Nor were interwar narratives of pain and redemption always uniform. Whereas Patricia Stokes in this volume addresses the way in which the discussions of female bodies and the birthing experience took on heightened significance during and after World War I, Peter Fritzsche reveals how urban and national memories ("cities forget, nations remember") often ran on very different registers. The point, though, is that the war and its legacy of mass death and mourning spawned all kinds of novel political narratives and powerful cultural memories based on the imaginary bonds of pain and prosperity. Indeed, these imaginary bonds rested at the heart of the twentieth-century cycle of German crisis and calm, sacrifice and satisfaction, ruination and renewal.

At this juncture it would be useful to say a few words about *pain* and *prosperity* as historical terms. Traditionally these phenomena have been defined in relation to opposing terms. Clinical and experimental psychology, for instance, have typically opposed pain with pleasure, seeing the two as the fundamental building blocks of human motivation.[9] Prosperity most often serves as one end of an imagined continuum of consumption, whose other pole is famine or poverty.[10] What is so striking about the case of contemporary Germany, however, is how frequently institutions and individuals have paired pain with prosperity, and vice versa. This hints at a fact acknowledged by a wide range of scholars in the humanities and social sciences: that pain and prosperity are not fixed, immutable states, but "plastic" ideals and norms whose functions, forms, and values differ over time.[11] In short, they are figures inherent to no one field of human activity and therefore the property of no single line of inquiry. Historians have shown, for example, that consumer behavior toward and emotional investments in products have been quite diverse, passing through at least three major structural transformations in the West since the seventeenth century.[12] Nor can the development of a thriving consumer society in the late twentieth century be characterized as the result of a linear, progressive unfolding of capitalism. Modern Germany is a good case in point. Its economic history is punctuated by periods in which plenty and prosperity grew (1866–73, 1895–1915, 1924–29, 1934–41, 1949/1958–73) and others when dearth and pain have had to be distributed (1790–1850/ 1865, 1874/1879–90/94, 1916–23, 1930–33, 1942–48, 1973/1990–).[13] Over the course of the twentieth century these cycles of boom and bust took on particular political gravity, not least because—as Alon Confino and Rudy Koshar remark—"German governments, economic managers and labor leaders had had a long history of raising expectations about prosperity—and then reneging on their promises."[14]

What then have pain and prosperity meant over time? The terms themselves have only recently been the subject of scholarly investigation. On the one hand, the nouns *Schmerz* (pain) or *Leid* (suffering) and *Wohlstand* (prosperity) garner little if any attention in the leading historical studies of social language in modern Germany.[15] Historically, *Schmerz* has had somatic referents, from early on mostly invoking wounds, often located in particular body parts.[16] By contrast, the lexicon of "suffering" appears to have more explicitly social and psychological components and origins. Whereas the noun *Leid* is etymologically linked to ancient terms for sadness, shame, insult, disgust, and abomination, the verb *leiden* has traditionally been synonymous with enduring, experiencing, and going or making one's way through something.[17]

On the other hand, *Wohlstand*, like its kin *Wohlfahrt* (welfare), *Wohltat* (good deed), and *Wohltätigkeit* (charity), until the turn of the twentieth century, had had more to do with the cultivation of an economically and morally good public life than with the availability and consumption of products.[18] For even if the concept generally connoted wealth, eighteenth- and nineteenth-century policing, economics, and political science agreed that the "prosperity and good morals" of the people were invariably linked as matters of state. Between the mid-nineteenth and the mid-twentieth centuries, conversely, the social sciences pushed the notion of "doing well" into new directions, at once statistically objectifying and psychologically "subjectifying" it. By the 1970s and 1980s, as terms such as *Lebensstil* (lifestyle), *Lebensweise* (way of life), and *Lebensqualität* (quality of life) gained wide currency, the measure of well-being had expanded to take into account stages of life history, individual choices, and personal concerns.[19] Thus, the twentieth century has witnessed a broadening (across a greater variety of social spaces and institutions) as well as a deepening (into more intimate spheres of the lives of individuals) of the concepts of pain and prosperity.

By the same token, the study of consumer cultures has long remained at the outer edges of German historiography. On one level this is hardly unique to Germany, given that historians are only now seriously integrating consumerism into the larger framework of European historiography.[20] Until quite recently, the habits and habitus of European consumers were mostly left to economists and sociologists, thus the history of consumerism usually took the form of aggregate behavioral statistics or composite sketches of various professional organizations. Even those social historians who did venture into the terrain generally concentrated upon particular subjects, for example, industrial workers, nutrition and/or consumer cooperatives. But the last decade or so has witnessed a vigorous new cottage industry of books devoted to exploring the consumer practices of twentieth-century Europeans.[21] At the forefront of this trend is a young generation of social and cultural historians who have rescued consumerism from the appendix tables by reconsidering the ways in which modern consumerism radically reorders the relationship of politics and economics, citizen and state. In part, such scholarship is a predictable by-product of Western Europe's more general post-1945 experience, in which leisure and consumption slowly replaced work and production as the principal linchpins of cultural and personal self-understanding. New research on the former Eastern bloc has even shown that this Western European shift in identity formation enjoyed surprising parallels (despite chronic shortages of goods) behind the Iron Curtain as well.[22] For if nothing else, the events of 1989 made it quite clear to all just how much consumer desire and want undergirded the modern state's social stability and political legitimacy.

In this context, Germany affords a particularly instructive study. In recent years there has been a veritable flood of new books on the country's radically incongruous "consumer cultures" of the last century. Such a proliferation is all the more notable given that German historiography in this respect remained somewhat behind scholarly work in France, Britain, and the United States. Alone, the term *consumerism* first entered the German academic vocabulary—in stark contrast to its Western neighbors—only at the beginning of the last century.[23] And after World War II, when consumerism began to take wing in Western Europe and especially the United States as a new academic field, it remained marginalized in both German societies. In East Germany, for example, there was little interest in the subject beyond political propaganda about the socialist fulfillment of material needs and the denigration of capitalist overproduction, waste, and hedonism. Strikingly, such aversion found great purchase in West German academic circles, too. A good deal of this had to do with the long-standing antipathy toward "mass culture" within German academe ever since the turn of the century, which by and large viewed consumerism as a demeaning pastime of what later became known as the "culture industry." From the 1950s on this attitude acquired even more cultural weight, as both the West German left and right joined forces in denouncing the pleasure culture of the Economic Miracle as essentially American-style "Coca-Colonization" and/or immoral escapism.

All of this has changed since 1989. Themes of prosperity and consumer culture have now gained wide currency, as a rash of new studies on German automobile and "travel cultures," tourism, alcohol consumption, domestic life, housework, everyday objects, and the "dream of the good life" have appeared in the last decade.[24] While this international scholarly trend has certainly been shaped by the 1960s "style wars" of counterculture politics and the growing awareness of the limits of industrial growth resulting from the dramatic economic downturn of the early 1970s, the garish "conspicuous consumption" of 1980s lifestyles in the West and the dismantling of the Berlin Wall proved decisive in the German context. The widespread interpretation of the events of 1989, which saw the latter as essentially reflecting a collective East German yearning for the consumer fruits of West German liberalism, has helped spur the now prominent line of academic inquiry into twentieth-century material well-being. As Confino and Koshar put it, "The success of the West German model, its historical legitimacy as well as its power to reconstitute, for better or worse, the cities, markets and minds of the former East Germans, undoubtedly explains a good part of German historians' heightened interest in consumption as a social force."[25] In this regard the history of prosperity (and by implication the political effects of doing without) has attracted increasing attention as a revealing dimension of modern German history.

Such views are vividly on display in Bonn's recently built "House of History" museum (Haus der Geschichte), where the differences between the rival German republics are largely expressed through material culture and consumer goods. To be sure, such renditions of the past are still often shaped by Cold War ideology and prejudice, especially insofar as refracting East German history through the prism of its lackluster consumer culture had been a staple of Western propaganda throughout the Cold War (see the contribution by Ingrid Schenk in this volume). Yet the "rush to unity" exposed the surprising degree to which the narrative of material progress (or regression, as the case became) had shaped East German consciousness as well.[26] Indeed, it did this to such an extent that this oft-overlooked GDR link between materialism and identity has continued to color East German memories since Reunification, even if the judgment of its lost material culture has changed from a source of embarrassment to one of pride and solidarity.[27] Consumer desire and dreamworlds have thus moved to the center of historical inquiry about Germany's Cold War identities and differences.

As noted earlier, however, the themes of pain and prosperity in modern life are more ubiquitous than indicated by the historiography of consumer culture. As such, notice should be made of three prominent scholarly discussions in which pain and prosperity have occupied a central role. First, pain and prosperity have emerged as central themes in the historical literature on modern selfhood and identity. While Michel Foucault's *Discipline and Punish* has been the target of much criticism over the years, its main argument—that the old regime of deliberately spectacular, physically painful punishment was replaced by a (no less painful) modern system that sought to quietly adjust and train the "souls" of social deviants to accepted norms—has inspired a plethora of cultural histories of the body.[28] In this context, the sanctioned ways in which a society chooses to inflict or alleviate the pains of individuals offer insight into a community's most basic assumptions about human nature. Not that scholars easily agree on how reliable records of pain can be.[29] Historians of the body and medicine (see Stokes in this volume), in particular, have been engaged in sometimes acrimonious debate over the questions whether moderns are more or less tolerant of pain than their predecessors, whether pain thwarts or prompts articulation, and whether or not medicine has historically neglected the pains of patients and experimental subjects.[30]

The question of the extent to which pain can be tolerated, voiced, and heard leads directly into matters of self-presentation and self-representation. Every society offers its members a repertoire of available social responses to ill and good fortune. How a person or group reacts to his or their particular fate has often been assumed to reflect specific character.[31] Thus, for instance, the German soldier in World War I was supposed to face injury and death heroically with individual resolve, whereas those suffering from chronic illnesses in the last decades of the same century have been invited to share their pains with others in the form of consumer self-help groups.[32] In fact, as both examples suggest, psychic comfort and discomfort appear to have been peculiarly singled out as objects of twentieth-century concern. With the rise of mass production and consumption in the late nineteenth century, marketing specialists began providing adults and children with new models for expressing and coping with happiness, dissatisfaction, and anxiety through products themselves.[33] By the 1980s, the multi-billion dollar pharmaceutical industry had successfully engineered a new generation of psychiatric drugs (such as Prozac and Clozaril) that promised greater efficacy with fewer side effects. Such drugs, particularly the new antidepressants, raised the possibility of not just alleviating the emotional sufferings of the clinically ill, but enhancing the personality traits of the otherwise healthy in order to keep up with the demands of a high-growth, achievement-oriented society.[34]

Yet while such dilemmas of identity formation may well be the result of the globalizing effects of transnational enterprises, pain and prosperity have also played special roles in German ideals of national belonging.[35] As recent social histories demonstrate (see the essays by Eghigian and Fritzsche in this volume), the shortages, loss of limbs and lives, and widespread impoverishment brought on by World War I led many Germans to reconsider their conventional relationship to the state and to establish new bonds of solidarity on the basis of a presumed common fate.[36] National Socialism translated this sense of common fate into its own highly attractive notion of the German *Volksgemeinschaft*, that mystical community of Germans that was supposedly being vitiated by parasitic forces and inured by enormous sacrifice with little gratitude in return.[37] The Third Reich (see the contributions by Geoffrey Cocks and Sabine Behrenbeck in this volume) envisioned the solution to this supposed victimization in their own brutally eugenicized terms of *pain* and *prosperity*: those believed responsible for inflicting pain on the national community were to be systematically eliminated, while fecundity and the good life were to be promoted among the racially deserving citizenry.[38]

After World War II, pain and prosperity continued to occupy a prominent place in German national self-consciousness and narratives of belonging. However, the division of Germany into two sovereign states led to their highly bifurcated use in service of and response to the competing ideologies of social market liberalism and state socialism.[39] In West Germany, hoisting the heroic image of the so-called rubble women

(*Trümmerfrauen*)—women who took part in the massive clean-up of German cities in the years immediately after the war—to the status of national icon functioned to push aside troubling questions about everyday complicity with Nazi crimes.[40] In the memories of many West Germans, it also effectively consigned the suffering and hardships of both the war and the immediate postwar years to the prehistory of the Federal Republic (FRG) and its subsequent narratives of restored normality and pleasure. Introduction of the deutsche mark in 1948 thus became a pivotal moment: National identity and esteem became increasingly associated with social, familial, and individual prosperity. The formerly exclusive national ties of blood, as Erica Carter puts it, "began to shift toward a new definition of West German-ness as won through contributions to the economic welfare of the nation."[41] East Germany, which only abandoned food rationing in 1958, responded to images of West German affluence through a deliberate campaign in the 1940s, 1950s, and 1960s intended to present its own progressive picture of success. Even if East German happiness and prosperity were to be ensured through the socialist solidarity of workers and peasants, the GDR embraced its own version of "consumer socialism" and the pursuit of the good life.[42] As Ingrid Schenk and Katherine Pence show in this volume, West and East Germany offered their citizens distinctive models for escaping war and scarcity and securing national well-being and belonging. These "official" versions of the prosperous society had important normative consequences for men and women. New ideals of male wage-earners and housewife-consumers were formulated to fit these paths.[43] The highly politicized rival images of bounty and progress were always relational and competitive, marking the ways in which each Germany represented the present and imagined the future. Thus, despite the portrayal of the Cold War as primarily a battle of ideologies, political differences were often waged in the world of material culture. And it was here where the dialectic of pain and prosperity was most dramatically negotiated and showcased by both Germanys.

A second and related area in which the themes of pain and prosperity have figured prominently is in discussions over the history of values and moral discourse.[44] As noted, normative judgments about human experience and conduct have historically accompanied thinking about pain and prosperity. In an important recent study, John Crowley has shown that the ideal of "physical comfort—self-conscious satisfaction with the relationship between one's body and its immediate physical environment—was an innovative aspect of Anglo-American culture, one that had to be taught and learned."[45] Comfort only began to be assumed as an end-in-itself after political economists applied it to standards of living and their fulfillment. As a result, both comfort and discomfort became objects of rational improvement in the nineteenth century and, in the process, became new criteria of modern humanitarianism. Likewise, they served as important markers distinguishing the middle classes from rural and urban laboring households.[46] In the course of the twentieth century many observers believe pain and prosperity virtually replaced class in setting social distinctions.[47] Surveys have documented a remarkable shift since the 1960s in the values and standards of subjective well-being among those living in advanced industrial societies. As these societies distanced themselves from their violent and penurious pasts earlier in the century, they increasingly espoused what are commonly called "post-materialist" values: less dedicated to maintaining order, fighting inflation, and ensuring a strong defense and more inclined to prize quality of life, local autonomy, and a friendlier, less impersonal society.[48] Social movements associated with environmentalism, feminism, peace and nuclear disarmament, self-help, civil and gay rights, as well as religious fundamentalism are just some of the causes that came to international prominence in the last third of the twentieth century by advocating precisely these alternative values.[49]

Cold War Germany is, once again, a particularly interesting place to examine these shifts in attitudes, not least because Germans followed two radically divergent social paths.[50] The now legendary Economic Miracle that followed the war appears to have been pivotal in dissolving a diffuse crisis-mentality among West Germans. Whereas many identified the immediate postwar period with loss, pain, chaos, and need, the "return" of stability, prosperity, and family life in the 1950s and 1960s was widely seen as a sign of the successful reconstruction of "normal life."[51] Especially for the generation that had experienced the war, the availability, acquisition, and maximization of material prosperity became self-justifying goals. This consensus of sorts broke down, however, in the face of two challenges. The first came from young people and intellectuals in the 1950s and 1960s, who criticized it for its shallowness and self-centeredness. The second challenge came from the stagflation of the 1970s, which shattered the naive faith in permanent economic growth and social security.[52]

Conversely, such sentiments in East Germany, or for that matter in all of the former Eastern bloc countries, have been harder to gauge given the pronounced lack of openness in the former communist states. Nonetheless, a variety of sources, ranging from security police records to interviews, are providing scholars with information on everyday mentalities in the former GDR.[53] The relatively rapid Stalinization of East German society after the war meant official disavowal of Western-style consumerism —to say nothing of physical devastation, crushing reparation payments (until 1953), and the absence of any outside financial assistance from its superpower sponsor—and delayed any real material improvements until the 1960s.[54] Under a regime that governed primarily through rationing and privileges, East Germans often responded by withdrawing into small niches of intimates, taking part in the black market, and "recycling" products for repeated use. Such a stark bifurcation between official public culture and private life delegitimated the former and placed enormous pressures on the latter.[55] Even if by the mid-1970s and 1980s both party and people voiced many of the same desires for and grievances about prosperity and personal satisfaction, a basic tension remained within East German society between the collective and leveling pretensions of state policy and popular inclinations toward distinction and individualization.[56] Such tensions eventually surfaced in the 1980s in the form of the "civic movement" (*Bürgerbewegung*), an array of peace, human rights, women's, and environmentalist groups that publicly raised questions about social equality, freedom of speech, pollution, and nuclear proliferation.[57]

In both cases, recent research has moved away from the tired theses about the supposed "Americanization" and "Sovietization" of each German republic in favor of studies about how each country developed its own national idiom and self-understanding, often despite superpower influences.[58] The power of Cold War identities could be seen in the cultural difficulties in the wake of Reunification, where the initial fraternal language of 1989–90 about a renewed German–German identity quickly dissipated into acrimonious accusations and mutual misunderstandings.[59] However much many conservatives hoped to erase two generations of division and hostility through political fusion, it has been evident to everyone that inter-German difference, and not sameness, has dominated public discussion.

A third major theme that has significantly drawn on notions of pain and prosperity is that of memory and memorialization. Over the past decade and a half, there has been a veritable boom in scholarly and popular interest in history, memory, and identity.[60] At its most basic level, the preoccupation with collective memory has centered on the questions of how societies symbolically represent their pasts, who controls their representation, and the consequences.[61] This has led to some fresh perspectives on German memory in recent years.[62] Not surprisingly, discussions about collective memory in and of twentieth-century Germany have focused primarily on the representation of the Holocaust within political circles, intellectual debates, film, literature, popular media, and memorials.[63] All agree that the landscape of collective memory about the Third Reich is pockmarked with troubling silences. In the GDR, official sites and public occasions of remembrance deliberately obliterated Jewish victims from the story of National Socialism while mythologizing communists as heroic figures of opposition.[64] In the FRG, commentators have long noted the difficulties faced by older Germans in particular in raising the subject of Nazi atrocities.[65] This is not to say that memories of the war enjoyed no collective enunciation. However, most West German "war stories" tended to concentrate on the plight of German soldiers, refugees, and women as emblems of a "nation of victims."[66] Only with time—and with considerable difficulty—were German antifascist resistors included in this changing political articulation of the Nazi past.[67] Yet the knowledge and experience of mass killing found little public expression until the late 1960s. One influential perspective on this theme has seen such silence as, at least in part, a result of the desire to repress the psychic pain associated with traumatic (both direct and indirect) memories of the Holocaust.[68] In the now famous phrase of Alexander and Margarete Mitscherlich, the Third Reich presumably left most Germans with an "inability to mourn."[69]

Others, however, believe such historical "amnesia" about National Socialism has less to do with trauma than with the continuities in prosperity between the Third Reich and the Federal Republic. Public opinion surveys, government reports, and oral histories have shown that the majority of West Germans in the 1950s recalled the recent past as a period of good times (1935–41) sandwiched by bad times (1929–35 and 1941–49). Indeed, as Omer Bartov and Ulrich Herbert have observed, many Germans continue to recall the years under Allied occupation as even more painful than the last years of the war; it is the victims of Nazi persecution who have consistently lumped together the years 1933–45.[70] This is in many ways the forgotten origin of the Federal Republic's "recasting of bourgeois Germany."[71] But if this has cast a new light on West German memory, so too has it inspired new work on the Nazi period as its own "culture of pleasure."[72] In fact, as Michael Geyer points out, it was precisely this linkage between plunder and notions of racial entitlement, between "fantasies of unlimited consumption and excessive war," that effectively undergirded the Nazi regime.[73]

To speak of victims is to imply perpetrators. The task of distinguishing between the two—between those who killed and inflicted pain on others from those who were killed and subject to abuse and loss—has played a fundamental part in efforts at representing and memorializing Nazi Germany. Over the past two decades, such efforts have prompted a number of lively public debates on both sides of the Atlantic over which groups should be considered perpetrators and which victims.[74] The dilemma is itself a modern one. For the idiom of political victimhood—of using undeserved suffering as a vehicle for self-identification, expression, and making political demands—is one that became particularly authoritative and ubiquitous in the nineteenth and twentieth centuries.[75] As the status of victim has grown increasingly inclusive, it also has become easier to elide distinctions between oppressor and persecuted, as self-professed victims compete with one another for preeminence.[76]

The collapse of East Germany added yet another layer of painful memories to the burden of "coming to terms with or overcoming the past" (*Vergangenheitsbewältigung*). Similar to developments in Eastern Europe and South Africa in the 1990s, a reunified Germany both publicly and privately debated the culpability of individuals and institutions in enabling the former regime to exercise its authority. Journalists "outed" political figures, intellectuals questioned the conformity of colleagues, individual citizens examined their Stasi (state security) files, and so-called truth commissions (the most famous being the Gauck-Authority) attempted to ascertain accountability.[77] Once again, a bestselling book proclaimed that (East) Germans, psychologically scarred and emotionally underdeveloped by their years under totalitarianism, were finding it all too difficult to mourn, to come to terms with their fates.[78] The legacy of East Germany, however, has not overshadowed that of the Third Reich. Instead, it has been transposed on top of the collective memory of Nazi genocide and persecution, resulting in sometimes polemical debate over the comparative suffering of fascist and communist victims.[79] Concentration camps, public buildings, street names, and other landmarks in the East now can be associated with more than one unambiguous set of events.[80] This makes the "work of mourning" (*Trauerarbeit*) that much more difficult and treacherous.

The issue of memory can be seen in other ways as well. One of the most interesting is how narratives of pain and prosperity have been re-tooled after 1989. Given the disappointments for many (especially in the East) about Reunification, and given the ability and/or disinclination among East and West intellectuals and cultural brokers alike toward forging a new affective language of German-German solidarity, it is not surprising that the stories of pain and prosperity took on geographical expression. A recent popular exhibition on the history of the two Germanys makes this explicit.[81] For many, the events of 1989 only confirmed the old Cold War antinomy of the free and affluent West versus the oppressed and penniless East.[82] On the one hand, this was evident in the West German nostalgia after 1989 for their "Bonn Republic" and its patrimony of constitutional order, plurality and economic prosperity.[83] On the other hand, the serialized revelations about Stasi complicity, the cultural shock of "Kohl-onization," and the widespread feeling of second-class citizenship among *Ossis* (Easterners) was often expressed as a collective *Trauerspiel* of pain and trauma.[84] Yet there have been some noteworthy exceptions to this model. For one thing, the shrill chorus of

West German public complaints about the severity of the so-called Solidarity Tax—to say nothing of the larger German reluctance to give up the deutsche mark in the name of European Union—has made plain that narratives of pain and economic discontent have found popular expression in the West as well. By contrast, the enduring post–Berlin Wall East German *Ostalgie* (East German nostalgia), as Paul Betts explains in his contribution, has often turned on redeeming narratives of the GDR past as a lost culture of sharing and private pleasures. While Reunification may have spelled "the end of German longing" on the national political stage,[85] expressions of longing and nostalgia continue apace. Indeed, the Berlin exhibition of 1995 entitled *Wunderwirtschaft*, or Miracle Economy, which chronicles the febrile modernization of the GDR during the 1960s, has revealed that many East Germans—despite widespread knowledge at the time that they were not keeping pace with West German standards of living—often remember their own hothouse "economic miracle" as a period of increased affluence, optimism, and comfort. The recent project in the East German city of Eisenhüttenstadt to establish a new "East German Everyday Culture" museum (Dokumentationszentrum Alltagskultur der DDR) dedicated to preserving artifacts from GDR material culture is another example of the ongoing attempt to rethink East Germany's lost socialist modernity as something more than a culture of want and privation.[86] Even so, it is undeniable that the majority of post-1989 accounts of East German social history remain elegies of pain, suffering, and betrayal.[87]

How, when, and in what way these issues will change is of course the stuff of pure speculation. Yet it seems fair to say that it will necessitate a fundamental refashioning of the cultural construction of pain and prosperity, especially insofar as it affects the relationship between past and present. Already the efforts by a range of historians and publicists across the political spectrum to rewrite history as a means of instilling enthusiasm and confidence in Germany's bullish political future, to discard the old "special path" thesis of German pathological development, and to try to resurrect the long-tarnished ideas of national pride and "enlightened patriotism" are indications of these new cultural sea changes.[88] Whether or not this will be benign or dangerous, evidence of neoconservative nation-building, or simply by-product of the country's long-desired "normalization," is naturally open to question. But as new twenty-first century identities are devised along the axes of pain and prosperity, there is much to be gained by reconsidering how they relate to their twentieth-century forerunners.

Pain, Entitlement, and Social Citizenship in Modern Germany

Body, Nation, and the History of Pain and Suffering

A substantial literature has grown around the theme of the body and its relationship to modern politics.[1] Historians of modern Europe in particular have directed most of their attention to two themes: the representation of the polity as a body and the uses to which bodies have been put in the service of that polity. In the case of the former, historians have noted that both medieval and absolutist political thought saw the political realm in terms of a broader Christian cosmology. According to feudal and early modern legal traditions, the sovereign, subjects, and the natural and sacred worlds were organically linked with one another as part of an immutable and unified order of things. The person of the king himself, in turn, was understood as nothing short of the embodiment of the political order, the "body politic."[2] It was this very personalization of sovereignty, which liberalism labeled despotism, that the French Revolution symbolically and violently attempted to depose.[3] And while it has been common to cite the rise of impersonal, rational law as the direct result of democratic revolution, feminist historians and theorists have pointed out that liberal political discourse of the eighteenth and nineteenth centuries persisted in treating the polity as a body by ascribing it an explicit gender.[4]

If the medieval and early modern states developed the most elaborate justifications for treating the kingdom as a body, the modern state appears to have been more intrusive in practice. Scholars have questioned liberalism's founding myth of a free and independent civil society governed by a minimalist state. Democratic government, industrial capitalism, mass politics, and modern warfare have all been cited as requiring unprecedented degrees of social engineering in order to promote civil peace, economic productivity, and military prowess. In serving these goals, it is argued, modern political and social institutions have attempted to monitor, stigmatize, discipline, and mold human desires and conduct more intimately than ever before.[5]

The rise of nationalism and the nation-state appears then to have only augmented the links between body and polity. This is no more evident than in the conduct of warfare. Wars in the age of national belonging, as Michel Foucault has pointed out, "are no longer waged in the name of a sovereign who must be defended; they are waged on behalf of the existence of everyone; entire populations are mobilized for the purpose of wholesale slaughter in the name of life necessity: massacres have become vital."[6] Such a massive mobilization of people on behalf of the nation requires a sense of belonging that by no means came naturally. Individuals historically have had to learn how to feel, act, and be nationalist. Language, festivals, art, literature, currency, technology, maps, museums, and schooling have all been identified as important components in this process of "becoming national."[7] At the same time, the metaphor of the polity as body proved remarkably resilient, informing nineteenth-century fears about national decline and social degeneration.[8] These anxieties eventually expressed themselves in a late nineteenth- and early twentieth-century obsession of many European states with a perceived decline in fertility and bourgeois ideals of marriage.[9]

These sets of concerns about the relationship of the human body to the political community are also reflected in the specific historiography of modern Germany. The early modern German state drew no distinction between state, economy, and society. Rather, the ruler was enjoined to administer, maintain, and reproduce the human and natural resources of his realm as an extension of his own household. In order to foster peace, security, and welfare, so-called police ordinances were established to regiment and direct behavior. Under the influence of cameralist and absolutist doctrines, policing eventually regulated a dizzying array of economic, household, moral, medical, educational, and religious affairs and practices.[10] As elsewhere, however, nineteenth-century Prussia passed reforms that began the process of divorcing the competence of the state from any one person by making the state a legal institution standing "above individuals."[11]

Historians of modern Germany have been keen to point out, however, that the emergence of a bourgeoisie, a liberal movement, and a national state (1871) in nineteenth-century Germany did not have the same effects as similar events did in Western Europe. Imperial Germany (1871–1918), as one particularly influential history tells it, retained many of the vestiges of feudalism, setting Germany off on its own antidemocratic, reactionary "special path" into modernity.[12] To be sure, historians have recognized

late nineteenth- and early twentieth-century Germany as the site of remarkable industrial growth, vital social movements, and pioneering scientific and technological innovation. These developments, however, appear to many historians only to have reinforced and refined the
technologies that went into socially disciplining the bodies of boys and
girls, men and women, workers, housewives, and soldiers.[13]

Similar to the wider European literature on the subject, nationalism
figures prominently in explanations about the German state's increasing
vigilance toward the body. German nationalism is commonly categorized
as a form of "cultural" or "ethnic" nationalism: one that stands in direct
contrast to the "civic" or "political" nationalisms of England, France,
and the United States by defining the nation as a fixed community determined by nature, history, and blood.[14] This has imbued German definitions of national belonging with an inherent racial element that persists
to this day despite reforms in 1999.[15] Modern German national and political discourses thus have voiced recurrent anxieties about purity and
have been drawn to the image of shedding blood as a form of redress.[16]
Particularly during the first third of this century, the body assumed a host
of sacred, aesthetic, and erotic significances in German national culture:
at once an object of public policy intervention (women and reproduction), violent fantasy (sexual murder), imagined infection (Jews), pro-
and anti-Americanism and modernism (body-building and sport).[17]

Looming over all these histories is National Socialism and the Third
Reich. It is understandable if a teleology leading straight to the Holocaust
creeps into many of these narratives. The bureaucratically planned annihilation of Jews, *Sinti*, and Roma (Gypsies), the mentally ill, the de-
formed, and the decrepit offers an unavoidable and sobering example of
how far a modern state can go in trying to realize its dreams of a perfect
order. Nazism turned eugenics into political platform and state policy.
The notion of the "body politic" resurfaced with a vengeance. This time
it assumed the modern guise of a totalitarian and biologically chauvinis-
tic regime that purported to defend and nurture the sacred "national
community" by excluding the corrupt and irredeemable and encouraging
the racially pure and healthy.[18]

The considerable research done on the subject thus testifies to the fact
that modern European and German political life has been acutely concerned with the bodies of its citizens. Yet for all the talk about "the politics of the body," most studies have uniformly treated all such power relations as a one-way street, content to point out the homogenizing impact
of institutions on individuals. Even in those cases where scholars recognize
limits to official pretensions of regimentation, political relations are often
couched in terms of a linear (action-reaction) language of "resistance,"

"opposition," and "protest" to elite policies. Yet neither social institutions nor individuals and their bodies encounter one another in a vacuum. As products of society, they always act *within* society, able to call on a host of extrainstitutional values and often having access to wider audiences beyond their encounter. Moreover, even the most totalitarian political cultures appear to be more polyvocal than Michel Foucault conceded.[19] Thus, the purported "medicalization" and "social disciplining" of the masses may themselves be artifacts of historical methods and evidence. Reliance on the testimony of medical, legal, academic, and bureaucratic professionals is, at least in part, responsible for reproducing the top-down image of an authoritarian, nationalizing state and a largely silent, pliant citizenry.[20]

Indeed, modern government, law, medicine, and industry all have made claims on people's bodies. But did citizens, litigants, patients, and workers not reciprocate by making claims on these very same institutions? Too often it is forgotten that the human body is not only an object of political activities, but also the subject generating such endeavors. The fact that bodies are of profound symbolic value in society by no means precludes—in fact, only enhances—the possibility that individuals will creatively represent and use their own bodies for a variety of political purposes.[21]

This is nowhere more apparent than in the phenomenology and history of pain. Historical evidence confirms that the human body in affliction has rarely been silent. Western medicine since antiquity has understood pain as a sign communicating information about the locus, etiology (causes), and prognosis of an illness. During the nineteenth and twentieth centuries clinicians came to accept pain as an indirect form of communication by the self about its psychological state. At the same time, researchers began to award it the status of a scientific and medical problem sui generis.[22] Moreover, those afflicted have consistently voiced their agonies and discomforts. There may be times, as Scarry and Wear have argued, when pain has compelled silence.[23] But as Porter rightly points out, more often than not pain has prompted those afflicted to express it "with exactitude and eloquence" and "in great abundance."[24] Evidence for this can be found in autobiographies, art, literature, and clinical case studies.[25]

Pain and its barely distinguishable counterpart suffering are interesting for another reason: they serve as a bridge, not simply between the physical and the mental, but between the personal and the social, the private and the public, the individual and the collective. This has often been lost in the plethora of medical autobiographies that commonly give the impression that pain and suffering invariably lead to exclusion, heroic isolation, and self-absorption. Once again, however, clinical, ethnographic, and historical data indicate that pain and suffering have just as often served as bonds of social and political solidarity between individuals.[26] Thus, the ability of pain to help forge and cement (or by the same merit, loosen and unravel) community also has a history.

Pain and suffering therefore provide us with a unique inroad into the relationship between the body and the modern politics of the nation. As Ernest Renan pointed out in 1882:

> More valuable by far than common customs posts and frontiers conforming to strategic ideas is the fact of sharing, in the past, a glorious heritage and regrets, and of having, in the future, [a shared] programme to put into effect, or the fact of having suffered, enjoyed, and hoped together. . . . Where national memories are concerned, griefs are of more value than triumphs, for they impose duties and require a common effort. . . . A nation is therefore a large-scale solidarity, constituted by the feeling of the sacrifices that one has made in the past and of those that one is prepared to make in the future.[27]

Pain and sufferings in this context are more than conditions to be avoided or medicated. They are feelings and memories of feelings that are embraced and brought near as means by which to identify self and community. How then has pain been invoked in the service of political cause? Furthermore, What does pain say? Or better put, How is pain expressed in certain political contexts and to what ends and effects?

I therefore want to revisit the history of nation and body in Germany by examining how representations of painful experience were used toward political ends and were ultimately transformed in the process. In particular, I wish to locate the place of pain and suffering in the general discourse over social citizenship in Germany from roughly 1880 to 1970. Social insurance records reveal an intrinsic relationship among the modern German state, those it governed, and representations of the body. Germany's elaborate social security system, which awarded pensions and therapies to millions of disabled workers and their families beginning in the 1880s, was the pivotal instrument in the process of linking the fates of individuals with that of the German state. It did this by providing a highly litigious arena for the production and reproduction of national loyalty through its idiom of injury and compensation. By World War I, most of Germany's working population had come to assume certain social claims as rights and entitlements. The manner in which this sense of social entitlement was articulated underwent three major changes over the course of the twentieth century. First, social rights were subject to a *collectivization*—articulated as group entitlements—during World War I and the early Weimar Republic. Second, a process of *nationalization* occurred between roughly 1925 and 1949, in which social suffering and citizenship were represented in a heroic nationalist rhetoric. Finally, social entitlement went through a process of *consumerization* in the 1950s, 1960s, and 1970s. During this period, the ideals of social security were largely detached from those values associated with an economy of shortages (for example, pain, social misery) and linked to those associated with postwar prosperity (growth, maintenance of lifestyles). In effect, Germany's social security system transformed somatic pain into a medium of national belonging.

Personal Pains and Public Meanings in
Wilhelmian Disability Insurance, 1883–1914

The rhetoric of "social disciplining" and "medicalization" has dominated the historical study of German social insurance. The story of German disability insurance (established during the years 1883–91) traditionally has been written as one of subjugation and subterfuge: bourgeois liberals and conservative aristocrats establishing a system of social security in order to destroy worker loyalty to unions as well as to promote industrial peace, ultimately resulting in the placement of an unprecedented amount of power in the hands of German physicians.[28] These were among the ambitions of the founders, but they were not the only ones, and we have little reason to consider them successfully realized.[29] Social insurance was the linchpin in the process of forging worker loyalty to the new German state, but it was by no means a case of smoothly orchestrated "social imperialism."

To understand this, it is necessary to first appreciate the relationship of social insurance to the history of disability. Historians of medicine have pointed out that well into the nineteenth century Germans, like other Europeans, understood ill health within the framework of religion. Early modern individuals called on a Christian "illness theology," as Ute Frevert has put it, in awarding sacred and mundane meanings to their afflictions.[30] Perceiving sickness as part of Divine Providence, however, did not translate into patient passivity. The sick and injured actively sought out healers, medicated themselves, and demanded immediate results from doctors' cures.[31] The reports of sixteenth- and seventeenth-century physicians indicate that the afflicted were a generally impatient lot. Both acute and chronic patients routinely expressed the desire to get out of bed, go back to work, and resume pastimes such as Bible reading, all integrative functions served by local hospices. In this sense, one can say that early moderns had developed a prototypical, or "folk," sense of disability, expressed in the wish and attempts to treat impairing injuries and ailments.[32]

Pain was inextricably bound up with these folk attitudes. As Barbara

Duden has shown, eighteenth-century patients tended to reify pain as a single entity that traveled around the body and changed its form. For patient and doctor, pain was not merely a symptom. It was an affliction in and of itself and whose successful cessation was considered evidence of cure.[33] Pain was therefore treated as a source of impairment. Such impairment, however, extended beyond the individual's everyday life and normal bodily functions. Particularly in cases of chronic pain and illness, their disabling effects disrupted the lives of family members as well. It was therefore not uncommon for those debilitated to associate their symptoms with those of living and deceased family members and friends.[34]

The rise to prominence of what was referred to as the "social question" between 1820 and 1880 brought the first encroachments on these more or less private and highly personalized responses to pain and disability. Population growth, industrialization, urbanization, and widespread impoverishment were widely taken by German policy makers to be signs of a profound social crisis. Conservatives, progressive liberals, and socialists alike voiced grave concerns over the dissolution of traditional, feudal bonds of social affinity with little if nothing to replace them. Particularly after the failed revolution of 1848, as the "social question" became increasingly reduced to the "worker question," political groups, notables, industrialists, bureaucrats, and academics sought state intervention.[35]

The introduction of compulsory social insurance legislation in the 1880s and 1890s was offered by its supporters as evidence of the German state's commitment to its toiling classes. Worker, employer, and state contributions were mandated to fund a variety of health insurance schemes designed to provide short- and long-term cash benefits and treatment for sick and injured workers. The plan's obvious attempt to win the loyalty of labor led socialists in Germany to oppose it. The legislation was therefore the creation of an antisocialist alliance of liberals, Catholics, conservatives, and the Crown.

The fact that social insurance law in Germany came from a seemingly odd wedding of liberal and conservative ideologies had important repercussions for how the system ultimately came to understand pain and suffering. The two political ideologies shared some common attitudes toward human affliction and need. Both saw moral value in the satisfaction of human needs. But both also assumed there to be a natural system for the distribution of social products, one in which human want served as a powerful catalyst for individual betterment and charitable giving. In short, nineteenth-century German liberalism and conservatism believed pain and suffering played productive roles in German social life.[36]

These ideals found institutional expression in social insurance administration itself. Pension compensation was determined, not on the basis of a needs-assessment (as in poor relief), but on the basis of an individual worker's previous earnings and/or contributions. Moreover, pension levels had an upper limit (in accident insurance, two-thirds of the individual's annual income), so that a beneficiary's pension could never be equal to or greater than what he or she had earned on the job. This was to guarantee that individuals would not find dependence on the state more lucrative than working. The limit on compensation also assured anxious conservatives that pension levels would reflect the beneficiary's social rank. This carrot-and-stick approach was reinforced by periodic and compulsory physical examinations that monitored pensioners for improvement and malingering.

From an administrative standpoint then, pain and suffering played a strictly limited role in the social insurance system. Indeed, for the most part, they were understood to lay *outside* the system, as spurs for healing. *Within* the system, however, pain and suffering were largely invisible to insurers. Accident insurance boards, for instance, were adamant that disability was strictly an empirically verifiable condition. This meant that ailments needed to be, according to one insurance board, "outwardly visible."[37] The "subjective, entirely unverifiable complaints . . . of pain," as an official termed them, required "objective" corroboration.[38]

The epistemological assumptions of insurers therefore necessarily called into question personal experience and expression, inherently delegitimizing the laments of the injured. If it was true, as legislators and employers seemed to think, that self-interest and self-aggrandizement were the engines of society and the individual, then how could the testimony of claimants be believed? Insurance boards' mistrust translated into a case-by-case disparaging of motivations as they attempted to justify their daily rejections, settings, or diminutions of individual pensions.[39]

Workers, however, did not passively accept this bureaucratic understanding of their debilities and complaints. As mentioned earlier, laborers had a long history of perceiving their afflictions in much more personal, life-historical, less abstract terms than insurers.[40] In addition, those covered under Wilhelmian social insurance were among the most highly skilled and well-paid laborers in Germany. As Alf Lüdtke and Heide Gerstenberger have pointed out, such workers tended to consider themselves more "respectable" than most of the proletariat by virtue of their success in acquiring material security for their families.[41] Socially insured labor was therefore keenly attuned to matters of honor, status, and fairness.

It should therefore come as no surprise that pension claimants proved to be highly litigious. Imperial social insurance granted every worker the right to appeal insurance board pension decisions. This they did with increasing frequency. In 1901, workers appealed approximately one in every five accident insurance board decisions and one in every ten invalid insurance board decisions. By 1912 these figures had risen to approximately one in every three and one in every six, respectively.[42]

In order to appeal decisions, claimants had to testify to their reasons for deserving a pension (usually in both written and oral forms). These testimonials are striking for many reasons, but particularly noteworthy is how common it was for applicants to invoke their agonies and needs before authorities who, at least as official policy, showed no interest in them. Perhaps this was something of a residue from poor relief, where applicants were required to prove need in order to receive benefits. In any event, pension applicants routinely spoke of their pains. Steel worker Adolph Henckel insisted, "With continuous walking or standing, I am growing stronger, that is to say the right foot is, [but] the pains that go with it, which I usually have in [the foot], make using it unbearable."[43] Some, such as carpenter Wilhelm Keller, who lost part of his thumb, complained that his hand was so sensitive "that by the slightest touch, I feel sharp pains and therefore cannot handle anything."[44]

It was equally common for insured workers to invoke the economic hardships they and their households suffered as a result of their disabilities. Narratives frequently represented the injury as the beginning of a very slippery slope, usually ending in begging and poverty. Railman Ignatz Lang, for instance, complained after part of his left index finger was amputated, "I am mutilated for life; I can no longer do my job nor fetch the same wage as [I did] before the accident. . . . I was previously ordered to leave the hospital. For a long time I was without a job and the means to live. I could not find any work, and I had to earn my living by begging."[45] Impoverishment was the looming specter in their lives; it not only implied hard times, but would also signify a loss of honor, a backsliding into the mass of "unrespectable" paupers, beggars, and working poor from whom these skilled workers proudly distinguished themselves.

Social insurance therefore did not supplant the highly personal associations of pain and disability, but rather simultaneously incorporated and deflected them. Expressions of misery, need, and loss of status found their way into social insurance proceedings, but for the most part they fell on deaf ears. The administrative calculus needed to assign meaning to disability could hardly fit it into the compensatory logic of the system. In this regard, it is surprising that accident insurance did come to recognize human agony as a relevant factor in determining pension, but only insofar as it hindered the productivity of the individual worker.[46] Accident insurers drew a firm distinction then between a more narrowly conceived mental state of pain (*Schmerz*)—a phenomenon that correlated with clinically, legally, and bureaucratically verifiable physical symptoms—and that of suffering (*Elend, Leiden*), a phenomenon understood to lie outside the field of compensation since its etiology and consequences crossed the boundaries of the somatic and the social, the public and the private.

Early German social insurance, therefore, deemed that pain and suffering were all but meaningless in the guarantee of social rights. The official conception of social citizenship hinged on a nineteenth-century *thermodynamic* vision of work that linked entitlement to labor power. Pensioners and claimants, however, attempted to communicate the reality and relevance of their afflictions to insurance authorities in a *moral* idiom of suffering and theodicy.[47] Social insurance asked the insured to treat their ailments as a claim, a suit. Workers obliged, immersing themselves in the details of their own individual cases, seeking bureaucratic recognition of the perceived catastrophes that had befallen them. Millions of workers were in this way educated into a sense of social citizenship by the practice of social insurance itself, by pleading their cases and intrumentalizing their bodies.

The Collectivization of Social Suffering, 1914–1927

The years between the beginning of World War I and the creation of unemployment insurance in 1927 witnessed a growing emphasis on suffering as a vehicle of identity-formation and social belonging in German political culture.[48] Once again, the driving force behind this were those requesting or receiving social benefits. This time, however, individuals were supported by organized political action associations for veterans, war widows, and the disabled, all of which first began to form toward the end of the war. This "collectivization" of social politics was further fueled by profound changes to two of the principal symbolic means by which Germans related to one another and to the state: the language of citizenship and the German currency.

Among other things, the German state during World War I explicitly and deliberately invoked the sacred figure of sacrifice to mobilize its citizens. Both men and women were asked to perform acts of heroic self-sacrifice on the battlefield and on the home front in order to secure a German victory.[49] But this choice of rhetoric was fraught with complications. The German term *Opfer* means both "sacrifice" and "victim" (in addition to "casualty"). As a number of anthropologists of sacrifice have pointed out, ritual sacrifice not only implies a victim, but also represents a sacred contract between the one offering the sacrifice and the divinity. This means that the divinity (in this case, the nation-state) too has obligations.[50] Sacrifice, victimhood, and entitlement were therefore historically, linguistically, and ritually linked with one another. Invoking sacrifice necessarily meant invoking the idioms of victimization and entitlement as well.

The triad "sacrifice-victim-casualty" provided a powerful heuristic by which Germans after the war could understand and politically explain military defeat, the subsequent civil unrest, and the virtual universalization of loss, sickness, and impoverishment during the 1920s and 1930s.[51] Throughout the postwar period many questioned whether all Germans sacrificed equally and whether their own sacrifices had been worth it in the first place. War widows, veterans, orphans, and workers followed by civil servants, the young, the elderly, savers, and creditors all cast themselves as innocent victims of war, revolution, and economic disarray.[52] The task of repairing the damage fell most consistently to the nation-state since it had been in the name of the Reich that Germans had been called on to make their sacrifices.

As a result, the Weimar (1918–33) welfare state found itself inundated with demands.[53] Its task was made practically intractable, however, by the inflation and hyperinflation of the German mark during the decade from 1914 to 1924. Administrative costs, premiums, and pensions, legally and fiscally set in relation to one another, quickly lost all semblance of reciprocal calibration. The result was a financial disaster that shook the foundations of German social security.[54]

Social insurance pensioners, along with other welfare recipients, bore the brunt of the ensuing austerity measures. As one administrator explained to the Reich Ministry of Labor already in September 1920, "The present pension installment is so small that it still does *not in the least* suffice to cover *even the most modest necessities of life* for the pensioner."[55] In numerous petitions to government officials, pensioners and lobby groups voiced their demands for increased support in the familiar language of victimization. Seventy-five-year-old Robert Nagel, who was receiving a monthly pension of 184 marks, angrily wrote to the Prussian minister for public welfare: "It is deplorable after you have sacrificed [*geopfert*] your youth and health for society, and you still have to go hungry and starve during your final, declining days."[56]

Social pensioners, numbering around four million by 1924, thus were educated by and had a hand in fashioning this political culture in which victim status operated as symbolic capital.[57] This is most clearly evident in the changing manner in which activists represented themselves. Whereas the insured in Wilhelmian Germany tended to use bureaucratic terms to refer to themselves (most commonly *claimant, invalid, pensioner,* or *patient*), after the war a new vocabulary appeared in articles, petitions, posters, and correspondences. From 1920 onward, some disabled individuals and associations began making consistent references to themselves as "work invalids" (*Arbeitsinvaliden*), "work victims" (*Arbeitsopfer*), and "fellow sufferers" (*Leidensgenossen*). This shift in language was mirrored by a change in the organization of the disabled and their families. In the summer of 1920, the various local disabled and pensioner lobbying groups that had been established at the end of the war formed a national organization, the Central Association of German Invalids and Widows. Claiming sixty thousand members at its foundation, it announced its primary aim to organize "fellow sufferers" so that "no institution and no government will dare ignore the misery of those suffering and weak without their participation and without regard for their interests."[58]

The increasing bitterness about and loss of faith in the German national state that so characterized Weimar political culture was therefore the expression of many Germans' escalating and disappointed expectations of state action. The collapse of the German currency was particularly frustrating, for it destroyed the principal symbolic means by which state and citizen communicated with one another: monetary compensation. With a worthless currency, the Weimar welfare state appeared more than simply inept; it appeared deaf and dumb. Thus, by the second half of the 1920s, there was a widespread sense among citizens that the implicit social contract with the state had been broken, and, along with it, a fear that all the sacrifices had been in vain. Resentments converged as a creeping loss of faith.[59] The blending of the idioms of national sacrifice and social entitlement through mass privation and suffering therefore led simultaneously to an inflation of the sense of entitlement (in the form of greater expectations of state action) and to a widespread disenchantment with the state. Social entitlement and sacrifice thereby reinforced one another, placing questions of trust, responsibility, and reciprocity at the forefront of political debate.

Heroism and the Nationalization of Social Suffering, 1927–1949

The mass politics of victimization in Weimar Germany should be seen not as an indication of an anarchic civil war between narrow, self-centered interests, but rather as part of a broader national quest to find moral purpose in misfortune.[60] The German welfare state acted as a venue for individuals and groups to articulate their ideals of national belonging and their expectations of state action. Social policy became the object of and forum for discord over the proper constitution of the German polity. At

the policy level, this conflict was couched as an ideological battle between, on the one hand, those social service providers who defended the
traditional ameliorative welfare state and, on the other hand, those conservative, liberal, and eugenic critics who wished to, in one form or another, simultaneously privatize individual fate and remoralize state action
along nationalist lines. By the early 1930s, a discernible backlash against
the "mechanistic" and "bureaucratic" social welfare system had already
developed within intellectual and policy-making circles. It drew growing
support from confessional welfare organizations demanding the "repri-
vatization" of welfare activities and from local authorities on austerity
budgets looking to make spending cuts.[61]

While a great deal of critics' attention was directed at maternalist policy and youth programs, social insurance was nevertheless not immune
from the backlash that assailed the Weimar welfare state. Here, however,
criticisms of social policy dated back to a late-nineteenth century, but
continuing, debate over the causes and consequences of a somewhat
bizarre phenomenon—the so-called pension neurosis. The pension neurosis found its way into social insurance after a number of individuals
with nervous and hysterical symptoms made pension claims under accident insurance. Legally recognized in 1889, the phenomenon was a subject of debate among employers, workers, union officials, and physicians
who either perceived it as an illness or a wave of mass malingering. By
the end of the century, claimants were testing the boundaries of the diagnosis, and in a Kafkaesque turn of events, contended that the attempt to
acquire a pension itself was provoking nervous conditions. Disappointed
expectations, accusations of malingering, years of preoccupation with de-
fending claims, numerous court and medical hearings were all experiences endemic to the social insurance procedure, and the insured claimed
they triggered new neuroses and exacerbated existing ones. By the 1920s,
the phenomenon had come to symbolize the failure of treatment programs, the promotion of greed and dependency, and the overpoliticiza-
tion of insurance affairs. Debate about the efficacy and integrity of social
insurance coalesced around this evasive illness. With private insurers and
psychiatrists eventually conceding that compensation tended to promote,
not control, the affliction, the Reich Insurance Office in 1926 revoked
recognition of the pension neurosis, and acknowledged that the welfare
state itself had acted as a pathogen for the illness.[62]

The pension neurosis was invoked time and again by Weimar critics as
evidence of the ineffective, pathological, and "antisocial" (*unsozial*) nature of social insurance. Particularly following the stabilization of the
currency in 1924–25, administrators and policy makers were unrelent-
ingly challenged to justify the system. Supporters did just that, offering

philosophically expansive, morally valorized defenses of insurance and its social mission. Such justifications did not convince critics, and the latter appear to have gained an even more receptive audience after Germany introduced unemployment insurance in 1927.

Above all else, opponents of social policy were united in the conviction that social insurance had become an essentially perverse and perverting institution in modern German society. Time and again they contrasted the original pretensions of social insurance, frequently quoting Bismarck or Kaiser Wilhelm, with its "unintended consequences."[63] Rather than promoting loyalty to the state, public health, and high productivity, it had nurtured a host of unhealthy and immoral habits—greed, malingering, deceit, exaggeration, laziness, dependency, illness, hypochondria, sexual and moral depravity—while enfeebling the virtues of strength, self-help, responsibility, courage, joy in labor, and selflessness. A corrupt system, where administrators worked in palatial facilities and physicians indulged the hysterical complaints of workers, was purported to be having a corrupting influence on society in general.[64] From this perspective, the mass of discontented pensioners were indeed victims, but victims of an altruism gone wrong.

Thus, critics of the interwar German welfare state used the consumer rhetoric of sacrifice, victimization, and moral outrage, but in order to criticize social services and their beneficiaries. As the title of an influential work by Ernst Horneffer expressed it, social insurance had become an "abomination [*Frevel*] against the people."[65] It had destroyed the ethic of hard work ("the father of all virtues") and given license to abuse of public institutions, anxiety, cowardice, and parasitism (*Schmarotzertum*). Laying blame also on the "sentimental bourgeoisie" who had passed social legislation, Horneffer lamented the consequent "shameful effeminacy [*Verweichlichung*] of our time" and the "contemptible spiritual hedonists, the aesthetes," to which it gave rise.[66] The newly created unemployment insurance, he contended, best demonstrated to what extent the concern for social security had come to pervert the natural order of things. Risk, danger, poverty, and hunger, he argued, were "the indispensable driving forces of human life," making it "tragic, painful, hard." By trying to avoid and overcome such sufferings, "one was simply attempting to wipe out this heroic character of existence, out of a mawkish softness [*in süßlicher Weichheit*] to make life pleasant, safe, and secure for everyone."[67]

For critics such as Horneffer, it was time for social policy to "reheroicize" life and undermine the forces of social demoralization and national emasculation. This message was particularly near to the hearts of proponents of eugenics and race hygiene.[68] Social security, in their view, needed to be personalized by once again privatizing fate, in other words, making individuals and households responsible for securing their survival in cases of misfortune.[69] This, in turn, would eugenically promote stronger, healthier, and more responsible families and citizens.[70] Self-sacrifice, as it had been during the First World War, was once again invoked, this time in the hope of exercising a regenerative influence on what had supposedly become a degenerate national culture.

Nazi perspectives on pain, injury, and social citizenship assumed this heroic imagery of regenerative (self-)sacrifice, adding to it more overtly military and racial elements. As was true of almost every public issue in the Third Reich, however, Nazi leaders and policy makers never entirely agreed on one unifying understanding of social suffering. Rather, policies and debates vacillated between two poles.

At one end stood National Socialism's avowed loyalty to those "noble" Germans who had "sacrificed" so much over the previous decades.[71] Nazism's definition of the polity was the racially pure "national community" (*Volksgemeinschaft*). Members of the *Volksgemeinschaft* were believed to be linked with one another not only by a common genetic fund, however, but also by a common fate (*Schicksalsgemeinschaft*). According to the foundational myth of the Nazi party, members of the national community were long-suffering, taken advantage of by parasitic forces in society (socialists, Jews), and in recent times compelled to make enormous sacrifices with little gratitude in return. In response, National Socialism's approach to social welfare for "the deserving" emphasized self-help and responsibility as forms of national and racial self-defense.

In practice, this meant it was incumbent upon members of the national community not only to provide for themselves and their families, but also to come to the aid of less fortunate members. This ethos was at the heart of the Third Reich's enormously successful annual winter relief drive (*Winterhilfswerk des Deutschen Volkes*), a national collection of donations to help the needy with fuel, food, and clothes during the winter months.[72] Program director Erich Hilgenfeldt touted the drive as a form of collective giving that established "the feeling of responsibility as the duty of every German, [one] which he has to his nation, his family, and the future."[73] In language and ritual, the annual campaign was dominated by the idiom of collective, national sacrifice, as citizens were enjoined to show their "readiness to sacrifice" (*Opferbereitschaft*) for "needy comrades" (*notleidende Kameraden*) in a highly ritualized public event that, as Wieland Elffording has observed, translated the idea of the *Volksgemeinschaft* into an everyday practice.[74] To give, the Propaganda Ministry told its employees in 1933, "is a sacred duty for all those who have the good fortune to have work and bread, while millions of their fellow citizens still suffer in bitter misery through no fault of their own."[75]

Besides nationalizing the pathos of sympathy for the deserving needy, National Socialism also infused it with certain martial elements. Nazi leaders came to power in 1933 explicitly promising to make sure the sacrifices of disabled veterans "were not in vain." At the Nuremberg party rally of 1933, the director of the National Socialist Disabled Veterans Relief organization made it clear that the new Third Reich was not going to treat wounded veterans the same as "the unemployed, invalids, and other welfare recipients." Rather, veterans were to be granted the greater honor (and by extension, the larger pension) that was due them. Moreover, laws passed in 1938 and 1939 awarded greater benefits to active-duty soldiers injured in combat than to those injured either in peacetime or in rear-echelon duty.[76] These efforts were reinforced after the outbreak of war in 1939 by a change in administrative language. From 1940 on, German military and health administrations replaced the term *Kriegsbeschädigter* (a World War I term used to refer to those injured in combat and implying the notions of "damage" and "ruination") with the term *Kriegsversehrter* (a term whose etymology linked it to "pain," "wound," and "combat").[77] Thus Nazi military disability policy abandoned conventional principles of compensation (based on earning ability) and reoriented them toward militarized values of courage, heroism, and sacrifice.

Pain and suffering, however, could also have a very different set of connotations within Nazi discourse. From this other pole, pain and suffering were evidence of biological and psychological weakness. Eugenics and race hygiene provided the salient framework that contributed a measure of consistency among often competing and contradictory party, state, and local decision makers in their common quest to defend the racially pure and inherently productive *Volksgemeinschaft*.[78]

Policies could therefore have two aspects: a negative and a positive eugenic and race-hygienic outlook. Chronic illness, deformity, invalidism, decrepitude, and poverty all were to be met with the tactics of a negative eugenics. This meant identification, selection, and ultimately elimination. A host of Nazi campaigns, all initiated before 1941, brought the mass arrest and imprisonment of vagabonds, beggars, welfare recipients, "work slouches," and the congenitally disabled; the sterilization of hundreds of thousands of so-called hereditary ill; and the commencement of "euthanasia" programs that killed approximately 200,000 mentally ill, disabled, chronically ill, and racially undesirable men, women, and children.[79] The counterpart to these ventures was a positive eugenics that sought to nurture and enhance the productive and reproductive capacities of the community. Here emphasis was placed on rewarding ideal mothers, promoting competitive achievement among workers, and exploiting the service of foreign slave labor.[80]

Thus, from this eugenic and productivist standpoint, pain and affliction were indicators of potential pathology that threatened to corrupt the national community. It was therefore left to Nazi administrators and medical personnel to decide the fate of the individuals they encountered. Those deemed salvageable were "rehabilitated" by being placed in highly regimented environments (typically special military units or work camps).[81] For the millions of others considered hopelessly incapable of joining the *Volksgemeinschaft*, extermination was the Third Reich's "final solution."

The defeat of the Third Reich, of course, brought an end to Nazi genocide. Yet, Germany under occupation (1945–49), as it had been during the last years of the war, remained a society marked by shortages and need. More than anything else, hunger and social dislocation reinforced the continuity in the general perception that the German plight was one of suffering.[82] The politics of social entitlement after the Second World War were thereby quickly reduced to a politics of physical survival, as evidenced by the prominence of food strikes, hunger demonstrations, inflation riots, theft, and black marketeering.[83]

Once rationing ended, the collective and personal memories of Germans in the Federal Republic continued to invoke the heroic transcendence of pain and suffering as sources of national pride and belonging. Public opinion surveys, government reports, and oral histories have shown that the majority of Germans after the war recalled the recent past as a period of good times (1935–41) sandwiched by bad times (1929–35 and 1941–49).[84] Indeed, as Omer Bartov has noted, many Germans continue to recall the years under Allied occupation as even more painful than the last years of the war.[85] The postwar foundational myths of Zero Hour (*Stunde Null*, the idea that the end of the war gave Germans a clean slate) and the Economic Miracle (*Wirtschaftswunder*, West Germany's "miraculous" economic recovery of the 1950s and 1960s) were therefore not only attempts at erasing the immediate past of genocide and total war; they also represented a distancing from the pain and suffering of previous decades.

Pain, Prosperity, and Social Security in Twentieth-Century Germany

Over the course of the 1950s, 1960s, and 1970s, both East and West German societies began divorcing themselves from the economy of scarcity, albeit with differing degrees of success. West Germans quickly latched on to the consumerist ideals of economic prosperity and escalating social satisfaction. Introduction of the deutsche mark in 1948 ushered in a period in which national identity and esteem became increasingly associated with social, familial, and individual prosperity.[86] As Michael Wildt has expressed it, "The practice of consumption, which until well into the 1950s involved making much out of little, now consisted in the art of creating something of one's own out of much."[87] East Germany, which only abandoned food rationing in 1958, responded to images of West German affluence through a deliberate campaign in the 1940s, 1950s, and 1960s intended to present its own progressive picture of success. In contrast to the capitalist West, "happiness and prosperity" in the German Democratic Republic were to be ensured through the socialist solidarity of workers and peasants, an ascetic-functional ethos of production and consumption, and the guarantee of a basic living standard.[88]

Thus, West and East Germany offered their citizens distinctive models of the way out of war and scarcity and into prosperity and belonging. These "official" versions of the prosperous society had important normative consequences for men and women. As Katherine Pence observes, Germans worked out new ideals of male wage-earners and housewife-consumers to fit the new paths of prosperity: the stable, breadwinning husband and the dedicated, morally responsible housewife in the Federal Republic; and their counterparts in the GDR, the hardworking, physical laborer and the inventive, time- and budget-conscious homemaker/employee.[89]

As divergent as the West and East German ideals of the "good society" were, however, both political systems shared a dedication to the ideal of social entitlement through social security. During the 1960s and 1970s, the Federal Republic and the German Democratic Republic not only *quantitatively* increased social services and benefits, but moreover *qualitatively* broadened the operational definitions of social security and entitlement to incorporate the demands of increasingly consumption-minded citizens. Claims of social entitlement centered less on assuring a minimum income than on guaranteeing a growing standard of living and a "quality of life" envisioned as a comfortable "way of life."[90] The virtually universal support of a "social security" among Eastern and Western Germans during as well as after Reunification testifies to its unique allure as a political ideal capable of crossing the ideological divide of the Cold War.[91]

In social security, Germans of the postwar era found a concept of state action that bridged their dreams of prosperity with their anxieties about pain. Entitlement to social security, in principle at least, did away with the centuries-old plight and fear of precariously vacillating between the poles of abundance and hunger.[92] Now the rational management of individual and social fates made it seemingly possible for citizens to assume a secure medium of material comfort despite the vagaries of the political economy. Forged by social suffering at the beginning of the twentieth century, the German sense of social entitlement was thus reaffirmed in a climate of social prosperity by century's end. Social citizenship in Germany, then, has always been something more than simply an extension of civil rights into the realm of class and industrial relations. Body, pain, claim, resentment, and prosperity: a complex mix of somatic fates and emotive rhetorics have informed the way in which Germans have debated and continue to debate social belonging, moral obligation, and political responsibility.

3   PETER FRITZSCHE

Cities Forget, Nations Remember: Berlin and Germany and the Shock of Modernity

HOWEVER dramatic the rapid-fire motion of events in the revolutionary season 1918–19—the sudden realization that Germany had lost the war, the bitter terms of the armistice, the hurried departure of the empire's kings and princes, the struggles of the new socialist regime with radical factions and its desperate efforts to provision a malnourished, war-weary population—there was widespread suspicion that the revolution had not really taken hold and had been almost effortlessly absorbed by the routines of everyday life. Not only did the republic fail to strike deep roots among Germans but its leaders were relentlessly caricatured and mocked. There is no better image of the republic's first missteps than the cover of an illustrated magazine depicting the president and prime minister as bathing beauties. A trivial quality to the revolution was detected from the outset. Countless historians have quoted the sharp-eyed diarist, Harry Kessler, who on the first Sunday of the November 1918 Revolution watched bourgeois Berliners out for a stroll in the Tiergarten and recognized just how imperturbable they remained. It was only a few days later that Kessler spied the return of the first officers in uniform on Potsdamer Platz. Even traces of the bloody rebellion of the Spartakists in January 1919 faded quickly from the metropolitan scene. What astonished Kessler was the city's insouciance in the face of political upheaval. After a nighttime visit to a cabaret he remarked:

Not until the revolution did I begin to comprehend the Babylonian, immeasurably deep, chaotic, and powerful aspect of Berlin. This aspect became evident in the fact that this immense movement within the even more immense ebb and flow of Berlin caused only small, local disturbances, as if an elephant had been stabbed with a penknife. It shook itself but then moved on as if nothing had happened.[1]

The film historian Klaus Kreimeier approvingly cites Kessler, and adds: "The throngs that poured into the movie theaters night after night, Ufa's opulent premieres, the sometimes elegant, sometimes crudely comic achievements of Ernst Lubitsch—these were all part and parcel of that immense 'ebb and flow of Berlin,' of the leviathanlike, voracious, everyday life of the city. It was this everyday life that gave Berliners their equanimity and armed them against the impositions of history. In a state of civil war, it protected them against the icy winds of global historical changes."[2]

Cities Forget . . .

Both Kessler and Kreimeier describe a forgetful city. Leaving little more than scratches of a "penknife," which are barely felt by the metropolitan "elephant," history simply disappears amidst the hectic movements and popular entertainments of city people. This radical indifference is a central motif for interpreting the modern metropolis and particularly modern Berlin. The city is the space in which the "crisis of memory" manifested itself.[3] Karl Scheffler, author of the most famous survey of the city, *Berlin. Ein Stadtschicksal* (1910), concluded that the tragedy of Berlin was its fate "always to become and never to be." Scheffler's Berlin was always in transition and his Berliners were always resident nomads rather than recognizable bearers of culture and tradition. Even the city's physical geography effaced markings of time: "Berlin does not have natural points of reference or a dramatic physiognomy," Scheffler wrote, "the highs and lows that give a city charming and lively differences of altitude are completely missing."[4] The city's uniform layout swallowed up historical detours and cultural monuments, just as the elephant shook off the stabs of the penknife.

A more sociological but strikingly similar perspective was assumed by Scheffler's contemporary, Georg Simmel, who made his home on the busy corner of Leipziger and Friedrichstrasse. Simmel examined "The Metropolis and Mental Life" (1904) to argue that the fluctuations and contradictions of the big city required a dramatic process of psychological adjustment or "inner urbanization," which was distinguished by heightened sensual dexterity but also by emotional indifference.[5] In the barrage of new sensations, life in the metropolis amounted to a series of improvisations that foreclosed on secure and stable patterns. As a result, quotidian time measured in days and hours overwhelmed the historical time of anniversaries, reminiscence, and expectation. The extension of the money economy in the modern city accelerated this process of homogenization since the unimpeded circulation of money had created equivalencies for all standards of value and consequently leveled precapitalist distinctions and refinements as well as customs and obligations inherited from the past.

And Berliners knew just how right Simmel was: Throughout this period, they looked on aghast as stately eighteenth-century properties in the Friedrichstadt were bought up, torn down, and replaced by uniform, interchangeable commercial houses. "All things lie on the same level," Simmel instructed; they "differ from one another only in the size of the area which they cover."[6] It quickly became clear, as he argued in his *Philosophy of Money*, a highly influential text published with the new century, that one attribute of the modern economy was that "things do not last for any length of time."[7] For this reason, Simmel, like Charles Baudelaire, took the precarious and capricious quality of fashion to be the most telling indicator of modern time. What had become pleasurable at the beginning of the twentieth century were the "beginnings and ends," "the coming and going," the state of flux itself.[8]

The essays of Scheffler and Simmel remain astonishingly perceptive and have established the essential plot to the city. For the three generations of observers who have followed Scheffler and witnessed the devastation of two world wars, the thirty-year division of the city, and now the busy new start of Reunification, Berlin has remained a classically modern city because its character has been so forcefully determined by the experience of transience.[9] Given the horrors of Nazism, the terrible evacuation of the city's Jews in 1943, as well as the hardships of the socialist dictatorship in the East after 1949 and the erection of the Berlin Wall in 1961, it might seem fanciful to invoke the forgetfulness of a city in which, as Chancellor Gerhard Schroeder dutifully noted, "even the stones cry."[10] It is true, of course, that in the last decades municipal officials have struggled to create an appropriate memorial landscape.[11] Nonetheless the early analyses of Scheffler and Simmel, both of whom identified the modern city as a place of forgetting, a site in which nothing much endures, remain pertinent given the complete disappearance of the wall; the undoing of the strange juxtapositions between East and West, and center and periphery, and the tidy renovation of once wrecked and ruined, but evocative parts of the city that followed; and the whitewashed, prosperous exterior of urban improvements since 1989 generally. Reunification has steadily swept up the fragments of the past and dimmed the aura of the broken dreams and vivid nightmares that surrounded them.

The forgetful city should not be demonized. There is such a thing as too much past, and the passage from one generation to the next of the memories of civil war, whether in the former Yugoslavia, Northern Ireland, or Palestine, has an ominous, even stifling aspect.[12] Individuals felt this, too, and the disappearance of their personal pasts in the city could be enormously liberating. Men and women arrived in the city from the surrounding countryside, abandoning the lives they had once lived and the debts they owed to family and custom. The city was the blank slate for which the modern dreamer longed. And once in the city, people moved about with astonishing mobility, leaving behind unwelcome employers and unhappy situations in the security of anonymity. In a late-nineteenth century survey of young women who migrated to the city to work as maids, for example, more than half had switched employers after only twelve months. A number had found husbands, better-paying factory work, or more pleasant conditions in other households. Some slipped out of housework altogether, brought to term unexpected pregnancies, and perhaps made ends meet as prostitutes.[13] Waitresses, too, developed hard, but no less self-reliant strategies to adjust to the turbulence of city life, as Simmel predicted they might. Although newcomers easily found employment in hundreds of restaurants, cafés, and bars, they could be fired easily and subsisted mainly on meager tips. As a result, restaurant help rarely stayed in one place for more than several months. According to one 1893 sample of waitresses, more than three-quarters had changed places of work at least six times in a single year.[14] For all its distress, the tempo that scrubbed the past clean delighted Robert Walser, an enthusiastic emigrant and young writer from Switzerland. "The wonder of the city," he wrote in 1907, his first year in Berlin, "is that any particular bearing or behavior is drowned by all the thousands of variations, that opinion is completely fleeting, that while judgment is pronounced quickly, everything is forgotten as a matter of course." Surrounded by new facades and new fashions and new opportunities, city people moved restlessly forward and did not give the past a second thought. "What has passed?" Walser asked, "a facade from the Second Empire? Where? Back there? As if someone is going to stop, turn around, and look at the old-fashioned style one more time. Why? Move on, move on."[15]

Thanks to its solvent potentials and destructive mobility, the city provided the backdrop against which Hellmuth Plessner imagined a new social type in the 1920s. According to Plessner, modern life had withdrawn the conditions for returning home. To attempt such a return would result in a fixation on a single identity, refurbish reactionary politics, and inhibit the development of the individual person, who could live fully only as a traveler, a stranger, or, in other words, a metropolitan.[16] Here Plessner anticipated the figure of the postmodern fugitive, whose terrain is the brand-new, completely mobilized global cityscape. Zygmunt Bauman writes in similar fashion. Today, metropolitan life is lived as a succession of small, unending emergencies: "The hub of postmodern life strategy is not identity building, but the avoidance of being fixed."[17] Bauman's city people are on the move, "settling against," one might say, stability and rootedness.

Yet the forgetfulness of the city could also bewilder contemporaries. Designed to move goods and services and people quickly and efficiently, the industrial city of the late nineteenth and early twentieth centuries was in a constant state of renovation. It tore away the accretions of time and memory. The worn, smooth edges of the city of memory that Friedrich Nietzsche imagined in his description of antiquarian, commemorative history were abraded again and again by real-estate commodification, newly opened storefronts, and large-scale projects of urban renewal. Born in 1870, the journalist Arthur Eloesser mourned the precincts of his youth that had disappeared already by the 1890s. He had lost the marks and monuments of his city "in the ceaseless influx of new inhabitants who lived from day to day, without memory, without tradition, without a sense of duty to the past."[18] In many ways, he had become a stranger. The generations that followed made similar laments, so that one of the most remarkable aspects of the city was its forgetfulness or lack of history. There was no better exposition of the depletion of the past than Siegfried Kracauer's acclaimed essay from the year 1932. In "A Street Without Memory," Kracauer described a Kurfürstendamm that incorporated "emptily flowing time in which nothing endures." A never-ending train of new shops, new fashions, and new facades effaced any memory of what had been: "The new enterprises are absolutely new and those that have been displaced by them are totally extinguished." The prewar sandstone ornaments, themselves once completely up-to-date, now already "a bridge to yesterday," were simply knocked down.[19] Amidst ceaseless renovation, the Kurfürstendamm stood for a city that lived entirely without the past. As a sandstone city, both literally and imaginatively, Berlin was not so much newly modern as eternally new. For Kracauer this meant that metropolitans were never able to take their bearings or understand their historical circumstances, and thus could not act in politically liberating ways. Particularly the big-city public of clerks and employees, whom he studied more carefully, remained enthralled in the moment, their interests and passions and commitments pressed into the same sandstone forms as the city's facades.[20]

The city swallowed up tragedies, which were trivialized into natural occurrences rather than examined for social context and political meaning. Berliners devoured newspapers, and there were scores of daily and weekly papers from which to choose. But, as Kracauer noted, the items in the paper did not form a coherent line, just "a series of points," and today's poignant event became tomorrow's old news: "I know of no other city that is capable of so promptly shaking off what has just occurred," he concluded. This empty space was filled with fortuitous and coincidental events which lent the city excitement and dynamism, and made it a spectacle, but tore away at its history.[21] Gruesome murders, such as that of nine-year-old

Lucie Berlin in a crowded Ackerstrasse tenement in June 1904, for example, were quickly forgotten. No one cared to remember Lucie's life or tell her story, and some twenty years later, neighbors misstated her age and misplaced the date of the murder even further into time, to 1891.[22] Collective events slipped from metropolitan memory as well: the hunger demonstrations in 1890 or the anti-Jewish riots in the Scheunenviertel in 1923. Indeed, cities rarely remember their bruised and torn social histories: What collective frame of memory holds the story of the deadly race riots that erupted in the United States after World War I (in East St. Louis, Chicago, and Tulsa)? With its stress on newness, mobility, and adaptability, the city is a poor organ of remembrance.

The forgetful city threatened even the very sense of self by which people built a sense of identity and character. In this place of changing fortunes, inhabitants moved constantly, renting better apartments when times were good, finding more modest rooms when they turned bad. An astonishing one out of every two apartments turned over every year during the period (1879–94) of one survey. The result of this *Nomadenleben* was that Berliners grew up in and experienced the city from constantly shifting vantages.[23] Their memories lacked the stable of markers by which Walter Benjamin, for one, described his childhood in Berlin W., and they may well have faded altogether. Social Democratic reformers cited the case of one family that was almost completely imprisoned by the present, unable to make much sense of the life itinerary it had followed:

At first they found lodgings with a brother of the husband in Lichtenberg, at the time a rather insignificant village. Then they moved for two years to Pankow, where the husband found good work on a road crew for two years. Finally, they arrived in the city itself. The sick woman couldn't even keep the streets straight in which she had lived, didn't even know in which apartments her last two living children had been born. She could only say that the family moved about every six months. She had lived in some fifteen different apartments.[24]

In this particular case, hours and days, and the shifts of work and fortune, had deleted birthdays, anniversaries, and family celebrations. This is a remarkable and telling finding, one that indicates how little correspondence there was between life and geography. The structure of city life, the hasty movement of people and things, and the indifference of money, was presumed to have prompted a general crisis of memory that Kracauer, Benjamin, and other social theorists identified with the extremities, or the emergency, of modernity.[25] Transience, provisionality, or, in other words, the "lightness" of metropolitan life did not undo tragedy and pain but left it mute and without social sanction.[26] Insofar as the city denied its inhabitants a social frame for memory it left them without history or subjectivity.

There is reason, then, to think that Harry Kessler was right: that a neglected but striking aspect of the metropolis was its ability to move metropolitans on as if nothing had happened. But consider the time he is writing in: January 1919. What about the experience of mass death in World War I, the daily privations of scarce and rationed foodstuffs, and the mounting economic hardships of inflation? What about the November Revolution? Were these events simply swallowed up in the spectacle of city life, as we might take to understand from Kessler's description of a city that is as indifferent to history as an elephant is to the penknife? As it was, both the war and the inflation raised fundamental questions about the cohesion of the national collective as well as the pertinence of the traditions and customs that gave the nation its particular intimacy. Observers trembled at the prospect that without the integrative functions of national memory the sacrifices of Germans in the war would have been in vain. Throughout the 1920s, they anxiously reported on the force by which mass culture and everyday entertainments seemed to have stranded people in a permanent, unreflective present. The so-called dance craze, in particular, became the object of obsessive commentary, a symptom of a profound crisis of national memory in which the past and the sacrifices it had called forth were no longer woven into social identity. With its dance halls and unemployment lines, and its unsettled aspect, it was the postwar city that marked out the geography of oblivion that threatened to erase the vividness of German history.

In many ways, war in the years 1914–18 appeared to be an intensification of city life by ripping people from the moorings of the past, foreclosing on a predictable future, and stranding them in a terrifying, unending present. On leave and at home, veterans came to realize that the war amounted to a huge process of desacralization in which the unregulated flow of men and matériel, like the streams of money in the capitalist economy, abraded hierarchies of value and deflated concepts such as honor, service, and bravery. The postwar years did little to relieve the sense of erosion. Alfred Polgar surveyed Vienna after the war in ways that are suggestive for Berlin. He noted the dilapidated houses: "paint peels off and the facades crumble." "For years there has not been any new construction," he wrote. "No new apartments, no young, clean house grows out of this infertile ground. And the old ones give in without resistance to weathering and decay." The point is not whether Polgar accurately described postwar decay in the light of remembered prewar prosperity, but rather that he used city precincts to express the pointlessness and incommensurability of modern life. He went on to point out that clocks, which had once been so informative and calibrated, no longer told the same time: "The clocks on the streets, on church steeples, and on public buildings are fast or slow or do not work at all. Some are missing their face, others hands . . . those with bells chime at will."[27] Polgar depicted a city without plan or regulation or organization. In Vienna, and in Berlin as well, the center dropped out, leaving the city a tangle of side streets. "Her glitter is gone," concluded the *Berliner Illustrirte Zeitung* about Friedrichstrasse in 1919:

> The only thing that remains are the side streets, at which corners the street vendors stand peddling chocolate, shoe wax, pancakes, shoelaces, cigarettes, meat loaves, an endless chain along the building fronts from Belle-Alliance Platz to the Weidendammer Brücke. Even the shoe polishers are back home from the war.[28]

The emphatic attention paid to street vendors is revealing. The war had cheapened life not only by forcing people to sell their keepsakes, heirlooms, and other memory pieces but by turning treasures into junk as a result of curbside exchanges. Moreover, the war allegedly reduced countless city people to salesmen, who lived only by buying and selling in the most public and unadorned way. The widespread conviction that veterans in fact constituted the great majority of postwar vendors indicated how the national effort of 1914 had been completely drained of social meaning. All that was left five or six years later was ceaseless exchange. The hard cynicism by which observers repeatedly took veterans and particularly war cripples to be hustlers and fakes reveals that there was little in the way of a redemptive narrative to make sense of suffering. An unsympathetic psychiatric profession left victims of war trauma to fend for themselves, refusing in the main to acknowledge the damage the war had inflicted or to support pension claims, which they dismissed as pension scams.[29] Memories of the war were repeatedly debased into the tawdry terms of the market.

To be sure, families remembered lost sons and brothers and fathers, and placed commemorative photographs on mantle pieces and under Christmas trees. But just how enduring this vernacular culture of remembrance was is not at all clear. Without a broader political frame the losses were mainly a private matter, and private wounds eventually healed.[30] In fact, at war's end observers were struck by how quickly the war was repressed or forgotten. They repeatedly invoked the "dance craze" of the early 1920s to underscore the lightness of the memory of war, the insubstantiality of its effects among so many veterans and their families. According to Hans Ostwald, "Itzehoe"—this is a place in Schleswig-Holstein—"can claim the fame of having allowed dancing in five public halls already on the Sunday after the armistice."[31] Six weeks later, on New Year's Eve 1918, officials in the capital lifted the ban on public dances. "Berlin has never experienced such a New Year's Eve," commented the *Berliner Tageblatt*: "everywhere, here, there, and over there, on the northside, on the westside, on the southside, and in the suburbs, New Year's Eve balls." These commonplaces—and they littered newspapers in this period—were invariably contrasted with the political events they devalued: "Between three-four time and street disturbances, between confetti and red flags, dancers glide into the new year."[32] Throughout the city could be found disconcerting places where war and revolution had been forgotten.

The dramatic accounts of postwar inflation and hyperinflation also entailed suffering, and even greater confusion. They worked against popular conceptions of value and intuitive notions of monetary exchange, and therefore left people increasingly bewildered. Over the years 1919–23, the rapid devaluation of money intensified precisely the experience of the momentary and the transitory that social critics regarded as constitutive of modernity. Inflation declared a permanent state of emergency in which neither orthodox economic practices nor conventional economic values offered points of orientation; it invalidated experience. Like the war, then, the inflation entailed a huge process of desacralization in which the "misappropriation of money and goods" was accompanied by a more profound "misappropriation of spiritual values and a soiling" of what countless citizens "held to be holy."[33] At the same time, the inflationary spiral closed off long-range planning and held Germans to what became an elongated economic present in which money had to be spent as soon as it was acquired. As a result, even those Germans who did not speculate on the stock market became more or less skilled entrepreneurs of the moment in order to retain marginal value to the depreciating mark or to rapidly convert devalued marks into more reliable speculative instruments. Although workers, shopkeepers, and artisans denounced big capital and big finance, they too had become *Geldmenschen*, operating, comparing, and judging in their own spheres much like the traders and speculators whom Simmel had introduced as the characteristically free individuals of the modern metropolis. All sorts of constituents pursued the politics of narrow economic interest. Assessing the effects of the inflation, the respected economist Franz Eulenberg concluded in 1924 that "capitalist thinking" had in fact "advanced enormously" among all social groups.[34] The city itself incorporated the busyness of business. Hans Ostwald described the main streets of the big city reduced to little more than "money streets" in which a "ground-floor architecture" of "juice bars," "gin shops," and "cigarette and tobacco stands" flourished against a transitional backdrop of "posters and paper scraps."[35]

Given the permanent emergency, in which "capitalist thinking" mobilized more and more people, one of the consequences of inflation was to obscure the enormous damage it had wrought in the whirlwind of change it had introduced. The cumulative effect was to make yesterday's pain no worse than today's or tomorrow's. Moreover, the inflation demanded momentary, quick responses. "Slogans and facts, incidents and affairs . . . all the new things that bubbled to the surface! All the new things that arrived on the scene loudly and shrilly!" wrote Hans Ostwald in a brilliant summation of the spectacle of catastrophe. Inflation made credible the cool judgment of business and the mass culture of fashion and entertainment.[36] Not surprisingly, it was dance tunes and musical hits that caught the uninhibited spirit of the inflation—think of "*Wir verkaufen unser Oma ihr klein Häuschen*" or Claire Waldorf's "*Warum soll er nicht mit ihr?*"—and it was the tunes and hits, the "shimmies, foxtrots, one-steps, double foxes, African shimmies, Java dances, and Creole polkas," observed by Thomas Mann with such disconcertment in *Disorder and Early Sorrow* that best expressed the fortuitous and provisional aspects of the inflation.[37] Mass entertainment, not only the latest band hits, but also movies, fashion and body culture, and weekend outings, demarcated the extension of a culture of consumption that was "modern, ahistorical, [and] respectless."[38]

In a consumer culture that valued pragmatism and sobriety there was little room for the heaviness of remembrance and lamentation. As a result, individuals often recalled the losses of the inflation to themselves with shame or humiliation. "People prefer to hush them up or conceal them," wrote Elias Canetti, an attentive listener who during this time lived in a Frankfurt boarding house run by his mother.[39] Those witnesses who insisted on telling their tales of inflation seemed completely bewildered, or else distinctly unmodern and bound to tradition. They were like the widow Scharrenhöfer in Hans Fallada's *Kleiner Mann—was nun?* In rooms crowded with prewar bric-a-brac, the landlady cried alone in the dark and repeatedly asked why her money was "all gone." She was a forsaken character whom "the young people" she rents to quickly abandoned.[40]

The very "disorder" of the inflation militated against organizing its experiences into comprehensible order. Its violence ("all gone") had to be taken for granted—"but there was the devaluation of money" Scharrenhöfer is told, with the untranslatable *doch* serving to remind her of the obviousness and invariance of the facts. For Fallada's "young people," the contemporary world manifested itself in its obvious, that is, disheveled, or chaotic state. In this way, the shock of Weimar modernity, the illegitimacy of the past and the fleeting nature of the present, closely resembled the structures of city life investigated by Simmel and Kracauer. As Erich Kästner's character Fabian knew in 1931: "life is lived provisionally; the crisis will not end."[41] Still, there is something a little surprising in the merely muffled way that a pathetically caricatured widow objects to the given world and in the swiftness by which Fallada's "Lämmchen" unquestioningly accepts the catastrophe of inflation in her response. And yet the evidence from all sorts of metropolitan observers pointed to widespread indifference rather than sensitivity to the damage wrought by the inflation. (This forgetfulness is not unique: In the United States, the Great Depression surely mobilized Americans politically, but it also led millions of others, "the spawn of an individualist culture," to turn inward and blame themselves for their fate; and in the Soviet Union, the trauma of mass death in World War I was completely effaced by revolution and civil war.)[42] Indeed, one of the reasons Kracauer launched his exploration of mass culture in Weimar-era Berlin was to provide an account of the process by which the pain of experience was not turned into the narrative of evidence, but rather streamlined into ahistorical indifference, into facts and occasions.[43] Covering much the same terrain, Walter Benjamin toured the metropolitan sites of the German inflation, the little shops, the bank facades, and the littered streets, to demonstrate how historical and political events had been reified into wholly natural misfortune. For Benjamin the principal result of the twentieth-century's military and economic catastrophes was a disassembling of the categories of experience by which people made sense of their lives and gave evidence of their troubles: "never has experience been contradicted more thoroughly than strategic experience by tactical warfare, economic experience by inflation, bodily experience by hunger, and moral experience by those in power." Without the marks and pointers to understand these events, a whole generation that had still taken a "horse-drawn tram to school found itself under the open sky, in a landscape in which nothing remained unchanged but the clouds." Germans had been ripped from a comprehensible scene. "In a forcefield of destructive torrents and explosions," they had been stripped of history and reduced to "tiny, fragile human bodies."[44] As Peter Hughes argues, "Catastrophic violence destroys any stable sense of time and closes off that sense of a future without which history cannot be imagined." Catastrophe's victims "star[ed] at the camera of history like the refugees in contemporary photos." Their broken relations to the structures of temporality had turned them into modern-day analogues of the "primitive."[45]

Not least among the horrors of war and inflation, then, was the threat of oblivion, the death of social meaning and mutual understanding, so that all that was left were the "tiny, fragile human bodies" to which Benjamin referred, or the blank refugees in Hughes's account. While at first glance it seems counterintuitive that the unprecedented

sacrifices of Germans would be forgotten, it was precisely the total mobilization of the war that seemed to overwhelm the social imagination,
devalue collective concepts such as the state or the nation, and thus undercut the basis for social memory. Yet it was also the unwillingness to
accept the individual's total inability to take historical bearings that
prompted Kracauer and Benjamin to disembed the pain from the natu-
ralizing processes that hushed it away. Although they hardly wanted to
repair the nation, they actively sought to resist the disintegration of
memory and the invisibility of history. Kracauer himself detected resistance to oblivion. In a 1930 essay, "Screams of the Street," Kracauer focused on the "terror that is without an object" permeating the prosperous "streets in the west" precincts of Berlin: "their populace do not
belong together and the atmosphere in which communal actions emerge
is completely lacking in them." "Without content," Berlin W. expressed
the empty, ahistorical, and solitary aspect to the city that had been the
aim of so much of Kracauer's commentary. This overall muteness he contrasted to the sensible noise of a "National Socialist gang" and to the
"penetrating odor" of political riots in "Neukölln perhaps or Wedding,"
both distinctly left-wing proletarian districts.[46] It is not explicable why
Kracauer did not turn the corner and examine more closely the gang or
the riot, both of which do have "an object." His precisely observed reportage notwithstanding, Kracauer, like Kessler before him, is so taken
with the gloomy evidence of the crisis of postwar memory that he missed
the rehabilitative, if dangerous, efforts to reframe it.[47]

. . . Nations Remember

The very forgetfulness of the city generated ceaselessly renewed efforts
to create meaning and to restore memory. Discussing the postmodern
city in ways that are relevant to 1920s Berlin, the sociologist Zygmunt
Bauman observes that whenever people are constantly on guard, capable of moving through the crowd yet increasingly exhausted by the effort, "the thought of a refuge—a home—grows into a temptation ever
more difficult to resist." For all its provisional features, "city life," he
concludes, "cannot but render those dreams of home ever more intense."[48] It is in the city that "the enjoyment of protean, unbound identity and the desire for 'home,' for a community that binds and puts an
end to the perpetual exile of postmodern Proteus, are born, as twins."[49]
The search for new models of order validated notions of collective
morality and behavior, or community, and often quite exclusive visions
of nationhood, and they demonized the metropolitan figure of the fugitive and the stranger. If the city was pitiless in its forgetful, destructive

indifference, the nation redeemed suffering through memory and ritual. In other words, cities forget, nations remember.

The longing for memory in the forgetful city can be illustrated by the career of Hans Ostwald, one of the most well-known journalists in early twentieth-century Berlin, and, as already shown, after World War I, a major documenter of the inflation. For Ostwald, imperial Berlin had been an exciting journey of discovery, and his *flânerie* challenged the pretensions of the Wilhelmine establishment with sympathetic portraits of prostitutes, vagabonds, and other metropolitan marginals. But after World War I, the former vagabond, who had in fact tramped around Germany in the 1890s, mapped out a fearsome and disreputable cityscape in his influential *Sittengeschichte der Inflation*, or *Tales of the Inflation*. Many of the same characters introduced before the war reappear in the *Sittengeschichte*: criminals, gamblers, hustlers, prostitutes, musicians, occultists. But rather than exotic mutations on the shifting ground of the industrial city, they are vilified as extraneous parasites. Having given up the idea of expanding the notion of the *Volk* and making city people more familiar to each other—the explicit goal of Ostwald's prewar journalism— the *Sittengeschichte* polices the borders surrounding the *Volk*, at once distinguishing and segregating the margins in an effort to make more sanitary the core.[50] The diversity that had nourished a variety of ethnic, sexual, and cultural subjectivities in pre-1914 Berlin continued to be acknowledged, indeed was commented on in luxurious detail, but was now condemned for its hindrance of one particular subjectivity, that of the German people. Ostwald's vagabond longed to return home.

The face of Ostwald's new, postwar character, *das deutsche Volk* or *unser deutsches Volk*, remained mostly blank—Ostwald is more concerned with the physiognomical study of depravity—but its presentation to readers indicates a fundamental shift in the way Ostwald places Berlin in relationship to Germany. Whereas before the war, Ostwald endeavored to reveal the complexity of social existence and thereby elaborated a genre of realistic metropolitan reportage, after the war, he contrasted the intimacy, endurance, and transparency of "our" Germans to the indefinite, shifting, *Zeiterscheinungen* (temporary appearances) of the inflation; he opposed reliability to momentariness, the heaviness of the nation to the lightness of postwar disorder. The newly imagined national collective— "the brave little man, the letter carrier, and the train engineer, the seamstress and the washerwoman"—that Ostwald called together in the name of the *Volk* served to absorb the chaos of war, revolution, and inflation. It was an especially effective subject because it acknowledged the widespread suffering of ordinary, but "true" Germans. "Freezing Germany, its children and its women, who had to run out for coal for day and return so often with empty hands . . . the Germany that froze and suffered, that couldn't buy butter at usurious prices, couldn't buy goose and other delicacies"—all that hardship composed "the true picture of our country and its people." Sentimental images of deprived women and children stand in for Germany, and it is as Germans that their suffering is remembered and incorporated into a more stable future defined by hygiene, reliability, and work. Collective health is inextricably linked to national virtue: "The German people raised itself up again," Ostwald explained, "only because it was a people of work. Only through work could it create value and thereby build a new life."[51] Ostwald's text is exemplary of the way the twentieth-century idea of community and nation worked to redeem the pain of millions of individuals. The image of the nation validated individual suffering as national suffering, located individual misfortune in a common history, and thereby gave it social poignancy. It offered isolated and bewildered persons a collective understanding, and promised them a visible future. As Rudy Koshar explains, "Modernity's awful lightness, promoted by its unending production of societal resources outside experiential boundaries, has been countered, evoked, explained, and even facilitated by the nation's unbearable and enduring weight."[52]

National feeling among Germans dates back to the beginning of the nineteenth century and was certainly no invention of the 1910s and 1920s. But important cultural good as it was among the middle and even the working classes, identification with the nation was abstract and officious, and had very possibly diminished by the beginning of the twentieth century. The losses of World War I and later the hardships of military defeat, revolution, and inflation facilitated an intimate identification of the bodies of countless individuals with the particular body of the nation and aroused Germans (in various ways) to cultivate and guard the national idea.

The escalation of a Balkan conflict into a general European war, and the massive mobilization of men and matériel that ensued, insistently posed the question: How would the terrible losses of the battlefield and the home front be accounted? At the end of 1914, more than one million soldiers on both sides had been killed. By Christmastime, nearly every German family mourned the loss of a son, a brother, or a father. At the same time, the onset of the war caused massive disruption among working-class families. While the busy routines of the war economy quickly absorbed initial unemployment, long working hours on the shop floor and in the office, and an increasingly desperate food situation, assured the misery and unhealthy conditions of daily life during the war. Impoverished conditions prevailed until well into the 1920s, although social groups were variously effected. In these stressful circumstances, observers feared the overall fragmentation of the community; indeed historians have subsequently described national politics as a Hobbesian war of all against all in which interest groups mobilized to protect their advantages.[53] Yet it was not only narrow interests, that is to say, Simmel's quick-witted *Geldmenschen*, who indicated the damage incurred by Germany's military and economic catastrophe. The most authoritative means by which individuals made sense of their losses was by identifying their own fate with that of the nation. This identification allowed individuals to encounter each other as contemporaries, as nationals and Germans; to uphold their common rights through their common suffering; and to tell, share, and thus validate each other's stories. National feeling generated a common interest in the fate of individual Germans. It thereby created a nexus of memory in which to remember and commemorate the soldiers who died, the lives that had been disrupted, and the efforts that had been expended.

The idea of sacrifice to the nation is such a compelling "storied death" because the common bonds of national feeling preserved the memories of the fallen in the imagined continuity of the collective. History and particularly national history is something "told at the graveside" to make good the losses that would otherwise have been forgotten.[54] To be sure, the extent and endurance of the war, and the demands of the state, forced people to recognize the national idea. No newspaper reader or tavern bystander could help being caught up in a European war that was invariably cast in terms of "us" versus "them," Germans versus French or Russians. Given that 85 percent of all eligible males were mobilized at some point during the conflict, a total of some thirteen million German men, it is important to acknowledge the very personal ties that connected families to the fortunes of the nation and its armies.[55] Yet, at the same time, social contracts from below gave life to the functional requirements mandated from above. Such contracts were made from the most unexpected quarters. In the proletarian precinct of Prenzlauer Berg, for example, the artist and social activist Käthe Kollwitz commented in her diary that she "felt as if I were becoming new" as she watched her son report to his reserve unit in August 1914. The thought that accompanied the departure of her son was simply, "I felt ready to sacrifice myself." Four days later, Kollwitz began work in the "Aid Commission" of the National Women's Service, a newly founded patriotic group she in other circumstances would have certainly avoided. Despite the death of her son, already in autumn 1914, Kollwitz continued to follow, somewhat to her own surprise, "a sense of duty and responsibility toward the Fatherland."[56] Again and again, in her self-compositions, she linked her personal losses to the service and sacrifice to the nation.

The "storied death" that soldiers and the bereaved families of the dead told most often was that of the nation. As George L. Mosse has reaffirmed, the cult of the fallen soldier provided a way not only to romanticize the dead and lift their deaths out of the gruesome reality of the war but also to connect countless ordinary men with a larger collectivity, the nation, the endurance of which their sacrifices had insured. To a post–World War II generation that does not so easily recognize the romance of the war hero or acknowledge the dutifulness of the volunteer, it is hard to admit the attachment to the idea of the national cause. And yet it had tremendous force during World War I and the years that followed, which is precisely why the political Right succeeded where the Left did not. As Mosse puts it somewhat sharply, "the inability of the Left to forget the reality of the war and to enter into the Myth of the War Experience," to remember the war through the blinkered eyes of the nation, "was a gain for the political Right."[57] Again and again, the reply to the question "For what?" was "For Germany." It was not until the last months of the war that a more critical and cynical sentiment denied larger meanings to the carnage, but even then most Germans resisted the notion of "unstoried death" that it entailed; arrayed on the Left and the Right, citizens readily accepted the national terms of congratulation ("undefeated in battle") offered by Friedrich Ebert, the chancellor of the new republic, as he greeted the returning veterans at the Brandenburger Tor in December 1918. It is often forgotten how patriotic were the homecoming celebrations in the wake of military defeat; on Heidelberger Platz in the Berlin suburb of Wilmersdorf vendors did a smashing business selling red, black, and white imperial flags to gathered well-wishers. Even Käthe Kollwitz bumped into a parade on Prenzlauer Allee on 12 December: "Cannons, horses, helmets festooned with bright paper streamers. It looked so nice."[58] "It looked so nice"—after four terrible, terrifying years of war the blush of the nation for this Social Democrat and bereaved mother had not completely faded. In the years that followed the cult of the war dead remained credible because it recalled the deaths of individuals by invoking the national idea for which they were said to have sacrificed themselves.[59]

Of course, the nation commemorated in the streets of Berlin in December 1918 was hardly the same one that imperial officials had imagined when they reported with patriotic self-satisfaction four years earlier, when the kaiser's picture could seen everywhere.[60] Over the course of the war, a populist version of the nation had taken hold. The war was accompanied by a surge of public activism that historians have neglected to take seriously. Like Kollwitz, thousands of women volunteered to join the Red Cross, work in hospitals, and otherwise aid in war relief efforts. Concern for the people's health and welfare assembled unprecedented coalitions that brought together municipal officials, local socialists, and other activists long before imperial authorities moved into action. This work on the body of the nation generated a sense of national fellowship that for all its contradictions was genuine, and was treasured precisely because it was unofficial.[61] Indeed, public activism during the war anticipated Weimar's center-left parliamentary coalitions and provided the foundation for Weimar-era social policy. Long after the war was over, the so-called spirit of 1914 was remembered and embellished in patriotic ceremonies across Germany. This was the case for the Left as well as the Right: for the social-democratic *Reichsbanner*, August 1914 had been the first step toward the "*Volksgemeinschaft* of republicans" it struggled to realize in the Weimar Republic. To this end, the influential socialist group, with over 100,000 members, cultivated the wartime camaraderie of the trenches and rehearsed the wartime field services, training exercises, closed-formation marches, and patriotic songs ("*Ich hatt' einen Kameraden*," for example) that also composed the repertoire of its larger right-wing adversary, the *Stahlhelm*.[62] That the ideas of 1914 lived on so animatedly as a myth in the postwar imagination, even if contradicted by fact, confirmed just how effectively the idea of the nation valorized the efforts of ordinary people and, consequently, how forcefully it retrospectively organized postwar memories.

The "spirit of 1914" acquired credibility not least because it created a powerful vocabulary of political enfranchisement. However fictitious the idea of national harmony was during the war, it allowed poor people, and particularly working-class women and children, to lay claim on rights as Germans and compelled previously unsympathetic government officials to regard these claimants not as political opponents but as fellow citizens. Indeed, sentimental narratives of the nation at war, and the sacrifices of its mothers and soldiers, gave poignancy and voice to the suffering of "women of modest means." And, in turn, hungry women and children expressed the suffering and righteousness of the nation ringed by enemies and weakened by the Allied food blockade. As Belinda Davis shows, access to scarce goods such as food and pensions came to be regulated by one's capacity as a citizen rather than one's status as a widow or soldier's wife.[63] Giving authority to the image of the righteous, suffering people was its negative, the nearly ubiquitous metropolitan figure of the wartime profiteer, whose frequent portrayal as Jewish merely served to harden the opposition of national insiders versus corrupt outsiders.[64] The politics of food in wartime Berlin indicates just how quickly political

claims and public policy were made with reference to the imagined unity of the nation or the people (*Volk*). The endpoint of this process was realized with the November Revolution: the full and equal political enfranchisement and increasing social security for all Germans.

Furthermore, it would be a mistake to depreciate the role of the national idea as it was conceived in the war, even amidst the rancorous politics of the Weimar Republic. It was precisely as Germans, as bearers of the national ordeal of war and inflation, that Weimar-era constituents made social and economic claims and disputed the advantages of others. Nationalism guided the notions of right and justice that were at the very center of Weimar's economic disputes. For example, in the case of dispossessed creditors, whose loans had been paid back in worthless, depreciated currency, German judges shifted from "reason to morality."[65] "They abandoned the laissez-faire basis of contract," argues Michael Hughes, in favor of "vague, socially based, conceptions of equity" that favored the claims of creditors, which, I believe, can only be understood in light of newly validated notions of national community.[66] It was the war, more than anything else, that encouraged interest groups to see themselves as rightful claimants in national politics and to complain (loudly) if they felt disadvantaged; it was the nation at war that had annexed the sentimental narratives of pain and suffering in the first place. If the loss and suffering of wartime was "storied" as national sacrifice, the myth of national sacrifice functioned further to make loss and suffering visible, and politically potent. The national idea gave poignancy to the tribulations of previously disenfranchised constituents by including them in its discursive bounds. The nation therefore remembered the pain of the people, and the pain of the people embroidered the suffering and righteousness of the nation.

The war and the inflation revealed the particular ability of the nation to hold and make socially useful, or valid, in however tendentious a manner, the memories of Germans. The politics of food in the 1910s and the debate on the revaluation of debts in the 1920s suggest that the national idea made the pain of citizens more poignant and thus their particular claims on the public more compelling. What refurbished the idea of the nation, even if people did not agree on particulars, and what made it an intimate part of individual identity, was its effectiveness in making comprehensible the pain of war and inflation. The nation allowed individuals to encounter each other as nationals, to recognize each other on intimate terms, that is, as Germans who suffered similar misfortunes and who could therefore tell and share individual stories. Ostwald's *Sittengeschichte* worked precisely to create this mutual intimacy and recognition. National feeling, then, was not the result of the compelling accumulation of group experiences over time; it relied rather on the retrospective organization of loss to achieve intimacy among strangers who claimed to know about each other across time and space.

The difficult terms of war and peace imposed what Ernst Renan once referred to as the "daily plebiscite" of nationalism in which the abstract state that raised taxes and enacted laws was imagined as a living, breathing, injured collectivity.[67] By the 1920s, more and more Germans recognized themselves in the German nation because they remembered their suffering as a part of the nation's suffering. This recognition was not in unison and did not impose political harmony. But it did mean that individuals felt an extraordinary intimacy with the idea of the nation and worked to guard and cultivate it. How else to explain the depth of the resentments not simply at the Treaty of Versailles as such but at the creation of the Polish Corridor (1919), the partitioning of Silesia (1921), and the French invasion of the Ruhr (1923)? Over the course of four inflationary years, the accounting of the depreciation of the reichsmark in terms of U.S. dollars, and the widespread perception that the inflation was the result of Allied peacemaking rather than German warmongering, added to the pertinence of national identity. The effects of the hyperinflation in 1922–23 were so sweeping and the pain it inflicted so general, and its appearance so fused in the public mind with the Treaty of Versailles, that it exposed the national fate that all Germans shared, gave stark expression to national character and national suffering, and thereby spurred programs for national salvation. Precisely because they conflated their own suffering with that of the nation, Germans felt part of the body of the nation, and they felt the tearing of its borders. Reaction to these injuries, which can be shorthanded by the single word *Versailles*, was overwhelming: throughout the early 1920s, collections were taken up, young Rhenish children boarded in rural sanctuaries, and town squares filled with angry protestors of all parties. One reason why Germans continued to accept so readily any confirmation of the perfidy of the Allies and to protest so ardently their own innocence was that such melodramatic evidence maintained the sentimental narrative of the nation by which Germans articulated and understood their own private losses. The Germans to whom the American journalist H. R. Knickerbocker spoke in the early 1930s, in the depths of the Great Depression when reparations had for all practical purposes been suspended, still talked constantly about Versailles, reparations, France.[68] This fixation has less to do with the case Germans felt they had made *against* Versailles than with how Versailles served as a way for Germans to recognize and validate and remember their own tribulations to one another. In this way they might avoid falling completely into the domestic quarrels that threatened to separate and estrange them, and thereby to render them indifferent and thus forgetful. The humiliation of Versailles persisted as a nexus of collective memory. In a flawed and distorted manner, Versailles allowed Germans to remember the war and its losses.

The fate of the nation became the object of anguished personal concern. One of the remarkable consequences of the mobilization for the war was the degree to which Germans described the profound unsettlement of their individual lives in the light of new social relations and new collective commitments. Before the war, recalled the conservative Munich historian Karl Alexander von Müller, most people in his circle lived their lives as "private persons . . . the claims of the political community on the individual were held in bounds."[69] In his account, the war broke down the boundary between private and public so that more and more people quite self-consciously put their own lives in a national perspective. The year 1914 stood for the very discontinuities of history—the sudden, often disorienting invalidation of the past; the presence of alternative, even ominous futures; and the authority in any case of the subjunctive tense— that intensified the individual's awareness of and participation in a dramatic process of national jeopardy and reconstruction.

This process continued throughout the 1920s when Germans strained to figure out what was going on. In a struggle against oblivion, many devoted themselves to the study of the fate of the nation. Political activists retrospectively recalled their lively interest in public affairs. "World war . . . days of revolution . . . French occupation . . . Spartacists . . . Inflation"—we "were already quite interested in why these things had to happen," wrote Hermann Jung.[70] One future member of the Nazi Party, a teacher from Vorsfelde, explained that in the 1920s two books stood on his desk: "Adolf Hitler's *Mein Kampf* and Karl Marx. *Jawohl* Karl Marx! . . . Learning, reading, comparing. On top of that the bitter lessons of daily life. "Eventually, the teacher admitted that "Karl Marx disappeared" from his desk; Hitler did not.[71] Autobiographers also remembered their keen interest in history, frequently a favorite subject in school.[72] One indication of this informal study was the runaway success of Oswald Spengler's *The Decline of the West*, a title that became a household phrase during the Weimar years. Although Spengler's message was basically pessimistic, the two binary poles he identified and by which he structured contemporary history may well have aided Germans in reimagining the national community: To the circulatory life force of blood, which insured the stability and rootedness of family and *Volk*, Spengler imposed the menacing, expansionary dynamic of money, which he identified with the rise of the world economy, terms revived by the more explicit analysis of Hans Ostwald some years later.[73] In any case, the awareness and study of the ideological parameters of the postwar years—"learning, reading, comparing"—was characteristic and suggests the high degree to which the self was dramatized in terms of a new study of national history.

Between Marx and Hitler, Germans worked hard to make sense of their collective fate in the postwar years and to find the real truth. What Ulrich Linse calls "barefoot prophets" of the inflationary years grabbed repeatedly at the collars of passersby to provide complete answers.[74] Versailles was perhaps the most popular version of the vernacular "political science" by which Germans explained their fate. Homegrown economists, Gottfried Feder, for example, delivered strident calls for the abolition of interest, and otherwise delved into the inflation. The anti-Semitism of hundreds of local racial societies also made dramatic inroads among middle-class Germans precisely because it was such a "big lie" and thereby kept their own sentimental narratives intact.[75]

However muddled and tendentious the search for answers was in the 1920s, it has to be set against the evidence for indifference and forgetfulness. Already Kracauer suspected that there was more around the corner than he could see from the entertainment palaces on Potsdamer Platz: the noise of gangs, the odor of riot. In Berlin, as elsewhere, the cool, agile, light step of the metropolitan was followed by the heavy footfalls of nationalists, whose effort to remember loss and to create and recreate the nation must be considered an integral part of Weimar culture. In the early 1920s, Hitler, Spengler, and Feder were summoned up by countless men and women anxious to explain to themselves what was happening to the nation and ready to assume by virtue of their private reading and their local political efforts a kind guardianship over Germany. The personal commitment of thousands of Germans to this task is striking. Beginning in 1918, with the outbreak of the November Revolution, the meetings of the newly reorganized political parties were packed. And although interest in the established parties eventually ebbed, ordinary citizens remained unusually interested in politics and open to new perspectives, studying a variety of newspapers and pamphlets, auditing lectures, and casting their votes for new parliamentary lists. This was the case throughout the 1920s. In surveys of National Socialist members carried out in the 1930s, it is telling how many citizens became activists by the accident that reveals their political inquisitiveness: "In this time," remembered Emil Schlitz, "I read a lot and so one day, I don't remember which year, I came to hear about the new men in Munich who called themselves National Socialists."[76] "My newspaper at the time was the *Dortmunder General-Anzeiger*," which was Social Democratic, wrote one worker, but he once came across a copy of the *Völkischer Beobachter*. "The contents interested me a great deal," he recalled. "What I felt and thought was here expressed in words."[77] To be sure, most people did not become National Socialists, certainly not in the early 1920s, but these recollections confirm a general interest in exploring political alternatives and trying to place individual experiences into a larger social context and a common narrative.

The 1920s also marked a highpoint of nationalist festivity in Germany. Neighborhood festivity was dominated by patriotic and paramilitary associations, particularly the veterans' group *Stahlhelm*, and revolved around reenacted "field services" for the war dead, "German Evenings" which mixed politics and entertainment, and regional sport festivals. Among nonsocialists, clubs became more open and socially accepting; club life knit burghers together just as the "alternative culture" of the socialist movement captured the political allegiances of workers. At the same time, socialists also cultivated the idea of the nation, and activists from both camps considered themselves "soldiers" of the nation. The romantic-nationalist ideal of soldiering implied not just patriotic politics but also genuinely national service. Whether in the Social Democratic Reichsbanner or the right-wing Stahlhelm, men banded together, invited their sons or younger brothers and taught them wartime calisthenics and songs, and followed a geographical and political itinerary that took them far from their hometowns. Regional and national festivals attracted tens and even hundreds of thousands of citizens; special trains were pressed into service and local volunteers arranged sleeping quarters. This political tourism, whether to Munich, where the first large-scale nationalist athletic festival took place in July 1923; to Magdeburg, where the Reichsbanner marched in 1925 under the banner of Anschluss with Austria; and later to Hamburg, Koblenz, and Berlin, lent politics a spectacular quality, but also gave the abstract idea of the nation a genuine intimacy as activists traveled in uniforms to the point of destination, attracted the scorn or hurrahs of passersby at train stations, and got to know their counterparts from across the country. The exploration of wider, unfamiliar social precincts punctuated the autobiography of Weimar-era activists. "I walked through the city. I wandered through the Communist district. I talked to the people there a number of times," recalled a young middle-class youth, a Nazi.[78] And it was not only workers, but also farmers, artisans, and shopkeepers whom Nazi activists engaged. They did so not so much to appeal to specific occupational interests, as some scholars have suggested, but rather to cross social boundaries and to get to know the "little man," the "ordinary person," to reconstitute the nation as a collective, integral whole.[79]

There was no Sunday, reported Württemberg's representative in Munich, "on which one did not see brass bands marching in the morning through the streets, flags taken out of army museums, and everywhere people in uniform, or at least displaying their medals."[80] And Munich was not unique. Regimental meetings, commemorative services, and patriotic ceremonies took place in all German towns and cities, including very metropolitan Berlin, where parading Stahlhelmers dominated the streets sufficiently to merit inclusion in a few frames of Walter Ruttman's 1927 film *Berlin—Symphony of a Big City*. The metropolis was once again in the thrall of patriotic hoopla on the occasion of President Hindenburg's eightieth birthday in October 1928, and Stahlhelmers would return to the city in 1932. And while Berlin remained a basically "red" city, with Social Democratic and Communist voters constituting a majority, the German National People's Party and later the National Socialists did respectably well in its precincts.

In the end, National Socialist successes in the early 1930s were the culmination of the work on the nation performed by so many grassroots activists. For more than ten years, the notion of soldiering for the nation had animated the public sphere as paramilitary associations became increasingly influential on the Left and especially on the Right, and the various veterans' groups, nationalist societies, and the anti-Versailles protests they led gave local politics a distinctly patriotic cast. Heated debates flared in communities across Germany over which songs to sing (patriotic or folksy) or which flags to fly (the old black-white-red banner of the empire or the red-black-gold colors of the new republic). For all the economic hardship in this period, the fact is that the political Right in particular organized in an assertive and confident way and did so at the grassroots, so that German nationalism lost many of its officious, elitist associations. The world war and the struggles to redefine the political community in later years gave German nationalism the emotional depth it had hitherto lacked. This background of political mobilization is important to keep in mind when explaining the National Socialist seizure of power in January 1933. While Nazism was not inevitable, it was broadly consistent with the national idea that had been cultivated since the beginning of the war. The party made it clear that it would not represent special or single interests or give credence to the particular tales of tribulation that one group told against another. Nazi campaigners tended to address voters as Germans at huge rallies, rather than as constituents of parliamentary blocs. Again and again, Hitler and other leading Nazis hammered away at the theme of national solidarity, which would solve Germany's vexing problems: social reform, economic productivity, and the shameful peace. At the same time, no other party seemed as open to both working- and middle-class Germans, to speak the language of the proverbial "little people," to acknowledge the hardships they had suffered, and to create the spectacle of the resurgent nation in such compelling fashion.[81] In this way, the Nazis upheld the narrative of the sentimental nation, threatened as Germany allegedly was by pernicious internal enemies and international dangers, and provided individual Germans a plausible enough way to create a broader social and political meaning out of the particular losses they had suffered. After two decades of war, revolution, and inflation, Nazism offered one powerful version of remembrance around the concept of the *Volksgemeinschaft*. It was a version of national history that clearly excluded Jews, socialists, and others, but aimed to include and remember the so-called little people, "the letter carrier and the train engineer, the seamstress and the washerwoman" whom Ostwald had taken into protective custody in his *Tales of the Inflation*.

However much the Nazis benefited, the work on the nation was not a Nazi project. The identification of the individual with the imagined collective of the nation was so close because the idea of the nation offered individuals a way to think about and to organize the losses they had incurred. The larger narrative of national history was one way to ward off the threat of oblivion: It created a common story in which Germans could weave in the particulars of their own lives. The national idea served to give social poignancy to otherwise isolated incidents of misfortune. This idea never imposed political harmony on German politics, and it is a mistake to suppose that nationalism necessarily solves conflicts or erases differences of opinion. Indeed, nationalism may well have aggravated the fractiousness of German politics by giving legitimacy to the claims of so many constituents who now appeared before the public with a highly developed sense of entitlement of being German. What did concern individuals, however, was the fate of the idea of Germany, which was not simply an insubstantial, airy affection, even if it was an imagined fiction. Identification with the German nation was a powerful way to give narrative meaning to the horrible losses of the war and the inflation.

It needs to be quickly pointed out that the role of the nation was not simply to remember losses, but to remember loss in a sufficiently imprecise way so as not to aggravate the suspicions that one social group or religious community or geographical region had against another. The dominance of the political Right also led to a manifestly tendentious version of German history, one that paid little attention to the organized working-class movement and rewrote the November Revolution as conspiracy. The nation always forgot as much as it remembered. Whether this forgetfulness made it more difficult for (non-Jewish) Germans to recognize themselves in the national narrative is not clear: The power of the narrative probably rested more on the affinities it conjured up than on the verisimilitude it reproduced. Later on, during the Third Reich, it was the precision on which true believers insisted, rather than the vague or melo-dramatic quality to the national story, that disabled Nazi narrations: the highly stylized racial community, the easy identification of enemies in the present and the past, the prominent role given to specific characters such as early Nazis and the Freikorps. These partisan subplots, argues Rudy Koshar, threatened to undermine feelings of national unity and national continuity.[82] For the sake of the national narrative, it was all the more im-portant to preserve this imprecision, or forgetfulness, after World War II. As Koshar goes on to explain, a strong preservation movement emerged after 1945 in order "to help the German people 'recognize itself,' to see a 'most natural connection' between past and present" without focusing on "specific events or injustices," and particularly on war crimes and on the Holocaust; the point was "to remember to remember they *were* a people with a commitment to later generations."[83]

In an era when more and more Europeans are supposedly loyal to postnational constitutional forms, it is instructive to consider that in 1975 "West Germans were convinced that one of every twelve buildings in the Federal Republic had historical value."[84] This figure indicates the degree to which Germans moved around a landscape they felt they rec-ognized and in which they believed their shared history and traditions were present. It is remarkable evidence for the intimacy that the idea of the nation creates among strangers who are otherwise left mute in the face of loss and transience. Indeed the conditions of loss and the desire to mourn made the storytelling capacities of the nation all the more impor-tant in everyday life. What appears decisive is not so much whether the story of the nation is right or wrong, critical or not, but that it provides points of recognition for the misfortunes that are otherwise threatened with oblivion. During World War I and its bitter aftermath, the nation did, in fact, provide serviceable, if tentative and misleading, categories for comprehending "the competitive pushing and hauling and the mindless, ephemeral conditions that we now call social activity."[85] The misfortunes of the Germans made the national idea more, not less, compelling. And even after World War II, memory work, particularly in the vernacular set-tings that critical historical studies have often overlooked, concentrated around national themes: the sorrowful refugees from the East, the victims of the allied bombing campaigns, the German prisoners of war in the Soviet Union.[86] Even the highly self-critical reception of Daniel Jonah Goldhagen had as its main actors "ordinary Germans," those whom Benedict Anderson refers to as "our own."[87] For fifty years after World War II, the nation continued to produce a narrative of selective remem-brance, which is why historians found that *Vergangenheitsbewältigung*, the mastery of the past, was so incomplete and difficult to accomplish.

The city, of course, remains a physical site of remembrance, and the new capital of Berlin will continue to build a memorial landscape. But life in the city remains strongly disintegrative. The influx of migrants, the business of commerce, and the effort to rebuild and renovate have all proceeded at a quickened pace since 1989, working against remembrance. The disappearing acts of Berlin were already evident during the 750th anniversary of the city's founding in 1987 when the big exhibitions emphasized the city's ceaseless reinvention of itself. It is these disappearing acts that structure contemporary discourse about the new capital: the forgetting of forty years of the German Democratic Republic, the rapidity with which the evidence of disjuncture and disunion has been removed since 1989, the obliviousness with which Potsdamer Platz has been rebuilt, the demolition already of the first postunification "scenes" in Prenzlauer Berg and the Scheunenviertel.[88] It is the new city of the *Berliner Republik* that incorporates both the fear and the allure of the irrelevance of the past.

Purchasing Comfort: Patent Remedies
and the Alleviation of Labor Pain
in Germany Between 1914 and 1933

"IN sorrow thou shalt bring forth children." Even after the discovery of effective anesthesia around 1850, the biblical injunction of
Genesis 3:16 underpinned a view that women were destined to suffer in
childbirth. In Germany, this belief began to crumble only during World
War I, partly in response to the widespread and highly visible suffering
of soldiers during the war and its aftermath. During these years, an older
view that women had a moral duty to suffer gladly in the service of God,
nation, society, and family began to be contested by women's demands
for pain relief. The increasing number of women who wanted relief used
terms such as *choice* and *self-determination* to legitimate their desires—
language that, while influenced by feminism, also signified a nascent
consumerist orientation. Labor pain and its relief served as an arena in
which larger national themes were fought out but never fully resolved
between 1914 and 1933: pain versus its alleviation, self-sacrifice versus
self-fulfillment, hardship versus prosperity. At stake was the character of
evolving, modern female selfhood and its relation to the *Volkskörper*—
roughly translated as the social body—as well as the impact of apparently private choices upon public morality.

Can one rightly speak of prosperity, given that World War I and the
years that followed it brought hard times to most Germans? Wartime
food shortages were followed by inflation and then by hyperinflation.
From about 1924 through 1928, the Weimar Republic experienced a
time of relative prosperity. However, the world economic depression put
an abrupt end to this, leaving many families dependent on lower-paid female labor or without any steady income, and dashing individual and
collective hopes for a more comfortable living standard. If one defines
prosperity merely in terms of the availability of consumer goods, the term
has little relevance for most of the period from 1916 through 1933. Yet,

despite Germany's precarious economy and a persistent ambivalence toward mass consumption as being suspiciously American and thus "un-German," in some respects a cultural expectation of prosperity had begun to take root.[1] One way in which this expectation manifested itself was in a higher valuation of comfort. While one might imagine physical comfort to be a value that has been broadly shared over different cultures and historical eras, in fact comfort has come to be highly prized only in modern times. In the Anglo-American realm, as John Crowley has recently argued, the quest for comfort began to be pursued in earnest during the eighteenth century, when it supplanted earlier preferences for appearing fashionable or genteel. The prerequisite for this change was a burgeoning consumer culture.[2]

It is not clear just when a similar shift may have begun in Germany and other Central European countries. However, the 1920s appears to have been a time when many Germans sought to enhance their level of comfort. Many of the phenomena often understood as resulting from industrialization and urbanization—such as reduced family size, the enjoyment of leisure activities, or the desire for more comfortable living quarters—can also be read as a peculiarly modern pursuit of physical comfort.[3] In Germany, the number of children per family decreased from the 1870s onward, with the trend intensifying considerably after 1900. During the 1920s, a typical urban family had about two children. Larger families with four or more children were becoming rare in German cities, though many urban women would experience multiple pregnancies that terminated in abortion or spontaneous miscarriage.[4] The trend toward smaller families reflected an increasing aspiration to comfort in a number of respects. Families with fewer children could enjoy a higher overall living standard, which allowed for better housing, a more varied diet, and more leisure time. More energy and resources could be invested into each child's upbringing and education, thus enhancing the chances that one's offspring would also be better off, socially and economically. Not least, women who underwent fewer pregnancies and deliveries avoided considerable physical discomfort.[5]

The quest for comfort can fruitfully be viewed not just in terms of the relationship between a person and her environment, as Crowley conceives it, but also in terms of efforts to regulate the body's internal sensations, with the goal of minimizing those sensations that are painful or uncomfortable. Considered in this broader sense, comfort refers to a panoply of new techniques that aimed to harmonize the body with the prerogatives of nature: eating a more varied and nutritious diet, taking regular exercise, wearing healthful clothing, and the like. In short, modern desires for good health, together with the hygienic means toward achieving it, became an integral part of the pursuit of comfort. This notion of health is, of course, an individual one; notions of public or collective health were grounded in other desiderata that did not necessarily coincide with the prerequisites of individual health and that might call for suffering rather than comfort. In Germany, collective notions of health during this period often posited an abstract *Volkskörper*, whose demands often superseded those of individual health, most notably in wartime when the collective body required sacrifice: the starvation, dismemberment, and death of individual bodies.[6] Not least in the service of the *Volkskörper*, hygienic techniques were increasingly extended to women's bodies, particularly in their reproductive capacities. For example, a flourishing literature on right living during pregnancy promised not only healthier infants but also fewer discomforts during pregnancy and an easier delivery.[7] Social workers conveyed a similar set of health guidelines to expectant mothers in home visits and public prenatal clinics, as did doctors in their private practices.[8] In the case of prenatal advice, the health of mother, child, and *Volkskörper* were generally believed to coincide. This was often not the case for labor pain, where as we shall see, a conflict was widely perceived between individual comfort and the vigor of the *Volkskörper*.

Like comfort, suffering is also subject to cultural variation. Suffering can be defined as the experience of physical pain within a web of culturally defined meanings.[9] Culturally available forms of suffering are also historically specific. In the Middle Ages, for example, near-starvation was valued by some saints as a route to religious ecstasy and holiness— an interpretation that strikes the modern sensibility as strange, given current understandings of anorexia as a psychosexual, medicalized phenomenon.[10] Moreover, not all forms of suffering are necessarily interchangeable within a given culture and historical era. Suffering in childbirth can assume a unique status because it is linked with the continuation of a family, society, and state—with renewal and rejuvenation, rather than with illness, disability, and death. Aristocratic Englishwomen viewed the experience of labor pain as a badge of womanly heroism and honor prior to the nineteenth century. Suffering gave childbirth meaning and marked a woman's transition into full adulthood, thus serving as a rite of passage.[11] In the Christian tradition, suffering in labor has long been seen as a form of atonement for Eve's original lapse. Suffering can constitute an opportunity for heroism, a test of character, or a form of ritual purification. Historically, it has rarely been divested of moral dimensions. In the interwar period in Germany, the suffering of labor pain retained a strong moral quality that was inextricably intertwined with nationalist values.

The meanings attached to labor pain and its relief were themselves multiple and hotly contested by both physicians and mothers in Germany during the early part of this century. Some women clung to older, highly moralistic condemnations of painkillers in labor, a position that many family physicians supported at least in principle. Yet, a growing number of women wanted pain relief and actively sought it, and they too found allies among physicians, particularly elite, university-based obstetricians. The desire for relief expressed a rejection of maternity as an eternal pageant of suffering and self-sacrifice, in favor of a maternal ideal emphasizing voluntary altruism and self-fulfillment, congruent with new ideals of voluntary motherhood. Changing attitudes toward labor pain intersected with a shift from valuing the biological accomplishment of giving birth toward celebrating a mother's social contributions in child rearing—and a shift from maternal duty toward maternal love. Calls for pain relief both reflected and helped to constitute heightened demands for self-determination, which resonated not only with feminist sensibilities but also with Germany's first foray into democratic governance after the Great War. Finally, the attempt to minimize suffering in labor dovetailed with the mass pursuit of enhanced physical comfort. While some women sought the help of a doctor in this quest, others turned to consumer products that were available on the open market— what we would now regard as "quack" (*Kurpfuscher*) potions and patent medicines. The choices women made in their responses to labor pain contributed to their construction of two competing archetypes of the maternal self: a self-realized mother who embraced comfort, responsible above all to herself and her family, versus a self-sacrificial mother at the unquestioning service of *Volkskörper* and Fatherland, ready to suffer for an ostensibly greater cause.

Pain Relief in Labor:
Options under a Medical Monopoly

In demanding access to pain relief, women entered a field that was contested both on the level of politics writ large and on the more local level of medical practice. In practical terms, access to pain relief could be a problem for women because doctors exercised a monopoly over the more effective drugs. Midwives might help an attending physician administer analgesia (pain-relieving drugs) or anesthesia (drugs that obliterated pain). But the decision to supply any drug in the first place lay wholly within the doctor's purview. Physicians' attitudes toward the appropriateness of doing this varied widely, for reasons cultural as well as medical. Generally speaking, an elite, urban obstetrical specialist with left-leaning political convictions would have been more likely than a conservative general practitioner in a rural area to provide pain relief. Catholic physicians, coming from a milieu in which maternal suffering was greatly exalted, were more likely to oppose pain relief than were their Protestant and Jewish colleagues.

Elite German physicians devoted considerable efforts to developing pain-relief methods. During the early twentieth century, they arguably took the leading role worldwide in the area of obstetric pain relief. They thus had a professional stake in both providing analgesia and anesthesia (as part of a broad-based research agenda) and maintaining physician control over the most effective drugs available. By the 1920s German doctors had a wide spectrum of powerful anesthetics and analgesics at their disposal. The most commonly used in private practice were chloroform and ether, both of which had been available since the mid-nineteenth century.[12] The pharmacopoeia also included a variety of opium derivatives (such as morphine), sedatives, barbiturates, and even hypnosis. But discourse in medical circles and among the general public was shaped most strongly by a revolutionary technique dubbed "Twilight Sleep" (*Dämmerschlaf*), announced in 1906 by C. J. Gauss and Bernhard Krönig at the Freiburg University Women's Hospital.[13] Twilight Sleep combined morphine with scopolamine, a drug with potent sedative effects, to provide partial pain relief and to induce amnesia.[14] During labor, a woman received a set of injections designed to keep her in a state of semiconsciousness. Afterward, if the method had succeeded, she remembered nothing. Henceforth, Twilight Sleep served as the paradigm for obstetricians working on anesthetic methods. Women would not necessarily experience a pain-free birth, but they would later *believe* they had.

Twilight Sleep thus set a new medical standard for managing obstetrical pain by making women forget what they had experienced. Nonetheless, all but its most enthusiastic proponents acknowledged that it had numerous drawbacks regarding safety, effectiveness, and the physician's or midwife's ability to manage labor. Some disadvantages were relatively minor, such as women's frequent reports of dizziness or headaches afterward. Others were more serious. True pain relief was minimal, as most physicians admitted.[15] The drugs not only tended to weaken contractions and thus prolong the delivery (a problem common to most anesthetics) but also made women so groggy that they could not actively participate in labor. From one minute to the next, women would forget their attendants' exhortations to push. One physician observed a case where the infant was stuck in the birth canal for fifteen hours, until it was finally pulled out with forceps.[16] Nearly all obstetricians agreed that such prolonged labors increased the chances of infection.[17] While still drugged, some women also experienced visual hallucinations and thrashed about in their beds. In some cases, women threw themselves around so violently that attendants felt compelled to forcibly hold them or tie them to their beds. The woman whose baby was stuck for fifteen hours reportedly stood on her bed just before the forceps operation was to be performed and leapt through the room from one chair to another, "so that one positively had to hunt her down," according to her physician.[18] This thrashing interfered with the midwife's ability to catch the baby, to protect maternal tissues from tearing, and to maintain asepsis (germ-free conditions).[19] Doctors roundly criticized Twilight Sleep for causing women to grasp at their genitals, especially during contractions—a moral danger as well as a threat to asepsis.[20]

However, the greatest hazards of the method affected not laboring women but their newborn babies. A high percentage of infants encountered breathing problems, and some stopped breathing altogether. As a rule, these babies could be resuscitated. Still, some physicians attributed isolated instances of infant death to such breathing problems.[21] In addition to their risks, the drugs used in Twilight Sleep also posed formidable logistical challenges that made them unsuitable for use in home deliveries.[22] Hospital usage was also impractical, for laboring women had to be constantly supervised both to determine proper dosage and to prevent them from flying out of control, and the child needed continuous monitoring before and after its birth for signs of distress.[23] As a result of its drawbacks, Twilight Sleep never came close to being used universally, even in hospitals, although its hospital use was moderately widespread during the 1920s and early 1930s. Only those hospitals deeply involved in developing Twilight Sleep, such as the Freiburg University Women's Hospital, continued to use it as a matter of course for all labors, as long as the laboring woman did not expressly reject it and physicians regarded it as safe for mother and child.[24]

Other drugs that could have substituted for Twilight Sleep with morphine and scopolamine also posed problems. The local and regional anesthetics that are widely used today (in epidural anesthesia, for instance) received relatively little attention from obstetricians, probably because they fell outside the powerful paradigm of Twilight Sleep.[25] Physicians used spinal anesthetics for cesarean sections but rarely for uncomplicated births.[26] Nitrous oxide (laughing gas), which was considered relatively safe and effective, could blunt pain and induce a semiconscious state, but it found little use because its administration required a bulky and inconvenient apparatus.[27] Among the anesthetics that promised to produce Twilight Sleep more safely, a number of drugs did achieve high rates of amnesia, yet each of these methods had serious drawbacks. The "Gwathmey method" provoked severe states of excitation in some women, who cried out that "they were about to die, they were completely drunk, they didn't know where they were and wanted to go home."[28] Avertin, an anesthetic that a few obstetricians touted for use by the general practitioner in home deliveries, reportedly slowed contractions, induced overexcitation, increased postpartum bleeding, failed to achieve amnesia, and allegedly had the highest mortality rate of all the competing techniques.[29] Twilight Sleep using Somnifen or Pernocton, both barbiturates, also induced excitation, although Pernocton reportedly achieved amnesia (in fifty of seventy cases, in one study) without affecting contractions.[30] Pernocton did begin to replace morphine and scopolamine because its side effects were less extreme.[31] But after a period of initial popularity—by 1930 it had been used for twenty to twenty-five thousand births—Pernocton was abandoned even in Tübingen, the hospital that researched and promoted it for obstetrical use, by 1935, due to the states of excitation it caused.[32] Not until 1939 would Pethidine, a drug of lasting obstetrical popularity, be synthesized in Germany.[33]

As a result of this lack of safe, new alternatives, those physicians in private practice who used anesthetics in home deliveries usually stuck with the oldest anesthetics, ether and chloroform, and a newer but similar compound called ethyl chloride. These required only that the midwife hold a cloth over the laboring woman's face and periodically add a drop of the drug to the cloth. Though relatively practical for use in home births, these drugs carried significant medical risks as well, quite apart from their potential to explode.[34] Both ether and chloroform could make the woman feel she was about to suffocate.[35] They could drastically reduce the effectiveness of contractions, thus lengthening labor and requiring the use of oxytocic drugs to stimulate contractions, potentially endangering the infant's well-being, and increasing the risk of postpartum hemorrhage.[36] Consequently, physicians used these drugs only for a few brief moments, just as the infant was about to emerge from the birth canal.

A conscientious physician could thus find plenty of medical reasons for opposing Twilight Sleep and the other available methods. However, quite apart from the question of medical risks, German physicians' attitudes toward obstetrical pain relief were also strongly influenced by their political and moral convictions, which partook of the available cultural meanings attached to pain, and by their professional interests. These interests and beliefs could underpin either support for or opposition to liberal provision of pain relief. Only a few physicians opposed the use of painkillers in complicated births that involved forceps deliveries or more complicated surgical techniques. The debate centered on "normal" deliveries—and by extension, "normal" motherhood.

Patriotic, pronatalist convictions were cited by physicians on both sides of the controversy. During the course of the war, as Germans watched with horror while an entire generation of young men fell at the front or returned from it maimed, a resurgence in the precipitously dropping birth rate seemed to many social commentators—including physicians—as the only way to revitalize the Fatherland. For all but a handful of socialist or left-leaning doctors, pronatalism came to appear synonymous with patriotism.[37] Not only physicians but also German society at large equated women's service to their country as childbearers with men's service as soldiers at the front.[38] Suffering was, of course, an obvious link between the two forms of service, as was the presumption that both childbearing and soldiering secured the future of the nation. Women had a moral duty to the nation and the *Volkskörper* to provide more children, regardless of risk and pain. But given that women increasingly refused this form of service, what could induce them to bear more children?

While some physicians trumpeted a renewed valorization of suffering, others proposed breaking the link between pain and childbirth. Hugo Sellheim, director of the University Women's Hospital in Leipzig and an early, outspoken advocate of more liberal pain relief in labor, argued in 1917: "The prospect of a more painless delivery removes some women's fear of giving birth and thus helps to increase the number of births. Of course, even better would be education and a way of life that would prevent this exaggerated anxiety from developing in the first place."[39] This was a relatively liberal position; in addition to his populationist concerns, Sellheim elsewhere expressed a measure of sympathy for moderate, maternalist feminism. Humanitarian motivations and support for women's freedom of choice thus merged with his more obvious professional stake as an active researcher in the development of analgesics. By 1930, Sellheim suggested midwives be authorized to administer a narcotic syrup called Scopan to the women in their care—a surprising proposal, since it ran counter to the professional interests of obstetricians.

Sellheim's Scopan proposal failed. Many elite physicians rightly perceived it as a threat to their monopoly over analgesic drugs, and they objected to ceding so much authority to laboring women and their midwives.[40] For many general practitioners, however, and for some elite doctors as well, moral and political concerns were even more decisive than were professional interests. It is notable that these nonacademic doctors, who otherwise never or rarely published in medical journals, were exercised enough by the issue to write about it. Because sources such as professional journals and hospital records are skewed strongly toward elite specialists, these outpourings are the best evidence available on most general practitioners' views. In response to the Scopan proposal, one GP in a small town in Holstein decried the pampering of modern women. Instead, he wrote, "Humanity must become tougher and more manly again. Learn to suffer without complaining."[41] This sort of language echoed worries that Germany had lost the Great War because its citizens, both male and female, had grown too soft—too concerned about their own comfort. In this view, withholding pain relief was the only patriotic thing to do. Otherwise, a nation of weaklings, afraid to suffer, would be doomed to decline both in numbers and in vigor.[42]

Another ethical concern prompted some physicians to question the amnesia paradigm. Many general practitioners argued that childbirth represented a high point in a woman's life, indeed the defining moment of her femininity, for which she should be fully conscious and aware. For example, Dr. Julius Eversmann of the Red Cross Hospital in Hamburg believed that painkillers were defensible only if they did not obliterate the memory of birth. Like many of his colleagues, he usually gave a few drops of ether or chloroform as the baby's head emerged: "This relieves the last and not least pains for the woman, but since she immediately regains consciousness, it does not take away the experience of the child's first cry, which is the greatest and purest joy for every normal woman who is not yet degenerate."[43] A similar point of view was expressed by a general practitioner in the Scopan debate: "Only a *Frau* who has given birth has truly become a '*Weib*,'" as one country doctor, Johannes Neumann in Dassow, Mecklenburg, wrote in response to Sellheim.[44] This was, in a sense, a double birth, for the woman was reborn as a mother. His use of two different terms for woman, *Frau* and *Weib*, is significant. The term *Weib* has an old-fashioned ring to it, an echo of a rapidly disappearing world in which each person knew his or her place. When contemporaries talked about the "New Woman" in Weimar Germany—a short-hand term for a liberated urban woman who earned her own money, enjoyed her leisure time, and was in no hurry to become a housewife—the word they chose was always *Frau*. In contrast, *Weib* implies womanliness, motherliness, and maturity; individualism has little place in its semantic field. This form of self-evident motherliness was understood to be rooted in the natural order. Arguing on the basis of his experience as a rural doctor, Neumann suggested that normal labor pain was "naturally necessary." He believed the transition from despair in late labor to ecstasy at the child's arrival was a peak experience in a woman's life, which she ought to experience fully and consciously. Otherwise, she risked disrupting her normal psychological development, which Neumann (and many of his contemporaries) believed depended especially on "processes in the genital sphere"—a notion that few physicians would have extended to men in such sweeping terms.

A good many doctors thus believed that the full experience of pain (and not just of the child's birth) was essential to the making of a good mother.[45] Labor pain exercised a transformative effect on the female self, reconstructing even a narcissistic young maiden as a properly selfless mother. From this perspective, physical and emotional comfort was something a mother should expect to give but not to receive. In the opinion of a Breslau obstetrician, pain gave substance to motherhood "because only that which struggles painfully to the light takes into account a deeper meaning of life."[46] Even some of the physicians who were generally sympathetic to the ideal of a painless birth wondered if mothers spared the pain of labor would love their babies as much. One physician claimed to know of a mother who had a wholly "groundless aversion" against the child she bore in Twilight Sleep, yet she "tenderly loved the other one, born in pain."[47] Similar beliefs persisted among some German physicians even after the Second World War.[48]

The consideration of medical ideas and practices thus far suggests that the 1910s and 1920s saw the development of a new regime of surveillance.[49] The introduction of Twilight Sleep and related forms of anesthesia subjected laboring women to medical scrutiny that was unprecedented in its intensity. Minimizing the risks of such drugs required constant monitoring of the laboring woman, who had now become a patient in a hospital setting reorganized to ensure that medical surveillance remained unbroken. Women who gave birth at home—and this was the majority—were usually exempted from the unwavering medical observation that increasingly characterized hospital birth. Yet, the contrast between home and hospital practices should not be overstated. Women with the means to afford a private physician had the option of ether or chloroform at home, a choice that also brought them under closer medical observation. The development of this new regime of surveillance was not simply a case of technological determinism. The problems inherent in Twilight Sleep and other anesthetics were solved in ways consonant with prevailing notions of medical and maternal propriety and existing modes of managing childbirth. For example, the need to prevent infection of the laboring woman merged with a moral concern to hinder her hands from touching her nether regions, with the result that she was physically restrained and kept under close observation. Moreover, the new regime also subjected obstetricians to intensified scrutiny, as professional norms dictated the publication of failures as well as successes with new anesthetic methods.[50]

At the same time, the new regime of surveillance converged with moralistic discourses on the characteristics of a good mother. In some quarters, particularly university-affiliated research hospitals, it was indeed the case—as Eghigian and Betts suggest in Chapter 1—that "psychic comfort and discomfort appear to have been peculiarly singled out as objects of twentieth-century concern." This concern cut in two directions, as the example of the medical management of labor pain shows; it could aim either to attenuate pain or to channel the experience and meaning of pain in a particular direction. On the one hand, Twilight Sleep and related techniques for inducing amnesia were intended to spare women the psychic torment of reliving the suffering of childbirth. They thus manifested an evolving humanitarian goal of eliminating or at least reducing pain. On the other hand, this goal remained in tension with the older but persistent idea that motherhood was defined by suffering and sacrifice. In this view, the tribulations of childbirth functioned as a crucible for remaking the maternal self.

Whatever values a physician held, there no longer existed a position of innocence from whence he or she could perceive an unmedicated birth as the sole possibility. A decision now had to be made either to provide pain relief or to withhold it. This practical dilemma mirrored the impossibility of maintaining a neutral position in the discursive realm. In fact, it flowed from what Foucault would call a new discourse formation, which created a new context for medical action. This discourse also redefined sacrifice and suffering. While the valorization of suffering has a tradition as long as recorded history, the articulation of sacrificial motherhood here took a peculiarly modern form. No longer was the maternal self subordinated to a cosmic order, an otherworldly god, or a royal body; it was now committed to the *Volkskörper*, the abstract embodiment of the modern German nation. Moreover, the new techniques of monitoring and surveillance of childbirth presented new opportunities for medical personnel to guide the remaking of the maternal self in a desired direction—opportunities that multiplied with the rising demand for pain relief in labor.

Women's Changing Attitudes: Sacrificial Motherhood vs. Comfort

The range of attitudes among doctors paralleled the range of views on suffering and comfort in German culture and society at large during these years. Many women, too, shared the idea that motherhood ought to combine stoicism and sacrifice with love; other women contended that it was cruel to exact suffering where it could be avoided. This sharp division of opinion is visible in women's published responses to Sellheim's proposal in the *Journal for Further Medical Education* (*Zeitschrift für ärztliche Fortbildung*). Most of these women were either physicians themselves or physicians' wives; as such, they wrote from personal experience in childbirth as well as from a professional viewpoint. Like the male physicians, these female participants in the discourse on pain relief couched their arguments ultimately in moral and ethical terms. Regardless of their position, they shared with one another (and with male physicians) a preoccupation with the health of the *Volkskörper* and with various forms of sacrifice as constitutive of maternal identity.

Among the opponents of analgesia in labor, Frau M. G. Oden of Aachen claimed that she would never consider asking for relief because this would be abnormal and unnatural. "Every woman knows that she will be in pain as she brings her child into the world, and certainly no woman who is physically and mentally healthy would want to renounce the highest fulfillment of her womanhood for that reason." Pain was not merely incidental to giving birth, it was the precondition for maternal love. "I would like to describe labor pain, which is impossible to compare with any other, as most deeply meaningful. For when something painfully detaches itself from our hearts, we will have to take it into our hearts afterwards with doubled intensity and joy." Frau Oden's own experience had only served to confirm her opinion. She claimed that during forty-six hours of labor it never even occurred to her to ask that the pain be relieved, for each pain gave her the "blissful feeling" of becoming a mother.[51]

Other women concurred. Annaliese Jensen of Itzehoe agreed that labor pains were "certainly exceedingly strong, yet meaningful"; childbirth was something purposeful and by no means an illness that simply had to be endured. Jensen argued further that giving birth was a thoroughly active process, which required women to be alert.[52] Johanna Maria Stabreit of Nennhausen (Westhavelland) also agreed that being fully conscious was the only healthy way to experience childbirth, so long as it progressed normally. Like most of the opponents of obstetrical pain relief, Stabreit insisted that labor pain was fundamentally different than pain that accompanied illness, and that women forgot it as soon as the baby arrived. "Today we women are made completely confused with too much sympathy. . . . Having babies is really not as awful as it is always made out to be." Like Oden, Stabreit believed that the suggestive powers of the physician and midwife helped "a thousand times more" than any narcosis.[53]

These women systematically conflated their moral prescriptions with the exigencies of nature as they perceived them. They all wrote of pain as something purposeful and inevitable, indeed preordained by nature, which a "healthy" mother would not try to evade. The healthy mother, they believed, was not only physically sound but also in possession of emotional and spiritual resources and a properly selfless attitude toward suffering and motherhood—a package of qualities that they viewed as all of one piece. Pain, in their view, was not merely a blank slate; it was meaningful because it was the essence of maternity. Suffering became an end in itself. Implicit in their writings was an exaltation of maternal heroism and self-sacrifice, which merged neatly with aggressive nationalist and militarist ideals. Like the soldier on the battlefield, the expectant mother ought to be prepared to give her very life. Yet heroism implies that women could choose to suffer, whereas these women believed that exercising a choice would transgress against a natural law that preordained women's suffering. Although this debate was couched in moral rather than in overtly religious terms, some religious women, particularly Catholics, continued to believe that relieving labor pain would break a divine law as well. As one (male) Catholic writer expressed it: "Is not every mother in fact a sacrificial altar, on which she must constantly sacrifice herself?"[54] From a secular position, the obstetrician Sellheim observed: "Admittedly a kind of change in world-view is necessary before laboring women themselves believe: We may do that which we have not dared to think, namely permit ourselves pain relief, without violating a divine order."[55]

However, a good many women welcomed the possibility of pain relief. For them, labor pain was suffused not so much with meaning as with terror. Some of these women had experienced a previous labor as so shatteringly painful that they retained few other memories of childbirth. They emphatically had not forgotten their suffering. Instead, in their experience, the raw memory of pain obliterated any positive moral dimension to suffering. One of the women who gave birth to her second child in the Heidelberg University Women's Hospital "thought of her first, very painful birth only with horror," according to her physician.[56] After the delivery, the pain receded but the fear remained. For these women, pain offered little or no potential for redemption. Worse yet, it threatened to undermine national strength. Elli Keller, a doctor's wife in Silesia, argued that pain relief must be made available to discourage the use of birth control and thus promote strong, large families. Quoting an old joke, Keller remarked tartly that if women and men took turns bearing children, each couple would have only three children: one borne by the woman, a second by the man, and a third by the woman. "But a fourth would not be born, because from the first time and forevermore the man would have had enough—the 'nose full,' as the Berliners so nicely put it."[57]

The fear of pain was, however, no joke. For some women, the fear was so strong that it contributed to their choosing abortion over childbirth. Frau K. H., a twenty-nine-year-old former sales clerk on trial for abortion in Berlin, testified that while economic uncertainty had been a motivation, fear of pain had been paramount, "because as a result of the narrow build of my pelvis I had to endure extraordinarily strong pain during the birth of my first child and consequently I was afraid of a second birth."[58] Indeed, the pain of childbirth, both anticipated and experienced, merged with its danger in many women's minds. As Frau K. H.'s testimony suggests, this association had a rational basis, particularly when excruciating pain resulted from complications such as hers that were likely to recur in a subsequent pregnancy. No matter how often physicians insisted that childbirth was a natural, physiological process, many women continued to believe it was fraught with potential danger and certain pain. Fear of death and disability lurked in many women's minds during pregnancy, and it was only logical that these fears would peak during labor itself.[59] According to theories of "natural" childbirth that would gain adherents later in the century, fear and pain could create a vicious circle in which tension and excess adrenaline magnified pain, which in turn intensified fear.[60] Even if one does not subscribe to all the precepts of "natural" childbirth, it seems highly plausible that such a fear-pain cycle could intensify labor pain when women already felt themselves to be in jeopardy.

The desire for pain relief transformed the customs surrounding birth, motivating some women to choose the hospital over a home setting. Women might also call a physician specifically to provide pain relief in a home birth.[61] However, since insurance covered a physician's assistance with childbirth only when medically necessary, pain relief at home remained beyond most women's reach. Moreover, they were aware that only a hospital could offer the most effective pain control. Until the early twentieth century, the hospital had remained the refuge of those who were impoverished or unmarried (and usually both).[62] Such unfortunates could still be admitted free as charity patients. But hospitals now attracted a new, more prosperous clientele as the promise of truly effective pain relief helped overcome the distrust and opprobrium that for generations had led respectable women to shun hospital birth. According to one physician in Heidelberg, women there embraced Twilight Sleep with "extraordinary" speed and enthusiasm.[63] In Tübingen, women encouraged one another to choose "painless birth" in the hospital. For these women, the experiential losses associated with amnesia appeared to be a fair trade if they could expect effective pain relief. Dr. Vogt at the University Women's Hospital reported:

The news of painless birth spread over the entire city like a psychological infection. As soon as the first women who were delivered in Twilight Sleep with Pernocton arrived in their homes, they told their relatives and neighbors about the new method of painless delivery. Thereupon whole series of women came to the clinic solely on account of Twilight Sleep.[64]

Vogt's account indicates how the experiences of a few women could snowball into a burgeoning trend, which some physicians derisively dismissed as mere fashion.[65] Women conferred with one another and then demanded that doctors give them what they believed they needed. The speed at which women reacted to the new pain relief method in Tübingen indicates that it was fulfilling an existing need, not creating a new one, as some critics suggested.

Although the demand for pain relief reflected an implicit claim to self-determination, only rarely was it couched in explicitly feminist form. At no point did this demand coalesce into a coordinated campaign comparable to the National Twilight Sleep Association in the United States, which lobbied for universal access to Twilight Sleep in labor in 1914 or 1915.[66] Indeed, when the League for the Protection of Mothers (*Bund für Mutterschutz*, a relatively radical German feminist organization) devoted a few pages to Twilight Sleep in its journal in 1914, the author of the article was Mary Sumner-Boyd, one of the leading advocates of the method in the United States. Sumner-Boyd, who traveled from New York to Freiburg in order to enjoy a "painless birth," declared that the voyage was well worth it. She described the method as not only completely safe but also downright beneficial to mothers, in allowing them to recover more quickly, and to infants, in preventing forceps deliveries and allowing the physician to manage labor rationally.[67] Publication of Sumner-Boyd's article placed the League for the Protection of Mothers among the proponents of relief on demand, but the organization never pursued the issue further in any systematic manner. However, advocates of pain relief on demand did sometimes avail themselves of implicitly feminist critiques of male-dominated medical knowledge. Louise Diel, a Berlin writer who chronicled her own pregnancy for publication, put a sharp point on this experientially grounded critique. Noting that many physicians regarded renal colic (*Nierenkolik*, a kidney affliction) as the most painful human experience, she asked rhetorically: "How do the gentlemen doctors intend to prove this? Has one of them ever had a child?"[68]

An outspoken feminist, Diel gave birth in a Berlin hospital as a second-class private patient, and she was anything but shy in demanding relief. In her quest for comfort, she drew eclectically on remedies that ranged from simple to sophisticated. At the beginning of labor, she concentrated on regulating her breathing as a way of pacing herself and gaining some control over the pain. Decades before the invention of the Lamaze method, Diel was convinced: "Regular, deep inhalation and exhalation strengthens, distracts, calms. By the time the next pain is coming on, the body has recovered somewhat and can better ride out the onslaught." Also in early labor, Diel appears to have been served wine by the nurses, for she reported requesting "another swallow of red wine." Prior to labor, she had made elaborate plans to have music played, but when she was actually in heavy labor she rejected a nurse's offer to play it. However, she found gentle massage by the midwife or nurse to be quite helpful in dealing with the pain. She derived great comfort from her intimate rapport with her midwife, Erika—so much so that she insisted Erika stay with her throughout the entire delivery rather than leaving at the end of her shift. Diel also gained considerable relief from screaming at the height of a contraction—a technique that the hospital staff regarded as most unwelcome.[69]

Finally, and most importantly for our purposes, Diel had exacted an advance promise from her attending physician to administer painkillers if she felt she could no longer handle the pain. Significantly, Diel insisted that analgesia be *her* choice. At one point, as she began to push the baby out, she cried out for labor to end by whatever means possible. Her doctor took this as a plea to use forceps. But surgical intervention was not her desire. In fact, she had nothing concrete in mind, for "the pain raged and robbed me of every calm thought."[70] Soon thereafter, though, she vociferously demanded analgesia. The doctor responded that there was no time; the baby was on its way and he needed to wash his hands. When she screamed again for relief, a nurse appeared to assist with analgesia, and Diel immediately felt better, "secure and at the end of the agony." A mask was placed over her face, and she hungrily inhaled. However, the pain failed to abate and she continued to scream until Erika announced: "A boy, a splendid lad"—an experience as ineffable as it was profound, which Diel regretted being unable to express in words.[71] Still, in the midst of her tearful joy, between assuring herself that the her son was healthy and insisting that the staff attend to him first, she asserted repeatedly: "What a swindle, that was no anesthesia whatsoever!"[72]

Perhaps the doctor really did fail to put any chloroform or ether on the mask, on the assumption that psychological suggestion would be enough to satisfy Diel. At least one of his colleagues advocated just this practice during the 1920s.[73] Whatever the facts in this particular case, Diel's account reveals the expectations of modern, urban, middle-class, feminist women like herself. They insisted medicine be at their service, not vice versa. They expected pain relief to be considerable, perhaps even complete. And they saw no conflict between their own comfort and the welfare of their children.

Women who favored having at least the option of analgesia in labor viewed the question as much less fraught with moral import than did the opponents of pain relief. To the extent that women favoring pain relief perceived a residual moral component to it, they tended—as the example of Elli Keller shows—to locate morality in the achievement of national pronatalist goals, by whatever means were available and effective. Insofar as it promised to raise the birth rate, obstetrical pain relief actually became invested with a positive moral force. This conception of morality allowed for instrumental reasoning by which the desired end of a vigorous *Volkskörper* legitimated the means. It also redefined the choice of obstetric pain relief as a matter of public morality rather than a challenge to private, individual virtue. Keller, for one, wrote from the perspective of a citizen at least as much as from that of a mother.

This reconception of the moral significance of anesthesia had implications for maternal identity as well. Particularly for first-time mothers, childbearing constitutes a transition that creates a maternal self—a new identity as a mother.[74] For many of these mothers, including such an avowed liberal as Diel, a strong component of this was a specific identity as a *German* mother. Prescriptive literature for pregnant women strongly reinforced a German maternal identity, often framing it in terms of a duty to raise the German birth rate.[75] Both maternal and German identities were malleable during the Weimar period, just as were the meanings of labor pain. For example, and perhaps most saliently, those women who embraced labor pain relief did not necessarily reject the notion of maternal sacrifice entirely, but they no longer regarded sacrifice and suffering as central to their identities as mothers. They did not reflexively believe that a suffering mother would be a more loving mother. Moreover, to the extent that they advocated pain relief on patriotic, pronatalist grounds, they shifted the arena of maternal sacrifice from childbearing to childrearing. Having more children would spare women suffering in the short run but exact a greater physical and financial toll in the course of their upbringing. Yet, sacrifice had its limits here, too; the larger families that liberal pronatalists had in mind would comprise three or four children, rather than a huge brood that would be impossible to nourish and educate properly by middle-class standards.[76] This reflected a shift toward valuing more highly the spiritual and emotional qualities of mothers as nurturers of their offspring, rather than appreciating mothers primarily for their fecundity and physical suffering.[77]

Comfort in the Marketplace: The Demand for "Quack" Potions

Perhaps the most compelling evidence that many women wanted pain relief—and wanted it on their own terms—was the booming market in patent medicines aimed at expectant mothers. One in particular, a remedy called Rad-Jo, led its competitors by a wide margin.[78] Available in pharmacies or by mail, Rad-Jo consisted of an extract of an African plant, Jogonie, for which it was named. Other ingredients included primarily additional plant extracts—up to forty or fifty of them—as well as alcohol. Its promoter and manufacturer, Vollrath Wasmuth, claimed that Rad-Jo could relieve complaints of pregnancy, give energy, calm the expectant mother's psyche, give a breastfeeding mother plenty of milk, and—most importantly—guarantee a quick, safe, and virtually painless delivery. Flashy brochures, magazine ads, and even a promotional film featured photos of healthy mothers and babies alongside glowing testimonials from mothers, their husbands, and doctors and midwives. Under pressure from the medical establishment, the courts in 1925 restricted the sale of Rad-Jo to pharmacies and banned its advertisement; a higher court reversed this decision in 1927, ruling that Rad-Jo was not a drug and therefore not subject to governmental regulation.[79] However, physicians were losing their campaign against Rad-Jo and other forms of "quackery" in the court that mattered most: the court of public opinion.

The best evidence for the popularity of Rad-Jo was its success in the marketplace. Monetary sales figures are hard to come by, and those available are not comparable over time or to other drugs because of the rapid rise in prices due to hyperinflation in the early 1920s. (In mid-March 1923, a single bottle cost fifteen thousand marks, and prices continued to increase astronomically until the currency reform in November 1923.) Still, records indicate that women bought hundreds of thousands of bottles of Rad-Jo each year. About a million bottles were sold between 1906 and 1920. By spring 1923, this figure had risen to a total of two million.[80] This trend suggests that the pace of sales was actually increasing over time. Rad-Jo faced a certain degree of direct competition after its inventor, a certain Dr. Hey, had a falling out with Wasmuth and began to market a similar potion (Uxorin) with similarly sensational advertisements.[81] Uxorin appears never to have seriously challenged the leading position of Rad-Jo, however.

In response to its popularity, elite obstetricians unanimously condemned Rad-Jo in a joint statement issued in 1920. To some degree, they were provoked into doing so by Wasmuth's advertising claim that Rad-Jo had been "tested and judged by outstanding physicians and professors, including its use with great success at a German university women's hospital." In response, the directors of all the university women's hospitals in Germany publicly condemned the potion as medically useless and effective only in enriching its manufacturer, as it was sold at a "very high price."[82] These prominent obstetricians issued their declaration partly at the behest of the editor of the *Munich Medical Weekly* (*Münchener medizinische Wochenschrift*), one of Germany's leading weekly medical journals, who conducted an ongoing campaign against Rad-Jo. Medical criticism of Rad-Jo spread well beyond the lofty circles of academic medicine, as well, and was often buttressed by practicing physicians' observations. A Dr. Schwarzwäller wrote in an advice manual for pregnant women: "Rad-Jo and similar substances, which are intended to make birth easier and bring forth beautiful children, are completely worthless. Among the difficult deliveries that I have attended was also a whole series of cases in which the women had taken Rad-Jo beforehand."[83] A short blurb in the *Journal for Further Medical Education* in 1922 exhorted physicians to warn patients who asked about Rad-Jo—"and this still occurs very frequently, even now."[84]

In a storm of counterpublicity, Wasmuth insulted the competence of these doctors and accused them of pursuing their own greedy interests at the expense of their patients'. He launched a contest for the "most apt description" of Rad-Jo, which elicited a flood of testimonials. In printing these, he referred to the medical opponents of Rad-Jo as "defilers of civilization," "criminals against the people," and "pirates of the people's health." Elsewhere, he denounced them as "mass murderers."[85] Wasmuth combined these insults with evocations of women's experiences of suffering in childbed. In open letters to editors of various medical journals that publicly opposed Rad-Jo, he wrote: "If you knowingly [deprive pregnant women of Rad-Jo], you belong on the gallows, or someone should cut open your belly once every year and rummage and poke around in there with forceps and then stitch it up again, so that you would know for once what it means to have babies without Rad-Jo."[86] Even given the usually tense relations between allopathic physicians and other health practitioners, this was exceptionally strong language.[87] His hyperbolic scorn resulted in his being tried on libel charges in the early 1920s, though the court ultimately acquitted him.[88] In other encounters with the courts, Wasmuth fared less well. As a plaintiff, he lost a libel suit in Munich in 1909 against opponents who had called Rad-Jo an "outright swindle." In another suit, he was fined for falsely claiming that the Dutch royal physician had successfully used Rad-Jo.[89] However, to dismiss Wasmuth as an unscrupulous swindler was unfair; he stood behind his product, honoring the money-back guarantee for dissatisfied customers. His advocacy of Rad-Jo took on the quality of a crusade, backed by a passionate belief that the potion really could protect women's health. This passion went so deep that he actually attempted suicide in 1922, which his son later attributed to his distress at being prosecuted for libel.[90]

The Rad-Jo controversy represented another instance of physicians attempting to consolidate their monopoly on pain relief and drive unlicensed "quack" practitioners out of the health marketplace.[91] But doctors

also had a valid point: However much Wasmuth may have been convinced of the efficacy of Rad-Jo, women were wasting their hard-earned
money on it. There are good reasons to believe that Rad-Jo came
nowhere near to achieving the claims of its creator and his allies. For one,
the composition of the potion changed from one batch to the next, sometimes quite dramatically. A chemical analysis performed in 1926 showed
considerable variation from the 1922 formula, including an increase in
alcohol content from 5.25 percent to more than 18 percent by volume.[92]
The original formula was based on African plants reputed among the lo-
cals to promote easier births. As supply lines were interrupted during and
after the Great War, other European and American plants were substituted. Again, in choosing these ingredients preference was given to plants
with a reputation for promoting birth and lactation, but no distinctions
were drawn among folk tradition, homeopathic principles, and regular
medical research. The only plants rejected out of hand were those whose
effectiveness was clearly buttressed by scientific evidence; the use of such
plants would likely have brought Rad-Jo under governmental regulation
as a drug. Both the ingredients themselves and their proportions varied in
a way that one pharmaceutical expert described as "arbitrary" and
"thoroughly amateurish and disallowed"—an assessment that was cor-
roborated even by Wasmuth's own expert.[93]

Moreover, prominent physicians surveyed agreed that the chief ingredients of Rad-Jo would be good for just one thing: relieving constipa-
tion.[94] Of course, this property alone might have helped numerous
women feel better, especially during late pregnancy when digestion tends
to slow down, but it fell far short of Wasmuth's extravagant claims. In
any event, much cheaper laxatives were available on the market. More
or less controlled experiments consistently found Rad-Jo to be ineffective for other purposes. Obstetricians at the Greifswald University
Women's Hospital surveyed their patients and found that the rate of
complications among women who reported drinking Rad-Jo during
their pregnancies was no lower than among other women.[95] An investigation at the Berlin University Women's Hospital in 1921 tested Rad-Jo
under controlled circumstances on twenty pregnant in-patient women.
Due to postwar shortages of meat, their diet was largely vegetarian, as
Wasmuth recommended. Their average length of labor was not noticeably different from that of patients who had not taken Rad-Jo, nor did
they suffer less pain, judging from their behavior during labor. Further
investigation found that two patients who later wrote testimonials for
Rad-Jo and gave birth in this Berlin hospital reported much shorter
labors than their hospital records showed. The physician who noted this
discrepancy attributed it to many women regarding only the pushing

phase of delivery as actual labor, a phase of childbirth that very commonly lasts two hours or less.[96]

Were women just credulous sheep, then—easy prey to a peddler of "quack" medicines? Closer scrutiny of their motivations reveals a much more complex story. Here, the testimonials—which Wasmuth swore under oath were genuine—provide some clues. In fact, no one claimed that the testimonials were fake, only that they exaggerated women's true level of satisfaction with Rad-Jo. By 1920, Wasmuth claimed to have received 4,944 testimonials, thirteen of which came from doctors. An unspecified number were penned by midwives, who received a commission for persuading women to purchase Rad-Jo. Customer testimonials were generally not rewarded, though "needy" women sometimes received a rebate on Rad-Jo. Most of the testimonials came in response to questionnaires that were periodically included in the product packaging. Since Rad-Jo came with a money-back guarantee, Wasmuth argued that the small number of refund requests proved that his potion lived up to its billing.[97]

Irrespective of the authenticity of the individual testimonials, the language they used partook of a larger discourse on suffering, maternity, and danger—all themes that would have resonated with the many women who feared giving birth. The ads juxtaposed "case studies" of deliveries with and without Rad-Jo. Frau Helene Brüderle of Freising was quoted as writing in 1920 that a friend of hers "trembled in fear of her 'hour of trial.' The first child was killed during its birth, two were forceps deliveries, the fourth had to be brought to the light of the world . . . through the artifice of three doctors, which happened only after three days and three nights. The Rad-Jo child arrived in three quarters of an hour, almost painlessly, and weighed eight pounds."[98] This testimonial is fairly typical in its conflation of pain with danger and fear of death, its portrayal of physicians as apt only to heighten pain and danger, and its representation of Rad-Jo as offering hope and deliverance. A similar account, written by a forester named Kufahl, told of his wife delivering seven children in great pain, often only by cesarean section. Only one of the infants survived. The eighth delivery went easily and painlessly, although the child weighed nine and a quarter pounds. Forester Kufahl attributed the health of both mother and child to Rad-Jo.[99] Not only cesarean section (a relatively infrequent procedure, greatly feared for its high risk of maternal death) but all sorts of surgical and instrumental deliveries, particularly forceps, were mentioned repeatedly in the brochures and flyers. Multiple testimonials affirmed that Rad-Jo had allowed women with a history of forceps deliveries to give birth easily and naturally, with no intervention at all. In contrast to these horror stories, many of the testimonials reported a "painless birth" thanks to Rad-Jo. Numerous women claimed to have given birth to their first child in as little as fifteen minutes. One woman reportedly noticed that the child had been born only when it started to cry.[100]

In these testimonials, the avoidance of pain was consistently equated with robust health for both mother and child. In tapping into women's desire for comfort, the Rad-Jo ads also undercut the linkage between suffering and morality. Now, comfort was brought into perfect harmony with the fulfillment of maternal duty. The pictures of charmingly chubby babies that ran alongside the testimonials suggested that the avoidance of pain would in fact go hand in hand with assuring the health of one's children, a laudable (and uncontroversial) goal for any mother. The psychological benefits of Rad-Jo would redound to the whole family, for the woman would be more stable emotionally and less likely to approach motherhood with reluctance. One woman wrote that after several excruciating labors that went on for days, she had been so desperate to avoid another that she had considered suicide.[101] The clear implication was that Rad-Jo had saved this woman's sanity and life, and prevented several children from becoming motherless. The testimonials also repeatedly stressed the avoidance of injuries to the mother during delivery. Many emphasized a quick recovery time, which enabled the new mother to nurse her child (copious milk was another central theme) and to resume her household work.[102] The testimonials show that the new mother's health was often valued precisely because it allowed her to fulfill her duties as mother and housewife. One farmer wrote that Rad-Jo allowed his wife to work in the fields until the last minute before delivering her fourth child and then return to milking the cows three days later. In her fifth pregnancy, she washed heavy laundry—which was onerous physical work without a washing machine—until a half hour before giving birth to a daughter.[103]

In purchasing Rad-Jo, women demonstrated faith in the healing power of nature. The belief in a benevolent nature dovetailed with various currents of the *Lebensreform* (life reform) movement, which encompassed (among other trends) vegetarianism, clothing reform, and other elements of healthy living. "Life reformers" and practitioners of "natural" medicine gained broad influence in Germany around the turn of the century and retained considerable influence throughout the 1920s.[104] Despite the seeming austerity of the coarse bread and cold showers that many *Lebensreformer* championed, the pursuit of health by ascetic means in fact served the larger goal of comfort. Here, too, Rad-Jo harmonized well with "natural" ideas of health. For one thing, it was composed entirely of plants and plant derivatives, rather than industrially produced chemicals. It was one of many herbal remedies, albeit an especially popular one, in a crowded and booming market that escaped governmental regulation.[105] Wasmuth explicitly claimed it was a healthful drink, a dietary supplement, and a natural stimulant—not a drug or patent remedy.[106] This claim both helped Rad-Jo dodge regulation and appealed to consumers who would have felt uncomfortable about taking a drug.[107] Furthermore, its proponents alleged that Rad-Jo had its origins in the traditional practices of African and American indigenous peoples. "Primitive" women were viewed as having easy deliveries, both in the popular imagination and in propaganda for Rad-Jo.[108] Wasmuth stated that he had made three trips to Africa and seen for himself that difficult births were unknown among native women who consumed the Jogonie root.[109]

This appeal to exoticism was at the same time an appeal to an idealized view of nature, which held that mother and child could expect safe deliverance if only the harmful influences of civilization could be counteracted. Laments about the degenerative influence of civilization on women's reproductive capacities were standard fare among allopathic physicians as well. Recall, for example, Hugo Sellheim's declaration that a different, less enervating way of life would do women even more good than his recommended painkiller, Scopan. From this standpoint, Rad-Jo represented one of several linked strategies for reverting to an ideal and idealized state of nature. One naturopathic health advice manual recommended Rad-Jo as the crux of healthy living in pregnancy. In addition, it advised expectant mothers to wear special maternity clothing that did not bind or constrict (as opposed to the still-common custom of wearing corsets), to get plenty of fresh air and mild exercise, to take cold sitz baths, and to eat a low-fat diet emphasizing fruit, vegetables, and whole grains.[110] By harnessing the powers of nature, Rad-Jo promised to transcend women's purportedly natural lot—suffering in labor—and to return childbirth to its ostensible natural state, consisting in comfort and safety.

Rad-Jo ads appealed to mistrust in orthodox medical authority, which for many people was the flip side of faith in natural medicine. Like many advocates of natural medicine, Wasmuth and his allies usually addressed the patient/consumer directly, bypassing all middlemen.[111] The proponents of Rad-Jo favorably compared its gentle effects to the dangers that Twilight Sleep posed to mother and child.[112] This argument harnessed the desires for greater comfort that the availability of Twilight Sleep had helped stoke. Rad-Jo promised comparable comfort without risk, while circumventing the regime of surveillance that was built into the administration of Twilight Sleep and other pharmaceutical forms of pain relief. Propaganda for Rad-Jo portrayed medical surveillance as untrustworthy and downright scary. At their most inflammatory, the ads accused doctors of trying to suppress Rad-Jo in order to continue receiving high fees for surgical and instrumental deliveries. While this allegation remained unsupported, the critique of Twilight Sleep as inadequately safe was borne out by a strong preponderance of the allopathic medical evidence.

At the same time, Rad-Jo propaganda attempted to mobilize medical authority in its favor. A handful of physicians, all of them specialists in natural medicine, publicly allied themselves with Wasmuth. But the ads for Rad-Jo also frequently suggested that leading university-based obstetricians had tested and endorsed the potion. The Rad-Jo promotional film, entitled *A Benefactor of Humanity*, claimed that scientific testing in university hospitals had proven the effectiveness of Rad-Jo. It further implied that even serious complications of childbirth could be prevented simply by drinking Rad-Jo in late pregnancy, thus obviating the need for surgical deliveries or indeed any sort of medical attention, no matter how dim the prospects for a safe, spontaneous delivery. A report by a Berlin medical official on behalf of the police censorship authorities—which recommended denying permission to screen this film in public—noted that such arguments were apt to dissuade expectant mothers from seeking medical assistance even if they really needed it. This official noted that "a large part of the public" mistrusted the methods of allopathic medicine.[113] While it is unclear whether this film was ever publicly shown, a similar tension ran through the printed brochures, which explicitly criticized physicians for doubling the number of obstetrical operations in the preceding few decades yet failing to reduce maternal mortality.[114] Women who had taken Rad-Jo were repeatedly described as defying physicians' dire predictions of a difficult delivery. Testimonials frequently told of Rad-Jo consumers giving birth in a university hospital, with professors, midwives, and medical students marveling at the ease of delivery.[115] Wasmuth also repeatedly referred to tests conducted by Professor Zangemeister in the Marburg University Women's Hospital, which allegedly convinced Zangemeister that Rad-Jo was effective.[116] Zangemeister later denied this claim—under coercion by his colleagues, said Wasmuth.[117]

Apart from this dialectic between suspicion of medical orthodoxy and respect for medical authority, the popularity of Rad-Jo suggests a radical, widespread rejection of the medical monopoly on prescription medicines.[118] Women using Rad-Jo circumvented the authority vested in physicians and midwives and insisted on their right to choose their own remedies. One flyer, aimed at government officials, asked who was qualified to judge the effectiveness of Rad-Jo. The answer: "Only the laboring women, for they feel childbirth on their own body; no professor or physician can do this, for the woman can merely tell the physicians how painlessly or painfully birth proceeded."[119] Thus, the marketers of Rad-Jo encouraged women to do what they were already doing: taking pain relief into their own hands. This tactic was undercut when Rad-Jo became re-classified as a prescription medicine in the wake of the various libel actions. From about 1930, its sales declined sharply once women could no longer purchase it freely, though it remained on the market until 1989.[120] During the National Socialist period the pendulum of cultural beliefs would swing back in the direction of greater stoicism. Thereafter, psychosomatic methods (such as Lamaze) would arguably fill the gap for self-directed relief of labor pain in Germany.

Conclusion: The Tentative Triumph of Comfort

The Rad-Jo story might too easily be read as a tale of an unscrupulous "quack" fleecing credulous and superstitious women. Numerous women did express dissatisfaction with its effectiveness, according to a midwife who agitated against Rad-Jo in Cologne.[121] As a result, the Prussian Midwives' Association issued a public statement in 1921 that condemned Rad-Jo as failing to live up to its claims.[122] The University Women's Hospital in Tübingen reported that husbands, in particular, were angry at what they felt to be a waste of their money.[123] Another midwife reported quite a different phenomenon, however: "Every woman wants to have Rad-Jo, one tells the next about it, and the women feel so good with it."[124] A woman in Frankfurt wrote Wasmuth that she did not let herself be deterred by midwives and doctors who told her that Rad-Jo was harmless but wholly ineffective. "By now I have met many women who have also taken your Rad-Jo and who all praise it very much. I myself have also recommended it to wives of colleagues who were very happy with it afterward. A cousin of mine took it, too, at my strong recommendation and after five bad confinements finally had a living child and has felt much healthier and fresher ever since."[125] Those women who were satisfied with Rad-Jo may well have experienced what is now referred to as the placebo effect, or possibly what one obstetrician called the power of "mass suggestion."[126] In conjunction with the increase in women who desired effective pain relief in labor, however, the popularity of Rad-Jo signaled the beginning of a new attitude toward maternity in Germany. This modern conception regarded suffering neither as inevitable nor as the quintessence of motherhood.

In the struggle between sacrificial and pleasurable motherhood—between suffering and comfort—much more was at stake than the finite temporary physical pain of labor. Women sought reassurance that they would not have to make the ultimate sacrifice: the loss of their babies or of their own life or health. The iconography of Rad-Jo advertisements sometimes reminded them that the very lives of mother and child hung in the balance during labor. One particularly dramatic ad portrayed a naked woman (who oddly looked not in the least pregnant) clinging to a doctor as the skeletal form of Death tried to snatch her away. A small inset picture showed a healthy looking woman holding a chubby toddler in one arm while nursing a robust infant. Another inset showed a relief portrait of Wasmuth in profile. The accompanying text explained the obvious: using Rad-Jo would cheat Death of its prey and guarantee happy motherhood.[127] In the context of double-digit infant mortality rates that spiked as high as 30 percent during the Great War, Rad-Jo promised that the mother would be able to enjoy her relationship with her new baby.[128] Her own health would be strong enough to cope with the challenge of infant care, and she would not have to worry constantly about the child's survival.

Women's responses to both experimental new analgesics and natural remedies show that they were willing to grapple with the morality of obstetric pain relief. But they wanted to do so on their own terms. Those women who continued to reject pain relief grounded their critiques experientially. Morality, in their view, was no more abstract than their notions about female nature. They perceived both as rooted in their personal experience, which had convinced them that maternal love and duty evolved only through suffering. Women who wanted pain relief also found moral arguments in its favor. Such arguments consistently identified a benefit beyond the obvious one of sparing the mother pain— be it the strength of the nation, the vigor of the *Volkskörper*, or the health and survival of individual infants. These women were not eager to abdicate their responsibilities and prerogatives to physicians. Instead, they perceived a trade-off between self-determination and the effectiveness of pain relief. They responded to this trade-off basically in two ways. Some women were willing to submit to intensified medical observation in order to gain more effective relief. Others settled for a less potent drug that allowed them to continue to bear babies in a traditional setting without a physician calling the shots. This divided response prevented the new regime of surveillance over childbirth from spreading beyond a minority of women until roughly the 1960s, when hospital birth became nearly universal in Germany.

Electing pain relief, whether Twilight Sleep or Rad-Jo, entailed acceptance of the idea that bodily processes could be subjected to planned human control. This is a thoroughly modern idea, which presumes that an autonomous individual can manipulate her own or another body as an object. Not only physicians but also expectant mothers increasingly embraced this belief. Thus, recent feminist interpretations of pain relief in labor as the result of a (more or less explicit) conspiracy of male physicians to seize "control" over women's bodies in childbirth overlook the efforts women have made historically to obtain pain relief for themselves, often over the objections of their physicians. Some women, like Louise Diel, sought to persuade physicians to give them anesthetics or opiates upon demand. Among other women, a modern notion of control over one's body harmonized with a deep trust in nature—albeit a nature that had to be reclaimed by human means in order to defeat the degenerative influences of civilization. Their consumption of Rad-Jo affirmed that comfort was more natural than pain.

Compared to other countries, the mass pursuit of comfort and rejection of suffering and sacrifice in childbirth occurred relatively late in Germany. This trend gathered strength during the 1920s, as opposed to the late nineteenth century in the United States and Britain.[129] As a result, the new emphasis on comfort was too fragile to survive the National Socialist backlash against anything that smacked of softness. Under the new political system, the ideal of the suffering, self-abnegating mother would be re-inscribed upon women's bodies, reinforcing their subordination to husbands, the state, and the ostensible common good of a racially pure and militarily strong German people. The imagined health of the *Volkskörper*—a chimera that was ever-present but never uncontested during the Weimar period—would now incontrovertibly trump the well-being of individual mothers and children. After 1933, the ideal German mother was again to learn to "suffer without complaining," be it in enduring labor pain or in mourning the loss of sons in battle.

5 GEOFFREY COCKS

Modern Pain and Nazi Panic

PAIN is an intransmissible personal experience, but one that every human being knows. But pain is not the same experience in all cultures at all times. In the modern era, the predominant cultural trend in the West has been toward the separation of pain from the sorts of religious meaning it was imparted in medieval Europe.[1] After 1800 the human body and mind—as distinct from the soul—became the focus of unprecedented scientific, medical, institutional, and commercial concern in Western society. Pain was now understood in material and secular terms as something that often could and should be avoided in pursuit of physical and mental well-being. The Nazis attempted to reinvest pain with a broad cultural meaning. For the Nazis, the experience and endurance of pain was both the means and proof of racial superiority in the struggle with inferior races. But pain was also the anxious reminder for the Nazis of the morbidity and mortality of the human body regardless of nationality. This anxiety reveals Nazism as an act of massive cultural cowardice—of panic—a fear of life as well as of death. In the end, the rigors of the Nazi war for racial domination only increased the incidence of illness and pain—and ongoing individual and institutional strategies for their alleviation—in Germany and thus undermined the Nazi attempt to unify Germans into a common struggle for long-term "racial" well-being.

The Evolution of Modern Pain

The modern opposition between "pain" and "prosperity" was more than just the necessity of sacrifice for the sake of economic gain. Prosperity and well-being were now more than ever also a function of the relative assurance of physical comfort and health. More people in all classes now lived longer, and chronic illness and everyday aches and pains became a more common prolonged or episodic state than acute terminal disease. After the late nineteenth century in the West the incidence of epidemics declined markedly. Instead there emerged a host of new gradual stress-related illnesses and conditions along with the new common social roles of the patient and consumer of medical services.[2] While morbidity, too, declined, pain and well-being moved through people's private and public lives as a constant, an opposition, a pair, or a sequence, all of these manifestations having for individual and group a past, a present, and a future.[3]

The history of modern pain begins in ancient Greece with the Hippocratic turn from pain as part of the world of spirits to part of the world of nature. This formed the basis for the modern medical appreciation of a pain as a symptom of specific disorders. Only most recently has pain itself become a disorder with its own medical specialty, algology.[4] In fact, pain has always over time been a subject of contestation between an objective and subjective point of view. For Aristotle pain was an emotion, for Descartes a sensation. With the Enlightenment and the Scientific and Industrial Revolutions, mechanism and positivism came to dominate an increasingly medicalized view of the human organism. The world became secularized and "disenchanted."[5] In this brave new world of expertise, merchandising, and consumption, pain became a problem to be solved through the intervention of knowledge, material resources, and technology. All this built on the "eighteenth-century cult of sensibility [which] redefined pain as unacceptable."[6] It was also at the same time that individual pleasure came to be regarded as a legitimate human right in pursuit of earthly happiness through sensual indulgence and consumption of material goods and services.[7] The isolation of morphine in 1808, the discovery of the anesthetic properties of ether in 1847, and the chemical synthesis of aspirin in 1899 introduced the modern culture of effective pain alleviation and management in pursuit of quality of life.[8]

Pain, however, has always been inscribed with the history and culture of its bearer. This individual experience has become more important through the social construction of the modern self. While a human sense of self in some respects dates far back into history, the social dominance of personal identity dates from the early modern state's imposition of it as a means for purposes of taxation, military mobilization, and policing.[9] The Enlightenment subsequently raised the rights—and, often oppressively, the responsibilities—inherent in the individual to a central philosophical, moral, and legal principle. The growth of autobiography in the nineteenth century and the explosion of psychology in the twentieth were signs of preoccupation with the private self enhanced or threatened by the modern ethos of change and the new.[10] The historical creation of the individual self was, however, imprisoned within an individual body that became the object of an emphasis on healthful living. Moreover, many people became obsessed with the body as place and sign not only of individual pain and well-being but of collective threat and value.

European society also underwent a process of medicalization in the late nineteenth century whereby many social issues and problems were increasingly defined in medical terms and assigned to powerful professional and political medical authorities. The growth of transportation networks during the nineteenth century had magnified the danger of the spread of epidemic disease, particularly in Central Europe, the rapidly industrializing crossroad of the continent.[11] The professionalization of medicine contributed to the institutionalization of medical practice in state and society, as did the growth of both small and large pharmaceutical firms, especially after 1900. The expansion of industry required greater economic and political attention to productivity and disability. In 1883 Germany introduced a compulsory health insurance system for workers, in 1884 one for accidents, and in 1889 one for invalidism and retirement.[12] Both private and public concern with matters of health and illness had thus been heavily institutionalized in Europe by the first decades of the twentieth century. Although powerful social, economic, and political interests could prove to be an impediment to policies based on advances in medical knowledge, the general trend during this era was toward ever greater effectiveness of medical practice and public health.[13] The change most directly apparent to patients was the fact that doctors for the first time were able to treat and even cure an ever larger number of illnesses in a new beneficent "era of care."[14] This created significant popular demand for medical services and a general internalization of socially dominant bourgeois values and attitudes. There remained, however, popular resistance and recourse to alternative therapies (such as homeopathy), either by custom, the lack of access (especially in rural areas) to reliable or affordable medical care, physician class prejudice and authoritarianism, or—the preoccupation in Franz Kafka's "The Country Doctor"—the failure of modern medicine to solve the mysteries of pain and death.[15]

Whatever its capacities and outcomes, therefore, medicine by its very nature tends to intrude, and be invited, more deeply into people's lives than other official and professional entities, often leading to "antidiscipline" and "the polytheism of scattered practices."[16] Such struggles for autonomy within and against dominant structures of authority are a reminder that there is space—and thus degrees of agency—within structures. Pain and well-being in Nazi Germany was one such arena in which individuals and groups pursued interest, advantage, and protection from, within, without, and against authority. But the regime was also able to make a variety of effective appeals for allegiance on precisely the intimate and familiar ground of personal and familial physical well-being and security and amid the dissolution of traditional milieus. This took the form of "aestheticized politics" emphasizing exclusionary illusions of secure and healthy harmony and wholeness.[17]

These intersections took place against the background of particular historical developments in Germany. Although some have argued that it is uniquely "heroic in Germany to stand pain," it is difficult to establish a single consistent German style of, or German attitude toward, pain and well-being in the modern era.[18] Studies in the cultural specificity of pain have traditionally dealt with regional, religious, social or ethnic groups smaller or larger than national groupings. For example, in 1932 one German doctor complained that early diagnoses of illness in parts of northern Germany were impeded by a traditional reaction to illness of shame.[19] In Germany as elsewhere in the West beginning in the eighteenth century, pain and violence had become less a part of public life as a result of Enlightenment preference for imprisonment, deterrence, correction, treatment, and prevention over corporal punishment and execution, that is, "the growth of order and stability in German society. . . . [and] . . . the growing control of the state over its citizens."[20] Soon after, however, pain in private life began to be transformed from inexplicable or meaningful fate into meaningless natural—and possibly avoidable but thus increasingly ponderable—fact.

The First World War: The Fusion of Nation, Self, and Pain

The First World War had a huge effect on individuals' and societies' senses of pain, well-being, and self. Foremost were the devastating physical and mental effects of industrialized warfare on the millions of men deemed medically fit to serve in the national armies.[21] Such concerns built upon a traditional trepidation about war felt by many from the rural and urban masses.[22] During the war, civilians had come to know of the physical and psychological horrors at the front. And the mad, dying, and disabled veterans who survived the battlefields kept postwar society dreadfully aware of the costs.[23] Less evident but in the long run even more dangerous was the fact that the First World War was a brutalizing culmination of a modern trend by which nation-states sought to secure inward sovereignty and outward expansion, defining the individual and national in terms of enemies and victims.[24] Equally dangerous was the reaction of many soldiers, especially those from the middle classes, to the conditions of the new warfare: "a grim, probably inevitable glorification of one's helplessness, of pain and death, just as much of heroism and sacrifice."[25] This attitude was an understandable defensive reaction against the threat to bodily integrity and physical existence posed by mechanized combat.

But it often pitted soldiers against civilians and assumed misunderstanding, and—especially in Germany—even betrayal, behind the lines. In this construction pain was contrasted *experientially and ethically* with well-being. For many, the willingness to endure pain was proof of national sacrifice and loyalty while well-being became the province of traitors and even the racial Other.

These dynamics of "nation-building" in the psyche were particularly problematic in Germany. This is not surprising since "national identity is culturally, psychologically, and historically constructed."[26] The dislocations of the early years of the Weimar Republic only aggravated the tendency to think—or feel—in terms of the dangers of internal and external threats to the national "body." The German "stab-in-the-back" myth was fueled by such fantasies, and Jews in this sense too became a major focus of discontent for the German racist right. And there was, following Norbert Elias, some recrudescence of old feelings of German self-pity generated by the defeat of a national entity in which so much of the self had been invested.[27]

The German and Austrian experience of the First World War was all the more shattering because of the uniquely widespread experience of wartime malnutrition and disease due to the Allied sea blockade. The first wildcat strikes in the industrial Ruhr broke out over the "stomach question."[28] The effects were especially severe among infants and children. Birth weights fell significantly from 1916 onward, breastfeeding declined from 1915 through 1919, and diseases such as rickets and tuberculosis caused a precipitous rise in morbidity and mortality among children between the ages of five and fifteen. Gastrointestinal diseases as well as the incidence of worms, fleas, and lice showed marked increases. All of these afflictions were accompanied by psychological stress manifested in enuresis, "nervousness," and juvenile delinquency. Peter Loewenberg has argued that these conditions produced a generational cohort that supported Hitler. This was due to intensified oedipal conflict due to the absence of the father in the First World War, the increased dependence on a burdened mother, and the father's return (or death) in national defeat. The result was a generation of young males in particular whose early experiences had weakened their egos and superegos and whose reversion to "rage, sadism, and the defensive idealization of their absent parents, especially the father" in response to the new deprivations of the Great Depression made them peculiarly receptive "to the appeal of a mass movement utilizing the crudest devices of projection and displacement. . . . [and] submission to a total, charismatic leader."[29] Due to the demographic disaster of the First World War, there was an unprecedented bulge in the German population comprising precisely the most affected birth cohorts of 1900 to 1914.[30] Psychoanalytic self-psychology can further enrich this analysis in terms of pain, well-being, and identity. Self-psychology focuses on the development of the child's sense of self in relation to others and stresses the importance of parental empathy for the development of an affirmative and realistic sense of self. When such parental empathy is lacking or insufficient, the child develops a brittle grandiosity in place of genuine self-esteem. The wartime conditions Loewenberg describes—the absence of fathers and the alternating presence and absence (at work) of mothers, the material deprivation and damage, the psychological stresses—seem more than likely to have spawned such anxious and aggressive personalities that peopled the postwar radical German right.

Such private disappointments were also reflected in national identity. Although strong nationalism was universal in Europe, each nation had its own experiences with it. In Germany, national unity was more problematic than elsewhere. This was manifested in widespread scapegoating of Kaiser Wilhelm after the war, by which Germans denied their emotional dependence on him as a symbol of unity and strength. German national identity was all the more fragile because of its recent, tenuous, and brief realization in imperial Germany only since 1871. The kaiser's own anxious search for external validation took the form of peripatetic travel to celebrations and appearances around Germany. His concerns were mirrored by the Germans, who widely admired the kaiser for these trips, which were always enthusiastically well attended.[31] The Nazis, for their part, exerted a powerful appeal for a people that had gone through an era that rendered the human body and its disorders the center of much public and private attention, systematically endangered those bodies (and minds), and destroyed that form of a national body with which so many had identified. Especially those who at young ages during the war had endured material deprivation, physical distress, psychological damage, and national disappointment would respond to the Nazi appeal for German unity and strength. This was especially the case given the economic disasters of 1923 and 1929 that relived recent trauma to body, mind, and self. Identification with the nation through the Nazi movement allowed fears of weakness and danger to be projected onto the Other while assigning all vigor and virtue to a revived national body cleansed of elements of national and racial dissolution. This Nazi appeal to German men and women would be conducted largely on the intimate and familiar ground of health, hearth, and home. Just as the national "body" would be secure, so too would the private body of self and family.

Pain and Panic in Interwar Germany

By the 1920s Germany was a place where well-being and pain had become universalized and in the modern mode were opposed *materially* in a zero-sum equation. Numerous individuals and groups were seeking, and getting, compensation as victims of one sort or another. The Weimar Republic was committed to expanding the components of the state welfare system inherited from the Second Reich and the First World War. In response, those seeking such support organized into competing groups in the tradition of the old legal corporatism deeply embedded in German culture and the new economic corporatism inherent in modern industrial capitalism. The fiscal demands on the state became so great that by the end of the decade competition had replaced compensation as the chief determinant in the allocation of benefits. Pensions began to be based not on the cost of living but on the amount of contributions paid. Treatment and rehabilitation of both physical and psychological disorders were privileged over pensions. The ethic of productivity and social utility, also perceived and propagandized as a psychological benefit to the recipient, had become paramount. This ethic was reminiscent of the practice during the war of rationalization for purposes of efficiency; it was again imposed on the German economy as a condition of international loans under the Dawes Plan beginning in 1924.[32] Ostensibly, well-being was now placed over pain in terms of the encouragement of individual overcoming of pain and disability. But individual well-being was now subordinated to the endurance of pain in the fiscal, economic, and political interests of the state. This not only served the interests of the democratic Weimar government, but also helped pave the way for Nazi regimentation and exploitation of individuals' bodies and minds for purposes of national and "racial" aggrandizement.

Nazism radicalized contemporaneous eugenic fears of physical and mental degeneration. Such fears were aggravated by the new germ theory. The reality and image of invisible, invasive, or indwelling carriers of disease generated great anxiety, especially since antibiotics only came on the scene beginning in the 1930s and 1940s. Germ theory was an advance on older theories that posited sickness as a result of constitution, and epidemics the outcome of miasmas arising from an unclean environment. Microbes, however, were passed from person to person, and so it became commonplace to blame victims for not taking care of themselves and for endangering others as well. This censuring occurred in spite of the fact that bacteriology showed that infection was a random fact of natural conditions and historical events. Although many doctors and health-care workers sensibly spoke in nonjudgmental terms of "the socialism of the microbe," another view took hold: widespread polarization of worthy and unworthy, the careful and the careless, joined with racism and eugenic discourse to reject imperfect social and political solutions and "perfect" humanity by eliminating its "weaker" members and groups.[33]

Reflecting the heightened awareness of health and illness now widely institutionalized in European society, diseases had assumed metaphorical as well as medical and political status. Cancer had been known for centuries, but during the early twentieth century became the disease with the greatest literal and metaphorical presence.[34] It was linked in the popular imagination with the lower body, with shame, and with repressed sexuality.[35] But it was the literal nature itself of cancer that gave it its most dangerous metaphorical potential. For cancer was—and is—the great silent and relentless internal and external agent of decomposition and death. In this it embodied the worst fears associated with germ theory. And, perhaps worst of all, cancer subverts the value of pain. With cancer, pain was most often not a warning signal but a death sentence. German surgeon Ferdinand Sauerbruch made just this point in 1936, while the Nazi regime sponsored a traveling play about cancer that was entitled *Zu Spät* (too late).[36]

Pain and well-being became modern cultural markers for individual and collective metaphors drawn from experience of disease and illness. And with no one did these markers and metaphors have more deadly effect than with those on the radical racist right wing after the First World War. Such groups shaped and were shaped by the defensive mythification and memorialization of mass death that was one popular and official response to the uncontrolled mass destructiveness of the First World War. While some reacted to the war's destruction of traditional forms and beliefs with a more or less responsible existentialism, radical nationalists indulged in an anxious brutalization of politics and celebration of the manliness of the warrior. The Nazis were dedicated to a particularly ruthless and vicious brand of social Darwinism that saw human life as a biological struggle for survival among superior and inferior racial groups. Hitler himself was preoccupied in this sense with disease, infection, and contagion. The pages of *Mein Kampf* ooze with graphic metaphorical and literal references to syphilis, cancer, bacteria, viruses, parasites, bacilli, and vermin, all of which are linked with an imagined Jewish conspiracy to pollute and destroy the racial substance of the Aryan race.[37] This hypermasculinized fear of the morbid, sexual (and thus also mortal) body was likewise expressed in Goebbels's description in 1942 of homosexuality as a "cancer."[38] On July 10, 1941, Hitler declared he felt himself to be "Robert Koch in politics," and in February

1942, just a month after the Wannsee Conference organized the Final Solution, he invoked the names of both Koch and Louis Pasteur in speaking of the extermination of the Jews:

The discovery of the Jewish virus is one of the greatest revolutions that have taken place in the world. The battle in which we are engaged today is of the same sort as the battle waged, during the last century, by Pasteur and Koch. How many diseases have their origin in the Jewish virus![39]

To be sure, Hitler's obsessions sprang in great measure from psychological disorders born of early personal experience.[40] But these disorders were filled with the content of the times that in Hitler's case too revolved around issues of physical and mental pain and well-being raised to the level of fantastic, fanatic obsession.[41] Hitler himself suffered from a variety of bodily ailments, worried mightily about various inherited and acquired diseases, and was heavily dosed with patent medicines and chemicals for most of his public life.[42] Not surprisingly, given what we know about the fears associated with cancer in particular, it also seems that Hitler was particularly interested in the Nazi public health campaign against cancer. He had personally approved funds for breast cancer research, a disease from which his mother had died in 1907 while under the care of a Jewish doctor.[43]

The First World War had of course aggravated popular concerns in general with injury, death, and pain. The extreme nationalism of the radical right was based in great part on a desire for the collective survival of the nation as defense against heightened fears of injury, debilitation, and death. Fears associated with war would be dealt with by means of celebration of war as active assertion against the passivity imposed upon men by modern industrial warfare. Even well before the war, moreover, national identity had been widely constructed as masculine, in opposition to the notion of the female body as the place of private physical desire and weakness. The bloody postwar misogynist fantasies of members of the Freikorps, many of whom became Nazis, magnified these concerns, revealing even more clearly the deep masculine fears of the castrating fluid interiority of the female body.[44] This misogyny built on a Prussian and hence national tradition of hypermasculinity, which the First World War aggravated through the demand for the militant identification of the individual with the nation. The result was the further marginalization and even vilification of other class and gender identifications.[45]

The Nazi denial of shared individual human frailty thus spawned a new construction of pain and well-being that replaced the pluralistic political discourse of the Weimar Republic. This new construction was itself comprised of two radically opposed concepts, both of which in an almost medieval sense sought to invest pain with collective and transcendent meaning. The first juxtaposed extinction for the racial Other (primarily, "the Jew")—finally by means of poison gas designed for use against the threat to hygiene represented by vermin—and posited physical inviolability for the racial community.[46] This collectivist thought denied the reality of individual morbidity and mortality by stressing the survival and prosperity of the organism of the *Volk*. In this, it paralleled—and derived instrumental support from—a like phenomenon among some doctors. Since medicine could still do nothing about death, many doctors (many of whom were already radicalized to the right) turned "from the individual, whose case in the long run was always hopeless, to the 'body' of the nation, the *Volkskörper*."[47] This was also the logic of liberal social hygiene in its emphasis upon prevention of disease and, in psychiatry, future "degeneration" and crime.[48] The Third Reich, as a regime built upon terror, of course invested in pain as an explicit means of control of opponents.[49] Yet the power of the Nazi fixation on the morbid and mortal body meant that pain could not be a means of correction for racial enemies of the state. *Reichsführer*-SS leader Heinrich Himmler expressly forbade any attempt to indoctrinate concentration camp prisoners.[50] Such people could not be "improved" since they were locked by the Nazis in an iron category of physical and mental inferiority—and, paradoxically, a threat—to a superior race. In this construction, pain was punishment and prelude to death for the diseased racial Other, leaving the "Master Race" secure in eternal well-being purchased with the noble pain of heroic sacrifice.

The second constituent of the Nazi construction of pain and well-being concerned the members of the racial *Volksgemeinschaft* alone. This part of the new construction of pain and well-being tried to *collapse* pain and well-being into a single entity. While the Nazis promised well-being for every member of the "Aryan" race, pain (as with the military idealizations of the First World War before and after 1918) was now a necessary means and accompaniment to the struggle for racial mastery in Germany, Europe, and—by extension—the world. Pain and its endurance would in and of itself be proof of racial worth. Well-being thus consisted of the will to heroic sacrifice for *Führer* and *Volk* as well as the eternal reward for victory in the struggle for survival against the inferior races. This Nazi construction of pain in truth represented an anxious denial of—and panic over—what pain at bottom signals: the fragility and ultimate failure of all human bodies regardless of the often hierarchical distinctions constructed around them.

The Everyday of Pain in Nazi Germany

Nazi ideological concerns with the morbid and mortal body were both heightened and complicated by the quotidian health concerns of the German people. Besides the Nazi leadership's determination to undertake a racial cleansing of the German body politic, the regime of course also wanted to "harden" the German *Volk* for the inevitable, necessary, and desirable war that would be the means and proof of Aryan racial supremacy. This task was rendered more difficult given the cumulative adverse health effects of the First World War, the inflation of 1923, and the Great Depression. This damage came on top of the generally poor health, especially when it came to teeth and feet, among the less affluent classes as a result of poor nutrition, poor housing, poor footwear, and rural overwork. The Nazis' own martial activities, designed to use pain to prove and strengthen racial solidarity and masculinity, exacerbated at least some of these conditions: Military inspectors and civilian medical officers complained about the damage done by such "hardening" exercises in the Hitler Youth as barefoot marches and bareheaded marches in the rain.[51] Throughout the war officials would argue about the physical and psychological costs and benefits of strenuous exercise and the general medical control exercised by party organizations.[52]

The Nazis promised to restore the prosperity of Germany in the broadest (and most fanciful racist) sense of the word. Germans would go back to work, Germany would regain the honor and military prestige and protection lost under the Treaty of Versailles, and the new government would ensure that only those fit and eager to work would prosper. In fact, what the Nazi regime delivered to its population were increased demands for productivity and a decline in the amount of social welfare. The Nazis offered as incentive long-term collective well-being at the allegedly minor expenses of individual short-term pleasure and well-being, although the regime was also constrained to accede to or even promote popular self-indulgences for the sake of morale and public support. The Nazis plundered the public health-care system and expelled administrators and physicians who were Jews or political opponents. The purging of Jews resulted in shortages of specialists to the degree that even before the war the military and the Reich health administration were toying with the idea of allowing some Jewish doctors to practice on non-Jewish patients.[53] Even with heavily propagandized measures to promote occupational health and safety, improve working conditions, and provide for leisure activities, both the tempo and the workday of industrial production increased, with predictable rises in stress, accidents, and injury.[54] The rise in employment only slowly diminished some health problems: the district medical officer in the industrial district of Glauchau near Chemnitz in his annual health reports for 1935 and 1936 reported an ongoing incidence of neurasthenia among those who had been unemployed for some time.[55] But the increase in employment itself brought with it a worrisome increase in smoking, especially among youth, and in drinking.[56]

The Nazi approach had definite attractions to the great mass of Germans, especially given the past twenty years or so of social, economic, and political disruption and pain. It was also in line with a growing expectation—promoted through advertising and propaganda—of effective treatment of pain and illness through doctors and drugs. The German state had long been looked upon to provide the means for well-being, either in terms of a pension or—increasingly—in terms of productive reintegration into society. The state itself had become a place of *therapy.*[57] The alleviation of—or compensation, whether through pension or specialized work, for—pain and the promotion and provision of well-being now had at its disposal not only an increasingly effective and powerful array of medical sciences but the unparalleled resources of the modern nation. Modern governments had to be concerned about popular health and illness. In 1940 the German Army Medical Service issued a report for the period 1933 to 1935 and noted that the numbers of sick soldiers were much greater than those for the period 1908–13. This was because until the 1930s the military did not count minor illnesses such as influenza and tonsillitis.[58] Now mobilization of a population for mass warfare demanded the careful and *extensive* monitoring and treatment of illness. Under the Nazis, the state became as well a place of racial exaltation that, whatever individual Germans' doubts about—and fears of—racial policy, was inherently flattering and, with ongoing economic recovery and remilitarization, apparently effective. Racism appeared to offer a systematic explanation of very complicated phenomena in comfortingly simple, dichotomous, and familiar terms. Nazi actions in the realm of the familiar were especially effective in respect to medicine since that field was by nature characterized by prescription, that is, what should, must, and, given modern medicine, could be done. Even pain could be exalted as proof of commitment and service to a seemingly revived Germany. "Racial health" resonated with the individual on the grounds of the comfortable and the familiar: the family, children, home, and daily concerns over health and illness. The Nazis could also exploit the desire for respectability and conformity that had long characterized bourgeois social and sexual attitudes in Germany and in Europe.[59]

The Nazis thus dichotomized well-being and pain along racial lines and further isolated those officially deemed as alien to the racial community as the following instance shows.[60] On October 29, 1940, the mayor

of Neuruppin, a town northwest of Berlin, wrote a short letter in his capacity as local civil defense chief to the district medical officer. The mayor
reported rumors that the rise in deaths in the town during the previous
year was due to the disruption caused by air raid alarms and asked if
there was any truth to these rumors. *Amtsarzt* Tietz, in a letter addressed
to the mayor in the latter's capacity as local police authority, responded
on November 9, marking the communication "private and confidential."
Tietz noted that it was true that deaths in the city were up significantly in
1940 from 1939. Some of the increase, he observed, was in fact due to
the rigors imposed by air raid precautions: the blackout regulations on
residences that reduced the amount of light and sun; the disruption of
sleep; nights spent in cold, damp cellars; and, for some unfortunates, recourse to slit trenches during air raid alarms. Other reasons included a
cold winter and food shortages, both of which rendered older people
more susceptible to illness and death, and those local men who had
"fallen" in combat. But the major reason for the increase in mortality, according to Tietz in an apparently unprompted discourse, lay within the
confines of the provincial mental asylum: in the first nine months of
1939, eighty-seven inmates had died there; the figure for the first nine
months of 1940 was 284. He noted that the chief reason for this particular increase was the shortages of strictly rationed food for the inmates.[61]

Tietz, significantly, had even more deaths in the asylum to record in his
annual district health report for 1940: "The high death rate [428] in the
Landesanstalt may be traced to the fact that many very old and infirm patients have been transferred in from other evacuated institutions."[62] Although the number of deaths in the asylum fell slightly the next year to
393, rising slightly in 1942 to 401, this was still many more than the 162
recorded for 1939; in the 1938 report no mention at all is made of asylum deaths.[63] We of course know exactly what was going on: these deaths
arose from the transport of mental patients to killing centers under the
"euthanasia" program ordered by Hitler under cover of the war that
broke out in September 1939. It was in the fall of 1940 that "transit institutions" were established to funnel patients from a number of other institutions to the killing centers. In order to make room for the incoming
patients, the patients at the transit institution had to be killed. Neuruppin was one of these new transit institutions, which explains why the
death rate there, reported in Tietz's official figures, went up even more
radically during the last three months of 1940.[64] These transit institutions
were set up in response to public discontent—particularly that of relatives—over the killing of mental patients to ensure "greater secrecy about
the final destination."[65] The protests, which eventually forced Hitler to
declare an end to the official program on August 24, 1941, had not been

stilled by official condolence letters that, in line with propaganda favoring euthanasia, emphasized the end to suffering and pain that the patient's "natural" death represented. Officials tried to cover the operation by ordering immediate cremation of the bodies without the relatives' approval or presence and with the argument in letters of condolence that this protected the public from infectious diseases.[66] The regime was attempting to exploit its own and the public's fear of the incidence of disease built on memories of the First World War and, later, highly propagandized threats to public health represented by slave laborers and returning soldiers from the East. In spite of Hitler's 1941 stop order, the killing went on until the end of the war, often in the form of local "wild euthanasia" by means of fatal doses of medication or by starvation.[67]

The tiny paper discourse carried on by the mayor of Neuruppin and the district medical officer reflects a larger discourse on relative pain and well-being in the first year of Hitler's war. Given what we know about the rumors and anxieties that accompanied the Nazi "euthanasia" program throughout Germany, it is legitimate to speculate that when the mayor began his letter with the phrase "According to rumors," he was communicating concerns not only about deaths in general but deaths connected in particular with the asylum. His concern most likely was a desire not to be associated with some public unhappiness over an official government program while still being able to transmit the fact of it. He could do this by burying it in another real concern, that of the health effects of air raid measures. This indirect discourse was likely the reason that medical official Tietz responded by *opening* his letter by acknowledging the increased death rates in the town and ascribing it primarily to the rise in mortality at the asylum, only *after* that turning to the subject ostensibly raised by the mayor, and then returning to the matter of the asylum by closing the letter with a brief discussion of rationing as the chief cause of increased mortality there. Clearly Tietz wanted the mayor to know—and perhaps discreetly spread the word—that the patients at the asylum were dying because of the shared privations brought to all Germans by the war. At the same time, of course, Tietz communicated by "private and confidential" means the importance the regime attached to the killing of mental patients and thus the responsibility of bureaucrats like himself and the mayor to obey the government. Since it was the relatives of the patients and residents of villages and small towns of fewer than ten thousand residents who constituted most of the opposition, Tietz and the mayor could hope that the larger city of Neuruppin would view the asylum inmates' pain (from the process of dying from starvation) as part of general wartime pain and decline in well-being. Indeed, one of the advantages of "wild euthanasia" of this sort was that it could "hide the deaths as a by-product of an escalating total war."[68] The very fact that the mortality figures from the asylum were recorded in the regular annual health report for the district of Ruppin underscores the intent and the effect of folding these deaths into the larger figures of German wartime mortality. By contrast, the statistics from the killing centers themselves were compiled separately for purposes of strict secrecy.[69] With so much pain so widely shared, the sufferings of strangers behind walls could become even less important to most of the populace as time wore on and most everyone faced ever greater threats to well-being. It was also probably the case that many individuals in Germany, especially during the war, might pity these mental patients (even more than previously), but they most likely would usually do so in terms of relief that there were people even worse off than they were. This was the case of German workers with regard to foreign laborers in Nazi Germany.[70] So even common pity separated people sharing varying degrees of pain, in other words, relative (lack of) well-being. More generally, shared wartime suffering for a time strengthened German national and patriotic solidarity. But such suffering also mobilized individuals and groups (for example, family, profession, firm) in a longer-term trend toward individual and corporate defense of their own interests—what Ulrich Herbert has called "communities of fate"—in competition with other individuals and groups.[71] This further diluted concern for others not seen as part of a given corporate body, and especially those who, like mental patients, had already been placed in a distinct medical or even criminal category most recently stigmatized by the Nazis.[72]

Among "Aryans," pain and well-being were places of popular conflict, accommodation, and negotiation. The great bulk of this was unpolitical in the sense of "resistance" and represented ways of coping with the escalating demands of living in Nazi Germany. This coping comprised mixtures of selfishness and inertia that constituted both friction and lubrication for the regime's means and ends. Individual negotiations concerning pain and well-being in the Third Reich represented some degree of "resistance" in the sense of "drag" on the regime, but occasional relief from the often painful or wearing obligations also refreshed people for collaboration in their roles within the Nazi system. Regardless of an individual's view of the regime, to function as part of the modern Nazi industrial state was to advance its actions and interests.[73] And although the conditions of everyday wartime life would progressively erode belief in, and actions on behalf of, the racial *Volksgemeinschaft*, the regime could also rely, especially during wartime, on the by now well-developed habit of individual linking of identity, fate, sacrifice, benefit, pain, and well-being with those of the nation.

The Second World War: The Separation of Nation, Self, and Pain

Nevertheless, the rigors of war still only aggravated all matters of pain and well-being in Germany. The regime now demanded health in the form of physical action and sacrifice as proof of loyalty and racial worth. The Nazis also demanded in effect the endurance, if not banishment, of mental pain through assertion and, when necessary through psychotherapeutic intervention, bolstering of an innately superior "racial" German strength of will. A Luftwaffe psychologist thus predicted a higher rate of suicide among soldiers fearful of the harsh punishment ensuing from being branded "a parasite on the nation" for not performing up to racial expectations.[74] Although the Prussian army in particular had a history of brutal discipline driving some of its men to suicide, the German military had more recently striven for professional efficiency and was determined to prevent suicide among its officers and men.[75] There was some new Nazi tension along these lines, however. In 1942 the Luftwaffe issued guidelines for the prevention of suicide and felt constrained in response to an opposing racial argument to observe that suicide did not constitute a "natural elimination" (*natürliche Ausmerzung*); a year later the Luftwaffe declared that attempted suicide was not a punishable offense.[76] Popular opposition to wartime plans for a *Gesundheitspass* (health certificate) was likewise based on a desire to hide "disabilities" from the regime.[77] Quotidian health in general, especially over time, of course worsened: for example, widespread stomach problems, menstrual difficulties, a general weakening of immune systems, and a higher incidence of colds, flu, and tuberculosis due to stays in damp air raid shelters.[78] The effects of shortages of food, vitamins, clothing, and housing were compounded by the decreasing number of doctors and drugs. For example, a report from the district medical officer in Solingen on February 1, 1943, summed up the effect of the general loss of weight as a disturbance of psychological well-being (*das subjektive Wohlbefinden*).[79] In the summer of 1942, Reich health leader Leonardo Conti likewise anxiously pointed at the disturbing loss of weight evident among boys attending the funeral in Berlin of Sicherheitsdienst (SD) chief Reinhard Heydrich.[80] And in Dresden in 1943 Eva Klemperer noted "how unhealthy the schoolchildren look."[81]

The health of women's bodies in the Third Reich was specially complicated by traditional attitudes and Nazi ideology. While women no less than men supported the regime, Nazi sterilization policies especially targeted women. Women comprised perhaps the majority of Jews slaughtered in the Nazi extermination campaign. Women who worked in armaments factories had higher sickness rates than men, while female slave laborers in particular were subject to abuse by male German supervisors.[82] Women in these situations could exercise some degree of agency, however, often abetted by male indulgence of stereotypical female "weakness," by using pain and sickness as an escape from some intolerable situations. Especially workers from the East could—and did—exploit intense German fears of typhus and other contagions from eastern lands by—however desperate and painful—faking or aggravating symptoms of illness through the introduction of any number of irritating substances onto or into their bodies.[83] Women could thereby also exploit associated fears of the female body upon which the Nazis projected weakness and passivity.

The wartime social trend for "Aryans" was toward individual and corporate struggle at the expense of loyalty to the racial *Volksgemeinschaft*, a loyalty already eroded before the war through widespread denunciation to the Gestapo and widening wage differentials between skilled and unskilled workers. This tore at the appeal of racism as a focus on the familiar and, in war, as defense of one's own against all that was foreign and—increasingly—threatening. The approach of enemy armies was prefigured in German life and Nazi propaganda by the brutally contained threat of infectious diseases brought into the body of the Reich by prisoners of war and slave laborers. Such a "racial" threat could serve to mobilize fear on behalf of the Nazi regime, but as part of more general and various individual concerns about health and illness this too reinforced popular individual and corporate "protectionism."

This individualized and corporatized place of pain and well-being in Nazi Germany is perhaps most clearly represented in the growing market for pharmaceuticals.[84] In Germany as elsewhere, alcohol remained the most common and available painkiller.[85] But a variety of amphetamines, barbiturates, and analgesics was becoming an important means of the management of pain and well-being. Though the great bulk of the century's mass production of drugs would occur after 1950, the modern ethic of pain avoidance in pursuit of physical and mental well-being had as of the 1930s received massive chemical reinforcement.[86] Since the 1920s in Germany drugs had been regularly covered by state and private health insurance plans.[87] Drug companies advertised widely and public demand for drugs was high.[88] The Nazi regime praised pain as a necessary means and proof of racial superiority, but the Nazis also encouraged the consumption of drugs, especially stimulants, in an attempt to heighten military and industrial productivity, a policy one pharmacologist rather boldly called "the chemical whip."[89] But as wartime shortages grew acute, the individual and the corporate began to prevail over the communal. In the social space left by the Nazi liquidation in 1941 of the last consumer cooperatives that had been particularly common within the German working class, individuals exploited doctors and pharmacies as sources for what drugs were available.[90] Factories hoarded drugs for their workers and the army manufactured its own.[91]

Soldiers of course were the most vulnerable to injury, pain, and death. The Wehrmacht, in a secret report of 1944, documented the fact that the ratio of deaths to injuries in the current war was much higher than during the previous war and that wounds were generally more severe due to the power of contemporary weaponry and the dangers inherent in mobile operations.[92] The realms of military pain and well-being had also been expanded during the First World War to include official diagnosis and treatment of psychological disorders. The very availability of psychiatric categories and capacities naturally provided an opportunity for use and abuse, even with internalized and severe external sanctions for "malingering."

The Wehrmacht's medical services were well prepared to address the problems of physical pain.[93] Surgeons were aided by the body's natural anesthesia (*Wundstupor*) in conjunction with severe wounds.[94] But the monstrous conditions of the war in Russia overwhelmed the medical services. One result, in the word of a postwar British observer, was a "Crimean" situation of the highest proportion of limbless veterans in Europe.[95] There was desperate improvisation: One German medic on the Eastern front recalled asepsis by cigarette.[96] But the Germans also displayed an understanding of the pain created by war that engaged psychological, cultural, and political considerations. German researchers anticipated the contemporary "gate theory" of pain as a complicated mix of dependent physical and psychological forms and functions. The Germans also put great cultural emphasis on the importance of mobilizing psychological will in the battle against pain. The body's natural anesthetic capacities had to be supplemented by a sense of duty and loyalty to the unit, the nation, the race. Contemporaneous German psychotherapeutic research, too, expressed this cultural bias in its holistic emphasis on pain as a symbol and an act as well as a signal and a perception. This was in line with a more general Western "neo-Freudian" emphasis on the importance of overcoming pain and disability pursuant to the integration of the happy and productive individual into society. In Nazi Germany this helped mobilize psychotherapists and their patients on behalf of a regime dedicated to the destruction of others and put the onus of overcoming dysfunctional behavior on the patient and his "will."[97] At least one older military surgeon noted in 1939 that younger surgeons tended to insist that wounded soldiers' complaints of pain were "all in the head" and that they should be encouraged and even coerced into getting control over themselves.[98] This approach clearly cohabited with Nazi racism. One account, otherwise not marked by enthusiasm for Nazi ideals, asserted that "the Nordic man fights pain" in contrast to the resignation found in Islamic culture.[99] The common Western notion that more highly developed cultures exhibit more sensitivity to—as well as restraint in expression of—pain is also reflected in this assertion.

The carnage and suffering of war thus put Nazi celebration of manly warfare to a severe test. The Nazis etherealized death as noble sacrifice for the nation and the race. But this appeal became problematic as suffering began to supplant commitment to the fraying *Volksgemeinschaft*. This was even more of a problem when it came to wounded and disabled soldiers. The Nazis censored references to gruesome wounds in soldiers' letters and accounts of combat.[100] Dead soldiers were easier to glorify as well as being much less expensive than injured ones. The physical presence of wounded soldiers also not only reminded the Nazis of the dysgenic effects of war (the fittest most often do not survive), but badly aggravated the anxieties about morbidity that underlay Nazism. Albert Speer recalled one occasion "when Hitler, sitting in his private train, saw some wounded soldiers outside . . . [and] immediately pulled down the blind."[101] It is true that with the defeat at Stalingrad and Goebbels's proclamation of the Total War Program properly vigorous wounded soldiers were used in newsreels to underscore the stakes. Even Hitler spoke with wounded soldiers in a radio broadcast of March 19, 1943. But in hiding in Amsterdam, Anne Frank heard it and perceptively called it a "pathetic. . . . [and] hideous puppet show."[102]

The Nazis even mobilized language to combat the morbid effects of their war. In 1938 the regime had introduced a revised Military Benefits and Pensions Law. This law privileged injuries at the front over others and made benefits dependent not, as originally under Weimar, on the calculation of loss of civilian earning power but, as in imperial Germany, on the severity of the injury and consequent employability.[103] A new official term, *Versehrtheit*, conflated heroism with utility and cowardice with disability.[104] The verb *versehren* is an obsolete term for injure (*verletzen*) or damage (*beschädigen*), derived from the Old German word for pain, *ser*; to wit, pain as in "only pain," that is, something that can and will be overcome. In 1944 the program was placed under the Reich labor minister to effect and propagandize the productive integration of *Kriegsversehrten* (the war disabled) into the war economy. One newspaper article featured one-armed typists under the title "Five Fingers Are Enough" (*Es geht auch mit fünf Fingern*).[105] In reality, there were widespread problems with placement, wages, and morale; one report on the

SS Rehabilitation Battalion in Feldbach near Graz complained that most of the men were just sitting around doing nothing.[106] There was also generational and political dispute over the new terminology. Labor Minister Franz Seldte ordered that the old term *Kriegsbeschädigten* should replace the dual use of it and *Kriegsversehrten*. Seldte, a former leader of the Nationalist Party's veterans organization, the Stahlhelm, argued that solidarity among soldiers was harmed by the use of one term for disabled veterans of the First World War and another for veterans disabled in the present conflict.[107] The army, conservative by tradition, by and large went along with this change. The SS and the Luftwaffe, as the chief military bastions of radical Nazi sentiment, apparently did not.[108]

There was more general debate about the impact of the sight of badly wounded soldiers on domestic morale. The army medical service, in arguing for public promotion of its work, asserted that propaganda on the care given to the wounded would strengthen popular war resolve, especially late in the war when victory celebrations ceased and people cared more about the fate of their loved ones at the front.[109] This represented a rather sober change in emphasis from an army medical service argument early in the war that the lives of disabled veterans must be saved so as to serve as living example of the endurance of pain and damage for sake of the *Volk*.[110] The regime also understood special popular sensitivity on this issue given the threat of forced sterilization and "euthanasia," which is why veterans were—on paper at least—exempt from these programs.[111] Even more sobering were the observations in Chemnitz in 1943 of a medical officer who criticized the transport of wounded soldiers from hospitals to factories because their appearance damaged popular confidence in victory (*Siegesstimmung*).[112] These quotidian realities tore at the pristine and sacramentalized Nazi propaganda about war and soldiers. Men in their damaged state had prosaic and ambiguous effects upon others struggling with pain and well-being and did not produce in society the heroic relief from worldly doubts and pains proclaimed by the Nazis.

The Social Restoration of Modern Pain

National Socialism in power ultimately produced physical and psychological pain for almost all Germans as well as for millions of other peoples. For most Germans, there was a brief period of relative peace and prosperity until 1939. If the Nazis had won their war, a certain large number of Germans would have prospered objectively and subjectively, but the regime's obsession with worthy and unworthy life would have affected ever larger numbers of individuals as well as groups. At the very least, the threat of persecution for this or that "hereditary" failing would

have compromised the psychological well-being even of many of the
"Aryans" in the Third Reich. In 1944 the Nazi government was finalizing
cruel sanctions for a wide categorization of so-called asocials (*Gemein-
schaftsfremde*), and before the war there had been estimates from within
the Nazi Party that at most only 30 percent of the entire population of
Germany constituted valuable racial stock worthy of reproducing.[113] It is
impossible to determine if there was consensus on this figure or if this
view would have prevailed after 1945, but all of this was born of a panic-
stricken Nazi fantasy of a racial community free from the pain of being
human.

Near the end of the war, however, the *Volksgemeinschaft* was fading
fast, along with the tradition of identification of the self with the nation.
This was the case even before the military collapse of the Third Reich in
1945 revived doubts created in 1918 about such identification. German
society became more and more a war of all against all, of individuals and
groups marshaling resources against pain and for whatever degrees of
well-being—or at least survival—might be gleaned from escalating social
chaos. While Germans still worked and fought—and exterminated—for
the Reich, there was also growing indifference, skepticism, and cynicism
toward a corrupt and failing regime and consequently an even greater desire to preserve one's self and family. In early 1943, for instance, the SS
Security Service reported that soldiers home on leave were complaining
about the poor health care afforded their families.[114] There was also
greater indifference (mixed with prejudice) to the fate of others, in particular the Jews, with the exception of indoctrinated and brutalized soldiers on the Eastern front and those running the concentration camps
committed to the struggle against "Jewish Bolshevism."[115] These tenden-
cies help explain why loyalty to the Nazi regime was absent after the
death of Hitler, whose popularity was in part a compensation for material disappointments; why—save for a few *Werwölfe*—there was no guerrilla warfare after the surrender; and why in both successor republics the
bulk of the population made a relatively easy transition to new forms of
governance based more on security and prosperity than on nationalism.
The *Volksgemeinschaft* had simply disappeared amid the ever more difficult realities of quotidian existence, especially with regard to the fundamental issues of pain and well-being. Pain and well-being had not only
become heavily secularized, institutionalized, and socialized in the modern era but had become especially problematic due to Nazi racism and
the physical dangers and difficulties of total war.[116]

In the course of the Second World War, therefore, pain became separated, perhaps especially but not exclusively in Germany, from the ideal
of sacrifice for the nation. Pain and well-being were again now largely left

in opposition in terms of the self. Even during the Third Reich, pain and well-being had also become a matter of commodification, commercialization, and consumption. In this respect it is correct to speak of the "atomization" of German society under Nazism.[117] The Nazi version of the modern Western material culture of purchasable individual well-being—at least via doctors and the brave new world of drugs—perpetrated certain continuities of structure, appetite, and expectation in the development of a consumer culture.[118] Along with individualism came the practice of corporatism: the assertion of various competing collective interests within, without, and against civic, legal, and commercial structures of territorial state and multinational company.[119] Postwar German indifference to Nazi genocide was thus not simply a matter of repression of guilt, the necessity of rebuilding, indulgence in Cold War prosperity, or their own status as "victims" of war, but was also a result of social habits around pain and well-being created by the modern era and by powerful related experiences in Germany, especially since 1914 and 1933. Preoccupation with one's own physical well-being was further magnified—as with the influenza pandemic of 1918—by the continuation and even intensification of problems of health and illness in the immediate postwar period.[120] The horrendous bloody defeats at the front and the terrible suffering of German urban populations from Allied strategic bombing came at the end of the war and thus formed the most lasting impressions upon the German populace. The Germans were already modern in their concern for secular and medical well-being of the self. First propagandized and then traumatized by invasive Nazi racist obsessions with the fictional purity of the individual and collective body, German society responded in the end by returning to the modern separation of pain and well-being.

6

SABINE BEHRENBECK

The Transformation of Sacrifice: German Identity
Between Heroic Narrative and Economic Success

IT is generally assumed that the path from heroism to hedonism is a long one. Yet the Germans covered this distance within a scant fifty years. For if it is true that thoroughness is a German virtue, it is only consistent that the Third Reich's radicalized expansion of the traditional narrative of heroism would be followed by its depoliticization and dramatic reduction after 1945. At the center of the heroic national narrative stood the sacrifice of the hero for the benefit of the community. It symbolized the supreme value of a heroic ethos defined less by victory and success than by selfless idealism and renunciation of personal happiness. To it was opposed the desire for personal gain and the maximization of personal pleasure, which were regarded as the expression of an egotistical materialism and a contemptible and amoral disposition.

This binary opposition was already part of the political domain in the days leading up to the First World War and was used in constructing a national identity in Wilhelmian Germany. Out of the intellectual discourse about civilization and culture[1] emerged the clichéd contrast of the English "merchants" and the German "heroes."[2] This stereotype clearly demonstrated the scorn German "men of power" (*Machtmenschen*) had for those seeking material gain and, in turn, indirect symbolic power. The proponents of this lofty ideal assumed the pose of heroes who unselfishly placed their lives at the service of the nation. Indeed, as the debate over German war aims soon made evident, this thinking also inspired the German war effort between 1914 and 1918, most notably through direct domination strategies over expanding spheres of influence, raw material procurement, and the elimination of economic rivals.[3] Nevertheless, the Germans claimed that their campaign went beyond merely finding a "place in the sun." It was also about realizing a larger idealistic goal: namely, the greatness and glory of the nation, one opposed to the egotistical, materialist motives that they imputed to their spiritually bankrupt enemies (*Krämerseelen*).

As it became clear over the course of the Great War that the campaign would not be won quickly nor ended easily, mainly because there was no imaginable alternative to "victorious peace" (*Siegfrieden*), catastrophe ensued. A mentality of violence prevailed.[4] In the end, 1.8 million soldiers were killed and the war was lost. But the disastrous defeat of 1918 and the unexpected victory of the "merchants" did find an explanation, though, within the existing narrative framework of German society at the time. For it was incomprehensible that the soldiers or the generals could have failed, precisely because they had borne enormous privation, fighting, and sacrifice. Only discord could have undermined the German "Siegfried." A traitor had stabbed him in the back.[5] According to this logic, one of the main causes of defeat was the civilian population had no longer been able to endure hunger and misery and by their hunger strikes helped bring about the end of the war. Furthermore, the mutinous soldiers and revolutionaries of 1918 were also guilty of having sabotaged a Germany victory. The wish for individual happiness and well-being, as well as care for one's own family, were seen as distracting full devotion to the Fatherland and thus were considered as treason against the nation.

This tragic fate, however, was not permitted to be the end of the story. Germany had to be resurrected from its shame and humiliation. To this end, any and all means were justified.[6] Not long thereafter one explanation emerged that transformed the dead's apparently senseless self-sacrifice for a lost cause into an obligation for those who survived: It was their duty to give meaning to the suffering and deaths of fallen soldiers. In this way, the failure of the military leadership in the war could be concealed and turned into a threat against any individual on whom blame for the millions of war dead could later be pinned.

The values of post-1918 society did not differ very substantively from those of pre-1914 society: only in their radical nature and detachment from reality did they appear different from those they displaced. Even if the nation was beset by perpetual conflict, there was a fairly broad consensus concerning one thing: postwar society was seen as a *Volksgemeinschaft* (national community) transformed by war and unified by fate. The individual counted only insofar as he contributed to the well-being of the common good.

It was this idea that helped bring about the victory of the National Socialist movement. The Third Reich was certainly tied to this understanding of the past, claiming to make good on their promise of salvation, to end class struggle, and to reestablish the international prestige of the Reich. In order to achieve these goals, the crusade had to be resumed; 1918 had only interrupted it. Only after courageous fighting and selfless sacrifice, so went the reasoning, would victory and world domination come to the Germans as a result of their racial superiority. The promises became more believable with the economic recovery following the disastrous economic crisis of the 1920s and early 1930s. Little attention was paid to the actual cause behind the new-found prosperity: preparation for the next war through massive rearmament.

Along with those who died in the First World War, Nazi Party martyrs from the so-called time of struggle (*Kampfzeit*) were supposed to embody the heroic ideal of the *Volksgemeinschaft*. Deed, duty, perseverance, sacrifice, and service were the watchwords of this collective identity. In order to survive life's struggles, a readiness both to kill others as well as to sacrifice oneself were requisite. With victory, the promises of political and economic supremacy for the Reich were to be united with the material welfare of the *Volk*.

But when the weapons fell silent in 1945, Germans found themselves in a very different situation. They had to acknowledge that all of their effort and sacrifice had not brought victory and prosperity, but only resulted in hunger and destruction, physical flight and political impotence. In other words, their struggle had been fought in vain and was now devoid of meaning. Their collective identity therefore necessitated fundamental reorientation. A totally different master narrative crystallized during the years following World War II. It revolved around the image of the powerless German victims who experienced great suffering in the wake of misrule and defeat, but still managed to build a new Germany out of the rubble.

For the "have-nots" who had to again build an existence from scratch, material values won new meaning and importance. The forty deutsche marks given to every West German on the day of the currency reform in 1948 served as the pearly gates of capitalism. Insofar as West Germans quickly took on the capitalistic profit-orientation of the victors, they became "Americanized," in other words, "civilized." This represented a sharp break from their previous barbarism. By the same token, the vanquished now overcame their old disdain for the "cultureless" Americans in face of the massive technical and material superiority of the U.S. occupational force. The German Economic Miracle of the 1950s was apparently the trigger for the successful reorientation of West Germans from heroes to gourmands.

This essay will outline the historical course that the master narrative of heroism assumed in the construction of collective identity in Germany between 1918 and 1960. In so doing, it will draw connections between two contrasting leitmotivs of German national identity in this century: on the one hand, the desire for "the good life" and personal prosperity, happiness, and success; and on the other, the willingness to go without, to sacrifice, and even die for the community.

1. The Heroic Narrative After 1918

Humans attempt to order chaos by using myths and symbols. As Clifford Geertz put it, "There are at least three points where chaos—a tumult of events which lack not just interpretation but interpretability—threatens to break in upon man: at the limits of his analytic capacities, at the limits of his powers of endurance, and at the limits of his moral insight."[7] The First World War and the German defeat, along with the postwar revolution, inflation, and economic crisis, forced many Germans into just such a "liminal experience." In their case, however, the experience was bound to the bitter collapse of illusions about the political and military potency of the Reich, the loss of loved ones, physical health, and property, as well as the ruination of ethical ideals and compass.

The welter of crises spawned the creation and spread of myriad political myths and symbols that were brought into the public sphere in the 1920s by various political parties and groups.[8] In this, the narrative of heroism, in combination with the Christian dogma of salvation, played a central role.[9] They appeared to offer an answer to one of the most pressing existential questions at the time, namely how to make sense of the war's dark legacy of mass death. Already in the nineteenth century an interpretive framework had been adopted for locating the death of the soldier in the scheme of Christian sacrifice. In most European states, sacrificing one's life on "the altar of the Fatherland" was a common trope in justifying a soldier's death.[10] Here the nation served as the highest ethical value, justifying and thus demanding any sacrifice. As the refrain of a famous soldier's song by Heinrich Lersch went, "Germany must live, even if we must die."

The experience of mass annihilation on the battlefields of the First World War led to a partial break with traditional images of death.[11] During and especially after the war, great artistic and literary energy was spent trying to find a new interpretative representation of it.[12] Out of these efforts came a new symbolic figure that appeared in virtually every nation involved in the war: "the unknown soldier" interned in national monuments such as the Arc de Triomphe in Paris, Westminster Abbey in London, and the Altar of the Fatherland in Rome.[13] This symbolic figure was supposed to help ensure that the death of the individual would not be submerged by the mass dying that characterized a war of attrition, but that one's individual fate would acquire meaning from the service one performed for the nation.

In Germany, however, a central memorial commemorating the devotion did not exist. The symbolic figure of "the unknown soldier" was rejected as "un-German," since it reflected "merely the political and spiritual attitude of our former opponents."[14] Instead, "the good comrade" from a famous soldier's song by Ludwig Uhland now assumed this function:

> Ich hatt' einen Kameraden,
> einen bessr'n findst' Du nit.
> Die Trommel schlug zum Streite.
> Er ging an meiner Seite
> im gleichen Schritt und Tritt.
>
> Eine Kugel kam geflogen.
> Gilt es mir oder gilt es dir?
> Ihn hat es weggerissen.
> Er liegt mir vor den Füßen,
> als wär's ein Stück von mir.
>
> Will mir die Hand noch reichen,
> derweil ich eben lad'.
> Kann dir die Hand nicht geben.
> Bleib Du im ew'gen Leben
> mein guter Kamerad.

A rough translation is:

> I had a comrade,
> a better one you'd never find.
> The drum called us to battle.
> He walked at my side
> together in lock step.
>
> A bullet came flying.
> Is it for me or is it for him?
> It was he that was ripped away.
> He lies at my feet,
> as if he were a part of me.
>
> Still tries to reach out his hand to me,
> just as I load.
> Can't give you my hand.
> Remain in eternal life
> my good comrade.

"The good comrade" had proven his idealism by dying instead of (and in a way "for the benefit of") his mate. Thus, he became a model image for a postwar society in which devotion and fulfillment of duty, obedience and service—not one's own interests—were to become the basis of communal life.[15]

It was young noncommissioned officers at the front who were mostly responsible for disseminating this interpretation of the war experience. After the war men such as Ernst Jünger, Werner Beumelburg, and Franz Schauwecker sought literary and social recognition by stylizing themselves as the very embodiment of the "heroic officer at the front."[16] In their view, battle had created "a new kind of human being, a man in whom the most elevated of all manly qualities were dominant."[17] The message of these novelistic war memories glorified the trench experience as a model for postwar society. By orienting society on the pattern of interpersonal relationships in war, all social conflicts were supposedly overcome and the people made ready for the next war.

Amid the fallout of defeat and the numerous crises that plagued the postwar years, the meaning of mass death and painful wartime experiences was hardly perceptible. Yet the ideal of the self-sacrificing hero was not abandoned; instead, its significance was projected into the future. First, the meaning of sacrifice still had to be redeemed. "The war became a moral challenge: coming to terms with it was described [by those involved in it] as a well-earned new sensibility to primal life forces, whose lived intensity offered a powerful salve against the threat of death."[18] In parallel to such an idealistic notion of personal benefit, a comparable moral regeneration of the Fatherland as an effect of war was expected. Within the context of the mythologized war experience, every soldier's death was understood not as a powerless and involuntary victimization, but rather as a willing self-sacrifice.[19] Even in defeat, the fallen had demonstrated their loyalty. The futility of their mission only bespoke their idealism, whose measure was less heroic deeds than character and conviction.

The crisis of meaning reinforced the value of the willingness to sacrifice as a virtue in and of itself, even if the question of "to what end?" remained largely unaddressed. Alone the values of bravery and a readiness to sacrifice were supposed to save the Reich and protect it from foreign enemies.[20] From this perspective, the fallen advanced as the elite of the nation. They symbolized the internal integrity of the Reich and kept society from further degenerating into a dissolute and fractious present. The idea of dying for the nation transformed their plural lives into a singular form of existence based on service and devotion to others (*Proexistenz*).[21]

Transferring this Christian model of sacrifice to a decidedly secular context surely altered the horizon of salvation. It was not a gift of the dead, but a duty of the survivors. Accordingly, most inscriptions on German war monuments invoked this obligation of the living to the dead.[22] Remembrance of the dead was supposed to elicit a willingness to sacrifice among the living. Living a life in their spirit and filled with the same dedication would guarantee the resurrection of the despairing and down-trodden Fatherland.[23]

This notion of a meaningful death in war shaped the mentality of not only veterans after the Great War. The application of the Christian concept of sacrifice to those who fell on the battlefield was by no means an exclusive affair of so-called *völkish*, nationalist groups. On the contrary, it suffused the new myth of "the front experience" that dominated perceptions of the war some ten years after its conclusion. A quotation from the conservative literary critic Friedrich Sieburg in 1932 attests to this, insomuch as his experience at the front is read as a ritual act in keeping with the scheme of Christian Holy Communion:

This was the hour of the great battle. With sunken eyelids, as one might regard the body of the Lord, we formed the living chain and felt the fraternal blood of all coursing through us. . . . For a second, we felt like a body. . . . We, we were the creators of this unity [of the nation], and it did not scare us in the least that we were so alone as sacrificial victims on the altar. . . . In complete innocence and purity, the nation rose out of our hearts as in the first days of creation. . . . For we knew and know that only he sees the nation who is prepared to sacrifice. We have shown Germany how to sacrifice. . . . And our silence points up above, in the same way the smoke of a sacrifice rises above, for which God is well pleased.[24]

Just as the Wars of Liberation of the nineteenth century had already been understood as a national Easter, so was the First World War often interpreted as a profane communion and revelation. Walter Flex's *Der Wanderer zwischen beiden Welten* or Julius Zerner's *Kriegmesse 1914* are good examples. Death on the battlefield was bestowed with the aura of a sacred act. The sacrificial death of the nation's best was a reenactment of Christ's Passion, as suffering was supposed to lead to resurrection.

2. The Cult Surrounding the Nazi Party Martyrs

Leading National Socialists, as witnesses to and participants in this cult of the dead, had observed at the end of the 1920s how unconscious psychical associations could be converted into strategies for political action. The cult surrounding dead party members who had been killed by police or political opponents in street fighting drew heavily upon the heroic narrative that gave sense to soldierly death. From very early on Hitler and other party spokesmen claimed to represent the interests of the fallen and to fulfill their legacy by continuing the fight until victory was achieved. The so-called blood witnesses of the movement were proof of the righteousness of their cause, and they exhibited the radical resolution and unqualified devotion with which the National Socialists pursued their goals.[25] To the extent that it adopted violence as a means of solving national political conflicts, the party consciously and deliberately put itself in the soldierly tradition of being prepared to kill and die. It conferred upon the struggle for political power the attributes of a life-and-death struggle.

Their own dead provided National Socialism with an auspicious opportunity. On the one hand, it helped the party draw connections with the socially accepted notion of the idealistic self-sacrifice of soldiers; on the other hand, it enabled the Nazis to distinguish themselves from other groups across the nationalist party spectrum—few of which had any martyrs—and in turn help consolidate their own identity. Just as remembering the fallen in the Great War brought surviving veterans closer together, so too did the party martyrs facilitate tighter cohesiveness among members.

Legends and myths about these dead party members from "the movement's time of struggle" had been floating around from the beginning. The most famous example was the Berlin Sturmabteilung (SA) leader Horst Wessel, who was systematically built up as a young heroic savior by his Gauleiter, Joseph Goebbels. Horst Wessel was born in 1907 as the eldest son of a minister in Bielefeld. His father took part in the First World War and afterward was active in a Berlin city parish. As a youth, Wessel was a member of the Bismarck League, a paramilitary youth group associated with the German National People's Party (DNVP). After completing his schooling at a humanistic *Gymnasium*, he began studying law in Berlin in 1926 and became a member of a student fencing association. Soon he and his younger brother Werner joined the SA. Because of his apparent talent as an organizer and speaker, Wessel made his career among the "brownshirts" and quickly rose to the rank of Sturmführer. In the middle of 1929, however, his plans changed radically on account of a romantic involvement that assumed much of his time. He interrupted his studies, earned money as an unskilled laborer, left his parents' middle-class home, and moved into a furnished room in a working-class neighborhood with his girlfriend. His involvement in the SA also fell off at this time. Nevertheless, Wessel remained well known within communist working-class circles as a formidable member of the SA. With the death of his brother in December 1929, Wessel fell into a deep psychological crisis. Three weeks later an assassination attempt was made on his life, the background of which has never been sufficiently clarified. On January 14, 1930, a pimp and former boyfriend of his lover shot Wessel. His landlady, whose husband was a member of the leftist Rot-Frontkämpferbund, had denounced him, which lent his shooting a political dimension. Five weeks after the attack, Wessel died of his wounds at the young age of twenty-two.[26]

Goebbels stylized Wessel's obituary along the lines of an abridged

version of the life of Jesus and giving it the knowing title "To the Very
End." Quotations from the Bible pepper the piece, so that its "literary basis" could hardly escape the notice of any reader:

A German mother gave birth to him in pain. She raised him in worry and
misery. . . . Out of a child came a young boy, and he soon matured into a man. . . .
He goes as a prophet in the desert. . . . And he reaps only hatred as his thanks,
only persecution as his recognition. . . . He must bear the sins and failings of a
guilty generation. He knows why, and takes it upon himself silently. He is ready
to the end. . . . He leaves his mother and parents' home, lives among those who
revile and spit at him. . . . Outside in a proletarian neighborhood . . . he ekes out
a young, meager existence. A Christian socialist! One who beckons through
deeds: "Come to me, I will save you!" . . . Something godlike is in him, so that he
can be and do nothing other. One must become an example and sacrifice himself!
. . . You find him again among a horde of street workers. There he stands in the
middle of these giants of labor . . . and implores: Believe in me! They were not
able to, they did not want to. He had to end his journey. One late evening, they
forced their way into his attic room and shot him with perfidious lead in his ar-
dent head. . . . Five weeks he lay in agony and at death's door . . . He did not
complain. . . . And then, finally, tired and in agonizing pain, he gave up his spirit.
They carried him to his grave. . . . Those whom he wanted to save threw stones at
the dead body. . . . He drank from the chalice of pains until the very end. He did
not let go of it, but took it willingly and full of devotion. This suffering I drink
for the Fatherland! Raise him on high, the dead one, and show him to all. And
call out, call out: Ecce homo! Never tire of pointing him out! Carry him wherever
you go and wherever you stand, over your heads, and when asked who this dead
man was, then give only this answer: *Germany*! Another Germany is rising. A
young one, a new one! We carry it already in us and over us. The dead man who
is with us raises his tired hand and points into the faint distance: Forward over
the graves! At the end lies Germany![27]

The myth of the National Socialist hero, as was popularized by the example of Horst Wessel, tells of the "resurrection and return" of the hero,
but his basic message refers less to his fate than to his redeeming function
for the community.[28] Wessel's death, too, was interpreted as a victory. To
it was ascribed the function of stirring the German people: "Germany
awake!" Just like the Nazi Party's original sixteen martyrs from the failed
1923 putsch, so too Wessel and his fated brethren were not supposed to
have died for the benefit of the party, but "for Germany."[29] Likewise, the
National Socialist "movement" described itself as the executor of the will
of the entire German people. New fighters were to be won over to the
cause by means of the mythic elevation of death, following in the foot-
steps of the movement's original hero. In Wessel's case, his song served as
an instrument of inspiration. Through his example a community would
be created between the dead hero and his admirers, as Goebbels himself

contended in his "vision" at the gravesite of the party hero: "In ten years, children in schools, workers in factories, soldiers in the field will sing his song. . . . I see in my mind columns marching, endlessly, endlessly. A humiliated people is rising and on the move. An awakening Germany demands its right: freedom and bread!"[30] Through the narrative motif of the righteous sufferer, the party hoped to redeem the brutality and criminal violence of the SA. What is more, the heroic victim served in practice as an effective means for recruiting new fighters, who were supposed to step in as avengers of the dead hero.[31] The myth served as an appeal to the violent potential of supporters and supplied them with the necessary moral justification as well as much-needed revolutionary fervor, unscrupulousness and willingness to sacrifice.

However, the "Christian socialist" Horst Wessel embodied only one aspect of the National Socialist hero, the heroic fighter and heroic victim. The Janus-faced image presented yet another visage: this one carried the very attributes of Adolf Hitler and represented the figure of the leader and victor.[32] After the Nazi seizure of power, this new image soon outshone the fallen party members, whereby the cult of the hero was gradually transformed into a Führer cult.

The more unbearable the experience of suffering and impotence, the stronger the wish for radical change becomes and more acute the longing for fulfillment and happiness. Under these circumstances grows the desire to realize this dream of power through violence.[33] National Socialist parlance called this transformation "revolution" at the social level, "conversion" to Nazi ideology at the personal level. According to the doctrine of the party leader and his followers, every individual was obliged to help bring about these changes at the risk of his own life. The breakthrough from suffering to happiness had to be possible, for the desire was so urgent. The preferred means were determined not by moral norms, but by the very force of suffering itself. An eloquent testimony to this was the writer Rudolf Binding's "Creed" (1933): "Germany—this Germany—was born from a raging longing, from an inner obsession, from the bloodiest throes. To want Germany: at any price, at the price of any danger. Any plaint pales before this."[34]

The modern sense of one's own nothingness was intensified by a pervasive feeling of loss of national meaning in the wake of the First World War defeat. This was to be compensated by something unusually monumental.[35] The more grandly the goal was conceived, the less inhibited people became about the means. Put differently: The hero, who has prepared himself for sacrificial death, now acquired the right to kill others on the grounds that it served the absolute goal. Heinrich Himmler's famous motto for the Schutzstaffel (SS) should also be seen in this light:

"Be ruthless with ourselves and others, kill and be killed" (*Hart sein gegen uns und andere, den Tod zu geben und zu nehmen*).

Secondary virtues such as a feeling of duty, toughness, loyalty, obedience, absolute dedication, honesty, decency, and bravery, which were publicly recognized as primarily soldierly virtues, belonged to this new ethic.[36] They were pressed into the service of a higher value, "Germany." It was only seemingly a secular national goal; in reality it was extraordinarily diffuse and always possessed religious qualities.[37] Out of this developed an extremely problematic hierarchy of values. "Secondary virtues of this kind have an instrumental character. Only a rational final objective turns them into actual virtues. If this end remains absent or indeterminate, then there is no rational ends-means relationship. The result is that the larger purposes, which are supposed to govern the practical world, are then sought within the virtues themselves."[38]

Within this heroic ethos, value was dependent upon and manifest through the successful realization of those secondary virtues, which were only originally supposed to serve it. "Germany" as a goal thus existed chiefly as an idea; only once the will to sacrifice, loyalty, submission, and fulfillment of duty were all performed on a mass scale would the larger value emerge to which they were all directed. This is why a devout "bearing" (*Haltung*) played a more important role than the substance of faith itself. In the words of Goebbels, "It is not all that important what we believe in; only that we believe."[39] Or as Ernst Jünger put it in 1921:

Death is the highest accomplishment for a belief. It is creed, deed, fulfillment, faith, love, hope, and goal. It is perfection and completion as such in an imperfect world. Thus, the content is nothing and conviction everything. One may die obsessed with a fatal error, yet he has achieved greatness. . . . Delusion and the world are one, and whoever dies for folly, still remains a hero.[40]

The value of "bearing" as a principle feature of National Socialist heroism played a central role in its ethos; occasionally it was called "the spirit of the SA" (*SA-Geist*) and replaced the nineteenth-century nationalist term "spirit of the people" (*Volksgeist*).[41] A more specific sense of the content of this bearing could be seen in the heroic dramas of the time; it was about the defiantly heroic attitude in a hopeless and tragic situation which best enabled the "idea" to break through and take form. In other words, it was a kind of martyrdom.[42]

The heroic myth thus presented its ethos with the help of symbolic figures, their actions and modes of behavior. The hero embodied a catalogue of virtues. At the top stood the qualities of loyalty, purity, and the willingness to sacrifice. For the National Socialists, the loyalty of the hero to the bitter end constituted a service to the Führer and the people. It was a sign of his idealism and a mythic surrogate for the perceived threat of a full dissolution of traditional social relations.[43] Thus all social relations were reduced to a hierarchically structured loyalty, without any attention paid to the complex structures of a modern social network. Unconditional loyalty was supposed to provide and maintain the unity of the Reich and the nation. The longing for this was especially pronounced given the cleavages that accompanied Germany's febrile urbanization and industrialization. Political salvation, it was hoped, would come from heroes willing to make sacrifices. Redemption could only be reached through an idealism that stood opposed to the prevailing vices of materialism and the desire for personal gain. The Third Reich cast itself as the final expression of this hoped-for salvation.[44]

The construction of the Nazi myth of heroism must also be seen in relation to the emergence of numerous "inflation saints" and prophets of crisis during the 1920s.[45] This politico-religious revival movement blossomed between the end of World War I and the hyperinflation of 1923, only to reappear with the beginning of the world economic crisis of 1929. Its cycles make clear the connection between material misery and ethical crisis, between the experience of suffering and the search for a compensatory heroic narrative.

The "barefoot prophets" of the Weimar Republic preached salvation through renewal and offered themselves not only as sacrifices for society, but also as political leaders. "The social gesture of sympathy [*Mitleidsgeste*] turns into the heroic pose of the social revolutionary and can rise to the level of a Caesarist cult of supermen [*Übermenschenkult*]."[46] Adolf Hitler was just one of many of these new messianic leader figures at the time. "Those contemporaries in the throes of anxiety did not seek their salvation in rational behavior and economic considerations, but rather partly took . . . refuge in the social myth of the messianic leaders. These were not swindlers, for they actually believed that their arrival would make everything anew. This inflated self-confidence, in turn, provided supporters with a foothold and prop, while also amplifying their readiness to suffer and sacrifice."[47] The belief in a politico-religious transformation of humanity and society appeared to be the solution to the crisis. "The general message of the crisis years lay in the will of the 'strong,' of the heroes, a message in which public institutions no longer sufficed as the providers of order and meaning."[48]

Hitler had tried to separate himself from the myriad inflation saints and warned his followers about the "*völkish* Johns" who continually sought contact with him and the Nazi Party.[49] Common to all of them was above all the "cult of the redeeming heroic leader personality."[50] The self-humiliation and the willing proletarianization of the "Christian socialist" that figured in Goebbels's variant of the heroic myth about Horst Wessel now reemerged in the asceticism of the inflation saints. By choosing poverty and sharing property, they firmly placed themselves within the legacy of Jesus and crusaded against those "new money" profiteers of the war and the inflation. In this way, they proved to those threatened by downward mobility and material loss that they would make a virtue of necessity. The impoverishment and degradation suffered would be re-narrativized as a prerequisite for spiritual reformation.[51]

The particular allure of the National Socialist message of salvation lay in its understanding of sacrifice. Hitler demanded much more of his followers than simply asceticism and inner reform. He offered the opportunity to brawl with political opponents as well as torment defenseless Jewish citizens. Here a vent was opened for pent-up aggressions, compensating for the experiences of impotence and downward mobility suffered in everyday life, while simultaneously offering a powerful sense of moral superiority.

This aspect of National Socialism rested on an ambivalence that inhered in the German concept of sacrifice. The German term *Opfer* does not differentiate between "sacrifice" as a cultural ritual and "victim" as the passive sufferer of an injury or loss. The term *Opfer* thus designates both the ritual as well as its object. In sacrifice, doing, and suffering, offering and receiving flow into one another.[52]

The level of meaning behind ritual sacrifice thus plays a special role. The victim of a battle may be on the losing side; yet according to the ritualistic understanding of sacrifice, his status as a victim is an honor. To be worthy of sacrifice is proof of his impeccable and even immaculate quality. In a violent struggle, moreover, the victim is at first glance in the morally integral position. Whoever is prepared to sacrifice himself is then no longer seen as a perpetrator and receives a quasi-automatic absolution for that which he has done to others before his own death. Since every victim in a struggle or in a ritual requires an active subject who victimizes him, this necessity excuses the subject from the responsibility of his action. For what the perpetrator does must take place: without him there can be no fruitful redemption.

In the National Socialist myth of the hero, both positions—sacrificer and victim—merged with one another. In fact, the Nazi hero was honored less for his deeds, which in the early years were basically acts of violence, than for his having suffered a sacrificial death. Nonetheless, the dead victims called on those who survived to become victimizers/perpetrators. The Nazi heroic myths contended that the dead were not victims in the sense of losers, but instead were heroes and future victors. The murderous aggression of brawling SA troops was represented as pure idealism for a good cause. The Nazi movement's brutality and lack of scruples formed one part of its attraction. Its brutality was effectively intimidating and repulsive, yet because of its physical strength it was also fascinating and admirable for many. To belong to a group that thus qualified as future victors might well be the morally weaker position, but the prospect of escaping victimhood could help overcome the reluctance to use violence.

3. Triumph and Death of the Hero

The promises of the National Socialist myth of the hero focused on an expectant new era. Circumstances of need, persecution, and oppression—as those who experienced the "time of struggle" subjectively perceived it—were supposed to be made bearable by the prospect of eventual victory in all struggles. The future triumph served as the justification for one's own sacrifices in the Nazi struggle as well as for the losses of their opponents. Alternatively, those sacrifices already made were supposed to lay the foundations for the party's claim to power: "Twelve years of struggle and courageous sacrifice lay behind us. By this achievement alone, we already have earned the right to lead the Reich."[53]

Once, however, Adolf Hitler became chancellor on January 30, 1933, this story of sacrifice and victory had to be modified. It had to be made concrete by linking religious hopes of salvation with concrete power relations. By equating a Hitler chancellorship with the arrival of the savior and the resurrection of the people, the Nazi Party had whetted expectations that it was neither willing nor able to fulfill.

The fruits of victory neither satisfied all followers, nor was it Hitler's intention to actually carry out the announced revolution. The need to justify the experiences of death also receded significantly along with the casualties within party ranks. The heroic myth in the Third Reich thus was confronted with tasks different from those during the "time of struggle," when it had served primarily to recruit, integrate, justify, and motivate fighters. Now, however, it was necessary to create other versions more oriented toward the needs and prerequisites of the entire population.[54]

The Third Reich saw itself as the fulfillment of German history. It represented the idea of an endpoint, after which there would be no further development. The Nazi leadership thought the establishment of their "eternal," "thousand-year" rule was a sign of announcing this "happy end" to the country's historical development. After the politically unstable circumstances of the postwar period, this image was attractive to a broad spectrum of the population who longed for orientation and security. Still, from these new desires for quiet and order emerged a new dilemma for the new leaders if they were to retain "struggle" as a life principle.

The solution to this problem appeared in a form for which the foundation had already been built well before 1933. The naming of Hitler as chancellor, so the story had it, was only the beginning of a development, whose end would be a new Reich and a new Human Being. Until then, there remained one other path, a path of more sacrifices and privations. For up to now, only the enemy inside Germany had been defeated. The struggle against foreign powers that had been interrupted in 1918 had yet to be brought to a victorious end.[55] Overcoming the internal conflict of the nation thus only represented a necessary precondition for its invincibility against external powers.

By the same token, this meant that "national elevation" (*nationale Erhebung*) had not yet brought about the complete transformation of a new way of life. On the contrary the qualitative jump was only to be accomplished through redoubled national effort and devotion. Within the Third Reich it was to be reached through creation of a "racially pure" national community; beyond German borders this new national campaign anticipated a major international confrontation aimed at overturning the defeat of 1918.

After 1933 the Nazi cult of heroes concentrated more and more upon the Führer as much as the surviving victor-heroes, while many sacrificial heroes were now relegated to the background.

> Einer geht und ist der Held.
> Und die andern folgen gern,
> Schreiten mit ihm durch das Feld,
> Schreiten unter gleichem Stern.
> Folgen in die Ewigkeit,
> Fragen nicht nach Leid und Tod;
> Denn sein Wort is ihre Zeit,
> Seine Taten sind ihr Brot.
> Einer geht und ist der Held,
> Seines Volkes Herr und Knecht,
> Und wie er die Fahne hält,
> Werden Schwur und Fluch zum Recht.
> Und er spricht es in die Zeit,
> Ehern wie ein Gott gebot,
> Und es flieht vor ihm das Leid,
> Und es stirbt an ihm der Tod.[56]

A rough translation is:

> One goes and becomes the hero.
> And others follow his lead
> Marching with him through the fields
> United under the same star

> Follow him to Eternity
> worry not of suffering and death
> Since his word is their time
> His deeds are their bread
> One goes and becomes the hero
> master and slave of his people
> As he holds his flag up high
> Vows and curses become law
> And he speaks into the time
> brazen like a god ordered
> And from him suffering runs away
> And in him death does die.

The present tense and direct diction of this text registers the timelessness of a hierarchical structure based upon the unconditional subjugation of all under the will of singular heroes, whose religious attributes as redeemers were capable of mitigating misery and even overcoming death.

Even if this heroic mission—so exalted that the history of humanity was believed to lay in the hands of the German race—saddled Germans with heavy demands, Hitler was not blind to the fact that such forced asceticism needed some material fulfillment in the here and now, or at least the prospect of some worldly prosperity and happiness. In order to secure mass support the regime understood that one task could not be deferred until the beginning of war, namely the improvement of Germany's dire economy. However much rearmament and the Reich's Four-Year Plan served as the mainspring of economic revival, there were other initiatives which effectively broadened the perception of economic takeoff.

One of these propaganda instruments was the construction of the Autobahns. Even today this project is remembered as one of Hitler's most positive achievements, not least because it radically curtailed the number of unemployed.[57] It has often been presumed that the importance of the Autobahn lay in its military potential for wartime mass mobilization. A closer look at its network, however, makes clear that its supposed strategic military importance played at best a subordinate role in the project.[58] Its objective was above all of aesthetic: it was designed for domestic tourism. For the privileged automobile owner the highways were supposed to make accessible the natural beauty of German town and country.[59] The layout of the freestone-formed Autobahn bridges and the Heimatschutz-style filling stations, together with its radial conception of roads leading out of the cities into the countryside, was intended to cultivate comfort and satisfy yearnings for luxurious experiences. The highway construction project was of course complemented by the regime's promise to deliver new automobiles—the famed Volkswagen—to the working masses.[60] In this sense, the Third Reich successfully marketed the Autobahn project as evidence of the regime's can-do productivity and technical progress. Although only 4 to 5 percent of the unemployed actually benefited from the program, to say nothing of the fact that three-quarters of the project's financing was siphoned off from unemployment insurance contributions, the project became an abiding symbol of economic vitality and dynamism.[61] Mobility, which citizens were promised in the name of the Autobahn, effectively replaced the freedom that had been taken away in the political sphere. This image of the Autobahn as an emblem of progress, dynamism, freedom, and prosperity still predominates, rendering these motorways all but immune to criticism.[62]

4. The Crisis of the Hero

During the prewar years there was a collective identification with the official cult of heroes. Large sections of the populace subscribed to the heroic narrative in a positive manner. It could clearly be used to raise people's sense of self-worth and to furnish convincing explanations for the past. This was especially important given that the national self-image and the need for self-affirmation were at odds. Thus the acceptance of war was inseparable from the notion of war as the very incarnation of heroic struggle. Yet this consent was mostly confined to war as an idea, an abstract principle, a mere hazy possibility. For the majority of Germans the heroic ethos of struggle was only appealing insofar as there were no actual bloody victims and it remained at the level of a vague "readiness to sacrifice oneself." It was effective so long as it was expressed through contributions to the Winter Assistance Program, "Family Soup Sundays," and daily rationing and performance of duties. Besides, the massive rearmament program had brought with it economic benefits (full employment, economic revival) and social progress, which effectively undermined resistance against the menace of war.

Despite the regime's long and careful war preparations (for example, universal conscription and increased military build-up), future war casualties on the German side had to be calculated and justified. The Nazi cult of heroes of the 1930s must therefore be seen in tandem with the regime's preparation for war. Already in the prewar years there emerged—especially among future soldiers—a positive popular attitude toward aggression, struggle, and violent death. For example, the celebration of the "blood witnesses from the time of struggle" and those who had fallen for the Fatherland during the Great War was not only intended to invoke past experiences, but always pointed toward future war sacrifices. Since the "people's will to military preparedness" (*Wehrwille*) could not be simply produced by means of crude, aggressive propaganda, the elaborate rites and symbols of the hero cult assumed the role of disseminating this new heroic ethos without explicitly naming any concrete goals of aggression.[63]

Already by the beginning of the conflict the lack of war enthusiasm among civilians and soldiers alike made it plain that an unconditional acceptance of the heroic ethos was hardly commonplace. Only the successes of the German army, particularly the quick victory over France, spurred a more positive attitude toward the war.[64] On the whole Germans regarded the war as more of a "fate," even if they exhibited a remarkable loyalty and willingness to obey and work hard for the Nazi state.

In the end, however, this reflected only a partial adaptation of the heroic ethos. In the few years before the outbreak of war it was impossible to remake the whole German *Volk* as a heroic elite. Amid the emergency conditions of war the majority of Germans were hardly enamored with the virtues of war; indeed, the affirmative heroic qualities (enthusiasm, purposeful action, brinkmanship, to say nothing of lust for war and killing) were confined to a small minority. Yet it was precisely this disparity that enabled the SS to construct its image as an indispensable wartime elite within the Nazi state.

Early on, the war possessed a rather pleasant side for many civilians and soldiers alike. The quick military victories brought the systematic exploitation of newly occupied countries, which was officially welcomed as a vital means of provisioning the war-rationed Fatherland and thus raising the standard of living for all Germans. Fearing the recurrence of the hunger strike of the First World War, the state was very keen on keeping the new home front satisfied this time. This was all the more critical given that the war might require long-term rationing and everyday privation. On the fighting front, soldiers were often rewarded with the plunder of foreign lands as material compensation for their suffering and service. For example, the extreme undervaluation of the French franc due to Germany's fixed rate of exchange made French consumer goods remarkably cheap, of which German soldiers took quick advantage. Soldiers were inundated with wish lists for French products from those back home, many of which were delivered through military parcels or by the soldiers themselves during their military leave.[65]

As long as the lightning victories were able to provide German soldiers free and virtually unthreatening visits to various European cities and landscapes, as long as they could impress their "girls" with French stockings and champagne, Belgian lace and pâté, as well as Dutch cheese, heroism was an easy attitude.[66] Over time, however, personal sacrifice was increasingly demanded and the prospects of subsequent material booty began to dwindle, with the result that the selfish will to survive began to crowd out other concerns. No doubt this affected the front soldiers less so, whose existence in a strict command-and-obey system left little choice or time to think about these alternatives. Yet the situation was different elsewhere. For instance, the Eastern front never offered any real possibility of material compensation, at least in terms of consumer goods or touristic leisure time. What plundering did take place there by the Wehrmacht was part and parcel of the larger annihilation strategy against the Soviet people.[67]

Hitler had calculated that he would have to force greatness upon the German people. But in order to pursue his unwavering plans for world dominion, he had to take his country into total war, a war in which the outcome could only be total victory or utter defeat. As long as the prospects of an imminent German victory looked plausible, the mythical stature of the rulers only grew. Many individual participants and civilians helped build the myth, since it enabled many people to put their own actions and suffering in a collective and comprehensive context. But as the possibility of military defeat loomed on the horizon, the heroic myth soon began to lose its pull and persuasive power. What now became clear to many was that clinging to such a mode of explanation ultimately meant assenting to one's own destruction. Of course this had always been the myth's logical conclusion, but it had been suppressed from consciousness for a long time. Thus the death of heroes was always linked to the death of others. The defeat at Stalingrad in 1943 was the turning point, for it made plain that Hitler was serious in demanding from his people unlimited sacrifice.[68]

Whether consciously or not, most soldiers and civilians recognized that the heroic myth ultimately did not make sense. What good would come from the sacrifice of soldiers at the front? To whose benefit was the destruction of women and children, if the country's own leadership (Hitler's "scorched earth" command) so utterly denied the people's very existence? Yet the heroic myth of self-sacrifice for the common weal was now taken to absurd extremes, and was done so through threat of punishment and without linking such sacrifice to any higher value. As a larger framework for interpreting actions and experiences, the myth lost its appeal; it could no longer justify the experience of mass death. The paradigm of the heroic single death was insufficient in the face of a continual and collective life-threatening situation. The absolute imperative of collective sacrifice stood in opposition to the more pragmatic wishes of the people to survive. But it was not the annihilation of other peoples or minorities that prompted the Germans to recoil from the inhumane and

reprehensible actions that this Nazi image of heroism implied and necessitated; instead, it came out only once German lives were threatened.

Hitler and Goebbels believed in and identified with this heroic ideal
until the very end. They pursued the suicidal consequences of this guiding heroic image with the conviction that their own lives as Führer-heroes
would bestow greatness upon their heroic sacrificial deaths and would
live forever in eternal memory for generations to come. The Führer and
his propaganda minister had themselves experienced the seductive power
of the call to sacrifice; it fulfilled the commonplace yearning for devotion.
Until the end of their lives they were convinced that the connective tissue
of the *Volk* was precisely its will to sacrifice. What they failed to understand, however, was that this will to sacrifice oneself was inseparable
from the hope for some sort of practical payoff or at least immaterial
benefit. When these things fell from sight, so too did the attractiveness of
sacrifice.

The myth began to pale in power as the logical consequence of the
self-annihilation revealed itself. By that time the Germans had immunized
themselves from being impressed by the "heroic death" of the Führer. His
"sacrifice" was hardly enough to inspire loyalty "until the very end"; so
much so that many began to see themselves as Hitler's main victims.[69]
They were deeply disappointed with the Nazi regime and angry about the
way in which the government had unjustly led them into a catastrophic
situation.[70] Many shielded any guilt by claiming that they only had done
what the government had demanded in the name of war victory. In effect
they argued in such a way as to dispel any notion of a second stab-in-the-
back legend about the betrayal of the home front. As opposed to the First
World War, so they reasoned, the home front fought to the bitter end.
Even so, its logical conclusion was rarely addressed: that one's own loyalty and obedience to this regime was perhaps mistaken, and that resistance and sabotage, refusal and desertion would have been the more
moral and responsible course of action.

The insufferable fact that the crimes of the Nazi regime had been possible only through the "heroism" of everyday Germans effectively led to
a split interpretation of responsibility.[71] This certainly presented problems
for the postwar era, since the Nazi heroic ideal (especially the sacrificial
element) remained partly intact. Out of the Nazi era image of the victim-
hero grew a new self-perception. By the end of the 1940s many Germans
saw themselves as victims of the occupying forces. Their political occupation, looting, and raping left an indelible mark on West German consciousness, while the similar practices of the German Wehrmacht at the
beginning of the war were summarily forgotten. More, they felt them-

selves victims of the newly liberated forced laborers and prisoners of war, whose plundering was not seen as a reaction to their violent displacement, incarceration, and long exploitation at the hands of the Nazis. "With lightning quickness a new attitude emerged about war and National Socialist rule: everything was viewed from the perspective of defeat, historical consequences were reversed, cause and effect inverted. After the defeat the one-time victor now saw itself as always having been the loser. By surprise attack the Germans usurped the role of victim."[72]

In sum, the attractive power of the heroic narrative can be explained so: it helped create clear lines demarcating internal and external, one's own group and designated foreigners. It necessitated a conflictual situation with a clearly defined enemy. Yet in fact it only worked with the help of material incentives. Without the economic boom of the 1930s, its binding power would surely have been much less. This is best confirmed by the fact that contemporaries to this day always cite the economic achievements of the regime (the end of unemployment, the construction of the Autobahn, and so on) as the pretext for their loyalty to Hitler. Just how weak the heroic myth had become for the wartime populace was clearly evidenced once the war came to Germany.

5. Where Have All the Heroes Gone . . .

"The collapse of National Socialism created . . . the deepest fissure in the twentieth-century history of victim myths."[73] This is not so surprising, if one recalls how much sacrifice was demanded of Germans both during and after the war. Apart from Nazi experience, from which many Germans felt disappointed, abused, and betrayed, the postwar period was characterized by an astounding disinclination against collective identities of any kind. Chief among them was the absence of collective West German victim and heroic narratives.

Many who believed in the Führer were faced in 1945 with the task of trying to understand their own suffering and the loss of belonging. Yet they had to do so without recourse to any interpretative structure from the state. The main question was: Could war sacrifices retain any signification in the aftermath of utter defeat? The self-destroying effect of the heroic myth was in part manifested in people's inability to integrate their war experiences in their lives after 1945.[74] Since their concrete experiences were without sense in and of themselves, the meaning of these events was usually passed over or bound to overarching institutions, such as the National Socialist system. In order to transform the "mass of unforgettable war experiences . . . into a comprehensible framework," postwar society lacked any real public structures of meaning that might have given expression to either positive or negative sentiments. Postwar West Germans thus felt themselves in a strange limbo, not least because the "fascist world of meaning no longer existed for the vast majority of people."[75]

Nevertheless, some elements of the old heroic myth were reused for interpreting the recent past. For example, the model of the inevitable victory of heroes enjoyed a place in East Germany's Socialist Unity Party ideology: "In the German Democratic Republic, National Socialism was reworked as a distinctive historico-philosophical theodicy. It was seen as a great evil, but in the end—despite its intentions—it helped to serve the good cause of bringing about the victory of socialism in East Germany. The brutal party slogan 'We come after Hitler' did little to question the meaning of history; instead, it ordered all events according to a 'dialectical' scheme," which resulted in "the broken heroization" of socialist realism.[76] The 1933 defeat of the working class was thus reinterpreted as a victory: "All's well that ends well" (*Ende gut—alles gut*). Like the National Socialists in 1933, the communists after 1945 devoted considerable energies to reconstructing a myth that imitated the "delayed victory" (*Parusieverzögerung*) of early Christianity so as to explain its coexistence with capitalism. And it was one in which sacrifice was placed in the foreground, even if this necessitated some ideological retooling. As one observer put it: "Marx's understanding of the liberation of the working class has in principle already taken place—yet the next phase of the struggle demands even higher sacrifice."[77]

In East Germany new heroes replaced old ones. The victors of war and history, the triumphal soldiers of the Red Army and the exiled or imprisoned communists now assumed center stage. They afforded new socialist citizens with a salutary identity, while at the same time whitewashing them from the brown stains of the past. Whoever was prepared to help build East Germany's socialist society was given a new historical myth, one that buried the real past under the rubble of forgetting. The antifascist consensus only perpetuated the aggressive friend-enemy dichotomy from the past; the Nazi concept of "national community" was simply dressed in red robes.[78]

In West Germany the heroic narrative's notion of victimhood persisted, even if the idea of active sacrifice was lost and reduced to the image of the passive, guiltless victim. Likewise, the concept of "death for the Fatherland" had to be reinterpreted. Horace's old couplet of "Dulce et decorum est/pro patria mori" [sweet and fitting it is/to die for one's country] no longer held sway, as historian Hermann Heimpel noted in 1955. A decade after the war he observed that most West Germans did not define themselves according to sacrifice and personal renunciation; in fact, they very much wished to live long and well. Modern Germans, so he argued, were a new "species, that accepts death but no longer wants to die."[79] Absent was the ideal of the sacrifice-loving and war-lusting heroes of old. A good example rested in the West German political holiday of June 17. On this occasion West Germans were encouraged to pay homage to the Cold War martyrs who died during the East German worker uprising of June 16–17, 1953. Yet there was little show of public solidarity with such heroes; indeed, most West Germans used the opportunity to enjoy a day trip in the countryside. Not "Unity in Freedom" (*Einheit in Freiheit*) was the focus of their concerns, but rather "Unity in Leisure" (*Einheit in Freizeit*).[80] So uninterested was the West German public in the larger meaning of the holiday that it eventually became an annual ritual for politicians and journalists to complain about the dangerously apolitical attitudes of West Germany's "pleasure-seeking" populace.[81]

A collective and binding association with the Second World War carried little power anymore. Nor was there any society-wide support after 1945 for private attempts to come to terms with the past. Wartime suffering and its effects had to be handled individually in the private sphere.[82] Here the values of postwar society radically diverged from those of Germany's prewar society: individual work and achievement determined one's social status, whose end was mostly the enjoyment of personal prosperity and leisure. The claims of community on singular individuals were shunted as much as possible.[83] Self-assurance no longer derived from military confrontations with neighbors, but rather from economic competition and pride in "German quality work" (*deutsche Wertarbeit*).

Democracy and the market economy were the twin postwar forces that West Germans after 1945 needed to integrate into their collective identity. Both were based upon the free choice of individuals. Yet there was an important contrast, nonetheless. While democracy was at least oriented toward a sense of community, market economics raised individual profit-seeking into a virtue in and of itself. But it was not only the intrinsic contradiction between civic and consumer virtues that bothered many West Germans; it was also the postwar period's stark contrast to the values and experiences of past epochs.

Because of its emphasis upon war preparation, the Nazi economy was an all-encompassing planned economy. Consumer goods for private households were strictly rationed during the war; ration cards for food and clothing were commonplace, a practice that of course continued through the first postwar years as well. No less important was that citizens had no real political choices during the Third Reich. Such an experience dramatically shaped the mentality of the war survivors. After the successive experiences of political fragmentation and quasi-civil war during the

Weimar Republic, followed by twelve years of political abstinence under Nazi domination and in turn widespread disillusionment accompanying the collapse of the regime, the post-1945 generation was deeply apathetic toward political questions.[84] For many the negative image of the National Socialist German Workers' Party (NSDAP) was transferred to the postwar political parties as well, while democracy itself was commonly viewed as an unwanted foreign system imposed by the victors who largely evoked suspicion and skepticism.[85]

Even so, a crass friend-or-foe attitude did remain as the residue of old political ideologies. With the intensification of the Cold War, the perceived enemy shifted from the Allies to the enemy in the East. Anticommunism ironically confirmed the view that (West) Germans had fought on the right side all along during the war. Hence they could participate in the victory. Which is to say that the old confrontation with communism was now carried on by other means. No doubt the political rivalry of both blocs found its most decisive symbolic manifestation in the economic arena. Consumerism thereby represented the second element of the Cold War mentality. In keeping with their apolitical attitude, West Germans generally experienced the new liberty as primarily consumer choice and freedom from communism; conversely, the free choice between different democratic parties figured much less prominently.

This mentality gave rise to a range of new values that broke from Nazi era ideology: status-seeking replaced the much-touted equality of "*Volk* comrades" (*Volksgenossen*); the profit motive supplanted social justice for and solidarity toward weak "special comrades" of the same race (*Artgenossen*); and the quest for material prosperity drowned out the dream of national greatness. And just as these "hedonistic" values crowded out the old heroic ideology, so too grew the wish for political relaxation. In order to enjoy its newly felt affluence, the state was not supposed to spend much taxpayer income on defense and security; instead, it should do everything in its power to leave its borders open and to encourage travel, traffic, and the unhindered stream of consumer goods. It was only fitting that West Germans later recalled the 1948 currency reform as the real turning point of West German history.[86] For them this was the event—not the 1945 cease-fire—that effectively brought the war to a close. Little wonder that the deutsche mark served as the country's unofficial state symbol.[87]

With time the pursuit of personal prosperity and the repulsion against the state's claim on its citizens—especially notable in the mid-1950s rearmament debate—was enshrined as a new German virtue. It all but replaced the old virtues of heroic asceticism and devotion to the common good. That is, the collapse of the Third Reich and the ensuing national division rendered obsolete the once-supreme value of heroic sacrifice.

In the heroic narrative the year 1948 afforded a kind of caesura. The end of the political purge and "atonement measures" (*Sühnemassnahmen*) was supposed to mark the end of the Allies' direct occupation, and of their former position in dictating their norms and values. This phase represented a new beginning, which also included a new understanding of the past.[88] In West Germany this meant that the heroes of war disappeared with the Nazis. Only war victims remained. The effects of war suffering were foregrounded instead of its causes. Otherwise, as it was argued, old wounds would give rise to new conflicts.[89] Consider for example the fact that war victims of the former enemies were honored in the early postwar years. This came about as a result of moral pressure from prisoners of war and concentration camp survivors along with their organizations, which dovetailed with the wishes of the occupying forces and the more general desire to elevate the country's international reputation. After 1949 these victims were remembered together with German victims. The foreign war victims thus functioned as a moral cloak under which different elements of German people's suffering (which included civilians killed by bombs and refugees, fallen Wehrmacht soldiers, and even casualties of various Nazi organizations) were lumped together.[90] The collective identification of West Germans as essentially war victims often led to a more or less secret empathy with condemned Nazi perpetrators and war criminals, with whom they felt much more affinity than with their countless victims.[91] Apparently, the old Nazi classification of peoples according to segregated categories of the elect community and "national enemies" (*Volksfremde*) persisted after 1945. Although the Allies only punished individual guilt, the Germans defended themselves passionately against the supposed assignation of collective guilt.[92] In such a defense they were well practiced, especially since the denial of war guilt after the First World War had been the one binding element of German society during the Weimar Republic.

After 1949 West Germans rejected the mantle as perpetrators, opting instead for the role of outside observers. Dividing the dead between perpetrators and victims must be stopped, so went the argument, since in death and suffering all are equal.[93] This of course had as much to do with the judgments upon the living as upon the dead. In the early 1950s the concerted campaign to free the "war condemned" (*Kriegsverurteilten*) was treated as a matter of national honor.[94] With it implicitly went the desire to defend the honor of dead soldiers without acknowledging their actions. This was especially the case regarding surviving Wehrmacht members.[95] It was all part of a larger postwar existential crisis of orientation that pivoted upon the question of how to make sense of one's own actions, suffering and uncertainty in face of defeat, political transformation and judicial condemnation.

Since National Socialism was not supposed to be remembered, it was unclear how to place the war in memory.[96] Fleeing responsibility for heinous crimes and a war of annihilation made it impossible to come to terms with experiences of suffering, violence, and mass death. The new political and economic beginning was used like a new name and identity bought at the expense of total amnesia. In the minds of many West Germans, it was pardonable to have been a Nazi as long as one now abandoned these convictions.[97] With time such an attitude became the basis for a new antitotalitarian consensus and helped ease the postwar transition. The reason for the widespread rejection of war was that both world wars were seen as having brought no tangible benefits. In light of the newly celebrated values of a postwar work and achievement society, war only represented destruction and the antithesis of these values. Yet it was also possible to compare the reconstruction achievements of the 1950s with the successes of the 1930s. In the 1950s, the pre-1939 "Economic Miracle" was particularly esteemed as the Third Reich's most positive achievement, even if its connection with war was largely ignored. In the early postwar years values like honor and Fatherland still played an important role. Only gradually were they replaced by personal freedom and prosperity. The Third Reich's "Heroes Commemoration Day" was renamed as the National Day of Mourning, while the fallen soldiers of the Second World War were honored for having defended the homeland. According to the new logic, they died in the name of freedom from Bolshevism. But their legacy was not at all a celebration of martial attributes. Precisely because the war was emptied of any larger meaning, the fallen served to admonish the survivors about the need for peace.

If we compare both postwar eras, it is plain that the legacy of each world war was treated quite differently. While the First World War provided an extraordinary source of signification in the interwar years for reinterpreting the relationship between German past and present, the Second World War afforded little corresponding narrative power and historical orientation for postwar Germans; in fact, its ability to furnish a compelling interpretative framework had already begun to collapse by the end of the war. By taking the Nazi ideology of heroic self-sacrifice for the community to its logical extreme, the war in turn exposed its absurd and suicidal dimension.

For a long time the guiding image behind German national mythology had been the tragic hero, who may have lost the struggle on the ground but in the end won the moral victory. It registered an ever-recurrent theme of German history that "heroism, that unwavering devotion to the Fatherland to which all Germans are obliged, invariably leads to defeat and death."[98] In Germany sacrifice without victory long acted as a "model of idealism and conscience." Even in moments of great success Germans were saddled with the memory of earlier generations, whose "loyalty and unquestioning faith steeled their hope in Germany's victory amid defeat and death." The Nibelungen legend, which was often invoked during both world wars as an inspirational symbol of identification, perfectly captured this fatalism. It certainly played a role in helping maintain support for Hitler's grandiose gamble, not least because people's feeling of impending defeat found a ready and age-old mythical model. Only through showing its self-destructive potential did the heroic myth lead to enlightenment. In any case, German peculiarities of the "victim syndrome" and the "lust for submission" (*Unterwerfungslust*) can be seen as historical phenomena. In their place stepped a postwar doctrinaire devotion to personal prosperity and material success, which have been subsequently hailed as the most important object lesson (*Lernerfolg*) for Germans from their whole twentieth-century experience.

Not to say that this dramatic transition from a violent will to sacrifice to the pursuit of prosperity was made so smoothly. Before 1945 there were certainly elements of hedonism, and some traces of sacrifice still persisted after 1945. On the one hand, the combat heroes took great pleasure in living the good life in France during the Nazi occupation; on the other, the labor of rebuilding Germany—including the image of the famed "rubble women" along with resistance against Hitler—served as key heroic episodes in the formation of the postwar's welfare state and "affluent society." Yet the charismatic heroic narrative had already collapsed. By the 1960s it was overrun by the obsession with personal gain within West Germany's burgeoning capitalist "achievement society," one that East Germans unthinkingly wished for and seized when the opportunity eventually arose.

KATHERINE PENCE

The Myth of a Suspended Present: Prosperity's Painful Shadow in 1950s East Germany

As we work today, so will we live tomorrow.
First produce more, then live better.

THESE optimistic slogans became central mottoes in the German Democratic Republic (GDR) in the 1950s, reflecting the country's narrative of national rebirth after World War II. Such widely publicized statements triumphantly proclaimed a trajectory for the new socialist state advancing out of the pain of the past toward a bright, prosperous utopian future. Within this narrative, collective pain became the starting point for this reemergence of the German nation. After the fall of the National Socialist regime, Germans faced the painful confrontation with the question of responsibility for the regime's criminality. Soon, however, the more immediate physical suffering from the prevalent hunger in the post-1945 rationing period eclipsed this existential dilemma in popular consciousness. Searching through the rubble of bombed cities for food allowed the defeated Germans to recast themselves as victims in the postwar era. The relief promised to hungry citizens was prosperity within socialism. East Germany claimed it would exceed even its neighbor and competitor, the Federal Republic (FRG), in bringing affluence to suffering Germans.

While this promise was certainly a splendid one, the above slogans also betray the central paradox of the GDR's reconstruction in its first decade: utopian prosperity would not come right away, and it would not come without work. "Today" would be characterized by "work," while East Germans would have to wait until "tomorrow" to "live better." While anticipating the promised utopia, civilians were called upon neither to despair nor to wait passively. Rather their ideological commitment and devoted labor in the present would help sustain the population in the face of ongoing painful shortages, or so the GDR regime hoped. Maintaining the population's commitment to the GDR in a present suspended between pain and prosperity became a major challenge for the regime in the 1950s, threatening the basis of its legitimacy.

The Legacy of Material Suffering

A sense of being mired in various forms of existential and material pain after the war made it possible for Germans to construct suffering as the foundation of their new society. Following the inflated national pride of the National Socialist period, Germans faced defeat, war crime tribunals, the loss of sovereignty, and dissolution of national unity. Even more pressing was the physical pain of endemic hunger resulting from the wartime disruption of production and distribution. Under such conditions, Germans faced the challenge of reconstructing a national identity under occupation by the Americans, British, French, and Soviets, who divided the country into four zones of military occupation in 1945.

Military occupiers forced Germans into an uneasy confrontation with the National Socialist past as a part of their goal to denazify and democratize the population. Their methods included group trips through concentration camps to witness the sites of mass killing, reeducation using propaganda films of death camps, and denazification trials to determine the party activity of each person.[1] Films produced in the Soviet Occupation Zone included *The Murderers are Among Us* (*Die Mörder sind unter uns*), which reflected this early struggle with questions of guilt and despair after Nazism.[2]

However, Germany's confrontation with its role as perpetrator soon gave way to a sense of German victimhood stemming from hardships of the occupation period. Alongside their democratizing goals, the military occupiers also attempted to exact retribution from Germans. The first, and perhaps most physically painful, sign of this thirst for revenge appeared when numerous occupying soldiers unleashed their rage during the final days of war against individual Germans. For many German women, especially in Berlin, the first encounter with their "liberators" was one of violence, brutality, and sexual violation.[3] Russian soldiers in particular became infamous for their calls of "*Frau, komm!*" that summoned German women to submit to rape. Although it will probably never be known how many women experienced this violation, estimates have ranged from between ten thousand to half of the 1.8 million women in the city of Berlin.[4]

Longer-term economic developments reinforced the sense of suffering at the hands of the occupiers. In the Soviet Zone, severe reparations resulted in the dismantling and transfer of entire East German factories to the Soviet Union. In a land already enduring severe shortages, the Soviet reparations highlighted the prioritization of punishment over rehabilitation in the first postwar years.[5]

Germans could and did blame their economic woes on the Allied occupiers. However Allied policies exacerbated economic disruptions brought by the Nazi-perpetrated war. Rationing began during the war and Nazi price controls hid inflation. These were both signs of future problems emerging from the war economy. Mass hunger came with the final defeat of the Nazi regime, when the agricultural, industrial, and distribution systems suffered severe collapse. The Allied occupiers inherited these limitations and could not immediately remedy them with their policies. As dictated by the 1945 Potsdam Conference Accords, each of the four Allies administered economics and agriculture separately in their occupation zones. This division impeded trade within Germany, thereby worsening supply of basic consumer goods.

The Nazi economy had profited from exploitation of slave labor and agricultural riches from the conquered Eastern territories. When this area was ceded to Poland in 1945, the Allied occupational economies had to compensate for this loss. With the end of criminal Nazi policies, food shortages emerged. The harsh winter of 1946–47 and bad harvests made these difficulties worse. Distribution of already scarce goods was difficult as a result of the destruction of railroad and other transport routes by Allied bombings. The influx of German refugees from the East and the chaotic mobility of the population returning to cities from evacuation sites and soldiers from the front placed extra burdens on the economy.[6]

Given these circumstances, hunger became a primary preoccupation of the German people. Faced with the ever-present *Magenfrage* ("stomach question"), Germans quickly turned from grappling with their role as perpetrators in the Holocaust to overcoming this period of shortages. A Berlin population survey from 1946 documented, for example, that attaining the basic commodities of food and fuel became the greatest difficulty and concern.[7] One German lamented in retrospect,

We had no more bomb attacks, but we also had nothing more to eat. Genuine starvation only really began for us in '45. The government that ruled over us [up until then] took care that there was at least enough to eat and that you could get full. But beginning in '45 that was no longer the case: then we starved, genuinely starved. You were never full. At no meal were you full. . . . When you met women standing in long lines in front of stores, their faces were all gray, almost black—that's how bad they looked, almost starved to death.[8]

Such accounts of starvation became common in the popular memory of the postwar period.

A central agenda for the occupiers would be to help assure provisions for the population. Each occupational zone instituted a rationing system to distribute scarce goods to the population. While preventing starvation on the one hand, these rationing schemes inadvertently reinforced a punitive stance toward the population through unequal distribution of goods.

The rationing systems differentiated among recipients based on criteria of age, occupation, social "value," and degree of involvement in the National Socialist regime. This differentiation was particularly stark in the Soviet Zone, where the system emphasized the differential value of labor by categorizing ration recipients in six levels according to "consideration of economic or social meaning of the work of the individual consumer."[9] The meager allotments varied slightly according to region and time, but in each case the discrepancy between the highest rung and the lowest was blatant. In Leipzig, for example, in December 1945, Category I received 2,186 calories per person per day and Category II 1,743 calories; members of these groups included heavy laborers working in industrial jobs such as coal mines and smelting furnaces or highly qualified professionals.[10] White collar workers in Category III received 1,382 calories and children in Category IV got 1,334 calories. The final group, labeled "others" (*die Sonstigen*), received only the starvation level of 1,171 calories, which earned this category the moniker the "hunger card" or the "graveyard card."[11] This category punished those who were either socially or productively less useful, such as the unemployed, retirees, disabled persons, "unemployed housewives," as well as those deemed responsible for the crimes of the previous regime, the Nazi Party members.[12]

From 1945 to 1947, the occupiers shared the common goal of denazification, punishment, and eventual reunification of the administrative zones.[13] As the Cold War started to drive a rift between the Western Allies and the Soviets, the terms for German reconstruction shifted from cooperation to competition between the two sides. Rather than continuing to focus on retribution and confrontation with Nazism, the occupiers now sought to rehabilitate the population for subsequent incorporation into the Western or Soviet blocs. In this context, the *Magenfrage* took on even greater significance. Rather than merely distributing scarce goods, the two regimes competed to rescue the German population from ongoing privation and ultimately to usher in an era of unsurpassed prosperity.

Food distribution was a critical first step toward prosperity. Undernourished workers exhibited low production levels, thus management of food shortages was basic to the reconstruction of industry and infrastructure. Food was also politically significant in the new Cold War climate. Consumer dissatisfaction could threaten the authority of the occupiers. In some cases, problems with provisions directly affected Germans' political views and attitudes toward the occupation regimes.[14] For example, low supplies became an issue in the efforts of the newly formed communist party, the Socialist Unity Party (SED), to establish itself as a popular leading party in the Soviet Zone. The SED feared dwindling support in the face of such shortages in 1947.[15] Economics official Josef Orlopp declared that "What moves the people, is not . . . the constitution, nor the question of socializing the big industries, but rather 400 or 600 grams of potatoes."[16] In other words, the population seemed politically motivated by problems of consumption, an acute source of their suffering, more so than by constitutional or structural agendas.

As the relief of hunger and the push toward greater prosperity became the defining agenda of the postwar German states, the regimes worked to downplay continuities with the Nazi past in order to declare the dawn of a new utopian era. The mythology of the Zero Hour (*Stunde Null*), an idea perpetuated throughout both halves of Germany, underscored the sense that 1945 constituted a break with the past. Lutz Niethammer argues that the German *Stunde Null* constituted a *Wunschtraum* (wish-dream) that the Nazi regime would be relegated to the past and forgotten.[17] The Cold War focus on progress and rehabilitation helped perpetuate this myth by downplaying the need for retribution for past Nazi crimes. Repressing the pain of confronting this past became a phenomenon that Alexander and Margarete Mitscherlich have called "the inability to mourn."[18] The repression of this guilt lingered in postwar German history and only gained attention in the *Historikerstreit* (historian's debate) of the 1980s and the neofascist violence of the 1990s.[19]

Equipped with the narrative of the *Stunde Null*, both East and West began to construct their own histories in ways that broke with the past in 1945.[20] In the Soviet Zone and its successor state, the GDR, however, the politics of socialism promoted a more extreme version of this break; structural transformation into an antifascist regime would purge the remnants of the capitalist, imperialist Third Reich. The GDR contrasted its own presumably successful rehabilitation with that of its Western neighbor by accusing the FRG of recycling old Nazis into leading economic and political positions. While the FRG remained tainted by unreconstructed Nazism, the GDR could focus wholeheartedly on overcoming the pain of hunger and shortages after 1945 by building socialism. Then the promise of future abundance—implicitly meant to prevent the population from ever going through the pain of hunger again—became the defining agenda for the new state as it competed with the West. Thus the shadow of the postwar years of shortage always lurked behind the bright future offered to the population.

The context of the Cold War gave this goal of abundance particular urgency and made it necessary for the regime to convince the population that their utopia was imminent. However, it became increasingly clear that the promised affluence would not be attainable immediately. Therefore, starting at the *Stunde Null*, the architects of the socialist utopia actively defined historical time as a series of steps through an interim period between the pain of the past and the successes of the future.

Marking Time: Selling
Socialism with the Promise of Prosperity

The *Stunde Null* transformed the long legacy of material want and deprivation into the ever-present backdrop of pain as the foundation of the two German states. It was incumbent upon the two emerging German states to construct a vision of legitimacy based on promised relief from pain. In the GDR, the process of establishing a socialist utopia on German soil was intrinsically connected with the process of converting a painful past to a more materially prosperous future. An outgrowth of the postwar experience, the definition of socialist utopia as the promised land of modern prosperity also reflected the Stalinist turn from Marxist "axioms of socialist emancipation" to the more immediate goals of industrialization and higher consumer standards.[21]

In the first decade of the GDR's existence, this prosperity was not yet attainable. Therefore, the process of transition itself was fraught with the pain of longing. Charles Maier has suggested that the postwar states had to transform public longing for a reunified German nation into something else.[22] The East German state had to transform public longing into the desire for future prosperity under socialism, which would motivate the population to work diligently for achievement of this goal.[23]

The East German regime constructed an image of the state that made the 1950s a period of suspended time between past and future in which the everyday pain of unfulfilled promises in the present was to be repressed in anticipation of things to come. In order to keep East German citizens from casting the early years of the GDR as painful, official propaganda described these years as an anticipatory time of waiting and wishing, in which the waiting would be filled with sacrifice and communal labor to help bring about the goal of prosperity. In this crossover period, the regime could claim to reconcile the contradictions of a promised equality and prosperity under socialism with the actual existing conditions of inequitable goods distribution and continuing need because the conclusion of utopia was still yet to be achieved. Meanwhile, the regime could claim to manufacture consensual forbearance of the population. However, basing the regime's early years on a promise of things to come gave the GDR a more tenuous hold on legitimacy that would be more difficult to maintain by the end of the decade.

In this period of suspended time between the *Stunde Null* and utopia, the regime structured economic development to mark out intervals of time until that utopia would be achieved. The planned economy itself worked to manage time in this way and the basic institutions of goods distribution underscored this creation of a forward-looking emphasis. Goods were distributed in a controlled way through the rationing system and as "free goods" sold outside the limits of rationing in the state-run franchise the Handelsorganisation (HO). These distribution systems each involved similar structuring of time through progressive intervals. Finally, the programs to improve the standard of living of the population reinforced this narrative of waiting for a future time.

The logic of the planned economy itself relied on building a consensus around intervals of time that would successively bring the population future satisfaction of needs and desires. These planning intervals embodied a progressive vision of transition from prewar and wartime standards of living to future unsurpassed prosperity. Propaganda literature promoted this idea to the GDR citizenry to bolster commitment to making the economy successful. Initially the primary goal for the economy was more backward looking. The first Two-Year Plan was ushered in by the German Economic Commission, the main institution for central planning established in 1948. This plan was based on the premise that the burgeoning economy would help East Germany overcome wartime need, regain prewar standards of living, and eventually lead to a period of unbounded prosperity for all citizens of the worker-and-peasant state. Propaganda promoting the first plan offered the "promise to present a construction plan that demonstrates what is to be done in order to come to a better life."[24]

A new time period of planning began in 1950 with the first Five-Year Plan. A brochure, called "Our Five-Year Plan," aimed to promote popular identification with the new economic system and described the steps toward future prosperity:

> The industrial production should be more than doubled by 1955 in relationship to the level in 1936. Already by next year, 1953, rationing will be eliminated, and all foodstuffs and consumer durables will be sold at uniform, reasonable prices. Two years later, in 1955, we will have more meat, sugar, milk, etc. available than in 1936.[25]

As this optimistic statement suggests, planning offered the population concrete goals for economic recovery within clearly marked time periods. Still using wartime deprivation as its reference point, these plans promised to lift the population out of its postwar nadir of provisioning to restore prewar standards of living.

As the decade progressed, the planned economy shifted its defining goals from restorative to progressive levels of prosperity. After the death of Stalin in March 1953 and the nationwide uprising against the GDR regime in June, the regime embarked upon a so-called New Course to increase production of consumer goods. In the New Course, East Germans' lives were supposed to become more pleasurable, attractive, and modern through better consumption.[26] The regime started to enumerate promises of a myriad of pleasurable commodities that would be made available by socialist production. Economic functionaries attended to details of daily life, offering goods that might improve consumption in the GDR, such as refreshing drinks such as fruity sparkling wines and ice cream with chocolate topping for the warm summer months.[27] The promise to provide future wish-fulfillment gained new impetus with the SED's promise to maintain an "open ear for all wishes and demands of the population" and to "take the ideas, suggestions, and critique of the population seriously."[28] Citizens participated in improving the consumer economy by expressing their commodity desires to the highest authorities. For example, some participants in a discussion of consumer issues complained in December 1953 that butter must be made cheaper, and that it made no sense when a suit cost one hundred marks to produce but it cost two hundred marks in the HO.[29] Authorities dealt with these complaints and perceived inadequacies by describing them as growing pains on the path to a hopeful future:

We possess the political and economic basis in order always to advance always further and even faster, because we are by no means satisfied with what has been reached. It still happens, that this or that commodity, which would fill important needs, is in short supply. The assortment of food is not diverse and constant enough; clothing and shoes often still don't meet our expectations in their quality, form, color and price. But the visible advances of the past year make it clear, that soon we will no longer hang back in these areas. Rather we can have and will have the best in sufficient variety.[30]

Although the New Course reinforced the commitment to building prosperity, this assessment suggests that the regime still expected its citizens to wait for that future time and to be heartened by the successive achievements on the road to that goal.

To underscore the importance of this entreaty to work toward future prosperity in the Cold War context, propaganda cast this effort as a sort of crusade. In a document labeled "material for propagandists" the SED Berlin leadership outlined how the GDR's steps toward prosperity were to be used against enemies of the regime, whether internal or external:

Fulfilling the plan and production of mass consumer goods [is an] important part of the people's fight. To the extent that we create new successes and new facts showing that we enrich the availability of goods and beautify our life through the production of mass consumer goods (refrigerators and vacuum cleaners, fruit presses, washing machines, mopeds, etc.), the house of lies of our opponents will be shattered.[31]

As this propaganda plan suggested, building a more pleasing and convincing consumer culture became key to winning the loyalty of the population and preventing further threats from political "saboteurs" such as those deemed responsible for the June 1953 uprising and from the lure of the West.

The year following the introduction of the New Course, 1954, was heralded as the "Year of the Great Initiative" in which modern technology would help fulfill the "steadily growing material and cultural needs" of society. The spirit of consumer modernization embodied in this initiative was carried on into the second Five-Year-Plan, which was declared at the Third Party Conference on March 24–30, 1956. The directive for the new Five-Year Plan pledged to raise consumer production by 40 percent and to actualize the new slogan "Modernization, Mechanization, Automatization."[32] These goals represent the shift toward aspiring to new levels of prosperity not yet known in German history.

The planning for greater prosperity reached new heights in 1958 with the Fifth Party Congress of the SED, where the push to increase commodity production gained new impetus. Here Party Secretary Walter Ulbricht declared that the "principal task" of the state was to overtake the West in per-capita consumption. The most important declaration of this congress explained:

The people's economy of the German Democratic Republic is to be developed within a few years so that the superiority of the socialist social order of the GDR, in comparison to the domination of the imperialist powers in the Bonn state, will be proven unambiguously. As a result the per-capita consumption of our working population of all important foodstuffs and consumer goods will reach and surpass the per-capita consumption of the whole population in West Germany.[33]

In sum, this grand statement of Ulbricht's new push for building socialism foregrounded the promotion of consumption by saying the GDR would raise its standard of living and "catch up with and overtake" (*einholen und überholen*) West Germany in per-capita consumption. Indeed, economic policy in the following months concentrated strongly on the consumer sector.[34] This announcement ushered in a new concentration on study of and comparison with worldwide living standards, especially those in West Germany, in order to improve the consumer opportunities for GDR citizens.[35] Besides quantitatively overtaking the West, the new development of consumer culture also aimed to raise quality of commodities and to modernize consumption. The focus of the "principal task" therefore placed new emphasis on the fashionability and diversity of goods. To enact this new program, economic planners stopped the second Five-Year Plan early and replaced it with a Seven-Year Plan, which aimed to fulfill these promises by 1965. Within this last planning period of the decade, the regime committed itself to completing the final stages of building socialism. Therefore, the intensified push to bring socialist utopia to fruition was interconnected with the overt goal of ushering in a period of prosperity.

Each of these planning periods marked out time during which particular steps toward prosperity would occur. Within each of these periods, the steps toward prosperity were enumerated in more detail through the implementation of a series of state-sponsored consumption programs. By mid-decade these programs concentrated on modernization of commodities and design to create what the regime called "selling culture" (*Verkaufskultur*). These programs promoted everything from new technologically advanced household appliances to commodities made from space-age synthetic materials. Specially designed campaigns celebrated these efforts, including one celebration in October 1955 called "Technology Month." Here, too, the state delineated periods of time as moments of material accumulation. These campaigns were touted as evidence of the transition from a period of pain and deprivation to a modern consumer "wonderland." New commodities were described in terms of the new prosperity they embodied. A prime example of this was the promotion of the chemical industry that brought new plastic commodities on the market.[36] The program to advocate chemical industry began in November 1958 and was popularized with the slogan "Chemistry brings bread, prosperity and beauty."[37]

Not only would aesthetic quality and advanced technology propel the GDR into a new age, but the regime emphasized that paucity of goods would be replaced by extreme quantity. This idea was also institutionalized in a program dating from 1959 called "The 1000 Little Things of Daily Life." Proliferation of available merchandise fitting every need or desire of the population became one of the core goals of the "economic principal task."[38] Economic functionaries took care to list in detail the dizzying array of goods to be produced in the Seven-Year Plan, as in one exemplary list from 1960: "kettle lids, laundry racks, flower boxes, sawhorses, handles, muzzles, baskets, curtain rods, oven leg supports, bicycle kick-stands, fireplace grills . . . fire pokers, door bolts, folding trellises . . . centrifugal pumps . . . hand-vices, particle board, garden fences . . . potato choppers, asparagus knives, etc."[39]

Ultimately, the result of this greater abundance and technological advancement would be an easier life for GDR citizens, especially women, who continued to be the members of the household who often primarily performed the daily shopping and housework. East German advertising reinforced this political message of how the SED regime represented a new affluent era. For example, in a shop window displaying the laundry agitating machines *Vibrette* and *Waschbär* the slogan "Modern technology in the household makes life more beautiful and easier for housewives" accompanied an image described in the advertising trade journal *Neue Werbung*, "A man's white shirt rises out of the wash-tub in an explanatory pose and says with reference to the sweating washer-woman at a tub 'Earlier one took pains; today one has it more comfortable!' "[40] This advertising display encapsulated the official narrative of GDR history from 1945 to 1961: a shift from pain to comfort. But as this description shows, the memory of pain remained the starting point for understanding what the GDR tried to offer in this new age.

The regime constantly chronicled its successful production of more and better commodities as evidence of prospects for greater prosperity, but access to these commodities, whether modern innovations or basic stables, and their accompanying comfort was contingent on the specific contours of East German retailing. Although socialism ultimately claimed to bring equal prosperity for all, the population faced a hierarchical division of commodity selection and pricing in the transitional phase of building socialism. The provisioning system in the GDR was divided into two levels: the low-priced, subsidized, but meager rationed goods, often sold in the consumer cooperative chain the Konsum; and the freely sold, more luxurious, and more expensive goods in the HO stores. The discrepancy between these two tracks of distribution highlighted the fact that equality and prosperity for all had not yet been achieved. Rather, the population was expected to bear this inconsistency as a necessary sacrifice on the road to utopia. Again, the population could only suspend its critique of this system if they agreed that prior to the dawn of utopia, the transitional phase from pain to prosperity would remain anticipatory, suspended time. Like the incremental planning years, the rationing and HO systems also incorporated gradated steps toward elimination of the painful inconsistencies they represented.

Both rationing and the HO relied on the population to endure delayed gratification. The rationing system involved the allotment of food and clothing over regular intervals so that basic subsistence could be maintained. The regime hoped eventually to eliminate rationing to restore "normal" conditions of selling, thereby replacing this remnant of wartime deprivation. In 1950 the regime pledged to eliminate rationing on all goods by 1953 at the latest.[41] In 1950 and 1951 important commodities were opened to purchase without rations.[42] The SED leadership also managed to raise the ration quota for much-desired foodstuffs such as meat and fat.[43] However, it was not possible to eliminate rationing fully in the GDR until 1958, eight years after the neighboring Federal Republic was able to do so. This condition left the East German population in a state of suspension waiting for the restoration of "normal" market conditions throughout most of the decade. Inherent in the rationing system was the expectation of future relief from it, and to this was added the promise of future prosperity.

The other part of the distribution system, the HO, was originally meant to offer an alternative to the black market. However, the HO essentially highlighted the problems of the rationing system, heightening the desire for scarce goods while postponing gratification until some indeterminate future time. This paradox was due to the pricing system. To soak up excess currency that was flowing into the black market in the 1940s, the HO set its prices just slightly below the black market prices so that speculators couldn't buy out the stock.[44] Most average consumers could not, therefore, afford the goods in the HO. However, prices in the HO would drop successively in systematic increments.[45] According to the propaganda, higher production would eventually enable "always wider circles of the population" to utilize this source of provision.[46] In the meantime, the HO divided the population into more and less privileged consumers, a far cry from the vision of utopian equality of ideal socialism.

From Suffering to Sacrifice:
Building Consensus for Building Prosperity

While waiting for prosperity to arrive, the population still had to cope with the suffering of continued rationing and shortages. To bolster the legitimizing myth that the new regime represented a departure from this sort of pain, it was necessary to recast this experience of shortage in the 1950s to fit the narrative of progress. To do this the regime reconfigured this period of extended suffering as a time of willing sacrifice, in which East German citizens would collectively bring about the socialist utopia. The implication of the slogan "First produce more—then live better" was that as active participants in the construction of socialism, the population itself would bear responsibility if the fulfillment of prosperity was long in coming. While the regime took an active role in defining historical time between pain and prosperity by marking out periods of the planned economy, the SED constructed this commitment to labor as something generated by the population itself. Even the responsibility for coining slogans to set this agenda fell to the average citizen, for example, Frida Hockauf, a textile worker who modeled forward-looking self-sacrifice with the maxim "As we work today, so shall we live tomorrow."[47] The regime publicized this slogan widely to build consensus around the concept of laboring for the future. Devotion to building socialism would fill the time prior to the prosperity of "tomorrow" to sublimate the sense of painful continuity with the postwar period.

The most important arena in which the population had to labor for future abundance was in agricultural and industrial production. The ideal worker in the GDR was the *Aktivist*, a worker modeled on the Soviet figure Stakhanov, who gained acclaim by achieving rates of production above the specified quotas, ideally through technical innovation and rationalization. Urged on by the slogan introduced at the Second Party Congress of the SED in 1947, "Produce more, distribute more justly, live better!" (*Mehr produzieren—gerechter verteilen—besser leben!*), workers were encouraged to surpass their required work quotas and achieve the distinction of *Aktivist* in order to create the better life to which they aspired.[48]

The workers in factories were themselves key to the plan to produce new commodities especially toward the end of the decade as part of the program "1000 Little Things of Daily Life." Ideally factory managers consulted with workers to find out the needs of consumers; factories would then add these goods to the originally scheduled output.[49] In this sense workers were addressed as consumers.[50] This combined role of worker/consumer, symbolized in the slogan "Your Hand for Your Product," potentially aimed in part to eliminate the worker's alienation from the products of his or her labor, which Marx saw as a problem of capitalism.[51] It also placed responsibility on the worker for determining the course of production and for assessing the needs of the consumer. Slogans such as "One Suggestion from Everyone" pressured workers to come up with ideas for new commodities. Workers received premiums for workable ideas.[52] Often the workers bore the burden to fulfill the factory's pledge to add consumer goods to its production. To do so they had to work more efficiently or work overtime. In one case, workers volunteered 1,500 extra hours to produce new commodities.[53]

Although a primary goal of the regime was to encourage workers to increase production, the shortcomings of the economy made it necessary for additional segments of the population to perform compensatory labor to make the consumer economy function smoothly. In some cases this may have been due to labor shortages. Without the market forces of supply and demand determining production, economic planners had to establish mechanisms for determining demand, sometimes by soliciting the population of consumers to declare their wishes. Also, as the economy made the transition to socialism by requiring private entrepreneurs to sign on with the state-run HO chain or the consumer cooperatives, the management of retail became more cumbersome and problematic. Thus, those assumed to be the primary household consumers, women, were enlisted to aid the transforming economy to determine the consumer's desires and to help fulfill them. Not only were women to be integrated into the workforce, but they were also brought into state-sponsored organizations in which they could use their presumed consumer expertise to bring about the consumer utopia.

Working women and unemployed housewives alike were organized into groups to fix the problems of the consumer economy. The SED politburo aimed to incorporate working women into the task of helping themselves when it decreed on January 8, 1952, that industrial firms should set up women's committees (*Frauenausschüsse*). These committees were to be made responsible for implementing the measures for women entailed in the collective agreements, including better shopping opportunities for working women.[54] When the men in the official trade union, the Free German Trade Union (FDGB), didn't pay enough attention to problems such as assortment of merchandise in the factory store,[55] women in the committees could step in and agitate for change and improvement of the stores, kindergartens and day-care centers, laundries and shoe repair.[56] A woman at a 1955 SED meeting to celebrate the anniversary of the women's committees professed to her committee's successful establishment of a factory store:

We were successful in achieving, with good cooperation with the HO and Konsum, that more and better goods are obtainable in our firm's shops. We fought for half a year to lengthen the opening hours of the Konsum store so that our women could take part in social life and still procure their purchases. Three days a week the Konsum firm is open until 7:00 P.M., and the Konsum store in the city of Radeberg is open until 7:00 P.M. on two days as well.[57]

Such achievements certainly had the potential to improve women's housework and to empower them as *Aktivist* workers. Women could combine their roles as workers and as consumers to improve their own lives within the general campaign to build the socialist utopia. Though the women's committees had limited power, they allowed women to work to help themselves to solve the "women's question" when other GDR institutions fell short.[58]

Housewives were potentially the most excluded from socialist communal life, which often centered around employment. Yet they were the ones considered most attune to problems of consumption. Therefore, the state-sponsored women's mass organization, the Democratic Women's Union of Germany (DFD), took on the role of incorporating unemployed women into socialist labor while using their presumed penchant for consumption to help fix the ills of the economy. Women in the DFD staged sales exhibitions, fashion shows, housewife and female farmer gatherings, at which they collected suggestions for improving merchandise quality, assortment, and fashion design. DFD women worked to improve the provision of certain commodities, as reported by its members in periodic reports, such as these from 1954:

In Lübben, our Friends have achieved, in common deliberation with female workers, enterprise managers, and the trade organs, that the knit undergarments produced in the Venus Factories would be directly delivered to the stores in Lübben. Previously there were hardly ever knit goods to be bought in Lübben.

The residents of Schwenda say, "We always had a very limited offering of fish and fish products. Nothing helped. Now the DFD spoke up about this, and that at least did something."

Innumerable Konsum stores, especially in the country, have been established due to the initiative of our women, such as in the districts of Döblen, Oschatz, Torgau, Eggesin, Althagen, etc.[59]

Through the combination of such local initiatives and centralized support, these women made incremental changes to improve consumption around the GDR.

These women became an even more integral part of retailing improvement by joining HO councils that began forming in 1954 and became an official part of the DFD's agenda on February 22, 1955.[60] By 1957, the GDR's districts reported HO-Councils in 2,600 stores and restaurants, in which nine thousand women and men were working.[61] These councils still attained only mixed success. In some cases, the DFD women worked to be agents of modernization in the stores, helping bring about renovations including refrigerated cases, shelving, sausage-slicing machines, and ventilators. They agitated for a better overview of goods in the stores, clear display of price tags, and partial self-service to help ease the shopping tasks for working women. When bad quality goods were delivered, DFD women saw to it that they were sent back to the distributors.[62]

The DFD used its attention to consumer improvements to help forge women's commitment to the party and the planned economy and the overall project of building future prosperity. For example, they interpreted rationing improvements as a gift from the regime directly to women to encourage women to feel bonded to the regime. On behalf of all women, the organization drafted letters thanking the regime for eliminating rationing of certain goods:

Over one million women and mothers, who are organized in the Democratic Women's Union of Germany, took notice with joy and thankfulness of the termination of food ration cards for products made from grain and legumes starting on January 1, 1951. We are happy about this measure, which brings considerable relief to all women and mothers in nourishing their families. . . . Through this the proof is furnished anew, that our government has taken the right path to peace, reconstruction and the improvement of our lives. We promise to use our whole power in the new year for the great peace plan—the Five-Year Plan—especially for the qualification of women in all professions.[63]

This letter demonstrates how the DFD worked to interpret the regime's achievements in improving consumption as a direct relief for women in particular. The letter aimed to create a reciprocal relationship between women and the state in which movements toward prosperity led women to seal their commitment to the task of building socialism in the Five-Year Plan. Many of the DFD's initiatives reiterated this goal of both improving women's lives and showing them that their lives would be best improved by the SED's brand of socialist reconstruction.

This delayed gratification meant that the promise of prosperity would be inextricably linked to the heritage of deprivation out of which the GDR was hoping to emerge. Before abundance would be possible, the citizens would have to be content with gradual steps out of material shortages. Socialism itself would remain a somewhat distant goal. The regime mobilized a number of strategies to assure the population of future fulfillment of desires if they stayed committed to the project of building socialism. Party propaganda continually reemphasized the assurance that socialism was the only true path to prosperity for everyone.

However, by the end of the decade it became increasingly clear that the promises of abundance would not come to fruition as had been expected. The economy continued to struggle with shortages and logjams of production and distribution. Consumers continued to queue before shops in order to obtain scarce items. The regime also failed to match its promises for consumer development with real commitment to investment in consumer industries. Rather, heavy industry continued to retain official privileging. This discrepancy between promise and reality became increasingly apparent with the continuation of domestic problems in the consumer economy and with the constant comparison between East Germany and its more prosperous neighbor to the West.

Between Pain and Prosperity

The 1950s were characterized by a striving to emerge from a past of pain and the attainment of a prosperous future. The GDR regime shaped its history in the 1950s as an interim period marked out as a series of steps toward prosperity. To gain consensus for this progressive narrative and to assure its own legitimacy, the state needed to show that the country was leaving the painful past behind and that wealth would soon arrive. This strategy required the population to live in limbo, suppressing both any sense of continuing pain and any desire for immediate fulfillment of consumer desires. Rather, this suspended time would be spent concentrating on work. Labor, seen as sacrifice rather than suffering, would bind the population to the project of building socialism.

Just as the regime had planned to end rationing in 1953 and could not do so until 1958, the date for achievement of this prosperity was repeatedly put off, but extended anticipation of future rewards could not be maintained indefinitely. By promising prosperity, the regime helped to mobilize desires for material gratification, which increasingly seemed more and more elusive. The further breakdown of any possible consensus came with the relative material abundance achieved in the West by the end of the decade.

At the beginning of the decade, the two new states seemed relatively matched in their abilities to deliver material goods to the population. Both East and West Germany materialized out of the painful period of shortages, and both faced difficult reconstructions. The first years of the West German Social Market Economy, launched in 1948, were characterized by unemployment and a concentration on filling basic consumer needs. When unemployment peaked in 1950 in the West, Western consumers, especially in divided Berlin, strayed across the border to the East to buy goods cheaply, taking advantage of the lower exchange rate.[64] This trend demonstrated how East Germans could afford to be optimistic about the prospects of their economy in comparison to the West. However, by the beginning of the 1950s, the Marshall Plan and the Korean War boom brought stabilization to the West German economy, particularly after 1953.[65] Although shortages continued to mark the bulk of the decade in the daily lives of West Germans, by 1959 the Economic Miracle began to live up to its name by making modern mass consumption accessible to much more of the population. Michael Wildt has analyzed this as an "end of modesty" when average Germans could afford more luxuries and didn't have to worry about fulfilling basic needs.[66] The so-called Golden West began to appear genuinely more golden.

The GDR also managed to achieve a modicum of prosperity by the end of the decade. By the mid-1950s, many households had already recovered a basic standard of living. Bombing victims had replaced their furniture, people generally had sufficient clothing, and food provision was relatively constant. As housing standards improved, household durables such as large appliances began to take on increasing importance for satisfaction of household needs.[67] More people could afford appliances and other hallmarks of the modern household.

Another important marker of normalization of the consumer arena was the elimination of rationing for remaining food and commodities on

May 28, 1958. This decree by the *Volkskammer* ended an era in which GDR citizens had experienced rationing in some form since 1939, and it marked a symbolic end to the immediate postwar period.[68]

However, three problems complicated and limited the dawn of prosperity. First, the problems within the planning system itself made it difficult for the economy to meet desires or needs of shoppers. Ina Merkel describes how the

basic guidelines of economic policy that led to a structural neglect of consumer goods branches, a systematic decay of middle class small businesses, and the lack of inducement for consumer production according to needs, had an aggravating effect on the permanent default of the [economic] plans and a discontinuous provisional situation. Reasons for disturbance of production also included the sometimes fully obsolete mechanical equipment, which often led to breakdowns, the halting and low quality flow of material (due to a lack of currency, they would fall back on low quality) and work force shortages.[69]

The continuing problems in production and affordability are reflected in a report from August 1958 from the trade union, the FDGB, about the inability of the economy to fulfill the needs and desires of consumers:

The indiscriminate manufacture of mass commodities in the years 1956 and 1957 is one of the reasons that our women are still always heavily burdened by running the household. To this is added the extreme expense of acquiring an appliance such as a washing machine. The current development in mass commodity manufacturing still doesn't guarantee that the need will be most extensively covered. Many appliances are very urgently desired by women—such as electrical household appliances, washing machines, vacuum cleaners, and electric and gas stoves. The current planning for production of household appliances cannot be seen as sufficient. Therefore attainment of greater free time for women still remains hampered.[70]

The second problem, which compounded these struggles of the planned economy, was the project to complete the stages of building socialism. Walter Ulbricht pushed this development first in 1952 at the Second Party Congress, when the regime coercively collectivized agriculture, industry, and trade. This state interference disrupted economic progress of the early 1950s, creating increasing shortages. The result was the biggest challenge to the GDR regime until 1989: the uprising of June 17, 1953. As a response to this unrest the regime ushered in a New Course, as described above, to focus more on consumer goods and to scale back some of the most severe measures of the transition to socialism, such as the repression of the private sector. However, in 1958, the same year that Ulbricht vowed to surpass the West in per-capita consumption, the SED also declared once again the campaign to complete the process of building socialism. Again private sectors of the economy were subjected to pressure to join the state-run franchises. Despite greater investment in the consumer sector, the state lacked sufficient funds to raise consumer production. Without desired imports from the Soviet Union and due to the difficulties of collectivizing agriculture, the economy suffered a crisis in 1960–61 that was most visible in the major gaps in merchandise assortment.[71] Just as the regime was declaring that the population would exceed the per-capita consumption of the West, supplies of butter, meat, and other basic products were severely lacking.[72]

The other progressive element of the economy, the gradual reduction of prices in the HO stores, also failed to live up to its promise of providing overall affordability. The state chain was unable to provide cheap goods for the general population, as it had claimed it would. While socialist ideology claimed to work toward a democratic leveling of society, the system of consumption embodied by the HO was actually rife with hierarchical categorizations. The gap caused by the double pricing system between the rationed goods affordable to the average person and the exorbitant HO goods constituted the most glaring hierarchy. Thus, the HO put the regime into a paradoxical trap. As a state-run institution, it was meant to symbolize the utopian quality of the new society, but precisely this symbolic weight made the HO a popular icon of the whole regime's failures when it failed to make good on its promises. Ultimately, rather than providing a socialist alternative to Western consumer culture, the HO emphasized continuing inequities and hierarchies in East German society.

The culture of consumption set up by the HO also reinforced and redefined other societal hierarchies within the ranks of laborers and consumers. It was the apparent injustice of these hierarchies that created some of the public's harshest critiques of the HO. As a popular poll taken by party leaders suggests, some East Germans were happy to have a chance to buy some new goods, but numerous reactions often revealed acute recognition of the HO's inequities. The aspersions cast on the HO reflected resentment of the hierarchy established by the East German labor and wage system, which differentiated between normal workers and the *Aktivisten*, often recipients of the progressive piece-wage (*progressiver Leistungslohn*). Indeed, all members of the population were encouraged to raise productivity and to become *Aktivisten*. However, the Stalinist system of distinguishing most productive workers from the "average" worker divided the workforce and intensified this hierarchical division with unequal distribution of material rewards.[73] Moreover, this division of workers into separate groups was heightened by the fact that the *progressiver Leistungslohn*, which in theory would most enable workers to buy HO goods at their high prices, was not available to all workers.

At the end of the decade, the regime tried various strategies to speed up the advent of promised prosperity. While the planned economies had been shaped by regular intervals of improvement, the modern innovations of the late 1950s emphasized the greater velocity of these improvements. Stemming from a desire to engineer a technical revolution in production and consumption, the Ministry of Trade and Provisioning sponsored various efforts at rationalization and standardization to make production, distribution, and shopping smoother, easier, and quicker. A prime example of this trend was the movement toward self-service supermarkets, an international development emphasizing rationalization and speed by introducing packaged goods on accessible shelves, thereby eliminating the need for shopkeepers as intermediaries between shoppers and merchandise.[74] The GDR also experimented with a number of shopping innovations that focused on speed of purchase. One of these was "minute shopping" in which employed women would order desired merchandise at a store in the morning to be picked up later.[75] Finally, the production of new "modern" goods themselves reiterated this desire for speed. Quick cooking and preprepared meals were designed to allow housewives to complete their household tasks quickly in order to take on the additional role as productive laborer. The aptly named "tempo lentils" (*Tempo Linsen*), lentils cooked in a brief ten-minute time span, exemplified this trend so clearly that it became a central icon at a 1996 retrospective exhibition of East German consumer culture.[76] The modern ethic of speed enhanced the image that prosperity and a more comfortable life would arrive sooner.

To convince the population that this utopia was indeed imminent, the regime started to revel in triumphalist celebrations of achievements already attained by 1959. The most prominent expression of this trend was the Trade Conference of 1959, at which the achievements of the past decade were displayed for political functionaries and the general population. Here such advancements as self-service food shopping were taken to the extreme through the erection of automatic vending machines, especially in plants for use by workers.[77] Walter Ulbricht and trade functionaries viewed displays of self-service shelving, floor plans, and modern store furnishings. Within modern renovated self-service stores, goods in high quality and quantity, contained in alluring packaging, showed how the GDR had reached international standards of marketing. In the post-rationing society, the GDR hoped to show how East Germans were now well fed on more plentiful, higher quality, and healthier food. Quantity was clearly important, since Ulbricht declared that the calorie intake in the GDR had reached that of the United States, "the land with the highest standard of living." A proud symbol of the GDR's ability to overcome the postwar hunger years was the increasingly stout population, for which Ulbricht found evidence in the need for larger dress sizes: "You will understand, that you absolutely will no longer manage with your current stock of size 42."[78]

The other strategy to salvage GDR legitimacy was to employ Cold War belligerence to disarm the allure of the West. The parallels between atomic-age commodities and weapons in the GDR's fight against capitalism became especially palpable at its Trade Conference in the form of a special gift from the HO delegation from Leipzig. To display their commitment to their culture of selling (*Verkaufskultur*), the delegation placed lists of their pledges inside model rockets labeled with the names of each HO store.[79] In the decade in which socialist technology was epitomized by the ultimate triumph in the "space war" (the launch of Sputnik), the use of the rocket as a symbol of retailing progress brought consumption into the modern space age. Ulbricht welcomed these rockets as an "expression of great progress."[80] However, rockets in the 1950s were not used just for space exploration but were also weapons for nuclear war. Thus, the HO represented its achievements in creating socialist consumer culture as a threatening attack on capitalism. The HO rockets gave concrete form to Ulbricht's threat to overtake the West in consumption. The juxtaposition of commodities and rockets at the GDR Trade Conference was in effect like a reworking of Kruschchev's famous phrase to say "we will bury you" with our "1000 little things."

The GDR's initiatives to improve and modernize consumption at the end of the decade aimed to show that prosperity had indeed arrived in a way that was, if less dazzling than in the West, at least more honest and less exploitative than capitalism. However, the trumpeting of GDR successes set a standard of achievement that put the regime in a difficult position since the juxtaposition of abundant displays and bold promises with concomitant economic failings made the discrepancy between promise and reality increasingly glaring, especially with the West next door. A sign that GDR citizens were perhaps no longer as content with the idea of laborious sacrifice and delayed gratification was the proliferation of illegal forms of consumption. East German consumers took part in a wide variety of informal networks of distribution, including smuggling goods from the West. Some people smuggled western commodities such as televisions via subway, streetcar, or private car for private use or resale.[81]

Popular recognition of this gap between promise and reality was expressed more severely in the massive flight from the GDR to the West, which increased in 1959 and 1960. Between 1949 and 1961 reportedly 2.6 million people left East Germany for the West.[82] This exodus was only stemmed by the construction of the Berlin Wall in August 1961.

The flight to the West showed how by promising consumer abundance, the GDR mobilized desires for material satisfaction that it could not fully satisfy. Like their desires, the population itself could not be contained until the Berlin Wall penned them in by force. The building of the wall signified the failure of the project of constructing the 1950s as a period of suspension between pain and prosperity. Instead, it became increasingly evident that the 1950s were in fact the foundational moment of the GDR, not a moment of crisis but rather the actual character of the regime. In other words, the future was now and the life of the regime would continue to be plagued by shortages and contradictions. The presence of the West directly across the border heightened this sense of the GDR's shortcomings.

Abandoning Utopia? The Lingering Shadow of Pain in the Era of Prosperity

The popular flight from the GDR and its termination with the erection of the wall became a sign that the population could no longer sustain the fantasy that life in the GDR was a suspension of time between pain and prosperity in the 1950s. The promise of prosperity had raised expectations for a better standard of living under socialism that could not be fully met. The display of GDR successes, such as those in the Trade Conference, were increasingly revealed to be a Potemkin Village of sorts, a façade behind which hid the true reality of the GDR: the utopia of equality and abundance would remain mostly illusory. Michael Burawoy and Janos Lukacs describes this paradox of socialism by suggesting that workers were exhorted to "build socialism" but ended up "painting socialism" to maintain the appearance of utopia:

> By its own logic, building socialism turns into its painting, reminding all of the gap between what is and what should be, deepening the critical consciousness of workers and managers alike. . . . Ironically, in the name of uniting appearance and reality, state socialism digs an unbridgeable chasm between the two, inciting workers to recognize how the world could be but isn't.[83]

By the end of the 1950s this logic of painting socialism had become more evident to the population, particularly because of the presence of the capitalist German state directly across the border.

Therefore, the greatest pain of the 1950s was perhaps the loss of idealism entailed in the unmasking of the GDR's self-generated mythology of suspended time. East Germans were confronted with the reality that, contrary to the promises of the regime, not only had they failed to escape a context of pain, but the standards of prosperity available by that time could not surpass those of the West. Continuing shortages and a hierarchy of consumer opportunities would not be a characteristic of the preutopian purgatory but would continue to plague the GDR throughout its history.[84]

This is not to say that prosperity was not enjoyed in the GDR on some level. Ironically, the construction of the wall enabled the salad days of GDR prosperity to flourish in the 1960s. Ulbricht's regime ushered in a so-called New Economic System in 1965 to experiment with a mixture of market forces and socialist planning in order to enable greater levels of consumption. For this reason, historians have focused their study of the consumption in the GDR primarily on the 1960s.[85]

In the optimistic 1950s, the dialectical opposition of pain and prosperity implied an ability to progress from one to the other. In the 1950s, when neither of these so-called poles of experience was available, the maintenance of this opposition relied on the idea of living for the future rather than in the present crossover period. However, the continuing problems reaching the goal of prosperity by the end of the decade collapsed this myth of living for the future. The building of the wall represented a revelation that GDR citizens could not expect to keep waiting for imminent utopia, but that they would have to start living in the present-day "real existing socialism." And the dialectical opposition of pain and prosperity gave way to the coming to terms with a situation in which relative prosperity arrived still embedded in the pain of recognition that the utopian quality of German state socialism was ultimately incomplete. Rather than achieving desired prosperity for all, the population would face continuation of inconsistent provisions and consumer hierarchies, which had burdened consumers in the 1940s. These continuities with the rationing period also laid bare the wider continuities with the Nazi period itself, so that the legacy of war and the burden of guilt could not be erased from memory. Finally, the Berlin Wall itself embodied the painful nature of GDR society. It was the ultimate cynical representation of the failures of the utopian vision. Even though society prospered behind the wall, its presence would be a constant reminder of the legacy of pain overshadowing GDR society.

8   INGRID M. SCHENK

Scarcity and Success: The East According to the West During the 1950s

AT the end of the Second World War, Germany lay in ruins. In Berlin, it was estimated that the removal of rubble "would require sixteen years with ten trains of fifty cars operating daily."[1] One eyewitness account described postwar Germany as a "country without mail or telephone services; 754 sunken barges . . . choked navigation on the Rhine; 885 railroad bridges dangled meaningless[ly] across spanless voids. . . . in the American [Z]one only 1,200 factories out of 12,000 still worked."[2] With the cessation of hostilities, those still living shifted their energies from surviving the war to the difficult work of regaining the life they remembered during peacetime. For all the residents of occupied Germany, finding adequate food, shelter, and clothing were primary concerns. While the end of the war may have seemed a new beginning, everyday life also went on as it had in terms of cramped quarters, inadequate sanitation, rationing, and black marketeering. In all four zones of occupied Germany, military forces and subsequent civilian governments had to secure basic physical needs for the population. As they did so, the two emerging countries both used the provisioning of the population as a means to underscore an ideological commitment to a new society, one that could be touted as better than its neighbor.

Both German states connected ideology with everyday life when providing opportunities for their residents to fulfill essential needs. The Christian Democrats in West Germany could use the mere suggestion of greater economic planning to imply an immediate and disastrous return to the deprivation experienced before the pivotal June 1948 currency reform. Nevertheless, the Federal Republic's Social Market Economy and the German Democratic Republic's Two- and Five-Year Plans held some assumptions in common. Both states depended on the productivity of workers to secure long-term economic success, and, especially by the early 1960s, both sought to transform those workers to consumers as a sign of progress.

While both German states invested heavily in an idea of progress as it related to the circumstances of everyday life, the West German sense of progress defined itself in large part against developments in East Germany. This sense of progress emphasized the superiority of Western capitalism over Soviet-style planning; a narrative of national identity stressing individual triumphs over collective scarcity emerged amidst ever-improving economic circumstances. Such a formulation of national identity—one based on individual transcendence of postwar scarcity—provided a broad enough umbrella to encompass recent arrivals from the East. Whether they left in 1945, 1948, 1953, or 1961, what made these Easterners into Westerners was that in leaving, they, like their Western counterparts of 1945, made a leap from current confusion and scarcity into an unknown and possibly better future. In addition, the West German state's use of economic progress in order to establish a sense of distance from the immediate postwar past as well as current circumstances in East Germany offered a way to orient residents toward a prosperous future without having to revisit wartime experiences. Nevertheless, relying on socioeconomic conditions to drive patriotic consensus depended on holding together a diffuse and potentially fragile coalition of forces with subtler means than those at the disposal of the German Democratic Republic (GDR).

However, the pen is often mightier than the sword, and reports from the East played a particularly important role in consolidating a West German sense of progress. As early as 1953, the West German press boasted about how far the postwar period of suffering had receded by noting that those conditions still existed in the GDR and motivated emigration. In addition, the West German sense of returning to global prominence not only depended on improved material circumstances for all consumers, but also relied on a particular apportioning of labor within the home. Advertising supportive of the Christian Democrats touted the benefits of Ludwig Erhard's Social Market Economy, depicting contented male wage-earners and their comfortably consuming wives. Since female participation in the West German labor force increased steadily during the 1950s, this advertising was likely more prescriptive than descriptive. Nevertheless, this divergence between image and reality fueled a myth of West German national progress.

From Zero Hour to Day X

As the Second World War ended, the allied powers divided Germany into four zones of occupation: the British administered the northwestern corner, which included the highly industrialized Ruhr Valley; the French administered the southwestern corner closest to France; the United States the midsection and southeastern corner including Frankfurt am Main and Munich; and the Soviets administered what had roughly been the midsection of Germany according to the borders of 1937. Incorporating Easterners into the West and finding a myth of national progress broad enough to include both older and newer citizens necessitated a turn to triumph over deprivation, since this provided a positive alternative to a focus on the pain of wartime destruction and the bonds of blood, territory, and ethnicity behind the National Socialist state.

In the three western zones of occupation, the allied military governments faced the daunting challenge of providing adequate food, clothing, shelter, and access to sanitary water supplies to the defeated population. A commission headed by former United States president Herbert Hoover discovered that only 75 percent of the urban population had shelter. This 75 percent housed the remaining 25 percent who were homeless.[3] Though the popular weekly *Der Spiegel* reported typhus outbreaks in Bavaria as late as July 1948,[4] and though a city official in Düsseldorf estimated that the existing clothing stocks would allow for the next distribution of new underwear to be in twenty-nine years,[5] getting enough to eat remained the most pressing concern. Although ration policies differed among the three western zones, most held onto the ration structure put in place by the National Socialist regime. This structure apportioned rations according to physical needs. For example, after April 1946, the population in the U.S. and British Zones was divided between those who could receive supplements as partially heavy laborers, heavy laborers, heaviest laborers, pregnant and/or nursing mothers, and everyone else—the "normal consumers." Nevertheless, as reported by the *Hamburger Freie Presse* in April 1946, the normal consumer ration in the three zones ranged between 927 and 1,275 calories a day—barely enough to prevent starvation, and in many cases certainly less than half the 2,300 calories per day established by an international nutrition conference as the minimum needed for survival.[6] Charity provided one means of filling the gap. However, despite their broad emotional appeal, only one in 25.5 persons in the western zones of occupation had received a CARE package by 1947.[7] In the absence of satisfactory legal options for obtaining foodstuffs, residents of the western zones turned to barter and black marketeering, as did their eastern counterparts.

While the *Hamburger Freie Presse*'s report assumed that the average caloric intake in the Soviet Zone was as low as in the western zones, it noted that no data was available with which to make a comparison. However, with respect to rationing, the establishment of an ideology compatible with occupation, denazification, and economic reorganization, residents of the Soviet Zone experienced upheavals similar to their western counterparts. Berliners, like other urban dwellers bearing the brunt of destroyed distribution networks, expressed complete dissatisfaction with their rations when surveyed by the U.S. Military Government.[8] Rationing in the Soviet Zone was based on ideological rather than physiological criteria: included in the highest ration category (2,023 daily calories) were the leaders of antifascist party organizations, antifascist artists and poets, as well as the mayors of Dresden and Leipzig. The lowest category (allotted only 1,407 calories per day) included those who ran private businesses, pensioners, invalids, the physically handicapped, former members of National Socialist party organizations, and housewives who were not also employed outside the home.[9] Despite an early influx of Soviet grain, distribution difficulties meant that the actual rations and reported rations often differed dramatically.[10] At least on paper, however, residents of the Soviet Zone were provided with a ration schedule that would guarantee productivity.

In the three western zones, politics and economics were interwoven as tightly as in the Soviet Zone. In many respects, political union in the West proceeded through efforts to link the zones economically. While denazification, democratization, and demilitarization were key goals among all three western zones, the U.S. stance on achieving these ends changed radically between 1945 and 1949. In terms of denazification, U.S. authorities initially determined guilt according to occupational title, but by September 1945 their method of ascertaining guilt shifted to assessing individual beliefs. In addition, denazification efforts varied across the zones, with nearly 90 percent of those in the British Zone classified as "exonerated," and only about a third receiving that designation in the U.S. Zone. Not surprisingly, the unevenness of denazification efforts generated cynicism, and as entrepreneurial expertise became increasingly desired in the late 1940s, former Nazis returned to positions of power and influence. In fact, by the early1950s, Article 131 of the Federal Republic's Basic Law returned former National Socialists to government positions. Democraticization began with the licensing of political parties and campaigns for local elections beginning as early as August 1945, with the Socialist Party (SPD) and the Christian Democratic Union/Christian Social Union (CDU/CSU) emerging as the two largest parties of a plurality. The Liberal Party (FDP), Communist Party, and a special interest party for refugees—the League of Expellees and Disenfranchised (BHE)—completed a variegated political landscape. The heads of the three zonal military governments charged regional leaders to call a constitutional convention in September 1948; the resulting document was named the Basic Law (*Grundgesetz*), rather than the constitution, because a sovereign Germany had not yet signed an official peace with the victors.

Economically, the United States initially favored a harsh peace that would prevent Germany from again becoming a military threat. Echoes of the Morgenthau Plan's effort to return Germany to pasture were evident as late as the March 1946 Level of Industry Plan, which limited German industrial capacity to approximately 50 percent of 1938 levels. However, both U.S. and British officials noted that dismantling operable factories would only contribute to unemployment and thereby irritate a hungry population already dependent on its occupiers' increasingly limited resources. U.S. Secretary of State James F. Byrnes's speech in Stuttgart in September 1946 indicated the first public signal of a change in policy; in order to harness the resources to help Germany help itself, the U.S. and British Zones officially merged into an economic Bizone on January 1, 1947. However, the Bizone's Economic Council served as a quasi-parliamentary body with representation from both zones. Ludwig Erhard's assumption of the leadership of this body in January 1948 sealed a domestic shift toward developing a market allowing industry relatively free reign while balancing competition with a safety net of social welfare programs. Finally, George C. Marshall's announcement of the European Recovery Program at Harvard University's commencement on June 5, 1947, clinched the shift from hard peace to self-help on an international level.

By mid-1948 administrative pressures and the Cold War made it nearly impossible to unify all four zones without one or another of the occupation powers losing face diplomatically or by setting up a potentially fatal disturbance in the European balance of power. The Soviets viewed the decision by the United States and Great Britain to abandon dismantlement in their zones by mid-1946 as a significant violation of the Potsdam Agreement. The creation of the Bizone and the Economic Council also strained relations. To further complicate matters, the French possessed a de facto veto power over decisions regarding occupation policy since they were not bound to the terms of the Potsdam Agreement. Rifts developed early on among the occupied as well. In early 1947, at a meeting of German regional prime ministers, western zone representatives refused to allow Soviet Zone delegates the opportunity to make a prepared statement before the start of the proceedings.[11]

Day X and the Division into Two States

During the late 1940s, Germany was divided more by economics than by politics—more specifically, the dual currency reforms of June 1948. As part of an ongoing reform of the banking system in the Soviet Zone, a revaluation of the reichsmark (RM) at a 10:1 ratio was to go into force on June 21, 1948. This revaluation applied to private savings; the savings of state organizations were converted at a 1:1 ratio. All regional banks were centralized under the Deutsche Notenbank, and the new currency issued in 1948 was officially named the Mark der Deutschen Notenbank (MDN) and popularly known as the Ostmark. The Deutsche Notenbank had full control over production and trade in what would become the GDR. It served as an arm of the state's economic planning efforts, since a business's account at the bank indicated how efficiently it functioned within the framework of a planned economy. If the business made a profit, its bank balance would grow; if it ran a deficit, the balance would decrease.[12]

At approximately the same time that the banking system in the Soviet Zone became integrated into a centrally planned economy, the head of the western zones' Economic Council, Ludwig Erhard, engaged in discussion with the U.S. Military Government regarding the possibility of currency reform in the western zones to soften the effects of black marketeering and encourage legitimate economic development. Though foreign aid might temporarily support the population, the lack of a recognized and reliable means of exchange would greatly inhibit long-term economic recovery and economic growth. The effort to bring in and store the new money in the western zones was code-named "Operation Bird Dog" and proved to be the largest logistical operation faced by the U.S. military since the D-Day landing. In the three western zones, "Bird Dog," launched on "Day X," on June 20, 1948; the western sectors of Berlin were scheduled to receive their new deutsche marks on June 24. For the Soviets, the introduction of a western currency into Berlin precipitated a decisive rupture in four-power relations and necessitated one of the more spectacular episodes in the Cold War: the Berlin Blockade. By the time the Berlin Airlift ended in May 1949, more than 200,000 CARE parcels, 782,000 metric tons of coal, 374,000 metric tons of food, twenty-seven thousand tons of fuel, and eight thousand tons of newspaper had been transported into Berlin. In the course of 275,000 flights, over 2.3 million tons of goods had been brought into the city and forty-eight pilots had given their lives to ensure the operation's success.[13]

Into the Economic Miracle

The arrival of a new currency signaled the start of a new era in the western zones. Before June 1948, cigarettes served as the western zones' unofficial currency. Those who could not trade cigarettes for staples or other needed goods could try the black market, where a kilogram of butter cost at least RM 200, a kilogram of coffee RM 300, and a pair of dress shoes RM 1000–1500. By way of comparison, twenty American cigarettes traded on the Frankfurt am Main black market for RM 91.20. A laborer at a construction site told a reporter for the *Süddeutsche Zeitung* that his weekly wage in August 1947 "amounted to eight American cigarettes."[14] Many people who could not afford to purchase on their local black market went on "hamstering" trips into the countryside, trading family heirlooms for sacks of potatoes and hoping that their "purchases" would not be confiscated by the authorities on their return home. The arrival of a recognized means of exchange gave merchants an incentive to display rather than hoard their wares, and the simultaneous lifting of most ration restrictions provided an even greater boost to retailers. As one eyewitness described it:

Instead of the old junk, instead of ashtrays, lighters, candlesticks, mousetraps and similar things that there had always been enough of even in those years of scarcity, there were [now] cooking pans, bicycles, shoelaces, light bulbs. These were things that one ran in search of from store to store and only futilely; suddenly, everything was available.[15]

Concerns about nothing to buy were soon replaced by not having enough cash in one's wallet to buy what was now available. Ludwig Erhard responded to one American official's concern about loosening ration restrictions: "Henceforth, the only rationing ticket the people will need will be the deutschemark [*sic*]. And they will work hard to get these deutschemarks, just wait and see."[16] Yet the currency reform made it difficult for workers to make ends meet. One housewife with two school-age children told an interviewer, "If one really thinks about it, I can't afford the tasty new potatoes. But Mr. Schäfer [her husband] simply has to eat something after standing around at work for eight hours."[17]

The currency reform in the western zones (as was the case in the Soviet Zone) privileged owners of real estate over wage earners and those living on fixed incomes.[18] While bank balances up to RM 5000 were converted at a 10:1 rate, wages and rents carried over 1:1. Real estate values remained constant. Since wages remained frozen until November 1948 and prices continued to rise, most workers who remained employed found it difficult to purchase what they needed on a wage that bought less and less. A general strike was called for November 12, 1948, to protest the gap between wages and prices, to support the reintroduction of rationing, and to encourage the prosecution of tax evaders. Despite the doubling of unemployment between June 1948 and January 1949, popular discontent did not translate into major changes in price or ration policy in the western zones. Yet until the boom created by the outbreak of the Korean War in June 1950 and a simultaneous easing of import/export credit, the economic and political success of the western German currency reform remained uncertain. After that point, however, the West German Economic Miracle pushed postwar uncertainty and instability far into the past.

Building support for a burgeoning marketplace, even when one's choices within it might still be quite limited, became a key concern for authorities in the three western zones, soon to become the Federal Republic of Germany (FRG). Even before the zones emerged as separate nations with differing governmental structures in 1949, comparisons based on the distance from a past marked by scarcity provided a political shorthand with which to normatively distinguish West from East. The persistence of rationing, scarcity, and black marketeering in the Soviet Zone provided a foil for any complaints about the current situation in the West. A correspondent from the *Süddeutsche Zeitung* who reported on Leipzig's 1948 Trade Fair in 1948 noted, "The store windows in Leipzig after the Eastern currency reform look like those in Munich before the 20th of June . . . one cannot buy anything useful and the black market thrives with nearly unchanged prices. Textiles and shoes are to be had only with ration cards, with which the authorities are extremely stingy."[19] There was no immediate change in the East that occurred with the introduction of its new currency, and the perception that life stood still was further reinforced by casual conversation. At the 1948 Leipzig Trade Fair, a reporter from the West noted, "As a Trade Fair visitor . . . one was always asked if 'over there' it was really the case that normal consumers received 500 grams of fat and three pounds of sugar per month, and if it was in fact possible to purchase potatoes, vegetables, and fruit at other than black market prices."[20] The reporter underscored his assertion that life in the East remained as it had been in the West where "the insufficient provisions drive [people] to hoarding. Therefore the trains to neighboring Sachsen-Anhalt, where more vegetables are available, are as overfilled as ours before the currency reform."[21] In addition to front yards still filled with vegetables and windows still missing glass, the persistence of the black market, hoarding, and rationing in the East underscored their comparative absence in the West. Thus, the West's claim that a market offering provision for all, variety for most, and luxury for some proved especially convincing when compared with a system in which supposedly guaranteed norms could only be met illegally.

These differences escalated by early 1949. *Quick*'s issue of January 9, 1949, contained a photo essay with commentary illustrating the divisions between East and West, even as it attempted a dialog between the zones. A photographer from the Soviet Zone had been contracted "to photograph what struck him and provoked his criticism. Here are his most interesting pictures."[22] Although "We Don't Have this at Home" included gripes about the price of a Christmas goose and illustrated a begging war veteran ignored by well-dressed and well-fed passersby,[23] this photo essay generally expressed wonderment at the material situation of the British and U.S. Zones. For example, store windows were filled with shoes for the unbelievable price of DM 22. Even though the West German public would pass over similar shoes for more stylish offerings just nine months later,[24] their appearance in store windows at the end of 1948 would have made the eastern photographer's acquaintances back home green with envy.[25] The variety offered at the newsstand was even more significant. As the photographer observed, "The abundance of papers from all parts of Germany and the world is stunning. Back home the voice of the world is muted. . . . When one travels from the Kurfürstendamm to the Alexanderplatz in Berlin one cannot but notice the difference."[26] This was a difference highlighting how freedom in the marketplace could translate into societal freedom and therefore reinforce a sense of zonal or national superiority.

In the West German marketplace, eastern shortcomings often served as a baseline for comparison. Similarities between the current situation in the East and western experiences of deprivation before 1948 reinforced a national narrative of progress tied to the distance, either geographical or temporal, from scarcity. That the East was like the western past was hammered home in a series of advertisements appearing in the West German popular press during the early 1950s. Paid for by an association sympathetic to Erhard's economic policy, these advertisements highlighted the superiority of variety and ambition over regulation and security, and thereby cemented the connection between Erhard's Social Market Economy and national superiority. In these advertisements, two working-class fellows discussed the benefits of the Social Market Economy in various leisure settings. While fishing one day, Fritz and Otto debated the pros and cons of a planned economy:

> *Otto:* If we have the money to buy something.
>
> *Fritz:* That is the case in every sort of economy, only those who have money can buy—only those who earn can spend.
>
> *Otto:* But in the socialistic planned economy the state dictates the prices, then you can buy . . .
>
> *Fritz:* What's been allotted to you from above—and that is little and worthless. And what you can buy without restrictions is sinfully expensive.[27]

Interesting here is the elision between quality and quantity. Rather than mentioning that price controls might be a good thing for certain items,[28] Fritz interprets the issue of planned pricing as general economic planning. He then stresses how a planned economy creates undesirable shortages of unwanted goods on the one hand, while fostering the inequality of an alternative market system (either black-, barter-, or for hard western currency) on the other. Those who can pay outrageous sums can get around the restrictions planned for all.

Crucial in Fritz's interpretation is his all-or-nothing approach toward planning and/or price controls. This elision among planning, distribution, and the superiority of the West German socioeconomic system is driven home as Fritz continued, "Otto we've already experienced this. Think about the time before 1948." Otto responded, "Yes, yes, my wife had to strip our home of many fine things in order to satisfy the children's hunger."[29] This comparison of the West before 1948 and an image of the East as of July 1953 (when this advertisement ran) shows how closely the advertisers intended market choice and national progress to be equated in the minds of West Germans. Perhaps the Social Market Economy may have necessitated delayed gratification, but the justification—only those who can pay get the goods, regardless—pointed to the hypocrisy behind the supposed equality in a socialist planned economy.

Though supporters of Erhard's Social Market Economy used the threat of a return to the deprivation of the immediate postwar period or invoked hardships of a planned economy as they currently existed in the GDR, the Social Market Economy's focus on private ownership coupled with minimal state control did not initially receive a universal welcome. As Erhard had quipped, the deutsche mark became the yardstick according to which workers measured their ability to secure basic needs and to dream about future luxuries. As was the case with rations for coal miners in the period before the June 1948 currency reform, prices became a point of contention afterward. While miners struck in 1947 to protest the lack of food, by November 1948 a key concern for all industries was the gap between frozen wages and rapidly rising prices for food and clothing. By the end of 1948, 5.3 percent of the West German labor force was unemployed, with unemployment escalating to 12.2 percent by 1950.[30] However, most jobs lost were in low productivity sectors of the economy such as agriculture and forestry; employment in manufacturing and construction actually increased. Since codetermination policies had been in place in the mining industry as early as 1946,[31] workers in key heavy industries would play a role in their enterprises' affairs, especially after the passage of the 1951 Codetermination Law. While certain workers would play an important role in the management of their firms, at the same time the ever-increasing labor pool made it unlikely that workers would be able to effect price restrictions or reductions through punitive union actions. Whether pushed by instability or pulled by the lure of building a new life, West German workers toiled long hours even after full employment had been reached. As late as 1957 less than a third of workers in the FRG worked a five-day week.[32] However, those long hours at the end of the 1950s meant leaps in familial standards of living, as greater numbers of West German households found television sets and automobiles within their reach.

If the November 1948 general strike had been a brief but serious expression of worker discontent in West Germany, the uprising of June 17, 1953 in the GDR illustrated even greater dissatisfaction with increased production demands. Without any advance notice or discussion, workers at the Stalinallee housing development site were told that the amount of sweat equity needed to make them eligible for a state-subsidized apartment would increase substantially. Though around 6 percent of all East German workers went on strike on June 17, 1953, their spontaneous expressions of discontent were not organized enough to counter a governmental display of force backed by Soviet troops. Walther Ulbricht thus received an opportunity to solidify his control of East Germany by purging any government officials who were perceived to have contributed to the uprising. Those discontented by the hard-line crackdown as well as those displaced by greater state planning of individual enterprises and the collectivization of agriculture streamed out of the GDR through the border in Berlin. By the end of 1953, over 330,000 refugees had fled the GDR.[33] If workers in the FRG remained skeptical about their government's management of the economy, those concerns were put in perspective by comparing hardships with their neighbors in the East. The presence of another wave of refugees underscored how individual triumphs over pain and scarcity could, when taken collectively, provide a basis for a national narrative of triumph over the past while omitting an examination of issues of wartime actions and responsibility.

By 1953, things taken for granted or within easy reach in West Germany underscored the distance between the present and the past—which lay five years behind, or a few hundred kilometers east. Two months before the appearance of Fritz and Otto's conversation about the differences between planned and Social Market Economies, an article in *Süddeutsche Zeitung* announced, "Carrots are a Rarity in Leipzig," and quoted a nineteen-year-old refugee: "[W]hy we fled? Because there was no more grub for us." Since his father had been a craftsman and had privately sold some of the wares he produced, the entire family had been stripped of their ration cards. The article estimated that about 14 percent of the population in the area would have been similarly affected. Obviously, this situation had a profound impact on the family's everyday life. "The ration cards were taken away from us and [our] money wasn't enough to buy in the HO shops, and over in the state shops there has been neither butter nor margarine for months, no oil, and lard only very rarely. For us it is worse than in 1945."[34]

For western readers, this account of the disruption of this family's occupational life emphasized three key points of contrast between West and East. First, the arbitrariness of the East German government's administration in stripping such workers of their ration cards. Second, ration cards were still used in the East and essential for many who could not make purchases in cash (and even in that case, elite stores still did not always stock essentials). Third, life in East Germany now was worse than at the end of the war—in some respects, the "future" did not start until this family had moved westward. Here again, West German readers could feel confident that their government provided a better life for its citizens than did that of the GDR: rationing no longer existed, only one relatively transparent market offered a wide range of goods for sale, the government supported entrepreneurial ventures, and the continuity of a family's occupational identity usually remained intact. Just as rationing was seen by readers in the Federal Republic to be a sign of the immediate postwar past, so was governmentally sanctioned black marketeering as well as arbitrary governmental control over the livelihoods of business owners.

Not only could West Germans feel confident that they had progressed while East Germans had not, but with the influx of refugees, particularly in 1953, West Germans could play the role held by affluent occupiers just eight years earlier. Again, West German progress was expressed not only in terms of triumph over the past but in terms of the preservation of a harmonious and happy family life. For example, an article in *Stern*, a popular West German newsweekly, described the circumstances of a recent arrival: "At home, that is, over in the East Zone, her mother could never give her enough to eat. Here in the camp, for the first time in her life, Helga had an orange and a proper bar of chocolate."[35] Though the article painted a picture of success, it asked, "Who will help the other children?"[36]

In detailing the disruption of "normal" family life, especially a normal childhood, this article stressed that having a comfortable home and a childhood filled with sunshine, dolls, and new clothing were part of the pattern of life now common in the West and impossible in the East. Refugees had to leave their homes

under cover of night and fog, leaving the pot on the still-warm stove, and in a stolen nighttime hour, sneaking through the familiar streets like criminals. [F]or all of them the [refugee] camp is the great basin of their hopes. We do not wish to ask why thousands come over every day, whether they are in danger for their safety or their person, or whether they want to participate in the better life here with us in the West, a life in freedom, fearlessness, and peace.[37]

Life in East Germany precluded the safety, security and normality of life in West Germany. West German children had no difficulty finding a warm, sunny spot to recover from an illness; West German families were not driven from warm stoves and familiar streets to secure their basic needs. What the refugees did not possess stressed the superiority of life where they chose to resettle.

Not only did refugees find themselves unable to provide for basic physical needs, they also lacked material comforts that encouraged the emotional responses that were an integral part of everyday life in the West. Such a transformation overcame Gisela, a girl who had arrived in the camp with double pneumonia. As she unpacked the boxes containing a new doll, a teddy bear, and new clothes, Gisela's "serious, sad face began to melt . . . and [then] what no one thought possible [happened]: she could smile again!"[38] The planned economy and her flight from it had left Gisela without the material sources of childhood joy. Just in time for the 1952 Christmas shopping season, *Stern* carried a cartoon feature offering a particularly scathing indictment of the East German economic and political system in the form of an imaginary "SED Toy Catalog." This included a sketch of a red-cheeked doll with a ribbon in her hair with the caption "Character doll Anni, talks, 54 cm tall, real hair." The doll was labeled "no longer available." Next to her, the same doll, without a head, was captioned "'Anna Pauker' doll, characterless, mute, one head shorter." It bore the label "New!"[39] A music box containing trumpeting angels accompanied by floral decoration underwent a similar transformation. The new version, labeled "Party Purge," held four hanging figures on a gallows.[40] Finally, even the stereotypically German garden dwarf had been reformed from a reclining, smiling figure to a wind-up, multiple armed and legged "Movable Garden Functionary, Model 'Aktivist': progressive, ambitious, constructive, [and] colorfast."[41]

If the planned economy depressed children, the West German popular press also portrayed it as degrading women. For example, a West German advertisement published in 1951 showed a rough sketch of a woman holding a pickaxe in a tunnel seated next to a cart of coal. It read, "In the Soviet Zone: 137,900 women in hard labor, 27,100 female coal miners. " The advertisement concluded, "Grotewohl [the GDR's prime minister] calls this equality of the sexes."[42] This particularly stark example highlighted the debate about appropriate jobs for women in the West German workforce by presenting a job clearly beyond the pale of acceptability and reinforcing the contention that the planned economy corrupted family life.[43] Women should be busying themselves in the home, or possibly in part-time white-collar positions rather than working in heavy industry or as functionaries of the state.[44] Women should also be spared the difficulty of long journeys and harassment of border guards in order to secure necessities for their families. Just such a tale was told in July 1953 of Frau B., who had traveled from the surrounding countryside into West Berlin to obtain a relief package. She "was not to be trifled with." In fact, "if someone wanted to take away the lard, cans of milk, flour, or white beans [that] she haul[ed] home for her children, [then] the fearless courage and new sense of self-awareness that almost all occupants of the Soviet Zone have felt since the 17th of June would probably give her arm the needed strength."[45] If cartoons and stories about refugee children may have attempted to reassure westerners of their superiority, the difference between West and East was also more boldly reflected in Frau B.'s grim determination. Here remained the woman, like so many women in West Germany, who braved checkpoints between 1945 and 1948 in order to bring home what was needed to feed her children. Traveling to the West to pick up relief packages may have involved risk, but it was also a practical and economical way to get what was necessary. Again, the role of refugees, particularly women forced beyond their homes for their family's sake, highlighted how a West German national narrative of belonging through economic opportunity (here translated into familial support) could pull together a diverse constituency with a positive focus.

If the *Süddeutsche Zeitung* described how "A Box of Lard is Worth a Day Trip" on page three of its July 28, 1953, issue, noting that "up to this time, 1600 [persons] have already received their boxes of lard, their four cans of condensed milk, their kilo of flour, and their pound of peas,"[46] page four told a very different story. "Even in the early morning hours, eager shoppers streamed into the department stores—many came on the first suburban train and with suitcases and backpacks."[47] These shoppers were determined to take advantage of that Never-Never Land for those eager to buy—Munich's summer closeout sales. When lines appeared in front of Munich stores in July 1953, it was because the stores were closed for lunch. At one point, "early in the morning, the rush on one clothing store was already so great that emergency exits had to be opened in order to facilitate the business's normal operation."[48]

Travelers seeking goods in both German states sought to make the most of opportunities that were available to them, but it was precisely the difference in opportunities that fueled comparisons of supremacy based on standards of living. Since these material standards were also linked to overcoming experiences rooted in the recent past, they became not only the yardstick by which current superiority was justified, but also measured the distance from a past when such deprivations had been commonplace. The race to summer sales rather than a journey for staples illustrated the distance between recent past and possible future for West Germans. However, that residents in both German states raced to acquire very different sorts of necessities illustrates that the impulse to overcome deprivation, present or past, remained an important drive during the 1950s, and one that played a pivotal role in national comparisons.

The Berlin Wall and
Escalation of East/West Comparisons

During the late 1950s the question of who did and who should control Berlin returned to the foreground of Cold War diplomacy. After Nikita Khrushchev announced that control of the entire city would be given to the GDR, a series of conferences failed to decisively resolve the issue of a change in the city's administration. In the summer of 1961 subway and train service in Berlin had been interrupted as part of an effort to stem the tide of those leaving East Germany by entering West Berlin. However, few expected the decisive rupture that came on Sunday, August 13, 1961. Marshall Dill describes a conversation between two men in a West Berlin bar on the evening of Saturday, August 12th. One man (who lived and worked in West Berlin) pleaded with his companion (who worked in West Berlin but lived in East Berlin) to move to West Berlin. At the very least he should stay in West Berlin that evening since he had already had too much to drink to get home safely. As Dill puts it, "If the invitation was accepted that youth woke up with only the clothes he had on, his job, and a chance to make a new life in the West; if not he woke up with his possessions, no job, and an indefinite span of years ahead of him in Ulbricht Germany."[49] Such was the swiftness with which the gateway between the two states closed.

While two separate German states had existed since 1949, the construction of the Berlin Wall meant that West Germany could no longer count on a steady stream of refugees to provide eyewitness accounts of ongoing deprivation or infringement of civil liberties. Nor could East Germany ignore the demands of a population no longer able to express extreme discontent by emigrating west. Though material circumstances in GDR improved steadily during the 1960s, the role of the planned economy in providing a comparatively comfortable standard of living remained a contentious point of comparison for the West German media, but with new criteria. Instead of carrots or cans of beans, now cars and television sets served as the yardsticks for measuring progress.

By 1963, assertions of western superiority made during the late 1940s and 1950s had solidified into comparisons connecting living standards with freedom of expression and freedom from interference in familial life.

By the 1960s competition between East and West had accelerated into questions of relative deprivation with consumer goods and lifestyles as the criteria for comparison. To take one brief example from the popular West German press, *Stern* included a feature about women in Czechoslovakia, juxtaposing a large photograph of four women in elegant dresses with a smaller one of a woman in a gatekeeper's uniform and explaining, "nearly all women in Czechoslovakia have to work." This was the case since "male income only covers food and rent—not beautiful dresses, not [a] television, and definitely not an automobile."[50] The assumptions implicit here—that the husband's income could support luxuries such as fashionable dresses, televisions, and car payments stressed the superiority of the West German wage structure. Even in the "Red East's Golden West," these women, one of whom was married to a doctor, were glad to be earning extra money as models. Posing in the garden of the Wallenstein palace was "a welcome second job." Czech women also worked as functionaries of the state, sweeping Wenceslas Square and working as gatekeepers; others worked as lathe operators.[51] Not only were these jobs a strain on the women, the article described their negative impact on family life. For example, "Many of them work too hard. The children are cared for in state-run homes. Therefore, the families are only united during the evening and on weekends."[52] Here again, the theme of the planned economy and its toll on private life is stressed to highlight the comfort offered by the West. Not only are luxuries necessities in the West, but, most importantly, the West German Social Market Economy allowed families to remain together without the direct interference of the state in child rearing.

Access to opportunities and a lack of direct interference in family life were especially important points, since it was not always the case in West German households that the husband's income alone could cover necessities and the acquisition of consumer durables such as televisions, refrigerators, and possibly automobiles. In many two-parent households (to say nothing of homes headed by single women) the acquisition of consumer goods was possible only with the second income of a wife working at least part time.[53] In fact, the percentage of married women who worked in the Federal Republic rose from 26.4 percent in 1950 to 36.5 percent by 1961.[54] Using the East bloc to reflect the horrors of state intervention in the economy and in family life ironically highlighted parallels in the reconstruction of both East and West Germany. However ambivalent they felt about working outside the home, many married women in the FRG saw their wages as essential contributions to the family's progress, especially to afford "luxury goods" like washing machines and radios.[55] In this respect, the drive to succeed could sustain those not yet having reached affluence just as comparisons of the hopelessly behind (and potentially dangerous) East bloc could reinforce a sense of superior difference.

Conclusion

Though both the western and eastern zones of occupied Germany experienced a period of deprivation after the Second World War, in the West, the currency reform of June 20, 1948, transformed want into desire, deprivation into possibility. This is not to say the FRG's early years passed without trouble—the conversion of wages and rents at a 1:1 rate while savings were converted at a 10:1 rate left many working-class families at a disadvantage. Despite the general strike of November 1948, and though there was tension until the outbreak of hostilities in Korea in 1950, neither collapse nor severe crisis threatened the stability of the FRG during the 1950s. The continuous stream of refugees from East Germany during the late 1940s and early 1950s reinforced claims of the Social Market Economy's superiority, since it was difficult to argue with success when regularly confronted with the very real consequences of failure. Not only did the refugees strengthen assertions about the majority CDU/CSU economic and political policies, but they also fortified a sense of progress at the core of West German identity. Since rationing and deprivation no longer existed in the West, the state had moved forward, and it could be described as progressive. While those conditions persisted in East Germany, that state remained in the past, providing a convenient foil against which West German claims of superiority could be gauged. Yet by the 1960s, material conditions in the East had improved to the point where one journalist commented, "The people over there were not only well-nourished, but that they were, indeed, grossly overfed."[56]

Since basic material comparisons would no longer prove persuasive, the criteria for western declarations of progress shifted: wives at home, television sets, fashionable clothing. Luxuries may have become necessities by the 1960s, but the ease or difficulty of their acquisition remained a theme of critique, as did the influence of planned economies on family life. Closely interleaved with the better opportunities offered in the West's freer marketplace were all the intangible benefits promised by life in the West. Included among these was the support for an updated version of the traditional division between public and private spheres: men earned the family's income in the public sphere, while women managed the monetary and emotional needs within the private sphere of the home. The interference of the state in the life of the family was one particularly sore point often exploited in East/West comparisons, yet the market made its influence felt in patterns of courtship, marriage, and family life in the West during the 1960s as the percentage of married female workers in the West German labor force increased steadily. This increase may have prompted a look toward the East, where conditions were comparatively dire.

Looking backward from the perspective of 1989 and beyond, East and West Germany emerge as undeniably different, yet one can now compare two seemingly different cases of individuals attempting to realize a state ethic in their daily lives. In the one case, an ethic mandated politically and backed by coercion when necessary; in the other, an ethic reinforced through socioeconomic norms and societal expectations. It may well be that these two situations have more compelling similarities at the level of everyday life than the differences held up by their respective Cold War media to stress a sense of national difference and superiority. Paradoxically, the most compelling factor reinforcing a sense of division between the two German states during the Cold War was that they both transformed postwar scarcity into abundance, but that they did the same thing so differently.

9 PAUL BETTS

Remembrance of Things Past: Nostalgia in West and East Germany, 1980–2000

EVER since Reunification, there has been a great deal of international discussion about the meaning of Germany's transformed political presence. Its new status within the North Atlantic Treaty Organization (NATO), the European Union, and post–Cold War Europe more generally has continued to generate passionate debate on both sides of the Atlantic. While Germany's present and future have been the subject of intense scrutiny and speculation, so too has its past. In many ways this was a predictable by-product of the *Wende*, or political turn, itself, which abruptly released German history from its Cold War confines. Practically overnight the whole postwar era was summarily shuttled off to the museum, rendering instantly obsolete the woolly political logic long used to explain the historical peculiarities of a divided nation. No sooner had the Berlin Wall been dismantled than new assessments of the German past, be they the legacies of the Third Reich, Holocaust, and most notably the German Democratic Republic (GDR) itself, were redrawn from fresh post–Cold War perspectives. But despite initial apprehension about a brown specter rehaunting German culture and historiography, post-1989 histories thus far have not invoked the past to underwrite new nationalist politics. No one would deny that a "renationalization" of German history writing has taken place, but it has gained little appeal beyond a limited circle of conservative academics. In part this has to do with the fact that constructing a new German national identity is still confounded (for many, thankfully so) by the Nazi and Cold War legacies. The difficulty for post-Reunification Germans of articulating a new vocabulary of political collectivity, social solidarity, and "enlightened" patriotism beyond the shadows of Hitler and Auschwitz underscores this point.[1] Equally important is the seemingly insurmountable antagonism between *Wessis* and *Ossis* that has plagued German-German relations since the heady days of 1989, making it quite plain that there is little national unity to affirm and celebrate. So intractable has been this mental Berlin Wall that most German histories written after 1989 have dispensed altogether with myths of common culture and national solidarity in favor of addressing the more pressing issue at hand, namely the roots of German-German difference.

Such a political change of focus has also been accompanied by a shift in methodology. To best analyze the origins of these nettlesome differences, scholars have devoted considerable attention to studying the very incongruity of history and memory during the Cold War. Often this has meant peeling back the accumulated layers of political propaganda and Cold War clichés in order to explore how individual and collective identities were shaped by postwar experiences. New oral histories together with a batch of innovative case studies of public commemorations, everyday cultures, and private recollections of the postwar era have sharply exposed the artifice behind the periodizations and platitudes of old. A good deal of the new scholarship has unsurprisingly concentrated upon the transformations and traumas of former GDR citizens.[2] Not that this impulse to focus on personal histories is simply the offspring of Reunification: It owes its inspiration to the two decade-old work of West Germany's pioneering "historians of everyday life," who were the first to troll the netherworld of private German memories (usually through oral history) beneath the faceless generalizations of traditional social history.[3] Still, there is no question that the last decade has witnessed an impressive output of new histories of Cold War Germany, the effect of which has been to push the German past to the center of cutting-edge historical anthropology and postmodern cultural studies.

But in view of growing scholarly interest in the interface of German history and memory, it is curious that the subject of nostalgia has curried relatively scant attention. This is all the more perplexing, not least because memory and nostalgia are plainly kindred spirits. New studies of the German past (apart from occasional remarks about post-Wall East German *Ostalgie*, or nostalgia, as we shall see) have nonetheless ignored it as a serious avenue of inquiry. What of course separates nostalgia from memory (and even more so from history proper) is the specific relationship between historical subject and object. It is worth recalling that nostalgia is etymologically defined as the "painful longing for home," underscoring the extent to which its condition is born of displacement and exile. While its first real cultural expression arguably can be traced back to *The Odyssey*, modern nostalgia first emerged in the mid-seventeenth century as a newly named medical pathology used to diagnose those suffering from the psychological anguish of being away from one's homeland. Originally it mostly referred to the classification and treatment of homesick Swiss mercenaries, which accounts for nostalgia's more popular assignation as the "Swiss disease." With time the term broadened considerably. During the Napoleonic wars, for example, French soldiers commonly used the term *nostalgie* to describe their chronic separation anxiety.[4] Over the course of the 18th and 19th centuries nostalgia was further expanded to include all of those abroad pining for home.[5] In its new rendering, it no longer was understood as only a symptom of restive homesickness; what increasingly distinguished nostalgia was the compulsive desire to overcome such alienation. It is precisely this element that forever links modern nostalgia to nineteenth-century romanticism. Not only did this marriage shift the focus of such estrangement from space (geographical remove) to time (lost historical eras and experiences), disaffected literati replaced soldiers as the new subjects of afflicted passion, with the consequence that nostalgia was no longer defined as a medical condition, but instead emerged as a new cultural language of loss and longing. For this reason the nineteenth century was the real crucible for modern nostalgia; it provided a cultural compass for many Europeans ravaged by the twin forces of the French and Industrial Revolutions.[6]

Germany naturally played host to a great deal of this romantic nostalgia. Given that both revolutions arrived so suddenly there, tearing asunder native traditions of political and economic life, Germany became and remained fertile soil for sundry nostalgic fantasies and romantic dreamworlds right up to the first half of the twentieth century. The longing for a lost agrarian *Volkskultur* in the aftermath of the 1871 unification; the fin de siècle nostalgia for classical culture; the cult of Frederick the Great and the backward glances toward Wilhelmine propriety during the Weimar Republic; as well as the Third Reich's (albeit contradictory) cultural desire for Teutonic idylls, preindustrial peasant folkways and above all the "front experience" of the "nation in the trenches" were among its most visible manifestations. What is so striking, however, is the relative absence of such nostalgia after 1945. True, each German republic devoted considerable cultural energy to reviving *Goethezeit* humanism as post-Nazi cultural ballast during the 1950s, and there were many rosy West German recollections about the Weimar Republic through the 1960s. Perhaps one could make the case that 1950s *Heimat* films, the postwar reconstruction of traditional building and city squares after 1945 as if the war never happened, and the 1970s rehashing of the glories of 1968 were also examples of postwar cultural longing for romanticized pasts.[7] Nevertheless, there is no denying that the post-1945 production of German nostalgia paled markedly in comparison to that in the first half of the century. Certainly this was evident in West German politics and culture; even the term *nostalgia* was dropped from West German encyclopedias during the 1950s and 1960s, only to be reinstated as a worthy entry in the mid-1970s. This sort of sentiment was all the more pronounced in East Germany, as the ruling Socialist Unity Party (SED) officially denounced backward-looking nostalgia as crass capitalist decadence and ideological cowardice in the face of the iron laws of Marxist historical progress. In both countries, the cultural enunciation of nostalgia practically disappeared until the 1970s.[8]

One obvious explanation lies in the Nazi legacy itself. The hardships, trauma, and subsequent revelations about the unparalleled atrocities committed by the Third Reich certainly killed off sentimental recuperation of Germany's immediate past; the overriding concern for both states (to say nothings of its citizens) was to establish as much distance as possible from the Nazi years. Not that all Germans yearned for a complete break with the pre-1945 past. Poll results as late as 1954, for instance, revealed that a good percentage of West Germans still harbored fond passions for the pre-war Nazi years.[9] The point, however, is that nostalgia enjoyed no real collective expression; indeed, it was precisely such nostalgia that was targeted for "reeducation" in both Germanys. As Charles Maier suggestively put it, "The point is that until 1989, postwar German history had to be a process of learning how not to long."[10] In a context in which most German national traditions and symbols were irreparably contaminated by Nazi association, the recovery of shared German pasts was often muted and made suspect. Geopolitical division and the onset of the Cold War only intensified German alienation from its history. The rash of West German Zero Hour proclamations perfectly expressed the strong disinclination toward looking to the past as inspiration and guidance; so did the Cold War revision of the famed "special path" thesis of German history, in which interwar pride in German cultural uniqueness was rewritten as pathological deviation from Western norms and ideals.[11] The present, so went the logic, was the long-needed rupture from a barbarous past. East Germany followed suit, constructing its founding national myth upon the triumph of the "worker state" and a clean break from the murderous domination of "monopoly capitalists." In each case, history no longer tethered German past and present. Instead, both German polities were recast as set pieces within larger rival stories of international modernism, for example, American-style liberalism or Soviet socialism. The upshot of which was that each republic became officially forward-looking, paying at best selective attention to certain cultural heroes and shining moments from the pre-1933 past. Only the victims of German history (and often from abroad) openly engaged in such nostalgic memory-work.[12] So even if history was regularly invoked in both Germanys as a source of Cold War justification and negative identity, it did not serve as a vehicle of collective longing and desire. Nation and nostalgia were officially divorced.

But this is not to say that nostalgia never surfaced after 1945. Yet it did so much later and in peculiar ways. There were two important popular manifestations of postwar German nostalgia: the West German longing for the "Golden 1950s" during the late 1970s and early 1980s, and East Germany's post-1989 *Ostalgie* for the comfort and security of the old German Democratic Republic. Common to both was/is the impulse to assuage the perceived pains of the present through romanticizing earlier decades of economic progress and political hope. For West Germans, these were the glory days of Adenauer's Germany, the first blush of postwar prosperity and optimism. East Germans by contrast have channeled their affections toward the faded dreams and relative affluence of the 1960s, when the country embarked upon its bold project of "consumer socialism." Both were also distinctly popular in nature. Given that the emotional longing for any German past was all but taboo after 1945, these often trivialized sentimental journeys act as decisive moments in each Germany's popular reworking of the meaning of history. Even more striking is the way that these nostalgia waves tended to center on pop culture relics from their respective "economic miracles." In this they afforded a far-reaching negotiation of the dialectic of memory and materialism undergirding each country's cultural identity.

While the events of 1989 occasioned a fundamental reshuffling of German history and identity, it pays to remember that such revisionism actually began a decade before. Nowhere was this more the case than in the Federal Republic (FRG) during the late 1970s and early 1980s. The period witnessed a steady stream of new histories boldly challenging what were then the Cold War pieties of West German politics and culture. The trend was duly noted at the time, not least because its neoconservative "rediscovery of history" often included a troubling reworking of the Nazi and Holocaust legacies. The Bitburg debacle, the conversion of Holocaust history into mass-media fodder, the so-called historians' debate as well as the more popular "Hitler fascination" all illustrated the decade's blurring of myth and memory, kitsch and death.[13] What is often forgotten, however, is that the early 1980s revisionism went hand in hand with a new nostalgia for the 1950s. While efforts to "normalize" the Nazi period understandably provoked great attention, the cultural construction of the fabled 1950s was just as significant. The wide appeal of what one famous 1978 exhibition suggestively called the "puberty of the republic" was echoed in the booming cultural industry of sentimental journeys back to Adenauer's Germany.[14] Everywhere were new exhibitions and publicized memoirs, magazine feature articles and television programs, social histories and fashion fairs about the decade. Crooners

from the era were back on tour, movie houses boasted 1950s retrospectives, old ads and television shows were rebroadcast, period furniture and
clothing knock-offs were reproduced and sold in department stores, retro
design boutiques popped up across the country, while collectors and pur-
veyors of yesteryear's detritus enjoyed their finest hour. The 1950s were
"in" and seemingly ubiquitous. How extensive it really was is of course
impossible to gauge precisely. Still, it was popular enough in 1978 to war-
rant a twenty-four-page cover story in *Der Spiegel*, West Germany's leading weekly newsmagazine. And it possessed enough staying power to be
the subject of two additional articles in the same magazine six years later;
in fact, one of the 1984 features was subtitled "The New Cult of the
1950s."[15] That such nostalgia was criticized as "false" and "mythic" (as
the 1978 *Spiegel* article had done) could by no means staunch it. On the
contrary, the very mythmaking of the past was the main point: it counted
as the country's first popular effort to conjoin history and happiness.

Unfortunately, this nostalgia wave has all but escaped scrutiny in West
German historiography. Part of the reason is that this romance with the
"nifty fifties" was common in Western Europe, Britain, and America.[16]
Across the Western countries was renewed interest in the cultural forms
and accomplishments of the postwar's first decade of peace and plenty. If
discussed at all, West German nostalgia was treated as a cultural equiva-
lent to the Reagan era mythology about the good old days of Eisenhower
America, particularly insofar as both Ronald Reagan and Helmut Kohl
explicitly invoked the political stability, can-do spirit, and moral order of
the 1950s as their political polestars. West Germany's economic recession
during the early 1980s, coupled with mounting clashes between the government and the newly found peace and ecological movements, only
deepened general anxiety about the present and future, fueling retrospective glances toward an innocent and idealized past.[17] Or this nostalgia
was casually dismissed as nothing but the natural expression of graying
baby boomers, who had reached an age of waxing sentimental about
their "rubble adolescence" and hothouse upbringings. Their histories, as
detractors scoffed, were thus less serious historiography than wistful autobiography. Still others intoned that such nostalgia could not be taken
at face value for the simple reason that it first emerged as a flea market
phenomenon. It was thus no "authentic" nostalgia, but really a tawdry
market ruse to empty attics full of dusty souvenirs of the not-so-distant
past and thereby converting, as Volker Fischer remarked, "history and
culture into flea market trinkets."[18]

No one would dispute the validity of some of these objections. This
1980s nostalgia was in fact quite international and by implication hardly
unique to West Germany; most of these accounts were written by baby-

boomers about lost youth amid the buoyant optimism of the Adenauer era; and the sentimental attachment to the 1950s did begin in the marketplace. Good proof that such historiography flowed easily into advertising was that some of the key publicists championing "1950s Modern" were themselves collectors.[19] However, to discard this new love affair with the 1950s as merely flea market economics is far too cavalier. For if nothing else, West German nostalgia was distinctive in the way it reclaimed the 1950s as affirmative national history. At first glance this may seem axiomatic and even quite natural, given the Federal Republic's stellar postwar political record and economic comeback. Yet it is worth recalling that the foundation myth of West German society was that it had been completely cleansed of all nationalist passion and pathos. No matter how much its origins may have been commercial, it was undeniable that the emotional floodgates about the past were suddenly opened. Out came a slew of testimonies about the 1950s that patently mixed memory and desire. While some argued that the decade was "the last unified epoch in which (almost) everyone strove for the same goals," others claimed that the 1950s was a time in which "life could be enjoyed a little again" since it built a "harmonious, sacred world" based on "being nice to one another" and "simple domestic bliss."[20] Another writer, in an article published in a top-selling pop-culture magazine, expressed this new sensibility toward the past:

The 1950s demanded a great deal from us, and precisely for that reason was it so beautiful. . . . Never were Germans so in sync [einverstanden] with their country as at that time. Never since has there been such a feeling of homeland [Heimatsgefühl]. . . . Life in this epoch was clearer, simpler and in large measure more sensible.[21]

As evidenced here, this pop-culture nostalgia went far beyond buying and selling old 1950s artifacts; together with this retro revival went a new tendency to remake early postwar experience and history as collective objects of desire.

Implicit in these accounts was a certain reappraisal of the early "Bonn Republic." Until the late 1970s the prevalent view of the 1950s was one dominated by the conservative mantras of privacy and propriety, where the postwar era's original promise of radical renewal soon gave way to a less-than-brave new world built upon security, conformity, and repressed memories. With time such unflattering portraits of the "Adenauer Restoration" were the stock in trade of the West German New Left. Not that the Right was altogether enthusiastic about the wonders of postwar life and culture either. While many conservatives may not have subscribed to Ernst Kästner's damning description of the era as a "motorized Biedermeier," they too voiced great misgivings about what they saw as the epoch's heedless consumer materialism, lack of *Kultur* and moral un-mooring. Which is to say that the postwar left and right were often quite indistinguishable in their denunciations of the coming of "Coca-Colonization" on the one hand, or the embarrassing return of petit bourgeois values, predilections, and lifestyles on the other. All of this changed during the late 1970s and early 1980s. The 1950s underwent a remarkable reversal from a contemptible source of laughter and forgetting to a beloved symbol of renewal and accomplishment. In fact, many of these new sentimental reflections about the 1950s amounted to quite blatant "*Wir sind wieder wer*" (we are somebody again) celebratory narratives. No doubt there were popular expressions of similar pride before, such as the outpouring accompanying West Germany's 1954 World Cup soccer championship. But what distinguished this 1980s nostalgia was that it venerated the past along with the present.

Its conversion of history into new national myth was perhaps best measured by its omissions. In many of these 1980s recollections, the era's refugee problems, widespread domestic violence, soaring divorce rates, protests against rearmament, and A-bomb anxiety were all but consigned to the margins.[22] So too were the persistent material misery and social insecurity coloring real 1950s life. Feminist historians were the first to challenge these 1980s fables of the reconstruction, showing that women in particular rarely experienced Adenauer's Germany as a resplendent golden age of renewed affluence and leisure. Rather than "Zero Hour" liberation, most women remembered the postwar period as predominantly one of long work hours and unstable employment, incessant domestic crises and personal dissatisfaction.[23] Others, notably former '68ers, tended to emphasize the suffocating atmosphere of conformity and sexual repression of 1950s social life.[24] Yet such critical revisions of the real 1950s were drowned out amid the flood of feel-good accounts about the period.[25] Even those factors that framed older postwar histories, such as Cold War politics, superpower dependence, and the once-ubiquitous "Americanization" of West German culture and society, were noticeably downplayed. Nineteen-fifties West Germany, long viewed as the forlorn object of history, now returned as its rejuvenated subject.

If these 1980s memories passed over many of the unpleasant aspects of the 1950s life, then what was remembered? However varied, one element common to almost all of the accounts was the centrality of consumer goods. Consider one typical 1980s recollection about the "Golden 1950s":

Is it at all possible to describe the feeling of the period? . . . I am not so sure, but one thing is certain: The day of the currency reform brought a new feeling for life, a new faith in the future, a new beginning. I was just thirty years old. Until then I led an improvised and chaotic existence. I was waiting for stability, security . . .

Now our shopping streets slowly regained their modish flair. Until then we had to go around in outdated old clothes. . . . Then suddenly arrived the super-comfortable nylon shirts and blouses, stockings and socks, Trevira skirts, small chic hats and—how beautiful!—embroidered white hand gloves! And then the plastic shoulder bags: everywhere the magic word was 'plastic'. . . . I was decked out with Bauhaus and WK-furniture. Rough-weave tapestries and String book-shelves—with these began the new lifestyle. . . . On the wall I hung prints from Nolde, van Gogh, and Klee. . . . [26]

What makes this passage so distinctive is the extent to which the "feeling of the period" was so closely connected with name-brand designer goods. On one level it neatly accords with the principal findings from several 1980s oral history projects on the 1940s and 1950s, which revealed above all that the 1948 Currency Reform—not the cease-fire of 1945 nor the 1949 achievement of statehood—represented the real end of the Second World War and the return of "normality" for most West Germans.[27] But it is wrong to argue, as many have, that the break with the past was solely measured by feverish and indiscriminate material acquisition, what Ludwig Erhard termed a new "will to consume." As noted in the quoted passage, style mattered. In the 1950s Bauhaus furniture, abstract art, and modern housewares were endlessly praised in West German public life as the very emblems of post-Nazi culture and "up to date" lifestyle. Invariably they were lauded as the visual complements to the postwar rehabilitation of jazz, modern literature, and those cultural wares that just a few years ago were vociferously condemned as "degenerate" art and culture. Upon reading these 1980s reminiscences, the strategy seems to have worked. Over and over again these things were singled out as valuable symbolic capital by an aspiring West German middle class (and business elite) intent on distancing themselves from both the fascist past and petit bourgeois present. In this they served as "memoried" markers of social distinction and successful cultural reeducation. The above passage is thus a typical 1980s remembrance in accentuating the conspicuous consumption of modern design objects as a narrative peg of West German social memory.

But these new cultural histories were not limited to Bauhaus and Braun. What is so compelling is that many of them focused on different design objects altogether. Frequently the attention was directed toward more commonplace relics from the early blush of restored prosperity. Rather than boxy Bauhaus design and International Style cutlery and furniture, the spotlight increasingly fell upon those things that never made it into the epoch's high-profile design venues showcasing a new-found West German modernity. Cheap domestic housewares found in many West German homes from the period occupied center stage in

1980s memoirs, exhibitions, and nostalgia boutiques. Favorite items included spindle-legged "bag lamps," foam-padded "cocktail chairs," bulbous portable radios, colorful ashtrays, curvy plastic furniture, abstract art-inspired tapestries, wallpaper and shower curtains, and, most famously, the three-legged kidney bean–shaped night table that came to symbolize 1950s domesticity, the *Nierentisch*. The cumulative effect of these pop-culture accounts was to challenge the presumed popularity of Bauhaus modernism, suggesting instead that the true style of the era was more accurately understood as a West German dialect of "organic modern" and "neo-Jugendstil."[28] It was thus the nonexported world of West German commodity culture—whose artifacts were relentlessly condemned as new *Gründerzeit* kitsch by its high design world through the 1970s—which suddenly emerged as the very vessels of 80s sentimentalism.[29] Not that "*Nierentisch* modernism" was all that provincial. After all, it took its formal cues largely from abstract expressionism and represented a discernible yearning to break free from the Nazi past by following new impulses in the world of international art and design.[30] Its colorful and dynamic repertoire of forms was clearly intended to counter what many remembered as the rigidity, rationing, and misery of both the war and immediate postwar years by celebrating a new *joie de vivre*.[31] But however much "Nierentisch modernism" was indebted to international trends, it was its distinctly West German inflection in 1950s home decoration that evoked such vivid recollections. So characterizing this 1980s rediscovery of the "other" 1950s as the genesis of West German postmodernism *avant la lettre*, as some did, misses the mark. Its belated celebration offered a serious reevaluation of the Federal Republic's early popular culture.[32] That one author insisted on dubbing the decade the "*Fuffziger Jahre*" [sic], one which patently was not "*hochdeutsch, sondern umgangssprachlich*" (not high German but rather informal and colloquial), summed up this broader desire to rehabilitate those pop culture forms and habits long banished from the standard academic representations of the epoch.[33]

Equally telling was how the 1950s were remembered. Quite often this nostalgia was chronicled as first-person accounts of material acquisition. Admittedly, the popular vogue of autobiography as a means of connecting past and present was one of the signature features of late-1970s and early-1980s West German culture; while most notable in fiction, it could also be seen in the explosion of autobiographies and memoirs.[34] Not to mention that the new cottage industry of oral histories published at this time foregrounded ordinary individual life stories as new sources of historical inquiry. The striking thing about these 1980s retrospectives (like the passage cited above) was that they almost invariably featured detailed personal reminiscences about the excitement and gravity of purchasing new consumer goods. Many of them naturally went beyond recollections of acquiring Braun phonographs or Nierentisch tables to include other major consumer items, such as washing machines, televisions, and later automobiles. But whatever the specific material markers in these narratives, the point is that these 1980s pop memories were largely based upon self-styled stories of consumer gain and social arrival.[35]

These new histories reveal a decisive issue in the 1950s reconstitution of popular memory: the affective relationship between people and things. It is often a forgotten dimension of the more general shift in social experience from wartime privation to postwar prosperity. The remarkable tale of the postwar Economic Miracle certainly gave great cause for nostalgia and identification, as many of the Nazis' material promises (affordable homes, vacations, automobiles, and modern design wares) had become reality for many West Germans by the mid-1960s.[36] On this point Michael Wildt has gone so far as to claim that such consumerism served as the real bedrock of West German political stability and democratic success, not least because it was the first time for Germans (as opposed to the harrowing experiences of the Weimar Republic) that political liberalism and economic prosperity occurred in tandem.[37] Add to this something else: West Germany's affluent consumer society signaled the full rupture with Nazism's war and labor economy, whereby goods and not bodies served as the principal objects of mass consumption.[38] In other words, the centrality of the relationship between people and products was a particular cultural consequence of postfascist liberalism. And insomuch as traditional markers of social difference such as education and *Kultur* had been badly disrupted and/or corrupted by the Nazi experience, the fine distinctions of individual identity were increasingly shaped by marketplace merchandise.[39] The widespread usage of the first person pronoun in these 1980s accounts of material desire and happiness bore testimony to these social developments. The emotional presence of these everyday objects as narrative signposts was thus much more than successful advertising or simply a reflection on the materialization of 1980s life. It represented a real reconfiguration of self and society in the 1950s, such that economics—not politics—functioned as the font of West German identity and identification.[40]

That the market had refashioned cultural memory in this manner was surely not lost on West German observers during the 1950s and 1960s. Many saw this coming and were extremely critical of these trends.[41] On the one side, conservatives such as Arnold Gehlen, Hans Freyer, Hans Sedlmayr, and Friedrich Sieburg condemned West German consumer culture for obstructing what they felt to be the necessary development of genuine (West) German solidarity based on a redemptive cultural past of humanist sensibility and moral teachings. In numerous writings they never tired of lamenting the absence of traditional German *Kultur* to stave off the corrosive effects of (an Americanized) industrial *Zivilisation*.[42] On the other side stood the Left, whose views were not so very dissimilar in this regard. Most influential for them was Max Horkheimer and Theodor Adorno's *Dialectic of Enlightenment* (1947), which effectively set the agenda for much West German cultural criticism through the 1950s and 1960s. In it they not only challenged the inherited wisdom about the emancipatory nature of the Enlightenment legacy, to saying nothing of their scandalous remarks about the "family resemblance" of Nazi culture and American mass culture, they also devoted considerable energy to addressing how bourgeois society "liquidated" cultural memory in the name of the all-pervasive commodity form.[43] Jürgen Habermas, Hans Magnus Enzensberger, Hans Werner Richter, and others extended their critique by arguing that modern consumerism had robbed the adversarial ethos of both *Kultur* and civil society, reducing the so-called public sphere to isolated islands of family intimacy and private spaces.[44] But it was the area of memory that became especially significant. Of great importance here was Alexander and Margarete Mitscherlich's best-seller, *The Inability to Mourn* (1967). In the book two leading West German psychologists diagnosed postwar society as chronically suffering from the effects of denying the horrors of the past, against which it has developed elaborate defense mechanisms to "de-realize" the entire Nazi period and suppress unwanted memories and guilty feelings. Leaving aside the historical value of this analysis, the relevant issue is that the Mitscherlichs singled out consumer hedonism as West Germany's escape from "working through" the catastrophes of Nazism, the war, and the Holocaust.[45] Not that such an argument was so unusual; on the contrary, *The Inability to Mourn* echoed a widely shared perception within West German academic circles that consumerism was antithetical to collective mourning and memory-work.[46] And despite widely divergent political agendas, these writers were united in upbraiding the "*Fresswelle 1950s*" for inhibiting the very possibility of postwar community, spiritual renewal, and reconciliation with the past.

These 1980s consumer histories broke sharply from this critical rendering of the 1950s. For one thing, they were overwhelmingly affirmative. Unlike most West German academic commentary through the 1970s, these new romances of the 1950s never subscribed to the idea that everyday West German culture was woefully deficient and/or a spin-off of American "cultural imperialism."[47] There was little antipathy toward "industrial civilization," nor any longing for preindustrial idylls and uncorrupted autonomous cultural spheres. Conversely, these narratives assumed and accepted the full industrialization of (West) German life and culture. That the 1980s renegotiation of West German identity centered on repossessing the very products of the long-denigrated "culture industry"—interior and industrial design, film, radio, television, fashion, advertising, tourism, and pop music—perfectly illustrated the ways in which mass-produced consumer goods now linked postwar experience and memory.[48] Hence these new cultural histories marked just how much the once-dominant place of work as the linchpin of German social experience and identity formation had been replaced by consumerism and leisure practices.[49] Underlying them was the assumption that West German cultural identity was first and foremost a product of affluence.[50] In this regard West German economist Werner Abelshauser was correct to say that "the history of the Federal Republic is above all its economic history" since it provided West Germans with a "vehicle for national identification or at least national self-understanding."[51] In light of this 1980s nostalgia, economics had also become culture.[52]

At stake is more than how the Economic Miracle successfully remade West German popular memory. The deeper issue is that the postwar period witnessed a radical reconstruction of identity from one of racist mission and collective sacrifice to that of individual choice and material well-being. As testified in these recollections, the grand master narratives of common purpose and imagined community (for example, nationalism, socialism, or for that matter, National Socialism) had been supplanted by countless autobiographies of physical satisfaction. The 1980s reworking of the 1950s thereby marked the degree to which West German memory had moved beyond Nietzsche's famous comment from *On the Genealogy of Morals* that "man could never do without blood, torture and sacrifices when he felt the need to create a memory for himself."[53] With it the long-standing German political ethic of deferred gratification (for example, socialism or fascism) seemingly evaporated with the historical end of the sacrificing "community of fate." Time horizons shrunk too, as the historical pathos of a collective German past and future had collapsed into the material demands and private pleasures of the immediate present. Once this 1950s preoccupation with the present became the past, once it became the subject of rosy reminiscence a generation later, it did so in a quite fitting manner. On one level, it may represent Clio's full modernization. To the extent that mass-produced consumer objects became the very repositories of postwar identity, it shows how popular memory itself had moved away from communal and transcendent *Kultur* toward materialist and individualist *Zivilisation*. Perhaps more importantly, it also radically revised the conventional expression of nostalgia itself. Unlike earlier forms of German nostalgia, the 1980s pop-culture variant was not really interested in turning back the clocks and returning to the desired era; in fact, it coolly accepted the historical distance between now and then. But to suggest that this only belies its inherent commercial spirit and faddish superficiality overlooks the key point. What made this West German nostalgia so unique was that it openly betrayed its etymological origins: it was not born of pain and exile, but gratitude and a newfound pride in a post-Nazi homeland. In this sense, this longing for the "Golden 1950s" had helped loosen the past from the difficult burden of pain, suffering, and guilt.

This reorganization of West German cultural memory offers several parallels to East Germany's post-1989 "*Ostalgie*." At first, the dissimilarities between the West German conservative turn during the early 1980s (*Tendenzwende*) and the East German *Wende* a decade later seem to defy comparison. Where the former was mainly shaped by the Christian Democrat Union's (CDU) resumption of power and a disturbing drift toward neoconservative nationalism, the latter was the by-product of the complete collapse of a political regime and semisovereign state. In the face of Reunification disappointments, East German *Ostalgie* originally arose as a fond glance backward to a fallen world based on socialist security and full employment, communal solidarity and progressive welfare programs.[54] Second, the perception of their respective consumer cultures diverged considerably. As opposed to the West German variant, East Germans could hardly advance stories of consumer satisfaction and material happiness. Even if many intellectuals insisted that the old GDR was somehow more noble in its austerity, these prized consumer goods were undeniably perceived as emblems of stagnation and suffering. In this, East German nostalgia remains loyal to the word's etymological roots. What the West and East German nostalgia waves have in common, though, was that material objects rested at the heart of these cultural longings. It not only confirmed how much each country's political legitimacy was closely linked to material well-being, but also that consumerism had radically shaped their respective cultural memories. And while GDR reminiscences have not been so blatant in freely inventing the past, there is a similar impulse to downplay memories of pain, suffering, and frustration in favor of more positive aspects of 1960s consumer culture.

Describing East German consumerism in these terms may strike some readers as quite surprising, especially since the former GDR was rarely perceived as a genuine consumer culture. Most observers (particularly those in the West) tended to characterize it as essentially a culture of privation, economic mismanagement, homogenized lifestyles, and East bloc ennui. The well-publicized day trips of wide-eyed East Berliners feverishly spending their "welcome money" on West German produce, furniture and VCRs during the heady days of 1989 only substantiated the long-standing Cold War image of East German suffering and consumer want.[55] While no one could dismiss the significance of such consumer tourism as an early expression of political liberation, it is only part of the story. Less well-known is that this initial Western shopping spree slowly gave way to a new desire among former GDR citizens for the very relics of their lost socialist world, be it everyday utensils, home furnishings, and/or pop-culture memorabilia. Yet such nostalgia, I would argue, is more than simply an escapist psychological defense against the chaos and disenchantment of Reunification itself. Rather, this ongoing remembrance of things past has been part and parcel of the changing nature of East German historical consciousness since that revolutionary autumn over a decade ago.

No doubt this East German nostalgia has been directly linked to the fact that the GDR has literally vanished from the political map. For it was this speedy absorption—what East German detractors often called "Kohl-onization"—that made the GDR story so unique. Unlike its East bloc neighbors, East Germany's so-called peaceful revolution did not result in the victory of diplomatic sovereignty and political independence. Of course this is not to trivialize the East German people's heroic participation in the collective East bloc campaign to free itself from Soviet oppression. What distinguishes the East German case, however, is that once the old regime collapsed, its citizens—to the great consternation of leftist intellectuals in both East and West Germany—voted for quick reunion with its Cold War enemy, thereby sacrificing any possibility of national autonomy and/or socialist reform. Whether or not this represented a missed opportunity for building a viable "third way" democratic socialism is immaterial at this juncture; the key point is that its "voluntary annexation" forever severed East German history and memory.[56]

In this regard East Germany remains quite singular. Unlike other East bloc countries, the GDR has not resuscitated dusty nationalist legends as post–Cold War ballast and orientation. For some this is the most salutary effect of its vaunted heritage of antifascism, which always served as the ideological touchstone of East Germany's socialist state and society. Uninspiring as this ideology may have become for many GDR citizens by the early 1970s, it remained East Germany's primary language of social solidarity and historical purpose. Erich Honecker's concerted campaign in the late 1970s to commemorate the milestones of German (and often Prussian) history—recostuming, for example, Frederick the Great, Goethe, and Beethoven as protosocialists—in a dual attempt to conjoin past and present as well as citizen and state was still limited to accentuating East

Germany's particular inflection of East bloc socialism.[57] That East German intellectuals worked to replace the older liberation theology of international socialism with the utopian dream of pan-European humanism during the late 1970s and early 1980s only reinforced this antinationalism. And while no one can discount the disturbing wave of immediate post-Reunification xenophobia and neo-Nazi violence, much of which took place in West Germany as well, it did stay at the margins and has continued to dissipate despite prolonged economic difficulties. What nationalist sentiment did animate in the post-1989 phase was less about the German political past than its promising economic future, what philosopher Jürgen Habermas rightly if derisively deemed "Deutschemark nationalism."[58]

But even this benign form of Reunification euphoria did not last long. Both West and East Germans soon realized that the heroic dismantling of the Berlin Wall was nothing compared with the more intractable mental wall dividing *Wessis* and *Ossis*. Already by the time Reunification was made official in October 1990 the televised fest of East-West German fraternity the year before had become a distant memory. German-German relations often degenerated instead into ugly bouts of repeated recriminations and mutual misunderstandings, thus exposing the illusory quality of the long-cherished Cold War dream of a so-called *Kulturnation* supposedly transcending geopolitical partition. In an atmosphere in which inter-German cultural difference, and not sameness, dominated post–Cold War historiography, the changes have been particularly pronounced in the former GDR. This is more than merely saying that the GDR past—like its currency and political culture—has suddenly become "instant history." East German history had been liberated from state surveillance and control. The deregulation of the East German past has unleashed a veritable free-for-all for new cultural squatters and carpetbaggers, whose historiographical perspectives have ranged from post-1989 exoticism about the "wild, wild East" to blatant exercises in political nostalgia. Just as the actual content of its history has been up for grabs, so too has the style of remembrance. Since the fall of the Berlin Wall, there has been a proliferation of new voices and alternative accounts challenging the state's manufactured monologue and former political economy of speech and script. New oral histories, museum retrospectives, and personal reminiscences abound about the "people's own experience."[59]

In this context the sphere of material culture has been and continues to be a favorite site of new memory production. Much of this has to do with the fact that it has played a decisive role in presenting and interpreting this German-German difference. One can see this plainly in the vitrine display of East and West German history at Bonn's "House of History" museum (Haus der Geschichte), where these one-time Cold War rivals are contrasted largely in terms of material output and commodity cultures.[60] Other more popular manifestations exist as well in which the design of consumer durables functions as visual shorthand for German-German dissimilarities. Examples include the satirical West German compilation of East German advertising films, *Flotter Ost*, or "Dashing East," as well as in the West German exhibition catalog mockingly entitled *SED: Schönes Einheit Design* and translated into English as "SED: Stunning Eastern Design." In the latter case, two West Germans journeyed to the GDR a few months before the dismantling of the Berlin Wall to undertake what they called a "lightning archaeological excursion." Having collected carloads of East German everyday objects, they exhibited these "real-existing commodities within the gray everyday life of the GDR" in a Frankfurt gallery in December 1989. Their fascination stemmed from the belief that the "GDR has unwittingly preserved fossil wares which, twenty or thirty years ago, were near and dear to us," confirming the degree to which the country became "a time warp zone in which product forms, now obsolescent in the West, could continue to mutate in some frozen limbo."[61] Indeed, casting East German culture as fundamentally living in a pre- or antimodern limbo of arrested development became a favorite West German parlor game in the wake of Reunification. Even if some tried to celebrate East German cultural life as less materialistic and more humane in its austere simplicity, the pseudoanthropology of modernity/unmodernity still dominates the academic construction of German-German difference.[62]

Yet this is not the way that East Germans remember their past. In fact, the GDR's consumer culture has undergone a transvaluation in the hearts and minds of many former citizens. Here it is worth recalling that in the old GDR, Western goods commonly served as unrivaled cultural capital. According to prominent East German psychiatrist Hans-Joachim Maaz, whose "psychogram of the GDR" became a best-seller in the wake of Reunification,

There was nothing that could beat the fetish value of western goods. Empty western beer or cola cans were placed as ornaments on the shelves of the wall unit, plastic bags bearing western advertisements were bartered, western clothes made the man. Real shortages and inferior merchandise in our country, and the surplus of items and quality luxuries in the West were the emotional background for a never-ending and never-satisfying spiral of consumption. Thus we played "Nouveau Riche Family," a variation of the children's game "mine is better than yours," in which western objects were the absolute measure.[63]

Even the party hierarchy reportedly succumbed to the same impulse, hoarding western imports (for example, Volvo sedans, Philips televisions, and Blaupunkt phonographs) as signs of status and power.[64] Little wonder that 1989 was often interpreted as simply the desire to enjoy long-sought Western goods after years of consumer frustration. Numerous eyewitness reports only confirmed this view by dramatizing East Germany's initial frenzied acquisition of western things along with the sidewalk accumulation of discarded GDR televisions and radios, furniture, and clothes.[65]

What is so striking is how quickly the former GDR's perceived relationship between East and West German goods changed a few years later. Where GDR goods once served as a source of perennial dissatisfaction and embarrassment, they later became emblems of pride and nostalgia. In part this was due to the fact that these formerly disdained articles suddenly became material reminders of a vanished world, newly idealized "fragments of a crumbled identity."[66] But more than this, the positive identification with these GDR goods was also a paradoxical result of post-1989 consumer frustration. For one thing, availability did not mean affordability. Steep price tags and West German condescension only intensified German-German differences and heightened the old East German self-perception of being second-class citizens. For another, East German nostalgia was fueled by the actual consumption of western goods. Once purchased, many of these coveted articles lost their nimbus of symbolic capital and political magic, thereafter returning to the "disenchanted" world of hyped exchange-value, credit payments, and planned obsolescence of consumer pleasure. The historical aura of German goods had been radically reversed: the former longing for the emblems of a glamorous Western present had now been replaced by those from a fading Eastern past.[67] Not to suggest that East German material culture nostalgia has been somehow universal and uniform, or that it has been the exclusive monopoly of East Germans. West Germans too have busily bought up these remaining former GDR objects. Admittedly, they often have done so for quite different reasons; for instance, West Germans tend not to collect old consumer goods, but rather more political memorabilia (SED pins and flags) as the preferred emblems of their own imagined GDR.[68] More, West German merchants were quick to spot the economic benefit of reviving former GDR brands (especially in processed food and small objects) as a market strategy for selling to former East Germans.[69] Like the West German nostalgia wave a decade before, the instant commercialization of GDR history at East Berlin museum shops, souvenir stores, and Sunday swap meets in Berlin and elsewhere gave rise to the same cry of despair about the demeaning commodification of GDR memory and culture. But even so, this *Ostalgie* remains a rallying point for East Germans.

The revived romance between East Germans and their own material culture emerged in a variety of forms. Notable samples include the founding of numerous Trabant automobile clubs and fan newsletters; the growing celebratory literature on GDR pop culture; the reissue of socialist-realist novels and East German rock albums; the conversion of the old GDR customs house into the "Palace of Tears" nightclub, whose decor and music explicitly evoked pre-1989 East Berlin; Frank Georgi's proposal for a Disney-esque East German theme park—aptly titled "Ossi Park"—in which barbed wire, Trabants, mock Stasi agents, currency exchanges, and even scratchy GDR toilet paper would all be part of this new amusement park of surrealized East German life; the increasing post-1989 tendency among East German consumers to prefer products and foodstuffs with old GDR labels as symbols of what Rainer Gries calls "East German continuity and identity"; the rash of "Ossi Parties" in Halle, Jena, Leipzig, and Berlin during the last few years, where party goers are required to bring old GDR trinkets for admission; as well as the grassroots campaign to save the former GDR radio station "DT-64" and the iconic "Ampelmännchen" (the little traffic light figure that adorned GDR city crosswalks).[70] That much of it is understood as a desperate gesture of cultural self-defense was perhaps best articulated in the words of the cofounder of the East Berlin "Save the Ampelmännchen" Committee: "If it's truly a Reunification, they need to recognize that the east has something to contribute, too—perhaps not governments or cars, but other things."[71]

But it is not as if the whole GDR consumer past has been awash in the warm glow of nostalgia. Much of the attention has significantly concentrated on the 1960s. The romanticization of this decade is hardly coincidental. In the memories of many East Germans, the 1960s stand out as a bright and hopeful decade between the exhausting production quotas of the 1950s and the widespread disillusionment of the 1970s.[72] Again this may seem strange to Western readers, particularly to the extent that the era opened with the 1961 construction of the Berlin Wall. Yet it is worth remembering that its construction acted as a short-term boon for the East German state insomuch as it effectively quelled West Germany's economic magnetism and stanched the embarrassing no-confidence demographic plebiscite of westward migration. Once the political system was "stabilized" in this manner, the SED concentrated on building a novel socialist industrial culture. The very title of one recent exhibition dedicated to recalling this decisive epoch—*Wunderwirtschaft* or "Miracle Economy"—is itself telling.[73] It refers to West Germany's better known Economic Miracle, but also to the surprising achievements of hothouse East German modernization. The buoyant optimism of the period makes more sense if we bear in mind that East Germany first announced the end of food and basic commodity rationing as late as 1958, bringing to a close twenty years of East German consumer privation.[74] Like West Germany, East Germany had been devastated by the war. But unlike its western counterpart, there was no Marshall Plan assistance; worse, Moscow demanded war reparation payments from the GDR until 1953. What little leftover capital did exist was invariably invested in heavy industry and export production in the name of economic recovery. Insofar as the state reasoned that investment in the consumer goods sector only diverted precious resources from all-important industrial production, GDR citizens were given the bare minimum in housing and consumer goods. By the early 1960s, however, the GDR economy had recovered and even posted impressive results. By 1965 it ranked among the world's ten most prolific industrial producers. Now the time had come when GDR citizens wanted a bigger piece of the pie, especially given the meteoric West German takeoff during the same period. At stake, however, was more than simply another replay of rising achievements breeding rising expectations. The oft-forgotten issue is that socialism itself was in part predicated on the idea of universal prosperity for all workers, who were supposedly finally free from the shackles of capitalist exploitation. It was therefore the materialist dimension of Marxism that became the vital concern for many East Germans, not least because the political revolution had already occurred some ten years before. Under pressure to deliver its promise, the ruling SED set out to remove the last vestiges of its postwar "rationing society" and embark on its consumer version of the Great Leap Forward; at the Fifth Party Conference the socialist slogan of "Work, Bread, and Housing" was significantly changed to the more expansive secular theology of "For Prosperity, Happiness, and Peace."[75]

Little wonder that 1960s modernization was shot through with paradoxes and contradictions. It was hard enough on a material basis to try to keep up with the Schmidts on the other side of the Berlin Wall by delivering modern washing machines, refrigerators, furniture, radios, televisions, and automobiles to GDR citizens. But East Germany's industrial economy was not built for consumer goods production, and thus consumers faced shortages and ever-increasing waiting lists for desired items. Closely linked to this was the thorny ideological problem of modern consumerism itself. The issue was not simply dumping various consumer products on GDR society as the deserved "fruit of socialist labor." The question was rather, How could consumerism be reconciled with state socialism's "dictatorship over needs?" Would it undermine or strengthen the relationship between citizen and state? The SED knew all too well that this was a dangerous wager, especially if the "consumer gap" with West Germany ever became too egregious (as it did).

Not surprisingly, it was precisely in the sphere of consumerism where a good deal of this political pressure surfaced. Much of this was the result of the fact that material prosperity and consumer satisfaction were often used as yardsticks by both German governments to measure progress and legitimacy. The SED was squeezed between market ideology from the West and the consumer demands from its own populace. By the end of the 1950s, preaching the virtues of deferred gratification (as one common 1950s slogan had it, "The way we work today is the way we will live tomorrow") was no longer tenable. Hoping to head off further popular disaffection, the state decided to hitch its destiny to the star of promised prosperity. The decade thus witnessed the great experiment not only in price planning, subsidized consumerism, and the introduction of the five-day work week, but also in the bold creation of a more attractive socialist consumer culture complete with state advertising agencies, snazzy product packaging, modern furniture, household decoration magazines and advice literature, self-service stores, mail-order clearinghouses, and even state travel bureaus. Though there were always problems, this venture in "refrigerator socialism" initially worked quite well in meeting the demands of export production and domestic consumption. Goods that were long considered luxury items—such as washing machines and refrigerators—became increasingly available to all levels of society, making it by far the most prosperous consumer culture in the East bloc.[76] On this score its windfall was as much political as economic in that the visible modernization of everyday life seemed to bespeak the future viability of the GDR's "consumer socialism."

Whatever else can be said about it, the upheaval of 1989 dramatized just how impossible this gamble had become. The remarkable boom eventually leveled off by the early 1970s, so much so that GDR consumer culture in the 1970s and 1980s was largely propped up by loans from IMF bankers and the West German government. By this time it was too late to turn back, however, mainly because the government knew that failing to continue to provide even increasingly sub-par consumer goods might breed further popular unrest. Although Honecker tried to curb this problem by investing more capital in consumerism following the Eighth Party Congress of 1971, the situation hardly improved. Before long it was plain that the state's effort to marry socialism and modern consumerism was a losing game, if only for the simple reason that there were—as one East German scholar put it—"always more consumer desires than consumer products."[77] The 1960s consumer modernization had indeed revolutionized everyday life in the GDR; but unfortunately for the SED, the newly unleashed consumer desire could not be so easily regulated or satisfied. The yearning for fashion, fantasy, and what Nietzsche once called the "eternal return of the new" eventually became an intractable political menace and liability.[78] Even if the GDR succeeded in providing its citizens with adequate housing, foodstuffs, and everyday necessities, the ever-present television images of West German consumer bonanza only pointed up the demoralizing differences in the availability and quality of GDR consumer articles. As another historian perceptively observed, "The discrepancy between material privation and verbal excess [by the SED] only succeeded in further arousing popular loathing and consumer appetite," in turn creating a runaway "inflation of desire" that scarcely could be controlled.[79] The SED's expansion of the country's special retail shops—*Exquisitläden, Intershops,* and the *Delikatläden*—during the 1980s as a measure to exploit high-end consumer demand, pent-up savings, and hard currency transfer from West to East only exacerbated popular resentment, not least because it flouted socialist ideals of social equality. The economic malaise of the 1970s and 1980s then went hand in hand with growing political disaffection, as state socialism (and this would be true throughout the East bloc) appeared to many as less the inheritor of the earth than an unrealizable pipe dream from a forgotten past.

Nevertheless, the post-1989 period has been marked by a new identification with this doomed experiment in socialist consumerism. The "miracle economy" exposition is only one of several examples chronicling the degree to which East Germans—despite the widespread perception that they were not keeping up with West German standards of living—often remember their own Economic Miracle as a period of increased affluence, optimism, and comfort.[80] What is so intriguing about these new histories is the very form of remembrance. Particularly notable was that the hallowed linchpins of socialist identity—the world of work and the laboring community—played a subordinate role in these new recollections. The individual socialist consumer occupied center stage instead. Lest there be any misunderstanding, I do not mean to imply that the construction of East German identity suddenly and completely changed from one of producer to consumer; numerous oral history projects since 1989 testify that the identity and self-worth of many former GDR citizens were closely linked to labor and production.[81] Yet it does indicate that consumerism played a significant role in East German culture as well, particularly in the memories of its citizens. Consider for example the following post-1989 recollection from the *Wunderwirtschaft* catalogue:

I had to save a long time for the motorcycle. The thing cost me 1,900 Mark at the time. But it was worth it. It was the absolute best! A 250 Pannonia with bench seat and radio. While I was braking my mother always slid off, something which—I must admit—always amused me. I still remember that I constantly drove to see my future wife in her village. Nobody had a motorbike there, which made mine a kind of status symbol. I even had additional footrests installed for my small son. After that, the three of us drove everywhere together! The people in the village thought that we were crazy to drive around like that with a child on board. My in-laws were actually rather hands-off and never interfered in our affairs or told us what to do—completely unlike my mother. She just didn't understand this kind of life, it was all so new. In any case I had this motorcycle twelve years, exactly during my whole adolescent rebellious period. We traveled all the time by bike and went everywhere with the thing. There are a lot of other stories to tell.[82]

Of foremost importance is the way in which the personal history of his motorcycle became the organizing principle of his narrated past and individual identity. Indeed, it is the very banality of the passage—one that is far removed from the worker heroism and collective destiny of "socialist realist" culture—that is so striking. While it is true that this impulse to reduce the trope of destiny from a collective to a highly personal one has characterized many East German recollection narratives since Reunification, the key point is that the narrative pivots upon the relationship between people and things.[83] Examples of this kind of subjectivized East German memory, featuring personal recollections, product biographies, and photographs about this lost socialist consumer culture abounded in the early 1990s. The significance resides in their novelty as post-GDR social history, where old things (even broken ones) live on as narrative vehicles conveying impressions of a collapsed world of social status, fashion, comfort, and security. Despite—or perhaps precisely because of—the abrupt "secularization" of GDR artifacts, where they no longer embody the dreams of a prosperous present and a hopeful socialist future, they now serve as the new repositories of private histories and sentimental reflections.

Such new consumer narratives implied a radical revision of the post-1989 East German relationship between self and society. For one thing, they revealed the extent to which GDR cultural memory—following the fate of its huge industrial combines after Reunification—had been repossessed and privatized. But this privatization of memory did not dissolve—as it has in the West—into subculture testimonies and affirmations of individual difference precisely because GDR consumer culture was not based on a market cult of differentiation. Not only was there little variety of goods nor brand-name competition, many of the products introduced in the consumer rush of the 1960s stayed in production until 1989 with little or no change in content or form. Regardless of how monotonous this may have been, this aesthetics of sameness was crucial in shaping the

GDR's collective memory. That is, the very lack of product innovation and repackaging assured that these objects—however privately experienced and remembered—would function as transgenerational markers of East German culture and identity. The display of these things in specifically public venues (restaurants and nightclubs, above all) along with the publication of these private memories as new post-GDR social history attest to the distinctly collective aspect of this pop culture nostalgia. That these new stories have downplayed gendered differences within GDR material culture, one that also emerged as a key element of East German social history immediately following the *Wende*, also belies the impulse to construct a more all-encompassing national experience and identity from this lost consumer culture.[84] This is why these socialist products have played an indispensable role in bridging individual and society, private and public memory since 1989. While markers of social distinction long existed within this allegedly classless society, most notably Western goods and travel privileges, the memories of GDR material culture have tended to reinforce, not undermine, East German solidarity. Such a formulation might seem somewhat odd, especially in light of Maier's claim that "the regime survived precisely by undermining solidarity with differential rewards such as travel and education, even by dividing up its supposedly loyal proletarian supporters into competitive work brigades, and by rewarding snooping."[85] True enough, but this nostalgia in effect has helped reconstruct this shattered East German solidarity after 1989. According to Ina Merkel, one of East Germany's foremost social historians, "East Germans still bond over certain standardized and mass-produced commodities. Catchwords are enough for mutual recognition. 'Remember the Multimax [drill]?' is enough to start a lively conversation . . . the discourse about specific brands is enough to re-establish an East German identity."[86]

What can we make of all this? Two comparative points deserve emphasis. The first concerns nationalism. Not that these nostalgia waves signaled a revival of the goose-stepping German nationalism of old. Yet they did implicitly challenge the cultural preeminence of their respective superpower patron. No coincidence that the new love for the Adenauer era coincided with drifting relations between the United States and West Germany. The Euromissile crisis and the anti-American peace movement, the advent of the Greens, the widespread founding of numerous local, regional, and national history museums, along with the more general "rediscovery" of German national identity in politics and culture all testified to this new transatlantic distancing.[87] Even the attitude toward "Americanism" changed. Not only did West German pop music legends Ted Herold and Peter Kraus take their place along Elvis Presley and James

Dean as the cherished icons of the era, the once-standard sociologies about the irreversible "Americanization" of the FRG now gave way to new studies of West German cultural negotiation and even self-defense.[88] Just as West German nostalgia focused upon the stuff of everyday West German life beneath the overlay of American modernism, so too did East German *Ostalgie* downplay emblems of Soviet-style modernism. Artifacts of East bloc internationalism (Soviet architecture, literature, magazines, film, and political culture) have been virtually ignored amid this post–Cold War refashioning of the GDR past.[89] That East Germans have shied away from remembering their past through Soviet memorabilia in favor of those goods "Made in the GDR" underlines this point. In this way, both German nostalgia waves were partly inspired by the desire to free their everyday cultures from the influence of official international modernism.

No less significant was that such nostalgia betrayed the elective affinity between consumerism and national identity. Surely this has long been noted in the West German case, given that economic prosperity became the main vehicle of identification in a country where traditional languages of affective solidarity had been destroyed. Less remarked, however, is that the same went for the former GDR. Certainly it can be argued that East German sentimentalism has enjoyed such little corresponding expression in the other former East bloc countries shows that the GDR (both before and after 1989) was more enamored by Western consumer dreams than its socialist brethren. The constant presence of West German consumer culture (whether actual goods or media images) as the universal yardstick of progress and prosperity, the disappointing economic realities and colonizing effects of Reunification, as well as the GDR's rejection of romantic nationalism as the polestar of pre-1989 political resistance and post-1989 national community largely account for the GDR's uniqueness. In the end, East Germany's political destiny was built with the same mortar that has underlain Western social politics for the last half century, namely consumerism as political legitimacy. Did not material dreams of the good life in large measure account for the backdrop for the 1953 uprising and the 1961 construction of the Berlin Wall, to say nothing of its dramatic dismantling a generation later? Indeed, it was the consumer dreams born amid pain and privation—like the West during the Great Depression—that eventually crowded out more socialist concerns. One Ministry of State Security report on popular attitudes toward the economy in June 1989 conveyed this deadly development on the eve of collapse. With great resignation, it conceded that the quantity and quality of consumer goods in the GDR "is increasingly becoming the basic criterion for the assessment of the attractiveness of socialism in comparison to capitalism."[90]

The fact that the 1989 reports of Erich Honecker's petit-bourgeois consumer lifestyle became such a highly publicized political scandal of party decadence (Wandlitz was often disparagingly referred to as "Volvograd" by the early 1980s) made clear how much consumer frustration and envy had shaped East German cultural consciousness. Surely the politicization of economics and consumer goods—which intensified as political idealism faded—was hardly special to East Germany; what is remarkable about the GDR is how these same begrudged objects became the common vessels of warmed-over cultural memory and political subjectivity a few short years later.

Second, this nostalgia marked a sharp turn in intellectual life in both countries. On the one hand, the West German variant pointed up the loosened hold of leftist intellectuals on national culture since the mid-1960s. In part this was a by-product of Kohl's election and the accompanying resurgence of intellectual neoconservativism. After all, it was precisely at this time that long-taboo issues such as patriotism, pride, and feel-good national identity were openly expressed and celebrated. Not to suggest that there was no pride expressed before; but it was done so privately, or at least in seemingly more apolitical forms such as pride in the country's economic take-off and high standard of living.[91] This 1980s nostalgia fully inverted this earlier logic and practice. As Rainer Gries noted, it was the first moment when the FRG freely "quoted itself" without shame or guilt.[92] No less significant was that this new sentimental populism also pointed to the wide chasm between the once-dominant leftist intellectuals and the general public. No longer did the old saws about the debilitating effects of 1950s materialism—that consumerism hampered authentic social life, political engagement, and even true "coming to terms with the past"—enjoy much purchase in public culture. While cultural criticism denouncing the evils of consumerism in "greasing morality and the soul" continued to be published, taking on board new ecological concerns about "false consciousness" and "life-threatening consumerism," they were clearly overrun by popular identification with the *Fresswelle* 1950s.[93] The motley assortment of publicists, collectors, and enthusiasts behind the new exhibitions and books about the "Golden 1950s" were by no means beholden to these older political crusades.

This was even more the case in the former GDR. Not only did the general public in 1989–90 pay little heed to older East German intellectuals, who implored them to stay put and reform socialism instead of succumbing to the siren songs of Western consumer capitalism. The gap between old-style GDR intellectuals and the public has become ever wider in the years since 1989.[94] Illustrative has been the renewed interest in the GDR consumer culture of the 1950s and 1960s; the group of intellectuals associated with Eisenhüttenstadt's recently founded East German Everyday Culture Documentation Center (Dokumentationszentrum Alltagskultur der DDR) neatly registers this shift. Unlike their predecessors, they no longer rail against the "culture industry" and the sins of consumption, but admit its mass appeal and powerful ability to forge new and lasting identities. For them the so-called Banana Revolution of 1989 is not a term of derision, but rather a starting point of historical inquiry. No doubt such interventions were originally fueled by a strong desire to re-vise the simplified and belittling portrayals of GDR everyday life peddled in the Western (and above all West German) media. On this score, the Everyday Culture Documentation Center partly functions as a counter-narrative to the one advanced in the vitrines of Bonn's "House of His-tory" museum. And if it is true that 1989 dramatically exposed the awk-ward distance between GDR intellectuals and the people, this post-1989 commemoration wave of East German material culture (Prenzlauer Berg's *Kulturbrauerei* has also hosted numerous shows on this theme) has effec-tively helped bridge the former chasm.[95] No finger wagging or scolding from intellectuals this time, nor any prescriptions of cultural enlighten-ment and consumer asceticism. In many ways this is the natural conse-quence of the sudden collapse of the GDR present and future, where only the past—and a material one at that—plays host to wistful rumination. As a result, the long-derided world of East German material culture (in large measure at the expense of pre-1989 *Kultur*) has ironically emerged amid the ruins of GDR politics and economics as a privileged site for con-veying the pathos of the GDR past both to themselves and others.

Even more striking is that these nostalgia waves also represented the demise of the antifascist consensus in both countries. In the wake of the implosion of the former Soviet Union, it is not surprising that scholars are now taking stock of the history and ideology of antifascism, not least because it underlay the self-understanding and justification of Cold War communism.[96] Nowhere was this truer than in divided Germany, where both countries—despite ideological rivalry—strove to build their new polities upon an antifascist consensus. The long-standing taboo against expressions of nationalism in both Germanies through the 1970s re-flected this shared mission. East Germany was naturally more extreme in this regard. While antifascism as the touchstone of official ideology had begun to lose its hold by the late 1970s, as evidenced in the "rediscovery" of German history and identity as well as the intellectuals' invention of "Europe" as the preferred language of solidarity in place of socialism, 1989 signaled the complete collapse of this antifascist consensus.[97] If nothing else, the *Wende* destroyed the state control of history and in turn the antifascist myth as the very ground of official East German identity and memory. Not only could this be seen in disturbing revival of xeno-phobic nationalism and neo-Nazism, but more benignly in the popular repossession of alternative pasts and long-suppressed subjective memo-ries. On this score Michael Rutschky is correct when he remarked that the 1990s reinvention of the GDR marks the genuine if belated emer-gence of the "GDR as culture," whose former citizens now form a real "experiential and storytelling community" based for the first time upon free, post-SED narrative exchange and uncontrolled communication.[98] All of which has shown that antifascism no longer occupies the center of these new myths and memories.

What is so compelling is that the same went for West Germany in the early 1980s. For the explosive new interest in German national identity and its attendant "normalization" of German history was in many ways only possible because of the weakening antifascist consensus that long dominated the FRG's world of letters and culture. Like in East Germany, this West German nostalgia belied the dramatic fact that the universities, *Kultur*, and the state no longer controlled the production of memory; in-deed, such retrospectives took place in the larger public sphere, including museums, design venues, television, urban boutiques, and weekend flea markets. But it was not only its popular dimension that was significant; "*Nierentisch* nostalgia" also played a role in challenging the antifascist consensus. This is best understood if we recall that in West Germany—like in East Germany—antifascist ideology was always predicated upon anticapitalism. The Left's perceived linkage of fascism and capitalism of course dates back to the 1930s; but it became a mainstay of West Ger-many's New Left through the 1970s. With the result that West German antifascism—like its East German counterpart—was often inseparable from denunciations against the dangers of consumerism. This 1980s nos-talgia had demonstrated that romantic consumer nationalism—the very inversion of antifascist ideology—had become for West Germans a key dimension of shared identity and memory. Not that there were not ear-lier attempts to reclaim the 1950s as new "heroic" national history; the first article lauding the "Golden 1950s" appeared as early as 1967.[99] Yet it was instructive that this first volley to romanticize the decade in these terms was steamrolled by a spate of New Left critiques of the "Adenauer Restoration" and the "CDU State" at the time, and it was this negative image of the 1950s—one emphasizing the continuities instead of the rup-tures—that prevailed until the 1970s.[100] The bluster surrounding the 1980s reshaping of cultural memory from one of production and pain to consumption and comfort was not only that it was fanciful. The reason why it was condemned so vehemently by leftists as naive neoconserva-tivism and flea-market fluff was precisely because it implicitly took issue with the time-worn legitimacy of older myths of postfascist identity and self-understanding.

Where this 1950s nostalgia mattered most, though, was how it related to the popular interest in other German pasts. It was one thing that this nostalgia wave was at the center of an alternative 1950s history. It was of course something else when it touched the Third Reich. The pop-culture fascination with Nazi culture first began in the early 1970s, when it emerged as a source of lurid curiosity in international sadomasochist sub-cultures and flea-market bazaars.[101] By the end of the decade there was a bumper crop of bold new Hitler biographies, films, and exhibitions about long-repressed historical subjects.[102] Yet there was a subtle connection be-tween fifties nostalgia and the more general revision of the Third Reich, which went beyond the fact that both began as mass-media phenomena far removed from the confines of university seminar rooms. The 1980s recollections of tranquil domestic life and private pleasures had begged the question of how far back such daydreams of wistful normality might go. It seems hardly coincidental that this new impulse to study Nazi so-cial history and everyday life—much of which pivoted upon the delicate concepts of normality and pleasure—first took place during the early and mid-1980s, a few years after the normal and pleasurable aspects of the 1950s had been successfully recovered. A revealing example is the way that Edgar Reitz's famous film, *Heimat*, which chronicles the life of a ru-ral German family over several generations, negotiated the past. Its novel and most controversial aspect was that it decentered the Holocaust as the linchpin of German experience and history, foregrounding instead the rel-atively unchanging and "normal" dimensions of everyday domestic life from the period.[103] Not that Reitz was alone in the reworking of the past; the so-called historians of everyday life uncovered much of the same sen-timent swirling beneath the official orthodoxies of West German state and society. This was why Reitz and these maverick historians were so severely criticized at the time, since they seemed to have wanted to reha-bilitate "normal" German society amid the emergency conditions of the Third Reich, and to reconfigure a Germany unknowing of or uninterested in Auschwitz.[104] But Reitz was hardly an isolated case; elsewhere the world of pop culture had overturned the inherited pieties about the past. Now the once-solemn industry of remembering was refashioned by the 1980s commodification of cultural memory, which baldly mass-produced the Nazi past as consumer object, visual entertainment, and political kitsch.[105] In this context the New Left's old conceptual vocabulary for un-derstanding German fascism—class and capitalism, Führerkult ideology and mass manipulation, psychological repression and the "authoritarian personality"—no longer enjoyed much sway in the public at large. Even the old stand-by of German history as a story of suffering, pain, and evil was being revised; instead, the new issues of normality and pleasure crowded to the front. It is precisely in these terms that Christopher Browning's *Ordinary Men*, Daniel Jonah Goldhagen's *Hitler's Willing Executioners*, and the controversial exhibition "The German Army and Genocide" have been so important, for they conjoined the concepts of normality, evil, and pleasure (in Goldhagen's case, the perverse pleasure of inflicting pain upon others) with the implementation of the Final Solution. Whatever the merits of these debates, the violation of this taboo subject—that German history was both normal and pleasurable—first occurred in the late 1970s with the discussions about the "Golden 1950s." Its success and power in liberating the past from the then-dominant anti-fascist consensus opened the door, I think, to the nostalgic ruminations about other German pasts.

These respective nostalgia waves reveal a great deal about the ongoing negotiation of German pasts and presents in the 1980s and 1990s. They represent key moments in the "popularization of history" in each country, one which arose from (and in the West German case, helped bring about) the broken monopoly on social history and memory enjoyed by the state, the universities, and the world of *Kultur*. This has been particularly poignant in the former GDR. That people would want to tell different stories after 1989 about "real existing socialism" was in itself predictable; what was so striking was the degree to which these consumer memories and objects have colored many of them. In so doing they throw light on the connective tissue binding self and society, and go a long way toward a sociology of German sentiments and passions. That the past in each case served as the very vehicle of psychological investment and warm recollection was no small matter, especially in view of the long-standing demonization of German history in both rival republics. In the end, these nostalgia waves emerged as real flash points of memory and materialism, illuminating how German postwar identities were born of postfascist promises and dreams of the good life.

Notes

CHAPTER I

1. Vaclav Havel, "Speech on 15 February 1990 on the Occasion of the Visit of President Richard von Weizsäcker to Prague," in *When the Wall Came Down: Reactions to German Unification*, ed. Harold James and Marla Stone (New York: Routledge, 1992), 312–13.

2. Tony Judt, "1989: The End of Which Europe?" *Daedalus* 123 (summer 1994): 15.

3. Mark Mazower, *Dark Continent: Europe's Twentieth Century* (New York: Knopf, 1998).

4. Tony Judt, "The Past is Another Country: Myth and Memory in Postwar Europe," *Daedalus* 121 (fall 1992): 83–119.

5. Henry Rousso, *The Vichy Syndrome: History and Memory in France since 1944* (Cambridge: Harvard University Press, 1991). See also Nancy Wood, *Vectors of Memory: Legacies of Trauma in Postwar Europe* (Oxford: Berg, 1999).

6. Eric Hobsbawm, *The Age of Extremes: A History of the World, 1914–1991* (New York: Vintage, 1994), 1–17.

7. Michael Huelshoff and Andrei Markovits, introduction to *From Bundesrepublik to Deutschland: German Politics after Reunification*, ed. Michael Huelshoff, Andrei Markowits, and Simon Reich (Ann Arbor: University of Michigan Press, 1993), 1. Note as well Eberhard Jäckel, *Das deutsche Jahrhundert: Eine historische Bilanz* (Frankfurt: Fischer, 1999); and Michael Geyer, "Germany, or the Twentieth Century as History," *South Atlantic Quarterly* 96 (fall 1997): 663–702.

8. Omer Bartov, *Murder in Our Midst* (New York: Oxford University Press, 1996). See also Scott Denham, *Visions of War: Ideologies and Images of War in German Literature before and after the Great War* (Bern: Peter Lang, 1992).

9. Sigmund Freud, *Civilization and its Discontents* (New York: Norton, 1961); Ernst Pöppel, *Lust und Schmerz: Grundlagen menschlichen Erlebens und Verhaltens* (Berlin: Severin und Siedler, 1982).

10. Massimo Montanari, *The Culture of Food* (Oxford: Blackwell, 1994).

11. Wolfgang Kaschuba, "Konsum—Lebensstil—Bedürfnis: Zum Problem materieller Indikatoren in der Kultur- und Mentalitätsgeschichte," *Sozialwissenschaftliche Informationen* 17 (1988): 133–38; Mary-Jo DelVecchio Good,

Paul E. Brodwin, Byron J. Good, and Arthur Kleinman, eds., *Pain as Human Experience: An Anthropological Perspective* (Berkeley: University of California Press, 1992); Hannes Siegrist, Jakob Tanner, and Beatrice Veyrassat, eds., *Geschichte der Konsumgesellschaft: Märkte, Kultur und Identität (15.–20. Jahrhundert)* (Zürich: Chronos, 1997); and Arthur Kleinman, Veena Das, and Margaret Lock, eds., *Social Suffering* (Berkeley: University of California Press, 1997).

12. John Brewer and Roy Porter, eds., *Consumption and the World of Goods* (London and New York: Routledge, 1993); Susan M. Pearce, ed., *Experiencing Material Culture in the Western World* (London and Washington, D.C.: Leicester University, 1997); Peter N. Stearns, "Stages of Consumerism: Recent Work on the Issues of Periodization," *Journal of Modern History* 69 (1997): 102–17; and Frank Mort, "Paths to Mass Consumption: Historical Perspectives," introduction to *Commercial Cultures: Economies, Practices, Spaces*, ed. Peter Jackson, Michelle Lowe, Daniel Miller, and Frank Mort (Oxford and New York: Berg, 2000). For a more global account of consumerism in terms of the relationship between Asia and the West in the early modern period, see Craig Clunas, "Modernity Global and Local: Consumption and the Rise of the West," *American Historical Review* 104 (December 1999): 1497–1511.

13. Volker R. Berghahn, *Imperial Germany, 1871–1914: Economy, Society, Culture, and Politics* (Providence, R.I., and Oxford: Berghahn, 1994), 11–17; Manfred Gailus and Heinrich Volkmann, "Einführung: Nahrungsmangel, Hunger, und Protest," in *Der Kampf um tägliche Brot: Nahrungsmangel, Versorgungspolitik, und Protest, 1770–1990*, ed. Manfred Gailus and Heinrich Volkmann (Opladen: Westdeutscher, 1994), 9–23; and Werner Abelshauser and D. Petzina, *Deutsche Wirtschaftsgeschichte im Industriezeitalter: Konjunktur, Krise, Wachstum* (Königstein/TS and Düsseldorf: Athenäum/Droste, 1981).

14. Alon Confino and Rudy Koshar, "Regimes of Consumer Culture: New Narratives in Twentieth Century German History," in *German History* 19 (2001): 135–61 (here 138). An excellent new study of the relationship between economic misery and German culture is Bernd Widdig, *Culture and Inflation in Weimar Germany* (Berkeley: University of California Press, 2001).

15. Otto Brunner, Werner Conze, and Reinhart Koselleck, eds., *Geschichtliche Grundbegriffe: Historisches Lexicon zur politisch-sozialen Sprache in Deutschland*, 8 vols. (Stuttgart: Klett-Cotta, 1982–97); Thomas Childers, "The Social Language of Politics in Germany: The Sociology of Political Discourse in the Weimar Republic," *American Historical Review* 95 (1990): 331–58.

16. Walter Hofmann, *Schmerz, Pein, und Weh* (Giessen: W. Schmitz, 1956).

17. Friedrich Kluge, *Etymologisches Wörterbuch der deutschen Sprache* (Berlin: de Gruyter, 1957), 432.

18. Mohammed Rassem, "Wohlfahrt, Wohltat, Wohltätigkeit, Caritas," in Bruner et al., eds., *Geschichtliche Grundbegriffe*, vol. 7 (1992): 595–636.

19. Armin Triebel, "Moral und Ökonomie: Zur modernen Semantik des Lebensstandards," in *Europäische Konsumgeschichte: Zur Gesellschafts- und Kulturgeschichte des Konsums (18. bis 20. Jahrhundert)*, ed. Hannes Siegrist, Hartmut Kaelble, and Jürgen Kocka (Frankfurt: Campus, 1997), 365–92.

20. Besides the edited collection by Siegrist et al. noted above, see also Susan

Strasser, Charles McGovern, and Matthias Judt, eds., *Getting and Spending: European and American Consumer Societies in the Twentieth Century* (Cambridge: Cambridge University Press, 1998).

21. Victoria DeGrazia and Ellen Furlough, eds., *The Sex of Things: Gender and Consumption* (Berkeley: University of California Press Press, 1996); Martin Daunton and Matthew Hilton, *The Politics of Consumption: Material Culture and Citizenship in Europe and America* (Oxford: Berg, 2001); Kaspar Maase, *Grenzloses Vergnügen: Der Aufstieg der Massenkultur, 1850–1970* (Frankfurt: Fischer, 1997); Geoffrey Crossick and Serge Jaumain, eds., *Cathedrals of Consumption: The European Department Store, 1850–1939* (Aldershot, U.K.: Ashgate, 1999). See also Mary Louise Roberts, "Gender, Consumption and Commodity Culture," *American Historical Review* 103 (June 1998): 817–44; Lisa Tiersten, "Redefining Consumer Culture: Recent Literature on Consumption and the Bourgeoisie in Western Europe," *Radical History Review* (fall 1993): 117–59.

22. Ina Merkel, *Utopie und Bedürfnis: Die Geschichte der Konsumkultur in der DDR* (Cologne: Böhlau, 1999).

23. Ulrich Wyrwa, "Consumption and Consumer Society: A Contribution to the History of Ideas," in Strasser et al., *Getting and Spending*, 431–48.

24. Wolfgang Sachs, *For the Love of the Automobile: Looking Back into the History of our Desires* (Berkeley: University of California Press, 1992); Rudy Koshar, *German Travel Cultures* (Oxford: Berg, 2000); Hasso Spode, *Alkohol und Zivilisation: Berauschung, Ernüchterung und Tischensitten in Deutschland bis zum Beginn des 20. Jahrhundert* (Berlin: Tara, 1991); Adelheid von Saldern, *Haüserleben: Zur Geschichte städtischen Arbeiterwohnens vom Kaiserreich bis heute* (Bonn: J. H. W. Dietz Nachf., 1995); Kristen Schlegel-Matthies, *"Im Haus und am Herd": Der Wandel des Hausfrauenbildes und der Hausarbeit, 1880–1930* (Stuttgart: Franz Steiner, 1995); Wolfgang Ruppert, ed., *Fahrrad, Auto, Fernseherschrank: Zur Kulturgeschichte der Alltagsdinge* (Frankfurt: Fischer, 1993); and Arne Andersen, *Der Traum vom guten Leben: Alltags- und Konsumgeschichte von Wirtschaftswunder bis heute* (Frankfurt: Campus, 1997).

25. Confino and Koshar, "Regimes of Consumer Culture," 138.

26. Jeffrey Kopstein, *The Politics of Economic Decline in East Germany, 1945–1989* (Chapel Hill: University of North Carolina, 1997); and Charles Maier, *Dissolution: The Crisis of Communism and the End of East Germany* (Princeton: Princeton University Press, 1997).

27. Paul Betts, "The Twilight of the Idols: East German Memory and Material Culture," *The Journal of Modern History* 72 (September 2000): 731–65.

28. Michel Foucault, *Discipline and Punish: The Birth of the Prison* (New York: Vintage, 1979); Martin Dinges, "Frühneuzeitliche Armenfürsorge als Sozialdisziplinierung? Probleme mit einem Konzept," *Geschichte und Gesellschaft* 17 (1991): 5–29; Roy Porter, "History of the Body," in *New Perspectives on Historical Writing*, ed. Peter Burke (University Park: Pennsylvania State University, 1991), 206–32; Petrus Spierenburg, *The Prison Experience: Disciplinary Institutions and Their Inmates in Early Modern Europe* (New Brunswick: Rutgers University Press, 1991); Norbert Finzsch and Robert Jütte, eds., *Institutions of Confinement: Hospitals, Asylums, and Prisons in Western*

Europe and North America, 1500–1950 (Cambridge: Cambridge University Press, 1996).

29. On contemporary debates over the notion of the archive, see the special issue "The Archive," *History of the Human Sciences* 11 (1998).

30. Daniel De Moulin, "A Historical-Phenomenological Study of Bodily Pain in Western Man," *Bulletin of the History of Medicine* 48 (1974): 540–70; David B. Morris, *The Culture of Pain* (Berkeley: University of California Press, 1993); Roy Porter, "Pain and Suffering," in *Companion Encyclopedia of the History of Medicine*, vol. 2, ed. W. F. Bynum and Roy Porter (London and New York: Routledge, 1993), 1574–91; Roselyne Rey, *The History of Pain* (Cambridge, Mass.: Harvard University Press, 1995); Elaine Scarry, *The Body in Pain: The Making and Unmaking of the World* (New York: Oxford University Press, 1995); "Schmerz und Schmerzerfahrung," special issue of *Medizin, Gesellschaft, und Geschichte* 15 (1998).

31. See, for instance, the classic work on table manners, Norbert Elias, *The Civilizing Process* (Oxford: Blackwell, 1994).

32. Claudine Herzlich and Janine Pierret, *Illness and Self in Society* (Baltimore: Johns Hopkins University Press, 1987), 210–35; Joachim Radkau, *Das Zeitalter der Nervosität: Deutschland zwischen Bismarck und Hitler* (Munich: Hanser, 1998), 357–455.

33. Peter N. Stearns and Timothy Haggerty, "The Role of Fear: Transitions in American Emotional Standards for Children, 1850–1950," *American Historical Review* 96 (1991): 63–94; Peter N. Stearns, "Konsumgesellschaft: Ein Kinderkreuzzug," in Siegrist et al., *Europäische Konsumgeschichte*, 139–68.

34. Peter D. Kramer, *Listening to Prozac: A Psychiatrist Explores Antidepressant Drugs and the Remaking of the Self* (New York: Penguin, 1993); Greg Critser, "Oh, How Happy We Will Be: Pills, Paradise, and the Profits of the Drug Companies," *Harper's Magazine* 292 (1996): 39–48; Siegfried Lenz, "Über den Schmerz," in *Über den Schmerz: Essays* (Hamburg: Hoffmann und Campe, 1998), 7–29.

35. On globalization and the writing of history, see Michael Geyer and Charles Bright, "World History in a Global Age," *American Historical Review* 100 (1995): 1034–60; Malcolm Water, *Globalization* (London: Routledge, 1995).

36. Robert Weldon Whalen, *Bitter Wounds: German Victims of the Great War, 1914–1939* (Ithaca: Cornell University Press, 1984); Richard Bessel, *Germany After the First World War* (New York: Oxford University Press, 1993); Gerald D. Feldman, *The Great Disorder: Politics, Economics, and Society in the German Inflation, 1914–1924* (Oxford: Oxford University Press, 1993); David F. Crew, *Germans on Welfare: From Weimar to Hitler* (Oxford: Oxford University Press, 1998); Belinda Davis, *Home Fires Burning: Food, Politics, and Daily Life in World War I Berlin* (Chapel Hill: University of North Carolina Press, 1999); Greg Eghigian, *Making Security Social: Disability, Insurance, and the Birth of the Social Entitlement State in Germany* (Ann Arbor: University of Michigan Press, 2000).

37. Peter Fritzsche, *Germans into Nazis* (Cambridge, Mass.: Harvard University Press, 1998). On the role of sacrifice as an organizing principle in German

and Nazi nationalism, see Sabine Behrenbeck, *Der Kult um die toten Helden: Nationalsozialistische Mythen, Riten, und Symbole* (Vierow bei Greifswald: S-H, 1996); Yvonne Karow, *Deutsches Opfer: Kultische Selbstauslöschung auf den Reichsparteitagen der NSDAP* (Berlin: Akademie, 1997); Greg Eghigian and Matthew Berg, eds., *Sacrifice and National Belonging in Twentieth-Century Germany* (College Station, Texas: Texas A&M University Press, 2002).

38. Gisela Bock, *Zwangssterilisation im Nationalsozialismus: Studien zur Rassenpolitik und Frauenpolitik* (Opladen: Westdeutscher, 1986); Klaus Dörner, *Tödliches Mitleid: Zur Frage der Unerträglichkeit des Lebens, oder die soziale Frage: Entstehung, Medizinisierung, NS-Endlösung heute morgen* (Gütersloh: Jakob von Hoddis, 1988); Hans-Walter Schmuhl, *Rassenhygiene, Nationalsozialismus, Euthanasie: Von der Verhütung zur Vernichtung "lebensunwerten Lebens," 1890–1945* (Göttingen: Vandenhoeck & Ruprecht, 1992); Peter Reichel, *Der schöne Schein des Dritten Reiches: Faszination und Gewalt des Faschismus* (Frankfurt: Fischer Taschenbuch, 1993); Michael Burleigh, *Death and Deliverance: "Euthanasia" in Germany, 1900–1945* (Cambridge, Mass.: Cambridge University Press, 1995); Henry Friedlander, *The Origins of Nazi Genocide: From Euthanasia to the Final Solution* (Chapel Hill: University of North Carolina Press, 1995); Geoffrey Cocks, *Psychotherapy in the Third Reich: The Göring Institute*, 2nd ed. (New Brunswick, N.J.: Transaction, 1997).

39. John Borneman, *Belonging in the Two Berlins: Kin, State, Nation* (New York: Cambridge University Press, 1992).

40. Elizabeth Heineman, "The Hour of the Woman: Memories of Germany's 'Crisis Years' and West German National Identity," *American Historical Review* 101 (1996): 354–95.

41. Erica Carter, *How German is She? Postwar West German Reconstruction and the Consuming Woman* (Ann Arbor: University of Michigan Press, 1997), 45.

42. Neue Gesellschaft für Bildende Kunst, ed., *Wunderwirtschaft: DDR-Konsumkultur in 1960er Jahren* (Cologne: Böhlau, 1996); Katherine Pence, "Schaufenster des sozialistischen Konsums: Texte der ostdeutschen 'consumer culture,'" in *Akten. Eingaben. Schaufenster. Die DDR und ihre Texte: Erkundungen zu Herrschaft und Alltag*, ed. Alf Lüdtke and Peter Becker (Berlin: Akademie, 1997), 91–118; Stephan Merl, "Staat und Konsum in der Zentralverwaltungswirtschaft: Rußland und die ostmitteleuropäischen Länder," in Siegrist et al., *Europäische Konsumgeschichte*, 205–41.

43. Katherine Pence, "Labours of Consumption: Gendered Consumers in Post-War East and West German Reconstruction," in *Gender Relations in German History: Power, Agency, and Experience From the Sixteenth to the Twentieth Century*, ed. Lynn Abrams and Elizabeth Harvey (Durham: Duke University Press, 1997), 211–38; Jennifer A. Loehlin, *From Rugs to Riches: Housework, Consumption and Modernity in Germany* (Oxford: Berg, 2000); and Michael Wildt, *Am Beginn der "Konsumgesellschaft": Mangelerfahrung, Lebenshaltung, Wohlstandshoffnung in Westdeutschland in den fünfziger Jahren* (Hamburg: Ergebnisse, 1994), 214–70.

44. For an introduction to the cultural history of values and morality, see Sonya O. Rose, "Cultural Analysis and Moral Discourses: Episodes, Continuities,

and Transformations," in *Beyond the Cultural Turn: New Directions in the Study of Society and Culture*, ed. Victoria E. Bonnell and Lynn Hunt (Berkeley: University of California Press, 1999), 217–38. Of related interest, see Alan Wolfe, *Whose Keeper? Social Science and Moral Obligation* (Berkeley: University of California Press, 1989).

45. John E. Crowley, "The Sensibility of Comfort," *American Historical Review* 104 (1999): 750. See his book, *The Invention of Comfort: Sensibility and Design in Early Modern Britain and Early America* (Baltimore: Johns Hopkins University Press, 2001).

46. Jonas Frykman and Orvar Löfgren, *Culture Builders: A Historical Anthropology of Middle-Class Life* (New Brunswick, N.J.: Rutgers University Press, 1987); Jürgen Kocka and Allan Mitchell, eds., *Bourgeois Society in Nineteenth-Century Europe* (Oxford: Berg, 1993).

47. On the notion of social distinction, see Pierre Bourdieu's highly influential *Distinction: A Social Critique of the Judgement of Taste* (London: Routledge & Kegan Paul, 1984).

48. Ronald Inglehart, *Culture Shift in Advanced Industrial Society* (Princeton: Princeton University Press, 1990); Göran Therborn, *European Modernity and Beyond: The Trajectory of European Societies, 1945–2000* (London: Sage, 1995), 272–303.

49. Claus Offe, "Challenging the Boundaries of Institutional Politics: Social Movements Since the 1960s," in *Changing Boundaries of the Political: Essays on the Evolving Balance Between the State and Society, Public and Private in Europe*, ed. Charles S. Maier (Cambridge: Cambridge University Press, 1987), 63–105; Martin E. Marty and R. Scott Appleby, eds., *Fundamentalisms Observed*, vol. 1 (Chicago: University of Chicago Press, 1991); Ulrich Beck, *Risk Society: Towards a New Modernity* (London: Sage, 1992); Gisela Kaplan, *Contemporary Western European Feminism* (New York: New York University Press, 1992); Enrique Larana, Hank Johnston, and Joseph Gusfield, eds., *New Social Movements: From Ideology to Identity* (Philadelphia: Temple University Press, 1994).

50. On the comparative history of prosperity and its values, see Gerald Diesener and Rainer Gries, "'Chic zum Geburtstag unserer Republik': Zwei Projekte zur Produkt- und Politikpropaganda im Deutsch-Deutschen Vergleich," *Geschichtswerkstatt* 25 (1992): 56–69.

51. Michael Wildt, *Der Traum vom Sattwerden: Hunger und Protest, Schwarzmarkt und Selbsthilfe* (Hamburg: VSA, 1986); Axel Schildt, *Moderne Zeiten: Freizeit, Massenmedien, und "Zeitgeist" in der Bundesrepublik der 50er Jahre* (Hamburg: Christians, 1995); and Hanna Schissler, "'Normalization' as Project: Some Thoughts on Gender Relations in West Germany during the 1950s," in her edited *Miracle Years: A Cultural History of West Germany, 1949–1968* (Princeton: Princeton University Press, 2001), 359–76.

52. Ursula A. J. Becher, *Geschichte des modernen Lebensstils: Essen—Wohnen—Freizeit—Reisen* (Munich: C. H. Beck, 1990); Andrei S. Markovits and Philip S. Gorski, *The German Left: Red, Green, and Beyond* (Cambridge: Polity, 1993); Alice Holmes Cooper, *Paradoxes of Peace: German Peace Movements Since 1945* (Ann Arbor: University of Michigan Press, 1996).

53. On sources in GDR history, see Lüdtke and Becker, *Akten*. See also *Dictatorship as Experience: Towards a Socio-Cultural History of the GDR*, ed. Konrad Jarausch (New York: Berghahn, 1999).

54. On Soviet policy in East Germany, see Norman M. Naimark, *The Russians in Germany: A History of the Soviet Zone of Occupation, 1945–1949* (Cambridge, Mass.: Belknap, 1995).

55. Günter Gaus, *Wo Deutschland liegt* (Munich: Deutscher Taschenbuch, 1983); Mary Fulbrook, *Anatomy of a Dictatorship: Inside the GDR, 1949–1989* (Oxford: Oxford University Press, 1995); and *Fortschritt, Norm & Eigensinn: Erkundungen im Alltag der DDR*, ed. Dokumentationszentrum Alltagskultur der DDR e.V. (Berlin: Ch. Links, 1999).

56. Lutz Niethammer et al., *Die eigene Volkserfahrung: Eine Archäologie des Lebens in der Industrieprovinz der DDR* (Berlin: Rowohlt, 1991); and Johannes Huinink and Karl Ulrich Mayer, eds., *Kollektiv und Eigensinn: Lebensläufe in der DDR und danach* (Berlin: Akademie, 1995).

57. Konrad H. Jarausch, *The Rush to German Unity* (New York: Oxford University Press, 1994), 33–52; Sabrina Petra Ramet, *Social Currents in Eastern Europe: The Sources and Consequences of the Great Transformation* (Durham: Duke University Press, 1995), 55–83.

58. Alf Lüdtke, Inge Marssolek, and Adelheid von Saldern, eds., *Amerikanisierung: Traum und Alptraum im Deutschland des 20. Jahrhunderts* (Stuttgart: Steiner, 1996); Konrad Jarausch and Hannes Siegrist, eds., *Amerikanisierung und Sowjetisierung in Deutschland, 1945–1970* (Frankfurt: Campus, 1997); Gerd Gemünden, *Framed Visions: Popular Culture, Americanization and the Contemporary German and Austrian Imagination* (Ann Arbor: University of Michigan Press, 1998); Reiner Pommerin, ed., *The American Impact on Postwar Germany* (Providence, R.I.: Berghahn, 1995); and Michael Ermarth, ed., *America and the Shaping of German Society, 1945–1955* (Providence, R.I.: Berg, 1993).

59. Lothar Prost, ed., *Differenz in der Einheit: Über die kulturellen Unterschiede der Deutschen in Ost und West* (Berlin: Ch. Links, 1999); and Patrick Stevenson and John Theobald, eds., *Relocating Germanness: Discursive Disunity in United Germany* (New York: St. Martin's, 2000).

60. For an excellent critical discussion of the subject, see Allan Megill, "History, Memory, Identity," *History of the Human Sciences* 11, no. 3 (1998): 37–62.

61. See the special AHR Forum, "History and Memory," *American History Review* 102 (1997): 1371–1412.

62. Rudy Koshar, *From Monuments to Traces: Artifacts of German Memory* (Berkeley: University of California Press, 2000); and Alon Confino and Peter Fritzsche, eds., *The Work of Memory: New Directions in the Study of German Society and Culture* (Urbana: University of Illinois Press, 2002).

63. Yosef Hayim Yerushalmi, *Zakhor: Jewish History and Jewish Memory* (Seattle: University of Washington Press, 1982); Charles S. Maier, *The Unmasterable Past: History, Holocaust, and German National Identity* (Cambridge, Mass.: Harvard University Press, 1988); Eric L. Santner, *Stranded Objects: Mourning, Memory, and Film in Postwar Germany* (Ithaca: Cornell University Press, 1990);

James E. Young, *The Texture of Memory: Holocaust Memorials and Meaning* (New Haven: Yale University Press, 1993); Tony Kushner, *The Holocaust and the Liberal Imagination: A Social and Cultural History* (Oxford: Blackwell, 1994); Peter Reichel, *Politik mit der Erinnerung: Gedächtnisorte im Streit um die Nationalsozialistische Vergangenheit* (Munich: Hanser, 1995); Rudy Koshar, *Germany's Transient Past: Preservation and National Memory in the Twentieth Century* (Chapel Hill: University of North Carolina Press, 1998); and Peter Novick, *The Holocaust in American Life* (Boston: Houghton Mifflin, 1999).

64. Claudia Koonz, "Between Memory and Oblivion: Concentration Camps in German Memory," in *Commemorations: The Politics of Identity*, ed. John R. Gillis (Princeton: Princeton University Press, 1994), 258–80; Julia Hell, *Post-Fascist Fantasies: Psychoanalysis, History, and the Literature of East Germany* (Durham: Duke University Press, 1997); Jeffrey Herf, *Divided Memory: The Nazi Past in the Two Germanys* (Cambridge, Mass.: Harvard University Press, 1997).

65. Dan Bar-On, *Legacy of Silence: Encounters with Children of the Third Reich* (Cambridge, Mass.: Harvard University Press, 1989).

66. Robert Moeller, "Remembering the War in a Nation of Victims: West German Pasts in the 1950s," in Schissler, *Miracle Years*, 83–109; and Atina Grossmann, "A Question of Silence: The Rape of German Women by Occupation Soldiers," in *West Germany under Construction: Politics, Society in the Adenauer Era*, ed. Robert G. Moeller (Ann Arbor: University of Michigan Press, 1997), 33–52.

67. Hans Mommsen, "The German Resistance against Hitler and the Restoration of Politics"; and David Clay Large, "'A Beacon in the German Darkness': The Anti-Nazi Resistance Legacy in West German Politics," both in *Resistance Against the Third Reich, 1933–1990*, ed. Michael Geyer and John Boyer (Chicago: University of Chicago Press, 1994), 151–66 and 43–256, respectively.

68. On the theme of trauma, collective memory, and repression, see Geoffrey Cocks, "Repressing, Remembering, Working Through: German Psychiatry, Psychotherapy, Psychoanalysis, and the 'Missed Resistance' in the Third Reich," in Geyer and Boyer, *Resistance*, 312–24; Michael S. Roth, *The Ironist's Cage: Memory, Trauma, and the Construction of History* (New York: Columbia University Press, 1995); Cathy Caruth, *Unclaimed Experience: Trauma, Narrative, and History* (Baltimore: Johns Hopkins University Press, 1996).

69. Alexander and Margarete Mitscherlich, *Die Unfähigkeit zu trauern: Grundlagen kollektiven Verhaltens* (Munich: Piper, 1977).

70. Ulrich Herbert, "'Die guten und die schlechten Zeiten': Überlegungen zur diachronen Analyse lebensgeschichtlicher Interviews," in *"Die Jahre weiß man nicht, wo man die heute hinsetzen soll": Faschismuserfahrungen im Ruhrgebiet. Lebensgeschichte und Sozialkultur im Ruhrgebiet 1930 bis 1960*, vol. 1, ed. Lutz Niethammer (Berlin: J. H. W. Dietz Nachf., 1986), 67–96; Lutz Niethammer, "'Normalisierung' im Westen: Erinnerungsspuren in die 50er Jahre," in *Ist der Nationalsozialismus Geschichte? Zu Historisierung und Historikerstreit*, ed. Dan Diner (Frankfurt: Fischer, 1987), 153–84; Omer Bartov, *Murder in Our Midst: The Holocaust, Industrial Killing, and Representation* (New York: Oxford University Press, 1996), 119–22.

71. Volker Berghahn, "Recasting Bourgeois Germany," in Schissler, *Miracle Years*, 326–40.

72. Hasso Spode, "Arbeiterurlaub im Dritten Reich," in *Angst, Belohnung, Zucht und Ordnung: Herrschaftsmechanismen im Nationalsozialismus* ed. Carola Sachse, Tilla Siegel, Hasso Spode, and Wolfgang Spohn (Opladen: Westdeutscher Verlag, 1982); Reichel, *Der schöne Schein*; Koshar, *German Travel Cultures*, esp. 115–34; Alon Confino, "Traveling as a Culture of Remembrance: Traces of National Socialism in West Germany, 1945–1960," *History and Memory* 12 (fall/winter 2000): 92–121; Shelley Baranowski, "Strength Through Joy: Tourism and National Integration in the Third Reich," in *Being Elsewhere: Tourism, Consumer Culture and Identity in Modern Europe and North America*, ed. S. Baranowski and Ellen Furlough (Ann Arbor: University of Michigan Press, 2001).

73. Geyer, "Germany," 693.

74. James Knowlton and Truett Cates, trans., *Forever in the Shadow of Hitler?* (Atlantic Highlands, N.J.: Humanities Press, 1993); Adelheid von Saldern, "Victims or Perpetrators? Controversies about the Role of Women in the Nazi State," in *Nazism and German Society, 1933–1945*, ed. David F. Crew (London: Routledge, 1994), 141–65; Angelika Ebbinghaus, ed., *Opfer und Täterinnen: Frauenbiographien des Nationalsozialismus* (Frankfurt: Fischer Taschenbuch, 1996); Robert R. Shandley, ed., *Unwilling Germans? The Goldhagen Debate* (Minneapolis: University of Minnesota Press, 1998).

75. Joseph A. Amato, *Victims and Values: A History and a Theory of Suffering* (New York: Praeger, 1990); Greg Eghigian, "The Politics of Victimization: Social Pensioners and the German Social State in the Inflation of 1914–1924," *Central European History* 26 (1993): 375–403; Omer Bartov, "Defining Enemies, Making Victims: Germans, Jews, and the Holocaust," *American Historical Review* 103 (1998): 771–816.

76. Andreas Huyssen, *Twilight Memories: Making Time in a Culture of Amnesia* (New York: Routledge, 1995), 249–60; Laurence Mordekhai Thomas, "Suffering as a Moral Beacon: Blacks and Jews," in *The Americanization of the Holocaust*, ed. Hilene Flanzbaum (Baltimore: Johns Hopkins University Press, 1999), 198–210; Silke Wenk, "Sacrifice and Victimization in the Commemorative Practices of Nazi Genocide After German Unification—Memorials and Visual Metaphors," in Eghigian and Berg, *Sacrifice*.

77. Robert von Hallberg, ed., *Literary Intellectuals and the Dissolution of the State: Professionalism and Conformity in the GDR* (Chicago: University of Chicago Press, 1996); John Borneman, *Settling Accounts: Violence, Justice, and Accountability in Postsocialist Europe* (Princeton: Princeton University Press, 1997); and Tina Rosenberg, *The Haunted Land: Facing Europe's Ghosts after Communism* (New York: Vintage, 1995).

78. Hans-Joachim Maaz, *Behind the Wall: The Inner Life of Communist Germany* (New York: Norton, 1995).

79. This was particularly evident in public reaction to the release of the German edition of Stephane Courtois, Nicolas Werth, and Jean-Louis Panne, *Das Schwarzbuch des Kommunismus: Unterdrückung, Verbrechung, und Terror*

(Munich: Piper, 1998). It argued that communism was historically more destructive than fascism in this century. On the ensuing debate in Germany, see Horst Möller, *Der Rote Holocaust und die Deutschen: Debatte um das "Schwarzbuch des Kommunismus"* (Munich: Piper, 1999).

80. Brian Ladd, *The Ghosts of Berlin: Confronting German History in the Urban Landscape* (Chicago: University of Chicago Press, 1997).

81. Deutsches Historisches Museum, ed., *Einigkeit und Recht und Freiheit: Wege der Deutschen, 1949–1999* (Reinbek bei Hamburg: Rowohlt, 1999).

82. Andreas Huyssen, "After the Wall: The Failure of German Intellectuals," *New German Critique* (winter 1991): 109–43.

83. Otthein Rammstedt and Gert Schmidt, eds., *BRD Ade! Vierzig Jahre in Rück-Ansichten* (Frankfurt: Suhrkamp, 1992).

84. Julia Hell, "History as Trauma, or Turning to the Past Once Again: Germany 1949/1989," *South Atlantic Quarterly* 96, no. 4 (1997): 911–47.

85. Charles Maier, "The End of Longing? (Notes Toward a History of Postwar German National Longing)," in *The Postwar Transformation of Germany: Democracy, Prosperity and Nationhood*, ed. John Brady, Beverly Crawford, and Sarah Elise Wiliarty (Ann Arbor: University of Michigan Press, 1999), 271–85.

86. This is not at all limited to East Germany. See for example Susan Reid and David Crowley, eds., *Style and Socialism: Modernity and Material Culture in Postwar Eastern Europe* (Oxford: Berg, 2000); and Daphne Berdahl, Matti Bunzl, and Martha Lampland, eds., *Altering States: Ethnographies of Transition in Eastern Europe and the Former Soviet Union* (Ann Arbor: University of Michigan Press, 2000).

87. John Borneman, *East Meets West in the New Berlin* (New York: Basic, 1991); Edeltraud Roller, *Einstellungen der Bürger zum Wohlfahrtsstaat der Bundesrepublik Deutschland* (Opladen: Westdeutscher, 1992); Daphne Berdahl, *Where the World Ended: Re-Unification and Identity in the German Borderland* (Berkeley: University of California Press, 1999).

88. Konrad Jarausch, "Normalization or Renationalization? On Reinterpreting the German Past," in *Rewriting the German Past: History and Identity in the New Germany*, ed. Reinhard Alter and Peter Montheath (Atlantic Highlands, N.J.: Humanities Press, 1997), 23–39.

CHAPTER 2

1. An earlier version of this paper was presented to the Symposium on Pain and Suffering in History: Narratives of Science, Medicine, and Culture at UCLA, 13–14 March 1998. I wish to thank Paul Betts, Geoff Cocks, Peter Fritzsche, Marcia Meldrum, Steven Reinhardt, Ingrid Schenk, and Melissa Watts for their helpful comments and criticisms. Funding for research was provided by the German Academic Exchange Service and International Research and Exchanges Board, neither of which is responsible for the views expressed here.

2. Ernst H. Kantorowicz, *The King's Two Bodies: A Study in Mediaeval Political Theology* (Princeton: Princeton University Press, 1957); Otto Gierke, *Political Theories of the Middle Age* (Cambridge: Cambridge University Press, 1958).

3. Ronald Paulson, *Representations of Revolution, 1789–1820* (New Haven: Yale University Press, 1983); Michael Walzer, *Regicide and Revolution: Speeches at the Trial of Louis XVI* (Cambridge: Cambridge University Press, 1974); Dorinda Outram, *The Body and the French Revolution: Sex, Class, and Political Culture* (New Haven: Yale University Press, 1989); Susan Dunn, *The Deaths of Louis XVI: Regicide and the French Political Imagination* (Princeton: Princeton University Press, 1994).

4. Susan Moller Okin, *Women in Western Political Thought* (Princeton: Princeton University Press, 1979); Jean Beth Elshtain, *Public Man, Private Woman: Women in Social and Political Thought* (Princeton: Princeton University Press, 1981); Joan B. Landes, *Women and the Public Sphere in the Age of the French Revolution* (Ithaca: Cornell University Press, 1988); Carole Pateman, *The Sexual Contract* (Stanford: Stanford University Press, 1988); Isabel V. Hull, *Sexuality, State, and Civil Society in Germany, 1700–1815* (Ithaca: Cornell University Press, 1996).

5. E. P. Thompson, "Time, Work-Discipline, and Industrial Capitalism," *Past and Present* 37 (1969): 109–45; Jacques Donzelot, *The Policing of Families* (New York: Pantheon, 1979); Michel Foucault, *Discipline and Punish: The Birth of the Prison* (New York: Vintage, 1979); Norbert Elias, *The Civilizing Process* (Oxford: Blackwell, 1994); William H. McNeill, *Keeping Together in Time: Dance and Drill in Human History* (Cambridge, Mass.: Harvard University Press, 1995).

6. Michel Foucault, *The History of Sexuality: Volume 1, An Introduction* (New York: Vintage, 1990), 137.

7. Eugen Weber, *Peasants into Frenchmen: The Modernization of Rural France, 1870–1914* (Stanford: Stanford University Press, 1976); Benedict Anderson, *Imagined Communities: Reflections on the Origin and Spread of Nationalism* (London: Verso, 1991); Geoff Eley and Ronald Grigor Suny, eds., *Becoming National: A Reader* (New York and Oxford: Oxford University Press, 1996).

8. Robert A. Nye, *Crime, Madness, and Politics in Modern France: The Medical Concept of National Decline* (Princeton: Princeton University Press, 1984); Daniel Pick, *Faces of Degeneration: A European Disorder, c. 1848–1918* (Cambridge: Cambridge University Press, 1989).

9. George L. Mosse, *Nationalism and Sexuality: Middle-Class Morality and Sexual Norms in Modern Europe* (Madison: University of Wisconsin Press, 1985); Gisela Bock and Pat Thane, eds., *Maternity and Gender Policies: Women and the Rise of the European Welfare States, 1880s–1950s* (London: Routledge, 1991); Seth Koven and Sonya Michel, eds., *Mothers of a New World: Maternalist Politics and the Origins of the Welfare State* (New York: Routledge, 1993); Susan Pedersen, *Family, Dependence, and the Origins of the Welfare State: Britain and France, 1914–1945* (Cambridge: Cambridge University Press, 1993).

10. Hans Maier, *Die ältere deutsche Staats- und Verwaltungslehre* (Munich: Beck, 1980); Marc Raeff, *The Well-Ordered Police State: Social and Institutional Change Through Law in the Germanies and Russia, 1600–1800* (New Haven: Yale University Press, 1983); Christoph Sachße and Florian Tennstedt, eds., *Soziale Sicherheit und soziale Disziplinierung: Beiträge zu einer historischen*

Theorie der Sozialpolitik (Frankfurt: Suhrkamp, 1986); Keith Tribe, *Governing Economy: The Reformation of German Economic Discourse, 1750–1840* (New York: Cambridge University Press, 1988).

11. Dieter Wyduckel, *Ius Publicum: Grundlage und Entwicklung des Öffentlichen Rechts und der deutschen Staatrechtswissenschaft* (Berlin: Duncker & Humblot, 1984); Reinhart Koselleck, *Preußen zwischen Reform und Revolution: Allgemeines Landrecht, Verwaltung, und soziale Bewegung von 1791 bis 1848* (Munich: dtv/Klett-Cotta, 1989).

12. This is the now classic view of Hans-Ulrich Wehler, *The German Empire, 1871–1918* (Leamington Spa/Dover: Berg, 1985). It has been summarily dismissed by the equally canonical David Blackbourn and Geoff Eley, *The Peculiarities of German History: Bourgeois Society and Politics in Nineteenth-Century Germany* (Oxford: Oxford University Press, 1984).

13. Gerd Göckenjan, *Kurieren und Staat machen: Gesundheit und Medizin in der bürgerlichen Welt* (Frankfurt: Suhrkamp, 1985); Detlev Peukert, *Grenzen der Sozialdisziplinierung: Aufstieg und Krise der deutschen Jugendfürsorge, 1878–1932* (Cologne: Bund, 1986); Paul Weindling, *Health, Race, and German Politics Between National Unification and Nazism, 1870–1945* (Cambridge: Cambridge University Press, 1989); Alfons Labisch, *Homo Hygienicus: Gesundheit und Medizin in der Neuzeit* (Frankfurt: Campus, 1992); and Kathleen Canning, *Languages of Labor and Gender: Female Factory Work in Germany, 1850–1914* (Ithaca: Cornell University Press, 1996).

14. Anthony D. Smith, *National Identity* (Reno: University of Nevada Press, 1991); Rogers Brubaker, *Citizenship and Nationhood in France and Germany* (Cambridge, Mass.: Harvard University Press, 1992). On the symbols and rituals that went into the nationalization process in Germany, see George L. Mosse, *The Nationalization of the Masses: Political Symbolism and Mass Movements in Germany from the Napoleonic Wars through the Third Reich* (Ithaca: Cornell University Press, 1975); and more recently Alon Confino, *The Nation as Local Metaphor: Württemberg, Imperial Germany, and National Memory, 1871–1918* (Chapel Hill: University of North Carolina Press, 1997).

15. Michelle Mattson, "Refugees in Germany," *New German Critique* 64 (winter 1995): 61–85; Stefan Senders, "Laws of Belonging: Legal Dimensions of National Inclusion in Germany," *New German Critique* 67 (winter 1996): 147–76; Uli Linke, "The Violence of Difference: Antisemitism, Misogyny, and Xenophobia," in *Sacrifice and National Belonging in Twentieth-Century Germany*, ed. Greg Eghigian and Matthew Berg (College Station: Texas A&M University Press, 2002).

16. Michael Geyer, "The Stigma of Violence, Nationalism, and War in Twentieth-Century Germany," *German Studies Review*, special issue (winter 1992): 75–110; Uli Linke, "Murderous Fantasies: Violence, Memory, and Selfhood in Germany," *New German Critique* 64 (winter 1995): 37–59; and Uli Linke, "Gendered Difference, Violent Imagination: Blood, Race, Nation," *American Anthropologist* 99 (1997): 559–73.

17. Klaus Theweleit, *Male Fantasies*, 2 vols. (Minneapolis: University of Minnesota Press, 1987–89); Sander Gilman, *The Jew's Body* (New York: Routledge,

1991); Cornelia Usborne, *The Politics of the Body in Weimar Germany: Women's Reproductive Right and Duties* (Ann Arbor: University of Michigan Press, 1992); Bernd Wedemeyer, "Body-Building or Man in the Making: Aspects of the German Bodybuilding Movement in the Kaiserreich and Weimar Republic," *International Journal of the History of Sport* 11 (1994): 472–84; Frank Becker, "Sportsmen in the Machine World: Models for Modernization in Weimar Germany," *International Journal of the History of Sport* 12 (1995): 153–68; Atina Grossmann, *Reforming Sex: The German Movement for Birth Control and Abortion Reform, 1920–1950* (New York: Oxford University Press, 1995); Maria Tatar, *Lustmord: Sexual Murder in Weimar Germany* (Princeton: Princeton University Press, 1995).

18. There is, of course, a huge literature on this subject. A good place to begin in English is Michael Burleigh and Wolfgang Wippermann, *The Racial State: Germany 1933–1945* (Cambridge: Cambridge University Press, 1991); and Henry Friedlander, *The Origins of Nazi Genocide: From Euthanasia to the Final Solution* (Chapel Hill: University of North Carolina Press, 1995).

19. Nazi social race policy provides a telling example. Throughout the regime's history, party experts and government officials in the Third Reich were divided into numerous competing, uncompromising factions over the shape and future of policies. More often than not this resulted in individual administrations and regions adopting their own rationale and systems, thereby contributing to a more general proliferation of centers of authority. See Michael Kater, "Dr. Leonardo Conti and His Nemesis: The Failure of Centralized Medicine in the Third Reich," *Central European History* 18 (1985): 299–325; Marie-Luise Recker, *Nationalsozialistische Sozialpolitik im Zweiten Weltkrieg* (Munich: Oldenbourg, 1985); Chistopher Browning, "Vernichtung und Arbeit: Zur Fraktionierung der planenden deutschen Intelligenz im besetzten Polen," in *"Vernichtungspolitik": Eine Debatte über den Zusammenhang von Sozialpolitik und Genozid im nationalsozialistischen Deutschland*, ed. Wolfgang Schneider (Hamburg: Junius, 1991), 37–51.

20. For a fresh look at these matters, see Norbert Finzsch and Robert Jütte, eds., *Institutions of Confinement: Hospitals, Asylums, and Prisons in Western Europe and North America, 1500–1950* (Cambridge: Cambridge University Press, 1996).

21. See, for instance, Mikhail Bakhtin, *Rabelais and His World* (Cambridge, Mass.: MIT Press, 1968); Pierre Bourdieu, *The Logic of Practice* (Stanford: Stanford University Press, 1990); Janice Boddy, *Wombs and Alien Spirits: Women, Men, and the Zar Cult in Northern Sudan* (Madison: University of Wisconsin Press, 1989); James C. Scott, *Domination and the Arts of Resistance: Hidden Transcripts* (New Haven: Yale University Press, 1990).

22. Daniel De Moulin, "A Historical-Phenomenological Study of Bodily Pain in Western Man," *Bulletin of the History of Medicine* 48 (1974): 540–70; Edward Shorter, *From Paralysis to Fatigue: A History of Psychosomatic Illness in the Modern Era* (New York: Free Press, 1992); Roselyne Rey, *The History of Pain* (Cambridge, Mass.: Harvard University Press, 1995).

23. Elaine Scarry, *The Body in Pain: The Making and Unmaking of the World* (New York: Oxford University Press, 1985); Andrew Wear, "Perceptions of Pain

in Seventeenth-Century England," *Society for the Social History of Medicine Bulletin* 36 (1985): 7–9.

24. Roy Porter, "History of the Body," in *New Historical Perspectives on Historical Writing*, ed. Peter Burke (University Park: Pennsylvania State University Press, 1991), 209.

25. Claudine Herzlich and Janine Pierret, *Illness and Self in Society* (Baltimore: Johns Hopkins University Press, 1987); Arthur Kleinman, *The Illness Narratives* (New York: Basic, 1988).

26. Paul Farmer, *AIDS and Accusation: Haiti and the Geography of Blame* (Berkeley: University of California Press, 1992); Roy Porter, "Pain and Suffering," in *Companion Encyclopedia of the History of Medicine*, vol. 2, ed. W. F. Bynum and Roy Porter (London: Routledge, 1993), 1574–91; Jay Winter, *Sites of Memory, Sites of Mourning: The Great War in European Cultural History* (Cambridge: Cambridge University Press, 1995); Arthur Kleinman, Veena Das, and Margaret Lock, eds., *Social Suffering* (Berkeley: University of California Press, 1997).

27. Ernest Renan, "What is a Nation?" in Eley and Suny, *Becoming National*, 52–53.

28. For a good introduction to this literature in English, see Gerhard Ritter, *Social Welfare in Germany and Britain: Origins and Development* (Leamington Spa/New York: Berg, 1986).

29. The workers' movement and the Social Democrats only grew in strength, and litigation consistently went up in subsequent years, while doctors were only one among several professional groups administering the programs.

30. Ute Frevert, *Krankheit als politisches Problem 1770–1880* (Göttingen: Vandenhoeck & Ruprecht, 1984), 55.

31. See Francisca Loetz, *Vom Kranken zum Patienten: "Medikalisierung" und medizinische Vergesellschaftung am Beispiel Badens 1750–1850* (Stuttgart: Franz Steiner, 1993).

32. See Annemarie Kinzelbach, *Gesundbleiben, Krankwerden, Armsein in der frühneuzeitlichen Gesellschaft: Gesunde und Kranke in den Reichsstädten Überlingen und Ulm, 1500–1700* (Stuttgart: Franz Steiner, 1995).

33. Barbara Duden, *The Woman Beneath the Skin: A Doctor's Patients in Eighteenth-Century Germany* (Cambridge, Mass.: Harvard University Press, 1991).

34. Robert Jütte, *Ärzte, Heiler, und Patienten: Medizinischer Alltag in der frühen Neuzeit* (Munich: Artemis & Winkler, 1991).

35. Eckart Pankoke, *Sociale Bewegung—Sociale Frage—Social Politik: Grundfragen der deutschen "Sozialwissenschaft" im 19. Jahrhundert* (Stuttgart: Ernst Klett, 1970); Christof Dipper, "Sozialreform: Geschichte eines umstrittenen Begriffs," *Archiv für Sozialgeschichte*, 32 (1992): 323–51.

36. Johann Baptist Müller, *Bedürfnis und Gesellschaft: Bedürfnis als Grundkategorie im Liberalismus, Konservatismus, und Sozialismus* (Stuttgart: Ernst Klett, 1971).

37. Bundesarchiv Berlin (hereafter BarchB), R89/21533, Vorstand, Strassen- und Kleinbahn-Berufsgenossenschaft (hereafter BG) to Reichsversicherungsamt (hereafter RVA), 13 January 1904.

38. BarchB, R89/20354, Vorsitzender, Ostdeutsche Binnenschiffahrts-BG to RVA, 18 September 1889.

39. For one example of this, see BarchB, R89/20240, Vorsitzender, Vorstand, Textil-BG von Elsaß-Lothringen to RVA, 11 February 1887.

40. This is also confirmed by working-class autobiographies; see Alfred Kelly, ed., *The German Worker: Working-Class Autobiographies from the Age of Industrialization* (Berkeley: University of California Press, 1987).

41. Heide Gerstenberger, "The Poor and the Respectable Worker: On the Introduction of Social Insurance in Germany," *Labour History* 48 (1985): 69–85; Alf Lüdtke, *Eigen-Sinn: Fabrikalltag, Arbeitererfahrungen, und Politik vom Kaiserreich bis in den Faschismus* (Hamburg: Ergebnisse, 1993), 136–51.

42. Kaiserliches Statistisches Amt, *Statistisches Jahrbuch für das gesamte deutsche Reich* (Berlin: Puttkammer & Mühlbrecht, 1906), 246; (1908) 264; (1915) 334–35.

43. BarchB, R89/20152, Adolph Henckel to RVA, 24 December 1887.

44. BarchB, R89/21087, Wilhelm Keller to RVA, 17 November 1896.

45. BarchB, R89/20051, Ignatz Lang to RVA, 17 October 1886.

46. The Reich Insurance Office awarded a 25 percent pension to a packer with an amputated left index finger because "the scar of the amputation incision . . . is painful where there is pressure or movement back and forth on the thumb and middle finger. [This] prevents the hand from closing and constitutes a considerable obstruction during work." See BarchB, R89/20683, *Friedrich Baehr v. Speditions-, Speicherei-, und Kellerei-BG*, RVA Senate, 25 January 1893.

47. I take the notion of theodicy in administrative process from Michael Herzfeld, *The Social Production of Indifference: Exploring the Symbolic Roots of Western Bureaucracy* (Chicago: University of Chicago Press, 1992).

48. An earlier version of the material presented in this section appears in Greg Eghigian, "The Politics of Victimization: Social Pensioners and the German Social State in the Inflation of 1914–1924," *Central European History* 26 (1993): 375–403.

49. George L. Mosse, *Fallen Soldiers: Reshaping the Memory of the World Wars* (New York: Oxford University Press, 1990); Kathrin Hoffmann-Curtius, "Opfermodelle am Altar des Vaterlandes seit der Französischen Revolution," in *Schrift der Flammen: Opfermythen und Weiblichkeitsentwürfe im 20. Jahrhundert*, ed. Gudrun Kohn-Waechter (Berlin: Orlando Frauenverlag, 1991), 57–92.

50. Henri Hubert and Marcel Mauss, *Sacrifice: Its Nature and Functions* (Chicago: University of Chicago, 1964); J. H. Beattie, "On Understanding Sacrifice," in *Sacrifice*, ed. M. F. C. Bourdillon and Meyer Fortes (London: Academic, 1980), 29–44.

51. This, as Jay Winter effectively shows, was part of a more general European reaction to the war marked by sacred and apocalyptic appeals to traditional rituals, myths, and imagery. See Winter, *Sites of Memory*.

52. Thomas Childers, *The Nazi Voter: The Social Foundations of Fascism in Germany, 1919–1933* (Chapel Hill: University of North Carolina Press, 1983); Robert Weldon Whalen, *Bitter Wounds: German Victims of the Great War, 1914–1939* (Ithaca: Cornell University Press, 1984); Gerald D. Feldman, *The*

Great Disorder: Politics, Economics, and Society in the German Inflation, 1914–1924 (Oxford: Oxford University Press, 1993).

53. Jürgen von Kruedener, "Die Überforderung der Weimarer Republik als Sozialstaat," *Geschichte und Gesellschaft* 11 (1985): 358–76.

54. Gerald D. Feldman, "The Fate of the Social Insurance System in the German Inflation, 1914 to 1923," in *Die Anpassung an die Inflation/The Adaptation to Inflation*, ed. Gerald D. Feldman, Carl-Ludwig Holtfrerich, Gerhard A. Ritter, and Peter-Christian Witt (Berlin: Walter de Gruyter, 1986), 433–47.

55. BarchB, RAM, Nr. 4532, Landesversicherungsanstalt Berlin to Reichsarbeitsministerium (hereafter RAM), 17 September 1920.

56. BarchB, RAM, Nr. 4547, Bl. 125–26, Robert Nagel to Preußischen Minister für Volkswohlfahrt, 1 September 1921.

57. On the notion of symbolic capital, see Pierre Bourdieu, *The Logic of Practice* (Stanford: Stanford University Press, 1990).

58. Geheimes Staatsarchiv Preussischer Kulturbesitz, Rep. 191, Nr. 4032, Hauptvorstand, Zentralverband der Invaliden und Witwen Deutschlands, Rundschreiben an die Ortsgruppen-Vorstände, August 1920.

59. On the role of resentment in German social political culture between the two world wars, see Greg Eghigian, "Injury, Fate, Resentment, and Sacrifice in German Political Culture, 1914–1939," in Eghigian and Berg, *Sacrifice*.

60. This point is also made by Richard Bessel, *Germany After the First World War* (New York: Oxford University Press, 1993).

61. Marcus Gräser, *Der blockierte Wohlfahrtsstaat: Unterschichtjugend und Jugendfürsorge in der Weimarer Republik* (Göttingen: Vandenhoeck & Ruprecht, 1995); 167–230; Edward Ross Dickinson, *The Politics of German Child Welfare From the Empire to the Federal Republic* (Cambridge, Mass.: Harvard University Press, 1996), 139–203; David Crew, *Germans on Welfare: From Weimar to Hitler* (New York: Oxford University Press, 1998), 152–65; Young-Sun Hong, *Welfare, Modernity, and the Weimar State, 1919–1933* (Princeton: Princeton University Press, 1998), 76–90.

62. Greg Eghigian, "The German Welfare State as a Discourse of Trauma," in *Traumatic Pasts: Studies in History, Psychiatry, and Trauma in the Modern Age*, ed. Mark S. Micale and Paul Lerner (Cambridge: Cambridge University Press, 2001).

63. On the invocation of Bismarck in Weimar debates over social insurance, see Martin H. Geyer, "Bismarcks Erbe—welches Erbe?" 280–309; and Lothar Machtan, "Hans Rothfels und die sozialpolitische Geschichtsschreibung in der Weimarer Republik," 310–84; both in *Bismarcks Sozialstaat*, ed. Lothar Machtan (Frankfurt: Campus, 1994).

64. See Gustav Hartz, *Irrwege der deutschen Sozialpolitik und der Weg zur sozialen Freiheit* (Berlin: August Scherl, 1928); Erwin Liek, *Die Schäden der sozialen Versicherungen und Wege zur Besserung* (Munich: J. F. Lehmann, 1928); Vereinigung der Deutschen Arbeitgeberverbände, *Die Reform der Sozialversicherung—eine Schicksalsfrage des deutschen Volkes* (Berlin: Vereinigung der Deutschen Arbeitgeberverbände, 1930).

65. Ernst Horneffer, *Frevel am Volk: Gedanken zur deutschen Sozialpolitik*

(Leipzig: R. Voigtländer, 1929). The term *"Frevel"* implies a sacrilege of some kind.

66. Ibid., 17–18.

67. Ibid., 41–42.

68. Peter Weingart, Jürgen Kroll, and Kurt Bayertz, *Rasse, Blut und Gene: Geschichte der Eugenik und Rassenhygiene in Deutschland* (Frankfurt: Suhrkamp, 1988), 188–273; Jürgen Reyer, *Alte Eugenik und Wohlfahrtspflege: Entwertung und Funktionalisierung der Fürsorge vom Ende des 19. Jahrhunderts bis zur Gegenwart* (Freiburg im Breisgau: Lambertus, 1991); Paul Weindling, "Eugenics and the Welfare State During the Weimar Republic," in *State, Social Policy, and Social Change in Germany, 1880–1994*, ed. W. R. Lee and Eve Rosenhaft (Oxford: Berg, 1997), 134–63.

69. Gustav Hartz, *Eigentum oder Rente? Eine Auseinandersetzung mit meinen Kritikern über das Thema: Sozialversicherung oder Sozialsparkasse?* (Berlin: August Scherl, 1930).

70. Erwin Liek, *Der Arzt und seine Sendung* (Munich: J. F. Lehmann, 1927).

71. Jay W. Baird, *To Die for Germany: Heroes in the Nazi Pantheon* (Bloomington: Indiana University Press, 1990); Sabine Behrenbeck, *Der Kult um die toten Helden: Nationalsozialistische Mythen, Riten, und Symbole* (Vierow bei Greifswald: S-H, 1996); Yvonne Karow, *Deutsches Opfer: Kultische Selbstauslöschung auf den Reichsparteitagen der NSDAP* (Berlin: Akademie, 1997). See also the contribution by Behrenbeck in this volume.

72. By 1939–40, the drive was taking in 610 million marks in donations. See Herwart Vorländer, "NS-Volkswohlfahrt und Winterhilfswerk des Deutschen Volkes," *Vierteljahreshefte für Zeitgeschichte* 34 (1986): 365; Florian Tennstedt, "Wohltat und Interesse. Das Winterhilfswerk des Deutschen Volkes: Die Weimarer Vorgeschichte und ihre Instrumentalisierung durch das NS-Regime," *Geschichte und Gesellschaft* 13 (1987): 157, 172–73.

73. Erich Hilgenfeldt, *Idee der nationalsozialistischen Wohlfahrtspflege* (Munich: Franz Eher Nachf., 1937), 12.

74. Wieland Elfferding, "Opferritual und Volksgemeinschaftsdiskurs am Beispiel des Winterhilfswerk (WHW)," in *Faschismus und Ideologie 2: Argument-Sonderband AS 62*, ed. Projekt Ideologie Theorie (Berlin: Argument, 1980), 199–226.

75. U.S. National Archives, RG 242, T-70/29, Reichsministerium für Volksaufklärung und Propaganda to Beamten, Angestellten, und Arbeiter des Hauses, 12 October 1933.

76. James M. Diehl, *The Thanks of the Fatherland: German Veterans After the Second World War* (Chapel Hill: University of North Carolina Press, 1993), 31–53.

77. See the contribution by Geoffrey Cocks in this volume.

78. See Burleigh and Wippermann, *Racial State*; Henry Friedlander, *The Origins of Nazi Genocide: From Euthanasia to the Final Solution* (Chapel Hill: University of North Carolina Press, 1995).

79. Gisela Bock, *Zwangssterilisation im Nationalsozialismus: Studien zur Rassenpolitik und Frauenpolitik* (Opladen: Westdeutscher, 1986); Wolfgang

Ayaß, *"Asoziale" im Nationalsozialismus* (Stuttgart: Klett-Cotta, 1995); Michael Burleigh, *Death and Deliverance: "Euthanasia" in Germany, 1900–1945* (Cambridge: Cambridge University Press, 1995).

80. Timothy W. Mason, *Social Policy in the Third Reich: The Working Class and the "National Community"* (Providence, R.I.: Berg, 1993); Irmgard Weyrather, *Muttertag und Mutterkreuz: Der Kult um die "deutsche Mutter" im Nationalsozialismus* (Frankfurt: Fischer, 1993); Ulrich Herbert, *Hitler's Foreign Workers: Enforced Foreign Labor in Germany Under the Third Reich* (Cambridge: Cambridge University Press, 1997).

81. See, for example, the case of "sickness batallions" in World War II, Rolf Valentin, *Die Krankenbataillone: Sonderformationen der deutschen Wehrmacht im Zweiten Weltkrieg* (Düsseldorf: Droste, 1981).

82. Rainer Gries, *Die Rationen-Gesellschaft. Versorgungskampf und Vergleichsmentalität: Leipzig, München, und Köln nach dem Kriege* (Münster: Westfälisches Dampfboot, 1991), 224; Alexander von Plato and Wolfgang Meinicke, *Alte Heimat—neue Zeit: Flüchtlinge, Umgesiedelte, Vertriebene in der Sowjetischen Besatzungszone und in der DDR* (Berlin: Verlags-Anstalt Union, 1991).

83. Günter J. Trittel, "Hungerkrise und kollektiver Protest in Westdeutschland (1945–1949)," in *Der Kampf um tägliche Brot: Nahrungsmangel, Versorgungspolitik, und Protest, 1770–1990* (Opladen: Westdeutscher, 1994), 377–91; Paul Erker, "Hunger und sozialer Konflikt in der Nachkriegszeit," in Ibid., 392–408; Elizabeth Heineman, "The Hour of the Woman: Memories of Germany's 'Crisis Years' and West German National Identity," *American Historical Review* 101 (1996): 354–95.

84. Ulrich Herbert, "'Die guten und die schlechten Zeiten': Überlegungen zur diachronen Analyse lebensgeschichtlicher Interviews," in *"Die Jahre weiß man nicht, wo man die heute hinsetzen soll": Faschismuserfahrungen im Ruhrgebiet. Lebensgeschichte und Sozialkultur im Ruhrgebiet 1930 bis 1960*, Bd. 1, ed. Lutz Niethammer (Berlin: J. H. W. Dietz Nachf., 1986), 67–96; Lutz Niethammer, "'Normalisierung' im Westen: Erinnerungsspuren in die 50er Jahre," in *Ist der Nationalsozialismus Geschichte? Zu Historisierung und Historikerstreit*, ed. Dan Diner (Frankfurt: Fischer, 1987), 153–84.

85. Omer Bartov, *Murder in Our Midst: The Holocaust, Industrial Killing, and Representation* (New York: Oxford University Press, 1996), 119–22.

86. Erica Carter, *How German is She? Postwar West German Reconstruction and the Consuming Woman* (Ann Arbor: University of Michigan Press, 1997), 45.

87. Michael Wildt, *Am Beginn der "Konsumgesellschaft": Mangelerfahrung, Lebenshaltung, Wohlstandshoffnung in Westdeutschland in den fünfziger Jahren* (Hamburg: Ergebnisse, 1994), 265.

88. Neue Gesellschaft für Bildende Kunst, ed., *Wunderwirtschaft: DDR-Konsumkultur in 1960er Jahren* (Cologne: Böhlau, 1996); Katherine Pence, "Schaufenster des sozialistischen Konsums: Texte der ostdeutschen 'consumer culture,'" in *Akten. Eingaben. Schaufenster. Die DDR und ihre Texte: Erkundungen zu Herrschaft und Alltag*, ed. Alf Lüdtke and Peter Becker (Berlin: Akademie, 1997), 91–118; Stephan Merl, "Staat und Konsum in der Zentralverwaltungswirtschaft: Rußland und die ostmitteleuropäischen Länder," in

Europäische Konsumgeschichte: Zur Gesellschafts- und Kulturgeschichte des Konsums (18. bis 20. Jahrhundert), ed. Hannes Siegrist, Hartmut Kaelbe, and Jürgen Kocka (Frankfurt: Campus, 1997), 205–41.

89. Katherine Pence, "Labours of Consumption: Gendered Consumers in Post-War East and West German Reconstruction," in *Gender Relations in German History: Power, Agency, and Experience From the Sixteenth to the Twentieth Century*, ed. Lynn Abrams and Elizabeth Harvey (Durham: Duke University Press, 1997), 211–38. See also Wildt, *Am Beginn der "Konsumgesellschaft,"* 214–70.

90. Akademie der Wissenschaften der DDR, *Probleme der sozialistischen Lebensweise: Ökonomische und soziale Probleme der weiteren Ausprägung der sozialistischen Lebensweise*, (Berlin [East]: Akademie, 1977); Jens Alber, *Der Sozialstaat in der Bundesrepublik, 1950–1983* (Frankfurt: Campus, 1989); Ernst-Wolfgang Böckenförde, *State, Society, and Liberty: Studies in Political Theory and Constitutional Law* (New York: Berg, 1991), 146–74; Merl, "Staat und Konsum."

91. Edeltraud Roller, *Einstellungen der Bürger zum Wohlfahrtsstaat der Bundesrepublik Deutschland* (Opladen: Westdeutscher, 1992); Winfried Schmähl, ed., *Sozialpolitik im Prozeß der deutschen Wiedervereinigung* (Frankfurt: Campus, 1992); Jürgen Zerche, ed., *Vom sozialistischen Versorgungsstaat zum Sozialstaat Bundesrepublik: Ausbau oder Abbau der sozialen Lage in den neuen Bundesländer?* (Regensburg: Transfer, 1994).

92. Massimo Montanari, *The Culture of Food* (Oxford: Blackwell, 1994).

CHAPTER 3

1. Klaus Kreimeier, *The Ufa Story: A History of Germany's Greatest Film Company, 1918–1945* (New York: Hill & Wing, 1996), 57.

2. Ibid.

3. On the notion of "memory crisis," see Richard Terdiman, *Present Past: Modernity and the Memory Crisis* (Ithaca: Cornell University Press, 1993).

4. Karl Scheffler, *Berlin. Ein Stadtschicksal* (Berlin: Reiss, 1910), 52, 59, 267.

5. Georg Simmel, "The Metropolis and Mental Life," in *The Sociology of Georg Simmel*, ed. Kurt Wolff (Glencoe: Free Press, 1950). See also Gottfried Korff, "Mentalität und Kommunikation in der Grossstadt. Berliner Notizen zur 'inneren' Urbanisation," in *Grossstadt: Aspekte empirischer Kulturforschung*, ed. Theodor Kohlmann and Hermann Bausinger (Berlin: Staatliche Museen Preussischer Kulturbesitz, 1985), 343–61; and Gottfried Korff, "'Die Stadt aber ist der Mensch . . . ',", in *Berlin, Berlin. Die Ausstellung zur Geschichte der Stadt*, ed. Reinhard Rürup and Korff (Berlin: Nicolai, 1987), 643–63.

6. Simmel, "The Metropolis and Mental Life."

7. Cited in David Frisby, *Fragments of Modernity: Theories of Modernity in the Work of Simmel, Kracauer, and Benjamin* (Cambridge, Mass.: MIT University Press, 1986), 87.

8. Georg Simmel, "Die Mode," in Simmel, *Philosophische Kultur* (Potsdam: Kiepenhauer, 1923), 42.

9. For a recent example, see the afterword to Michael Bienert, *Die eingebildete*

Metropole: Berlin im Feuilleton der Weimarer Republik (Stuttgart: Metzler, 1992), 212. See also the very familiar terms by which "Berlin. Metropole" is explored in *Kursbuch 137* (1999).

10. Quoted in *The International Herald Tribune*, 2 Dec. 1999.

11. Brian Ladd, *The Ghosts of Berlin: Confronting German History in the Urban Landscape* (Chicago: University of Chicago Press, 1997).

12. See, for example, Aleida Assmann, *Erinnerungsräume: Formen und Wandlungen des kulturellen Gedächtnisses* (Munich: Beck, 1999), 69–70; and Nicole Loraux, *Mothers in Mourning*, trans. Corinne Pache (Ithaca: Cornell University Press, 1998).

13. Oscar Stillich, *Die Lage der weiblichen Dienstboten in Berlin* (Berlin: Edelheim, 1902), 267.

14. Carl Schneidt, *Das Kellnerinnen-Elend in Berlin* (Berlin: Berlin Handpresse, 1893), 30.

15. Robert Walser, "Guten Tag, Riesin!" (1907); reprinted in *Die Berliner Moderne, 1885–1914*, ed. Jürgen Schutte and Peter Sprengel (Stuttgart: Reclam, 1987), 303.

16. Helmuth Plessner, *Grenzen der Gemeinschaft: Eine Kritik des sozialen Radikalismus* (Bonn: Cohen, 1924). See also Michael Makropoulos, *Modernität als ontologischer Ausnahmezustand? Walter Benjamins Theorie der Moderne* (Munich: Fink, 1989); Michael Makropoulos, "Haltlose Souveränität. Benjamin, Schmitt und die Klassische Moderne in Deutschland," in *Intellektuellendiskurse in der Weimarer Republik: Zur politischen Kultur einer Gemengelage*, ed. Manfred Gangl and Gérard Raulet (Darmstadt: Wissenschaftliche Buchgesellschaft, 1994), 197–211; and Helmut Lethen, *Verhaltenslehre der Kälte: Lebensversuche zwischen den Kriegen* (Frankfurt: Suhrkamp, 1994).

17. Zygmunt Bauman, *Life in Fragments* (London: Routledge, 1995), 88.

18. Arthur Eloesser, *Die Strasse meiner Jugend* (1919; reprint, Berlin: Arsenal, 1987), 7.

19. Siegfried Kracauer, "Strasse ohne Erinnerung," *Frankfurter Zeitung*, 16 Dec. 1932; reprinted in Kracauer, *Strassen in Berlin und anderswo* (Berlin: Arsenal, 1987), 19–24. Bernhard von Brentano, Kracauer's predecessor at the *Frankfurter Zeitung*, made the same observation earlier. See his "Berlin—von Süddeutschland aus gesehen," in *Wo in Europa ist Berlin? Bilder aus den zwanziger Jahren* (Frankfurt: Insel, 1981), 96–97.

20. See Siegfried Kracauer, *Die Angestellten: Aus dem neuesten Deutschland* (Frankfurt: Frankfurter Societäts-Druck, 1930); and Henri Band, *Mittelschichten und Massenkultur: Siegfried Krakauers publizistische Auseinandersetzung mit der populären Kultur und der Kultur der Mittelschichten in der Weimarer Republik* (Berlin: Lukas, 1999).

21. See Peter Fritzsche, *Reading Berlin 1900* (Cambridge, Mass.: Harvard University Press, 1996).

22. *Berliner Morgenpost*, 31 Oct. 1929; quoted in Johann Friedrich Geist and Klaus Kürvers, *Das Berliner Mietshaus, 1862–1945* (Munich: Prestel, 1984), 408. See also Peter Fritzsche, "Talk of the Town: The Murder of Lucie Berlin and the Production of Local Knowledge," in *Criminals and Their Scientists*, ed.

Peter Becker and Richard Wetzell (Cambridge: Cambridge University Press), forthcoming.

23. "Grossstadtkinder," *Berliner Lokal-Anzeiger*, no. 325, 4 July 1905.

24. Albert Südekum, *Grossstädtisches Wohnungselend* (Berlin: Seemann, 1908), 17.

25. Frisby, *Fragments of Modernity*, 185; Makropoulos, *Modernität als ontologischer Ausnahmezustand?*

26. On the "lightness" of modernity, see Rudy Koshar, *Germany's Transient Pasts: Preservation and National Memory in the Twentieth Century* (Chapel Hill: University of North Carolina Press, 1998), 330–31.

27. Alfred Polgar's *Hinterland*, cited in Hans Ostwald, *Sittengeschichte der Inflation* (Berlin: Neufeld & Henius, 1931), 241–42.

28. "Die Friedrichstrasse von heute," *Berliner Illustrirte Zeitung*, no. 36, 7 Sept. 1919.

29. Paul Lerner, "An Economy of Memory: Psychiatrists, Veterans, and Traumatic Narratives in Weimar Germany," in *The Work of Memory: New Directions in German History*, ed. Alon Confino and Peter Fritzsche (Urbana: University of Illinois Press, 2002).

30. Jay Winter, "Forms of Kinship and Remembrance in the Aftermath of the Great War," *War and Remembrance in the Twentieth Century*, ed. Winter and Emmanuel Sivan (Cambridge, Mass.: Cambridge University Press, 1999), 42–43, 60.

31. Ostwald, *Sittengeschichte*, 147.

32. Quoted in Ibid., 149. See also Ernst Troeltsch, *Die Fehlgeburt einer Republik. Spektator in Berlin 1918 bis 1922* (Frankfurt: Eichborn, 1994), 15.

33. Gerald D. Feldman, *The Great Disorder: Politics, Economics, and Society in the German Inflation* (New York: Oxford University Press, 1993), 858.

34. Martin Geyer, *Verkehrte Welt: Revolution, Inflation, und Moderne, München, 1914–1924* (Göttingen: Vandenhoeck & Ruprecht, 1998), 387.

35. Ostwald, *Sittengeschichte*, 231.

36. Ibid., 7. See also Helmut Lethen, *Neue Sachlichkeit 1924–1932. Studien zur Literatur des 'Weissen Sozialismus'* (Stuttgart: Metzler, 1970).

37. Thomas Mann quoted in and generally analyzed by Bernd Widdig, *Culture and Inflation in Weimar Germany* (Berkeley: University of California Press, 2000), 174.

38. Anton Kaes, "Die ökonomische Dimension der Literatur: Zum Strukturwandel der Institution Literatur in der Inflationszeit (1918–1923)," in *Consequences of Inflation*, ed. Gerald D. Feldman et al. (Berlin: Colloquium, 1989), 318.

39. Elias Canetti, *Crowds and Power* (New York: Farrar, Straus & Giroux, 1984), 183. See also his *The Torch in My Ear* (New York: Farrar, Straus & Giroux, 1982).

40. Hans Fallada, *Kleiner Mann—was nun?* (1932; reprint, Hamburg: Rowohlt, 1950), 39–41.

41. Erich Kästner, *Fabian: Die Geschichle eines Moralisten* (1931; reprinted, Zurich: Atrium, 1985), 62.

42. Michael Kazin, review of *The Hungry Years: A Narrative History of the*

Great Depression in America, by T. H. Watkins, *The New York Times Book Review*, 28 Nov. 1999, 23; Catherine Merridale, "War, Death, and Remembrance in Soviet Russia," in Winter and Sivan, *War and Remembrance*, 62.

43. On experience and narrative, see Joan Scott, "The Evidence of Experience," *Critical Inquiry* 17 (1991): 773–97.

44. Walter Benjamin, "Erfahrung und Armut," quoted in Geyer, *Verkehrte Welt*, 379.

45. Peter Hughes, "Ruins of Time: Estranging History and Ethnology in the Enlightenment and After," in *Time: Histories and Ethnologies*, ed. Diane Owen Hughes and Thomas R. Trautmann (Ann Arbor: University of Michigan Press, 1995), 271–72.

46. Siegfried Kracauer, "Schreie auf der Strasse," *Frankfurter Zeitung*, 19 July 1930; reprinted in Kracauer, *Strassen in Berlin*, 27–29.

47. Band, *Mittelschichten und Massenkultur*, provides the beginnings of a balanced critique of Kracauer.

48. Bauman, *Life in Fragments*, 135–36.

49. Ibid., 138.

50. Peter Fritzsche, "Vagabond in the Fugitive City: Hans Ostwald, Industrial Berlin, and the *Grossstadt-Dokumente*," *Journal of Contemporary History* 29 (1994): 385–402.

51. Ostwald, *Sittengeschichte*, 275, 8.

52. Koshar, *Germany's Transient Pasts*, 331.

53. Larry Eugene Jones, *German Liberalism and the Dissolution of the Weimar Party System, 1918–1933* (Chapel Hill: University of North Carolina Press, 1988).

54. John Whittier-Ferguson, "All or Nothing: Rebecca West, Gertrude Stein, and Writing About War," unpublished ms., 26–27.

55. Richard Bessel, *Germany after the First World War* (Oxford: Oxford University Press, 1993), 5–8.

56. See entries for 6 Aug. 1914, 10 Aug. 1914, and 15 Aug. 1915 in *Käthe Kollwitz. Die Tagebücher*, ed. Jutta Bohnke-Kollwitz (Berlin: Siedler, 1989).

57. George L. Mosse, *Fallen Soldiers: Reshaping the Memory of the World Wars* (New York: Oxford University Press, 1990), 106.

58. Peter Fritzsche, *Germans into Nazis* (Cambridge, Mass.: Harvard University Press, 1998), 103; entry for 12 Dec. 1918, Bohnke-Kollwitz, *Käthe Kollwitz*, 398. On the British public's insistence on meaning after World War I, see Adrian Gregory, *The Silence of Memory: Armistice Day, 1919–1946* (Oxford: Berg, 1994).

59. Michael Jeismann and Rolf Westheider, "Wofür Stirbt der Bürger? Nationaler Totenkult und Staatsbürgertum in Deutschland und Frankreich set der Französischen Revolution," in *Der politische Totenkult: Kriegerdenkmäler in der Moderne*, ed. Reinhart Koselleck and Jeismann (Munich: Fink, 1994), 43–44.

60. Fritzsche, *Germans*, 58; "Nachts vorm Schloss," *Tägliche Rundschau*, no. 356, 1 Aug. 1914.

61. Fritzsche, *Germans*, ch. 1; and also Jeffrey Verhey, *The Spirit of 1914: Militarism, Myth, and Mobilization in Germany* (Cambridge: Cambridge University Press, 2000).

62. On this theme, see David Bielanski, "Frontline Weimar: Civic Soldiers and Gender Relations in Paramilitary Life, 1924–1933" (Ph.D. diss., University of Illinois, forthcoming).

63. Belinda Davis, *Home Fires Burning: Food, Politics, and Everyday Life in World War I Berlin* (Chapel Hill: University of North Carolina Press, 2000).

64. See Jay Winter and Jean Louis Robert, eds., *Capital Cities at War: London, Paris, Berlin, 1914–1919* (Cambridge: Cambridge University Press, 1996).

65. David Southern quoted in Geyer, *Verkehrte Welt*, 210.

66. Michael L. Hughes, "Private Equity, Social Inequity: German Judges React to Inflation 1914–1924," *Central European History* 16 (1983): 82.

67. Ernst Renan, "What is a Nation?" reprinted in *Becoming National*, ed. Geoff Eley and Ronald Grigor Suny (New York: Oxford University Press, 1996), 53.

68. H. R. Knickerbocker, *The German Crisis* (New York: Farrar & Rinehart, 1932), 42–43, 76, 94, 97, 206–7, 209.

69. Quoted in Geyer, *Verkehrte Welt*, 31.

70. Hermann Jung, "Erinnerungen aus meiner Kampfzeit," January 1937, Bundesarchiv, NS26/532.

71. Rudolf Kahn, folder 31, Box 1, Theodore Abel Papers, Hoover Institution Archives, Stanford, California. See also Fritz Junghanss, folder 526, Box 7, ibid.

72. Hans Plath, folder 96, Box 2; Ernst Schmitt, folder 265, Box 5; Oskar Klinkusch, folder 349, Box 5, Theodore Abel Papers, Hoover Institution Archives, Stanford, California; Heinrich Wilkenloh, "Meine Kampferlebnisse," 31 Dec. 1936, Bundesarchiv, NS 26/531.

73. See Widdig, *Culture and Inflation*, ch. 4.

74. Ulrich Linse, *Barfüssige Propheten: Erlöser der Zwanziger Jahre* (Berlin: Siedler, 1983).

75. See, for example, Geyer, *Verkehrte Welt*, 281, 288, 300.

76. Emil Schlitz, untitled statement, 2 Nov. 1936, Bundesarchiv, NS 26/532.

77. Wilhelm Wittfeld, folder 15, Box 1, Theodore Abel Papers, Hoover Institution Archives, Stanford, California.

78. "The Story of a Middle-Class Youth," in Theodore Abel, *The Nazi Movement* (New York: Atherton, 1966), 269.

79. Thomas Childers emphasizes the importance of occupational politics; see his *The Nazi Voter: The Social Foundations of Fascism in Germany, 1919–1933* (Chapel Hill: University of North Carolina Press, 1983).

80. Quoted in Geyer, *Verkehrte Welt*, 123.

81. For a development of this thesis, see Fritzsche, *Germans*, 139–214.

82. Koshar, *Transient Pasts*, 148–52.

83. Ibid., 259.

84. Ibid., 5.

85. Bruce Jennings, "Tradition and the Politics of Remembering," *Georgia Review* 36 (spring 1982): 179–80.

86. Elizabeth Heinemann, "The Hour of the Woman: Memories of Germany's 'Crisis Years' and West German National Identity," *The American Historical Review* 101 (1996); and Robert Moeller, "War Stories: The Search for a Usable Past

in the Federal Republic of Germany," *The American Historical Review* 101 (1996), 1008–48.

87. Benedict Anderson, *Imagined Communities: Reflections on the Origin and Spread of Nationalism*, rev. ed. (New York: Verso, 1991), 202–6.

88. Rürup and Korff, *Berlin, Berlin*; and Klaus Hartung, "Doppelgesicht"; Stefanie Flamm, "Berliner Tempo"; and Karl Schlögel, "Kiosk Eurasia," all in *Kursbuch* 137 (1999).

CHAPTER 4

1. On Americanism and mass consumption, see Mary Nolan, *Visions of Modernity: American Business and the Modernization of Germany* (New York: Oxford University Press, 1994), esp. 108–27.

2. John E. Crowley, "The Sensibility of Comfort," *American Historical Review* 104, no. 3 (1999): 749–82.

3. On the development of leisure activities among the German working classes, see Lynn Abrams, *Workers' Culture in Imperial Germany: Leisure and Recreation in the Rhineland and Westphalia* (New York: Routledge, 1992).

4. For data on the declining birthrate, see John Knodel, *The Decline of Fertility in Germany, 1871–1939* (Princeton: Princeton University Press, 1974). On birth control and the triumph of the "two-child system," see Cornelie Usborne, *The Politics of the Body in Weimar Germany: Women's Reproductive Rights and Duties* (Ann Arbor: University of Michigan Press, 1992); Atina Grossmann, *Reforming Sex: The German Movement for Birth Control and Abortion Reform, 1920–1950* (New York: Oxford University Press, 1995); Anna Bergmann, *Die Verhütete Sexualität: Die Anfänge der modernen Geburtenkontrolle* (Hamburg: Rasch und Röhring, 1992); Karen Hagemann, ed., *Eine Frauensache: Alltagsleben und Geburtenpolitik, 1919–1933* (Pfaffenweiler: Centaurus-Verlagsgesellschaft, 1991); and James Woycke, *Birth Control in Germany, 1871–1933* (New York: Routledge, 1988).

5. These considerations all played a role in couples' preferring smaller families; see Max Marcuse, *Der eheliche Präventivverkehr: Seine Verbreitung, Verursachung und Methodik—Dargestellt und beleuchtet an 300 Ehen* (Stuttgart: Verlag von Ferdinand Enke, 1917).

6. See Elisabeth Domansky, "Militarization and Reproduction in World War I Germany," in *Society, Culture, and the State in Germany, 1870–1930*, ed. Geoff Eley (Ann Arbor: University of Michigan Press, 1996), 427–63.

7. The prescriptive literature is too extensive to list here. For an overview, see Maya Borkowsky, *Krankheit Schwangerschaft? Schwangerschaft, Geburt und Wochenbett aus ärztlicher Sicht seit 1800* (Zurich: Chronos Verlag, 1988); and Jördis Land, *Verhaltensempfehlungen für die Schwangerschaft im Spiegel der Ratgeberliteratur, 1880–1980* (Essen: Bosofo, 1989).

8. See for example Peter Reinicke, "Schwangerenberatung—Historischer Rückblick am Beispiel Berlins," *Soziale Arbeit* 33, no. 3 (1984): 97–112.

9. There is an extensive anthropological literature that treats suffering as a cultural phenomenon; see for example Mary-Jo DelVecchio Good, Paul E. Brodwin,

Byron J. Good, and Arthur Kleinman, eds., *Pain As Human Experience: An Anthropological Perspective* (Berkeley: University of California Press, 1992).

10. On medieval sainthood attained through fasting, see Caroline Walker Bynum, *Holy Feast and Holy Fast: The Religious Significance of Food to Medieval Women* (Berkeley: University of California Press, 1988). On modern anorexia, see Susan Bordo, *Unbearable Weight: Feminism, Western Culture, and the Body* (Berkeley: University of California Press, 1993).

11. Judith Schneid Lewis, *In the Family Way: Childbearing in the British Aristocracy, 1760–1860* (New Brunswick, N.J.: Rutgers University Press, 1986), 16, 154–61, 168.

12. On the introduction of chloroform in Great Britain, see Mary Poovey, "'Scenes of an Indelicate Character': The Medical 'Treatment' of Victorian Women," in *The Making of the Modern Body: Sexuality and Society in the Nineteenth Century*, ed. Thomas Laqueur and Catherine Gallagher (Berkeley: University of California Press, 1987), 137–68.

13. Actually, a Dr. Steinbüchel in Graz had discovered a similar method in 1902, but the names of Gauss and Krönig are most closely linked to Twilight Sleep because they refined it and publicized it widely. On the initial Freiburg study, see C. J. Gauss, "Geburten in künstlichem Dämmerschlaf," *Archiv für Gynäkologie* 78 (1906): 579–631.

14. Also known as hyoscine, scopolamine—a drug derived from plants in the nightshade family—is used today mostly to treat motion sickness.

15. See for example Ernst Baumann, "Untersuchungen über eine neue Methode zur Erleichterung der Geburt," *Monatsschrift für Geburtshilfe und Gynäkologie* (henceforth *MGG*) 45 (1917): 145.

16. Pauline Feldman, "Der schematische Dämmerschlaf nach Siegel," *Zentralblatt für Gynäkologie* (henceforth *ZfG*) 44, no. 3 (1920): 77. On protracted labors, see also Carl Meyer, "Über 100 Geburten im schematischen Scopolamin-Amnesindämmerschlaf," *ZfG* 45, no. 35 (1921): 1241–42; and Hermann Kossow, "Über die Geburt im Skopolamin-Paramorfandämmerschlaf," *ZfG* 46, no. 44 (1921): 1757.

17. Walther Schmitt, "Erfahrungen mit dem schematischen Dämmerschlaf," *ZfG* 44, no. 34 (1920): 942–43.

18. Feldman, "Der schematische Dämmerschlaf nach Siegel," 78.

19. Schmitt, "Erfahrungen mit dem schematischen Dämmerschlaf," 943; Meyer, "Über 100 Geburten," 1242–43; and Karl Abel, "Die schmerzlose Geburt," *Zeitschrift für ärztliche Fortbildung* (henceforth *ZfäF*) 27, no. 19 (1930): 626.

20. On the asepsis problem, see Feldman, "Der schematische Dämmerschlaf nach Siegel," 79; Schmitt, "Erfahrungen mit dem schematischen Dämmerschlaf," 943; Kossow, "Über die Geburt im Skopolamin-Paramorfandämmerschlaf," 1757; and Meyer, "Über 100 Geburten," 1243. The moral dimension had parallels to the controversy around chloroform in nineteenth-century Great Britain, in which its opponents alleged that laboring women displayed untoward signs of sexual arousal under its influence; Poovey, "'Scenes of an Indelicate Character,'" 142–44.

234 Notes to Pages 66–66

21. Baumann, "Untersuchungen über eine neue Methode," 141; Feldman, "Der schematische Dämmerschlaf nach Siegel," 80; and Kossow, "Über die Geburt im Skopolamin-Paramorfandämmerschlaf," 1758. For a case of infant death that remained unexplained (despite the attending physician's attributing it to Twilight Sleep), see Meyer, "Über 100 Geburten im schematischen Scopolamin-Amnesindämmerschlaf," 1240. For a counterargument, see Rudolf Theodor von Jaschke, "Der schematisierte Dämmerschlaf nach Krönig-Siegel in seiner neuen vereinfachten Form," ZfG 43, no. 46 (1919): 931.

22. On the problems in home use, see Paul Willy Siegel, "Tausend schmerzlose Entbindungen im vereinfachten, schematischen Dämmerschlaf," MGG 46 (1917): 506.

23. Feldman, "Der schematische Dämmerschlaf nach Siegel," 83.

24. The Freiburg University Women's Hospital had used Twilight Sleep routinely since 1906. Gerhard Horn, "Neue Erfahrungen über den vereinfachten schematischen Dämmerschlaf in der Geburtshilfe," ZfG 45, no. 8 (1921): 261.

25. For an exception to the general lack of excitement about local anesthesia to relieve labor pain, see M. Gutman and V. Metz, "Erfahrungen mit der Pudendusanästhesie in der Geburtshilfe," ZfG 53, no. 31 (1929): 1952–56. Physicians at one clinic objected to the need to inject drugs into highly sensitive tissues; see Erwin Strassmann, "Art und Technik der Narkose in Geburtshilfe und Gynäkologie," Die medizinische Welt 4, no. 42 (1930): 1505. For an overview of local anesthesia techniques, which were used mostly for gynecological procedures, see Konrad Heim, "Die örtlichen Betäubungsverfahren in der Frauenheilkunde," MGG 84 (1930): 45–63. Local and regional anesthetics available in the 1920s included not only injections of drugs such as novocaine near the area to be numbed, but also spinal and epidural injections. The more effective spinal and epidural methods posed risks of meningitis, encephalitis, and paralysis, as well as long-lasting, severe headaches; on the development of these methods, see Josef Waller, "Die Entwicklung der Schmerzbetäubung an der Universitäts-Frauenklinik in Tübingen" (Medical diss., University of Tübingen, 1946), 12–24. Although German physicians played a leading role in developing local and regional anesthetics, these methods appear to have enjoyed much greater popularity in the United States during these earlier years; see Madeleine H. Shearer, "Maternity Patients' Movements in the United States, 1820–1985," in Effective Care in Pregnancy and Childbirth, ed. Iain Chalmers et al. (New York: Oxford University Press, 1989), 117; and Wendy Savage, "The Management of Obstetric Pain," in The History of the Management of Pain, From Early Principles to Present Practice, ed. Ronald D. Mann (Carnforth, England: Parthenon, 1988), 192.

26. Strassmann, "Art und Technik der Narkose in Geburtshilfe und Gynäkologie," 1506.

27. Heinz Küstner, "Die Frage der Narkose und Anästhesie: Kritisches Sammelreferat," MGG 80 (1928): 31. See also Waller, Die Entwicklung der Schmerzbetäubung, 10–11. In 1933, British authorities approved the "Minnitt Gas and Air Machine," a device for administering nitrous oxide, for use in home births, but slow training of midwives hindered its dissemination; see Jennifer Beinart, "Obstetric Analgesia and the Control of Childbirth in Twentieth-Century

Britain," in *The Politics of Maternity Care: Services for Childbearing Women in Twentieth-Century Britain*, ed. Jo Garcia, Robert Kilpatrick, and Martin Richards (Oxford: Clarendon Press, 1990), 123–25; Savage, "The Management of Obstetric Pain," 192–93.

28. Paul Schumacher, "Praktische Erfahrungen mit der synergetischen geburtshilflichen Narkose nach Gwathmey," *MGG* 77 (1927): 319. This method entailed an ether oil enema and an injection of magnesium sulfate ($MgSO_4$).

29. Also known as tribromoethanol, Avertin is used today only in lab rodents. For the main booster of Avertin, see Eduard Martin, "Darf der Praktiker Avertin in der Geburtshilfe anwenden?" *ZfäF* 26, no. 17 (1929): 559–60. For critiques of Avertin, see Hellmut Kienlin, "Bestrebungen zum Ausbau des geburtshilflichen Dämmerschlafes," *ZfG* 52, no. 31 (1928): 1946–47; Carl Schroeder, "Die geburtshilfliche Schmerzlinderung mit Avertin," *Die medizinische Welt* 4, no. 22 (1930): 774; and Strassmann, "Art und Technik der Narkose in Geburtshilfe und Gynäkologie," 1505.

30. On Somnifen, see E. and Th. Better, "Beitrag zum Somnifendämmerschlaf in der Geburtshilfe," *ZfG* 53, no. 26 (1929): 1632–38. On Pernocton, see Kienlin, "Bestrebungen zum Ausbau des geburtshilflichen Dämmerschlafes," 1947–49; Hans Goldschmidt, "Der Einfluß des Pernoctons auf den Geburtsverlauf," *ZfG* 54, no. 6 (1930): 344–47; Emil Vogt, "Erfahrungen mit Pernocton beim geburtshilflichen Dämmerschlaf," *MGG* 80 (1928): 79–82; and Eugen Kulka, "Schmerzlinderung unter der Geburt," *Medizinische Klinik* 28, no. 32 (1932): 1233.

31. Emil Vogt, "Weitere Erfahrungen mit Pernocton beim geburtshilflichen Dämmerschlaf," *ZfG* 52, no. 44 (1928): 2808–19.

32. Waller, *Die Entwicklung der Schmerzbetäubung*, 27–29, 32. According to Waller, the Tübingen clinic did continue to use Pernocton in treating eclampsia.

33. Savage, "The Management of Obstetric Pain," 193.

34. Waller, *Die Entwicklung der Schmerzbetäubung*, 10.

35. Küstner, "Die Frage der Narkose und Anästhesie," 29.

36. Hermann Franken and Hans Schlossmann, "Der Einfluß der Narkose auf die Wehentätigkeit des puerperalen Uterus," *Archiv für Gynäkologie* 130 (1927): 215–20.

37. See for example Georg Winter, "Unsere Aufgaben in der Bevölkerungspolitik," *ZfG* 40, no. 5 (1916): 98–104; and Ernst Bumm, *Über das deutsche Bevölkerungsproblem: Rede zum Antritt des Rektorates der Königlichen Friedrich-Wilhelms-Universität in Berlin* (Berlin: Druck der Norddeutschen Buchdruckerei und Verlagsanstalt, 1916).

38. Cornelie Usborne, "'Pregnancy Is the Woman's Active Service': Pronatalism in Germany During the First World War," in *The Upheaval of War: Family, Work, and Welfare in Europe, 1914–1918*, ed. Richard Wall and Jay Winter (Cambridge, Mass.: Cambridge University Press, 1988), 389–416.

39. Hugo Sellheim, "Fortpflanzungspflege!" *MGG* 45 (1917): 377.

40. For a forum in which elite obstetricians responded to Sellheim's Scopan proposal, see "Schmerzlinderung bei Geburten außerhalb des Krankenhauses," *Die medizinische Welt* 4, nos. 9, 10, and 21 (1930): 288–92, 346, 739–41.

41. Sanitätsrat Dr. Bruhn, "Schmerzlinderung unter der Geburt," *ZfäF* 29, no. 8 (1932): 244.

42. As a group, German physicians were stronger advocates of bellicosity and authoritarianism than were other professions; see Michael Kater, "Professionalization and Socialization of Physicians in Wilhelmine and Weimar Germany," *Journal of Contemporary History* 20 (1985): 684–86.

43. Julius Evermann, "Medikamentöser Dämmerschlaf oder medikamentöse Schnellentbindung?" *ZfG* 49, no. 24 (1925): 1298.

44. Dr. Johannes Neumann, "Schmerzlinderung unter der Geburt," *ZfäF* 28, no. 24 (1931): 790.

45. This was also a common belief among nineteenth-century physicians in the United States; see Martin S. Pernick, *A Calculus of Suffering: Pain, Professionalism, and Anesthesia in Nineteenth-Century America* (New York: Columbia University Press, 1985), 47.

46. Hans Hoeland, "Schmerzlose Geburten und Wehenüberdruck," *MGG* 77 (1927): 6.

47. Ernst Ritter von Seuffert, "Über Schmerzstillung unter der Geburt," *ZfäF* 26, no. 21 (1929): 685.

48. Waller, *Die Entwicklung der Schmerzbetäubung*, 25.

49. On regimes of surveillance, see Michel Foucault, *Discipline and Punish: The Birth of the Prison*, trans. Alan Sheridan (New York: Vintage Books, 1979); and Alan Sheridan, *The Birth of the Clinic: An Archaeology of Medical Perception*, trans. A. M. Sheridan Smith (New York: Vintage Books, 1973). For fruitful applications of Foucault's theory in historical analyses of medicine and society, see David Armstrong, *Political Anatomy of the Body: Medical Knowledge in Britain in the Twentieth Century* (New York: Cambridge University Press, 1983); and William Ray Arney, *Power and the Profession of Obstetrics* (Chicago: University of Chicago Press, 1982).

50. For this argument, I am indebted to the discussion of fetal monitoring in Arney, *Power and the Profession of Obstetrics*.

51. M. G. Oden, "Schmerzlinderung unter der Geburt: Eine Erwiderung," *ZfäF* 29, no. 4 (1932): 113.

52. Anneliese Jensen, "Schmerzlinderung unter der Geburt," *ZfäF* 29, no. 8 (1932): 243.

53. Johanna Maria Stabreit, "Schmerzlinderung unter der Geburt!" *ZfäF* 29, no. 5 (1932): 150.

54. Peter Schmitz, *Weihevolle Mutterschaft* (Mödling bei Vienna: Missionsdruckerei St. Gabriel, 1925), 7. For a female Catholic view that exalted stoical suffering in labor, see the autobiography of the midwife Lisbeth Burger [pseud. Christine Strassner], *Vierzig Jahre Storchentante: Aus dem Tagebuch einer Hebamme* (1930; reprint, Olten: Verlag Otto Walter, 1943).

55. Hugo Sellheim, in "Schmerzlinderung bei Geburten außerhalb des Krankenhauses," *Die medizinische Welt* 4, no. 9 (1930): 280.

56. Karljohann von Oettingen, "Geburten im hypnotischen Dämmerschlaf," *Münchener medizinische Wochenschrift* 68, no. 9 (1921): 266.

57. Elli Keller, "Zum Thema 'Schmerzlinderung unter der Geburt' spricht eine Frau," *ZfäF* 29, no. 6 (1932): 182.

58. Landesarchiv Berlin 58, no. 416, vol. 3, 57.

59. On women's perceptions of childbirth as dangerous, see Patricia R. Stokes, "Pathology, Danger, and Power: Women's and Physicians' Views of Pregnancy and Childbirth in Weimar Germany," *Social History of Medicine* 13, no. 3 (2000): 359–80. For a contemporary diagnosis of an "epidemic of fear," see Ernst Bumm, "Zur Frage des künstlichen Abortus," *MGG* 43 (1916): 393–94.

60. Grantly Dick-Read, *Natural Childbirth* (London: Heinemann, 1933); Fernand Lamaze, *Painless Childbirth* (London: Burke, 1958). For a discussion of these and other architects of prepared childbirth, see Tess Cosslett, "Grantly Dick-Read and Sheila Kitzinger: Towards a Woman-Centered Story of Childbirth," *Journal of Gender Studies* 1 (1991): 29–44; and *Women Writing Childbirth: Modern Discourses of Motherhood* (Manchester: Manchester University Press, 1994), esp. 9–46.

61. Hugo Sellheim, in "Schmerzlinderung bei Geburten außerhalb des Krankenhauses," *Die medizinische Welt* 4, no. 9 (1930): 289.

62. Marita Metz-Becker, *Der verwaltete Körper: Die Medikalisierung schwangerer Frauen in den Gebärhäusern des frühen 19. Jahrhunderts* (Frankfurt: Campus, 1997); and Susanne Preussler, *Hinter verschlossenen Türen: Ledige Frauen in der Münchner Gebäranstalt (1832–1853)* (Munich: privately printed, 1985).

63. Karljohann von Oettingen, "Zur Frage der schmerzlosen Geburt," *Münchener medizinische Wochenschrift* 68, no. 51 (1921): 1654.

64. Vogt, "Weitere Erfahrungen mit Pernocton beim geburtshilflichen Dämmerschlaf," 2804.

65. For one contention that "painless birth" was a matter of "fashion," see von Oettingen, "Zur Frage der schmerzlosen Geburt," 1654.

66. See Judith Walzer Leavitt, *Brought to Bed: Childbearing in America, 1750–1950* (New York: Oxford University Press, 1986), 128–40; and Margarete Sandelowski, *Pain, Pleasure, and American Childbirth: From the Twilight Sleep to the Read Method, 1914–1960* (Westport, Conn.: Greenwood Press, 1984).

67. Mary Sumner-Boyd, "Dämmerschlaf," *Die neue Generation* 10, no. 6 (1914): 297–306.

68. Louise Diel, *Ich werde Mutter* (Dresden: Carl Reissner Verlag, 1932), 339–40.

69. Diel, *Ich werde Mutter*, 369–72.   70. Ibid., 373.

71. Ibid., 376.   72. Ibid., 377.

73. Max Nassauer, "Die schmerzlose Geburt," *Münchener medizinische Wochenschrift* 68, no. 42 (1921): 1366. He was rebuked on ethical grounds by a colleague; see O. Flöel, "Schmerzlose Entbindung in der Privatpraxis," *Münchener medizinische Wochenschrift* 68, no. 50 (1921): 1623.

74. For a theoretical perspective on this, see Reva Rubin, *Maternal Identity and the Maternal Experience* (New York: Springer, 1984).

75. An exemplary work in this regard was Johanna Haarer, *Die deutsche Mutter und ihr erstes Kind* (Munich: J. F. Lehmanns Verlag, 1934). Note, though, that

such literature commonly stressed a particular German maternal identity from at least 1914 onward.

76. Numerous bourgeois feminists advanced pronatalist ideals, especially but not only during World War I; Usborne, *The Politics of the Body*, 25, 39–41, 57–58, 66–67. Note that many of the socialist women cited by Usborne came from relatively privileged backgrounds, and thus it should come as no surprise that women across the political spectrum articulated similarly pronatalist, promaternity views.

77. This shift may have occurred first among middle-class Jews, who were better educated than most Germans; see Marion A. Kaplan, *The Making of the Jewish Middle Class: Women, Family, and Identity in Imperial Germany* (New York: Oxford University Press, 1991), 41–42.

78. Its proponents claimed that Rad-Jo had the highest sales ever for a potion that aimed to ease childbirth; "Rechtfertigung und Aufklärung über die Entwicklung des Kampfes um 'Rad-Jo,'" in Free University of Berlin library (hereafter FUB), Sammlung Rott, Box 138, L1/1a.

79. Bundesarchiv Berlin-Lichterfelde (hereafter BArchB) R86 1823.

80. W. Heubner, "Rad-Jo und ärztliche Berufsehre," *Klinische Wochenschrift* 2, no. 19 (1923): 906.

81. On Uxorin, see BArchB R86 1768. "Doctor" Hey had neither earned a doctoral degree, nor was he licensed to practice medicine as a physician; see "Gutachten" on the Rad-Jo film, October 29, 1920, BArchB R86 1689.

82. "Erklärung der Direktoren sämtlicher deutschen Universitäts-Frauenkliniken gegen Rad-Jo," *Archiv für Frauenkunde und Eugenetik* 6 (1920): 281.

83. Dr. Schwarzwäller, *Ratschläge für angehende Mütter* (Berlin: Carl Heymann's Verlag, 1928), 6.

84. *ZfäF* 9, no. 3 (1922): 88.

85. Heubner, "Rad-Jo und ärztliche Berufsehre," 905.

86. Open letter to Fa. Alwin Staude, June 4, 1920, BArchB R86 1689; see also the similar letter to Franz Jaeger, editor of the *Bayerische Hebammenzeitung*, June 20, 1920, in the same file.

87. However, sharp counterattacks against physicians had a long tradition among some proponents of natural medicine, extending back at least to the founder of homeopathy, Samuel Hahnemann, in the 1830s; see Hahnemann, "Homöopathik," in *Wege der Alternativen Medizin: Ein Lesebuch*, ed. Robert Jütte (Munich: C. H. Beck, 1996), 155–57.

88. Heubner, "Rad-Jo und ärztliche Berufsehre," 907.

89. "Gutachten," October 29, 1920; on permission to publicly screen the Rad-Jo promotional film, "Ein Wohltäter der Menschheit," BArchB R86 1689. The available evidence shows that Wasmuth landed in court multiple times; exactly how many is impossible to determine.

90. Personal communication from Dr. Lutz F. Wasmuth, son of Vollrath Wasmuth, October 13, 1999. Many thanks to Dr. Wasmuth for his kind assistance.

91. On physicians' fight against "quacks," see Cornelia Regin, *Selbsthilfe und Gesundheitspolitik: Die Naturheilbewegung im Kaiserreich (1889 bis 1914)* (Stuttgart: Steiner, 1995), ch. 3.

92. Chemical analysis addressed to Dr. E. Rost, February 10, 1926, BArchB R86 1823.

93. Heubner, "Rad-Jo und ärztliche Berufsehre," 906.

94. See for example the reports from the Universitäts-Frauenklinik in Munich, January 16, 1928, and from the Universitäts-Frauenklinik Greifswald, October 24, 1927, BArchB R86 1823.

95. Report from the Universitäts-Frauenklinik Greifswald, October 24, 1927, BArchB R86 1823.

96. Kurt-Otto von Stuckrad, report from the Universitäts-Frauenklinik Berlin, October 1, 1927, BArchB R86 1823. A similar argument about women's perceptions being influenced by the length of the pushing phase (second stage) of labor can be found in a letter from Wilhelm Liepmann to the Reichsgesundheitsamt, September 21, 1927, BArchB R86 1823.

97. Heubner, "Rad-Jo und ärztliche Berufsehre," 906.

98. Rad-Jo brochure, FUB Sammlung Rott, Box 138, L1/1a.

99. Testimonial of forester J. Kufahl, BArchB R86 1689.

100. Testimonials in BArchB R86 1823.

101. Frau L. Nagel, quoted in Werner Kautzsch, "Rad-Jo und kein Ende," BArchB R86 1823.

102. BArchB R86 1689.

103. Testimonial of Josef Karliczek, BArchB R86 1689.

104. On the *Lebensreform* movement and its relationship to "natural" medicine, see Regin, *Selbsthilfe und Gesundheitspolitik*; and Karl E. Rothschuh, *Naturheilbewegung—Reformbewegung—Alternativbewegung* (Stuttgart: Hippokrates Verlag, 1983).

105. On some of the other popular herbal remedies, see W. Peyer, "Über vegetabile Geheimmittel," offprint from the *Süddeutsche Apotheker-Zeitung* 5 (1929), BArchB R86 1730.

106. Vollrath Wasmuth, quoted in a health advice manual promoting Rad-Jo: Friedrich Hellmuth, *Das versiegelte Buch der Frau: Ein Ratgeber für Eheleben, Mutterschaft und Kindespflege* (Oranienberg: Orania Verlag, n.d. [c. 1914]), 33.

107. Unlike prescription drugs, patent remedies were almost entirely unregulated. The occasional (and fruitless) attempts to regulate them occured at the state rather than the federal level. They remained outside federal regulation until 1943. See Axel Murswieck, *Die staatliche Kontrolle der Arzneimittelsicherheit in der Bundesrepublik und den U.S.A.*, Beiträge zur sozialwissenschaftlichen Forschung, vol. 46 (Opladen: Westdeutscher Verlag, 1983), 267–79.

108. See Hellmuth, *Das versiegelte Buch der Frau*, 13–19; and "Wie erzielt man eine leichte Geburt?" BArchB R86 1768. Uxorin propaganda also promised that the civilized woman could give birth with the ease of a primitive if she only lived in harmony with nature and drank Uxorin; "Dr. Hey's 'Uxorin'" pamphlet, BArchB R86 1768.

109. Letter from Wasmuth to the Reichsgesundheitsamt, February 8, 1927, BArchB R86 1823.

110. Hellmuth, *Das versiegelte Buch der Frau*, 85–100. Wasmuth apparently had a hand in authoring this manual.

111. Rothschuh, *Naturheilbewegung*, 106.

112. Dr. H. Will, "Schmerzlose Geburten: Der Weg zur Erhöhung der Geburtenziffer und zur Rettung vor dem Volksuntergang," BArchB R86 1823.

113. "Gutachten" on the Rad-Jo film, October 29, 1920, BArchB R86 1689.

114. Article entitled "Hygiene der Mutterschaft," BArchB R86 1689.

115. Various brochures in BArchB R86 1689.

116. See for example the letter from Wasmuth to Dr. Schwalbe, July 19, 1927, BArchB R86 1823.

117. Letter to Franz Jaeger, editor of the *Bayerische Hebammenzeitung*, June 20, 1920, BArchB R86 1689.

118. This phenomenon, while particularly strong in Germany, could also be seen in the United States in the 1800s and early 1900s; on Lydia Pinkham's Vegetable Compound, a remedy similar to Rad-Jo, see Sarah Stage, *Female Complaints: Lydia Pinkham and the Business of Women's Medicine* (New York: Norton, 1979).

119. "An die Damen und Herren Reichstagsabgeordneten, an die Behörden und für die Gerichte bestimmt," FUB Sammlung Rott, Box 138, L1/1a.

120. Personal communication from Dr. Lutz F. Wasmuth, October 13, 1999.

121. Heubner, "Rad-Jo und ärztliche Berufsehre," 906.

122. Declarations of the Prussian Midwives' Association from December 16, 1921, FUB Sammlung Rott, Box 138, L1/1a.

123. Report from the Universitäts-Frauenklinik Tübingen, October 5, 1927, BArchB R86 1823.

124. Testimonial of Marie Brummer, BArchB R86 1689. On women clamoring for their midwives to provide Rad-Jo, see also Albert Niedermeyer, *Sozialhygienische Probleme in der Gynäkologie und Geburtshilfe: Ein Beitrag zur Sozialgynäkologie* (Leipzig: Kabitzsch, 1927), 132.

125. Gertrud Decker, letter to Wasmuth, February 17, 1927, BArchB R86 1823.

126. Report from the Universitäts-Frauenklinik Bonn, October 5, 1927, BArchB R86 1823.

127. Rad-Jo etching, FUB Sammlung Rott, Box 138, L1/1a.

128. The 30 percent estimate comes from Max Hirsch, "Staatskinder: Ein Vorschlag zur Bevölkerungspolitik im neuen Deutschland," *Archiv für Frauenkunde* 4, nos. 3–4 (1919): 184.

129. On the U.S. case, see Leavitt, *Brought to Bed*; Sandelowski, *Pain, Pleasure, and American Childbirth*; and Sylvia D. Hoffert, *Private Matters: American Attitudes Toward Childbearing and Infant Nurture in the Urban North, 1800–1860* (Urbana: University of Illinois Press, 1989). On Great Britain, see Lewis, *In the Family Way*.

CHAPTER 5

I am grateful to Greg Eghigian, Paul Betts, Richard Koenigsberg, Robert Weldon Whalen, and James Diehl for their expertise and to Albion College for the Royal G. Hall Chair in History.

1. Esther Cohen, "The Animated Pain of the Body," *American Historical Review* 105 (2000): 36–68.

2. Claudine Herzlich and Janine Pierret, *Illness and Self in Society*, trans. Elborg Forster (Baltimore: Johns Hopkins University Press, 1987), 190; Reinhard Spree, *Health and Social Class in Imperial Germany: A Social History of Mortality, Morbidity and Inequality* (Oxford: Berg, 1988), 49–50, 129, 143.

3. David Morris, *The Culture of Pain* (Berkeley: University of California Press, 1991), 87.

4. Ibid., 75.

5. Max Weber, "Science as a Vocation," in *From Max Weber: Essays in Sociology*, ed. H. H. Gerth and C. Wright Mills (New York: Oxford University Press, 1966), 106.

6. Karen Halttunen, "Humanitarianism and the Pornography of Pain in Anglo-American Culture," *American Historical Review* 100 (1995): 304.

7. Roy Porter and Marie Mulvey Roberts, eds. *Pleasure in the Eighteenth Century*, (New York: New York University Press, 1997).

8. Roselyne Rey, *The History of Pain* (Cambridge, Mass.: Harvard University Press, 1995), 171.

9. David Warren Sabean, *Power in the Blood: Popular Culture and Village Life in Early Modern Germany* (Cambridge: Cambridge University Press, 1984).

10. Peter Fritzsche, "Specters of History: On Nostalgia, Exile, and Modernity," *American Historical Review* 106 (2001): 1614–17.

11. Alfons Labisch, *Homo Hygienicus: Gesundheit und Medizin in der Neuzeit* (Frankfurt: Campus, 1992); Foreign Office and Ministry of Economic Warfare, "The Nazi System of Medicine and Public Health Organization" (London, 1944), 245, Microcopy 149/I62, Wiener Library, London.

12. Alfons Labisch, "From Traditional Individualism to Collective Professionalism: State, Patient, Compulsory Health Insurance, and the Panel Doctor Question in Germany, 1881–1931," in *Medicine and Modernity: Public Health and Medical Care in Nineteenth- and Twentieth-Century Germany*, ed. Manfred Berg and Geoffrey Cocks (Cambridge: Cambridge University Press, 1997), 35–54.

13. Richard J. Evans, *Death in Hamburg: Society and Politics in the Cholera Years, 1830–1910* (Oxford: Clarendon, 1987).

14. Edward Shorter quoted in "Wucherndes Dickicht," *Der Spiegel*, June 15, 1998, 199.

15. Robert Jütte, "The Professionalisation of Homeopathy in the Nineteenth Century," in *Coping with Sickness: Historical Aspects of Health Care in a European Perspective*, ed. John Woodward and Robert Jütte (Sheffield: European Association for the History of Medicine and Health Publications, 1995), 53.

16. Michel de Certeau, *The Practice of Everyday Life*, trans. Steven Rendall (Berkeley: University of California Press, 1984), 47; Richard J. Evans, "In Pursuit of the Untertanengeist: Crime, Law and Social Order in German History," in Evans, *Rethinking German History* (London: Allen & Unwin, 1987), 156–87.

17. Linda Schulte-Sasse, *Entertaining the Third Reich: Illusions of Wholeness in Nazi Germany* (Durham: Duke University Press, 1996).

18. Ralf Dahrendorf, *Society and Democracy in Germany* (Garden City, N.Y.: Anchor, 1969), 340.

19. A. Fraenkel, "Über die Krankheitsanfänge bei chronischen Leiden," *Deutsche medizinische Wochenschrift* 57 (1931): 1731–32.

20. Richard J. Evans, *Rituals of Retribution: Capital Punishment in Germany, 1600–1987* (Oxford: Oxford University Press, 1996), 118; Richard F. Wetzell, "The Medicalization of Criminal Law Reform in Imperial Germany," in *Institutions of Confinement: Hospitals, Asylums, and Prisons in Western Europe and North America, 1500–1950*, ed. Norbert Finzsch and Robert Jütte (Cambridge: Cambridge University Press, 1996), 276–77; Michel Foucault, *Discipline and Punish: The Birth of the Prison*, trans. Alan Sheridan (New York: Pantheon, 1977).

21. Joanna Burke, *Dismembering the Male: Men's Bodies, Britain, and the Great War* (Chicago: University of Chicago Press, 1996).

22. Christoph Nonn, "Oh What a Lovely War? German Common People and the First World War," *German History* 18 (2000): 104–9.

23. Jay Winter, *Sites of Mourning: The Great War in European Cultural History* (Cambridge: Cambridge University Press, 1995).

24. Omer Bartov, "Defining Enemies, Making Victims: Germans, Jews, and the Holocaust, "*American Historical Review* 103 (1998): 772.

25. Ibid., 774.

26. Peter Loewenberg, "The Construction of Identity," in *Psychoanalysis and Culture at the Millenium*, ed. Nancy Ginsburg and Roy Ginsburg (New Haven: Yale University Press, 1999), 42.

27. Norbert Elias, *The Germans: Power Struggles and the Development of Habitus in the Nineteenth and Twentieth Centuries*, ed. Michael Schröter and trans. Stephen Mennell (New York: Columbia University Press, 1996), 345; Martin H. Geyer, *Verkehrte Welt: Revolution, Inflation und Modern München, 1914–1924* (Göttingen: Vandenhoeck & Ruprecht, 1998).

28. Richard Bessel, *Germany After the First World War* (Oxford: Clarendon, 1993), 41.

29. Peter Loewenberg, "The Psychohistorical Origins of the Nazi Youth Cohort, " in Loewenberg, *Decoding the Past: The Psychohistorical Approach* (New York: Knopf, 1983), 279.

30. Ibid., 253.

31. Thomas A. Kohut, *Wilhelm II and the Germans: A Study in Leadership* (New York: Oxford University Press, 1991); see also Robert G. L. Waite, *Kaiser and Führer: A Comparative Study of Personality and Politics* (Toronto: Toronto University Press, 1998), 27–28, 196–97, 246, 252, 266–67, 285–86.

32. Greg A. Eghigian, "The Politics of Victimization: Social Pensioners and the German Social State in the Inflation of 1914–1924," *Central European History* 26 (1993): 375–403; David Blackbourn, *The Long Nineteenth Century: A History of Germany, 1780–1918* (New York: Oxford University Press,1998), 145, 341, 414, 473; Paul Lerner, "Rationalizing the Therapeutic Arsenal: German Neuropsychiatry in World War I," in Berg and Cocks, *Medicine and Modernity*, 121–48; David F. Crew, *Germans on Welfare: From Weimar to Hitler* (New York: Oxford University Press, 1998).

33. Roy Porter, "The Enemy Within," *New Republic*, April 20, 1998, 38–40; Bessel, *Germany After the First World War*, 39, 126, 141, 224. New epidemiological knowledge prevented epidemic outbreaks of infection among soldiers in World War I; see William H. McNeil, *Plagues and Peoples* (Garden City, N.Y.: Anchor, 1976), 220, 285.

34. Herzlich and Pierret, *Illness and Self in Society*, 54–58.

35. Susan Sontag, *Illness as Metaphor* (New York: Farrar, Straus & Giroux, 1978), 16–17, 22, 30–31, 63.

36. Ferdinand Sauerbruch and Hans Wenke, *Wesen und Bedeutung des Schmerzes* (Berlin: Junker & Dünnhaupt, 1936), 78; Gesundheitsamt Düsseldorf, Jahresgesundheitsbericht 1938, Allgemeine gesundheitliche Verhältnisse (hereafter Ga), Reg. Düsseldorf 54296 II, Nordrhein-Westfälisches Hauptstaatsarchiv, Düsseldorf (hereafter NWH).

37. Richard A. Koenigsberg, *Hitler's Ideology: A Study in Psychoanalytic Sociology* (New York: Social Science, 1975); and Richard A. Koenigsberg, "The German Body Politic and the Jewish Disease: Genocide as an Immunological Fantasy," unpublished ms., 1998.

38. *The Goebbels Diaries, 1942–1943*, ed. and trans. Louis P. Lochner (Garden City, N.Y.: Doubleday, 1948), 102.

39. *Hitler's Table Talk 1941–44: His Private Conversations*, trans. Norman Cameron and R. H. Stevens (London: Weidenfeld & Nicholson, 1973), 332; on the 1941 remark, see the note by Werner Koeppens, Irving Collection, Institut für Zeitgeschichte, Munich.

40. Robert G. L. Waite, *The Psychopathic God: Adolf Hitler* (New York: Basic, 1977).

41. Alan Beyerchen, "Rational Means and Irrational Ends: Thoughts on the Technology of Racism in the Third Reich," *Central European History* 30 (1997): 389.

42. Leonard L. Heston and Renate Heston, *The Medical Casebook of Adolf Hitler: His Illnesses, Doctors and Drugs* (New York: Stein & Day, 1980); Fritz K. Redlich, *Hitler: Diagnosis of a Destructive Prophet* (New York: Oxford University Press, 1999).

43. Ute Deichmann, *Biologists Under Hitler*, trans. Thomas Dunlap (Cambridge, Mass.: Cambridge University Press, 1996), 171, 399n61; Robert N. Proctor, *The Nazi War on Cancer* (Princeton: Princeton University Press, 1999). Rudolph Binion, *Hitler Among the Germans* (New York: Elsevier, 1976), argues that Klara Hitler actually died of the iodoform treatment used to burn out the cancer.

44. Klaus Theweleit, *Male Fantasies*, 2 vols., trans. Erica Carter et al. (Minneapolis: Minnesota University Press, 1987–89).

45. Sonya O. Rose, "Sex, Citizenship, and the Nation in World War II Britain," *American Historical Review* 103 (1998): 1148, 1159, 1162–63, 1165, 1173–74; George L. Mosse, *The Image of Man: The Creation of Modern Masculinity* (New York: Oxford University Press, 1996), 52–53; George L. Mosse, *Nationalism and Sexuality: Respectability and Abnormal Sexuality in Modern Europe* (New York: Fertig, 1985); Blackbourn, *The Long Nineteenth Century*, 367, 377, 379, 402,

407, 410, 427, 433, 467; Uli Linke, *German Bodies: Race and Representation After Hitler* (New York: Routledge, 1999), 45–46, 48–49, 124–32, 149–50.

46. Sontag, *Illness as Metaphor*, 74.

47. Detlev Peukert, "The Genesis of the 'Final Solution' from the Spirit of Science," in *Nazism and German Society, 1933–1945*, ed. David Crew (London: Routledge, 1994), 282; Michael Kater, *Doctors Under Hitler* (Chapel Hill: North Carolina University Press, 1989); Robert N. Proctor, *Racial Hygiene: Medicine Under the Nazis* (Cambridge, Mass.: Harvard University Press, 1988).

48. Wetzell, "Criminal Law Reform in Imperial Germany," 280–81.

49. David B. Morris, "How to Read *The Body in Pain*," *Literature and Medicine* 6 (1987): 139–55.

50. Hannah Arendt, "Social Science Techniques and the Study of Concentration Camps," in Arendt, *Essays in Understanding, 1930–1954*, ed. Jerome Kohn (New York: Harcourt, Brace, 1994), 241, 246n21.

51. Wehrwirtschafts-Inspektion VII (Munich), 1937, Microcopy T77, roll 248, frames 1067824–28, National Archives, Suitland, MD; Ga Grevenbroich-Neuss, 1937, Reg. Düsseldorf 54305 II; Ga Duisburg, 1939, Reg. Düsseldorf 54341, NWH.

52. Wehrwirtschafts-Inspektion VII; Dr. Liebenow, Die körperliche Leistungsfähigkeit eines Mannes im Alter von 17 bis 18 Jahren, n.d., Microcopy T354, roll 604, frames 260–62; Grundsätzliches über das Leistungsvermögen Jugendlicher bei der vormilitärischen Ertüchtigung, n.d., Microcopy T78, roll 187, frames 612865–65; Dr. Joppich, Die Leistungs-fähigkeit des Jugendlichen, n.d., Microcopy T78, roll 187, frames 612666–67, NA; Ga Duisburg,194, Reg. Düsseldorf 54292 II, NWH.

53. Geoffrey Cocks, "Partners and Pariahs: Jews and Medicine in Modern German Society," in Cocks, *Treating Mind and Body: Essays in the History of Science, Professions, and Society Under Extreme Conditions* (New Brunswick, N.J.: Transaction, 1998), 173–92.

54. *Deutschland-Berichte der Sozialdemokratischen Partei Deutschlands (Sopade)* (Salzhausen: Nettelbeck, 1980), 3:1592, 4:1319; Joan Campbell, *Joy in Work, German Work* (Princeton: Princeton University Press, 1989), 363–64.

55. Ga Glauchau Nr. 35, 38, Sächsisches Hauptstaatsarchiv, Dresden.

56. Ga Weilheim, 1934 & 1935, Gesundheitämter Nr. 583, 584, Staatsarchiv München; Ga Moers, 1938, Reg. Düsseldorf 54395 I, NWH.

57. Michael Geyer, "Ein Vorbote des Wohlfahrtstaates: Die Kriegsopferversorgung in Frankreich, Deutschland und Grossbritannien nach dem Ersten Weltkrieg," *Geschichte und Gesellschaft* 9 (1983): 248.

58. *Sanitätsbericht über das Reichsheer*, ed. Heeres-Sanitäts-Inspektion im O.K.H. (Berlin: N.p., 1940), 189; Microcopy T78, roll 187, frame 6128189, NA.

59. Mosse, *Nationalism and Sexuality*; George L. Mosse, "Beauty without Sensuality: The Exhibition *Entartete Kunst*," in *"Degenerate Art": The Fate of the Avant-Garde in Nazi Germany*, ed. Stephanie Barron et al. (Los Angeles and New York: Los Angeles County Museum of Art and Harry N. Abrams, Inc., 1991), 25–31.

60. David F. Lindenfeld, "The Prevalence of Irrational Thinking in the Third

Reich: Notes Toward the Reconstruction of Modern Value Rationality," *Central European History* 30 (1997): 371–72; Michael Burleigh and Wolfgang Wippermann, *The Racial State: Germany, 1933–1945* (Cambridge: Cambridge University Press, 1991); see also Alf Lüdtke, "The 'Honor of Labor': Industrial Workers and the Power of Symbols under National Socialism," in Crew, *Nazism and German Society*, 94; and Peter Gay, *My German Question: Growing Up in Nazi Berlin* (New Haven: Yale University Press, 1998), 144.

61. Kreisarzt Ruppin, Jahresgesundheitsbericht 1939–40, Pr. Br. Rep. 45D, folder 6, Brandenburgisches Landeshauptarchiv, Potsdam.

62. Allgemeine gesundheitliche Verhältnisse, Pr. Br. Rep. 45D, folder 7.

63. Allgemeine gesundheitliche Verhältnisse, Pr. Br. Rep. 45D, folders 5, 6, 9.

64. Henry Friedlander, *The Origins of Nazi Genocide: From Euthanasia to the Final Solution* (Chapel Hill: North Carolina University Press, 1995), 108.

65. Ibid.   66. Ibid., 104–5.

67. Ibid., 152.   68. Ibid., 188.

69. Ibid., 100.

70. Lüdtke, "The 'Honor of Labor'," 92–93; Ulrich Herbert, "Labor as Spoils of Conquest, 1933–1945," in Crew, *Nazism and German Society*, 268.

71. Quoted in Crew, introduction to his *Nazism and German Society*, 12.

72. Christa Wolf, *Patterns of Childhood*, trans. Ursule Molinaro and Hedwig Rappolt (New York: Farrar, Straus & Giroux, 1984), 200.

73. Michael Geyer, "Resistance as Ongoing Project: Visions of Order, Obligations to Strangers, and Struggles for Civil Society," in *Resistance Against the Third Reich, 1933–1990*, ed. Michael Geyer and John W. Boyer (Chicago: University of Chicago Press, 1994), 325–50.

74. Gustav Störring, "Die Verschiedenheiten der psycho-pathologischen Erfahrungen im Weltkriege und im jetzigen Krieg und ihre Ursachen," *Münchener medizinische Wochenschrift* 89 (1942): 27.

75. Geoffrey Cocks, *Psychotherapy in the Third Reich: The Göring Institute* (New Brunswick, N.J.: Transaction, 1997), 309; Blackbourn, *The Long Nineteenth Century*, 378.

76. Inspekteur des Sanitätswesens der Luftwaffe, Anweisung für Truppenärzte über Verhütung von Selbstmord, October 6, 1942, Microcopy T78, roll 191, frames 6135832–37; Microcopy T84, roll 181, frame 1549979, NA.

77. Leonardo Conti to Heinrich Himmler, March 18, 1942, Microcopy T175, roll 68, frames 2585201–4, NA; see also Himmler to Conti, April 1942, frame 2585191.

78. Leonardo Conti, *Stand der Volksgesundheit im 5. Kriegsjahr* (Berlin, 1944), Reg. Aachen 16486; Ga Krefeld, 1941, Reg. Düsseldorf 54292 II; Ga Rheydt, 1940, Reg. Düsseldorf 54295 I, NWH; United States Strategic Bombing Survey, Morale Division, Medical Branch Report, *The Effect of Bombing on Health and Medical Care in Germany* (Washington, D.C., October 30, 1945).

79. Reg. Düsseldorf 54291 I, NWH.

80. Conti to Martin Bormann, July 3, 1942, Microcopy T175, roll 68, frames 2585206–7, NA; see also Lisa Pine, *Nazi Family Policy, 1933–1945* (Oxford: Berg, 1997), 82.

81. Victor Klemperer, *I Will Bear Witness: A Diary of the Nazi Years, 1942–1945,* trans. Martin Chalmers (New York: Random House, 1999), 190.
82. Burleigh and Wippermann, *Racial State,* 242–66; Campbell, *Joy in Work,* 366, 368.
83. Hermann Köhler to Kurt Schössler, October 14, 1942, NSDAP, Kreisleitung Eisenach, folder 00014a: Adjutantur des Gauleiters, Myers Collection, University of Michigan; Ga Mülheim a.d. Ruhr, 1943, Reg. Düsseldorf 54291 I, NWH; Abensberg/Niederbayern to Conti, March 4, 1943, Microcopy T1021, roll 17, frames 128–31, NA; Deutscher Gemeindetag Berlin to Deutscher Gemeindetag Düsseldorf, September 1, 1942, RW 53/466, NWH.
84. See Peter Reichel, *Der schöne Schein des 3. Reiches: Faszination und Gewalt des Faschismus* (Frankfurt: Fischer, 1993), 374–75.
85. Carl Fervers, *Schmerzbetäubung und seelische Schonung* (Stuttgart: Enke, 1940), 152–53, 155.
86. Paul Ridder, *Im Spiegel der Arznei: Sozialgeschichte der Medizin* (Stuttgart: Hirzel, 1990), 11–25. See also the essay by Patricia R. Stokes in this volume (Chapter 4).
87. Ludwig Sievers, *Handbuch für Kassenärzte* (Hanover: Schlüchterschen, 1925), 37–45.
88. Meldungen aus dem Reich, February 20, 1941, Microcopy T175, roll 260, frame 2753286, NA; Auszug aus der Niederschrift über die 7. Sitzung der Rheinischen Arbeitsgemeinschaft für Wohlfahrtspflege am 4. Juli 1936 im Kreissparkassengebäude zu St.Goar, RW 53/455, NWH.
89. F. Eichholtz, "Ermüdungsbekämpfung: Über Stimulanten," *Deutsche medizinische Wochenschrift* 67 (1941): 56; Heeres-Sanitätsinspektion, Richtlinien zur Erkennung und Bekämpfung der Ermüdung (Anwendung und Wirkung des Pervitins), Nr. 120, June 18, 1942, Microcopy T78, roll 198, frames 614251114, NA; Cocks, *Psychotherapy in the Third Reich,* 242, 312–13; Vicki Baum, *Hotel Berlin '43* (Garden City, N.Y.: Doubleday, 1944), 11, 24, 26, 82, 85.
90. Brett Fairbairn, "The Rise and Fall of Consumer Cooperatives in Germany," in *Consumers Against Capitalism? Consumer Cooperatives in Europe, North America, and Japan, 1840–1990,* ed. Ellen Furlough and Carl Strikwerda (Lanham, Md.: Rowman & Littlefield, 1999), 295.
91. Reichsministerium des Innern to Reichswirtschaftsministerium, July 22, 1942, Reg. Düsseldorf 54364 III, NWH; Manfred Fischer, Die Eigenfertigung und die Betriebsleistung—Vergleich der Wehrkreis-Sanitätsparke, April 1, 1944, Microcopy T77, roll 297, frames 1125712–14; Meldungen aus dem Reich, May 9, 1940, Microcopy T175, roll 259, frame 2751485, and October 2, 1941, roll 261, frames 2754928–31, NA.
92. Der Heeres-Sanitätsinspekteur, *Der Wiedereinsatzfähigkeit nach Verwundungen, Erfrierungen, Erkrankungen* (Berlin, January 30, 1944), 6–7.
93. Ferdinand Sauerbruch, *Master Surgeon,* trans. Fernand G. Reiner and Anne Cliff (New York: Crowell, 1954), 236–37; Sauerbruch and Wenke, *Wesen und Bedeutung des Schmerzes,* 12–59; M. Kirschner, "Die operative Schmerzstillung im Kriege," *Der deutsche Militärarzt* 4 (1939): 153–63; Fritz Holle, "Praktische Erfahrungen über die Schmerzbekämpfung in der Kriegschirurgie des

Hauptverbandsplatz und Feldlazaretts," *Der deutsche Militärarzt* 7 (1942): 85–91; F. Hesse, "Die operative Schmerzbekämpfung im Kriege," *Der deutsche Militärarzt* 7 (1942): 185–91.

94. Sauerbruch and Wenke, *Wesen und Bedeutung des Schmerzes*, 12; Fervers, *Schmerzbetäubung und seelische Schonung*, 69.

95. "Crude German Surgery," *Manchester Guardian*, May 19, 1945, PC 5, reel 106, Wiener Library; Peter Bamm, *The Invisible Flag*, trans. Frank Herrmann (New York: NAL, 1958), 19, 24–25, 74–75.

96. Bamm, *The Invisible Flag*, 20.

97. Viktor von Weizsäcker, "Zur Klinik der Schmerzen," *Der Nervenarzt* 9 (1936): 553–59; Sauerbruch and Wenke, *Wesen und Bedeutung des Schmerzes*, 12–14.

98. Kirschner, "Die operative Schmerzstillung," 153.

99. Fervers, *Schmerzbetäubung und seelische Schonung*, 44.

100. Jay W. Baird, *To Die for Germany: Heroes in the Nazi Pantheon* (Bloomington: Indiana University Press, 1990), 231.

101. James M. Diehl, *The Thanks of the Fatherland: German Veterans After the Second World War* (Bloomington: Indiana University Press, 1993), 262n84.

102. Anne Frank, *The Diary of a Young Girl*, definitive edition, ed. Otto H. Frank and Mirjam Pressler, trans. Susan Masotty (New York: Doubleday, 1991), 93.

103. Diehl, *The Thanks of the Fatherland*, 43; Robert Weldon Whalen, *Bitter Wounds: German Victims of the Great War, 1914–1939* (Ithaca: Cornell University Press, 1984), 104; Young-Sun Hong, *Welfare, Modernity, and the Weimar State, 1919–1933* (Princeton: Princeton University Press, 1998), 94.

104. The same emphasis on disability was reflected in Nazi "euthanasia" bureaucrats' introduction of *Behinderte* in place of *Krüppel*: see Proctor, *Nazi War on Cancer*, 45.

105. See Microcopy T78, roll 191, frames 613571–659; and Arbeitsstelle der Reichsgruppe Industrie für Wiedereinschulung von Kriegsversehrten, Richtlinien für den Einsatz von Versehrten in Industriebetrieben, 1943, Microcopy T73, roll 109, frames 3267553–56, NA.

106. Meldungen aus dem Reich, June 21, 1943, Microcopy T175, roll 265, frame 2759739, NA; and Hauptfürsorge- und -versorgungsamt SS, June 10, 1943, Himmler File, 16/249, Library of Congress, Washington, D.C.

107. Microcopy T175, roll 188, frame 2726241, NA.

108. Justus Schneider, "Chirurgische Gesichtspunkte für den Wiedereinsatz der Versehrten im Flugzeug," *Der deutsche Militärarzt* 9 (1944): 536–38.

109. "Sanitätsdienst und Propaganda," c. 1943–44, Microcopy T78, roll 189, frames 613113–49, NA.

110. Dr. Wolff, "Die Betreuung unserer Schwerverletzten," *Deutsches Ärzteblatt* 71 (1941), offprint, Microcopy T78, roll 191, frames 6134677–82, NA.

111. Friedlander, *The Origins of Nazi Genocide*, 81–82.

112. Kommandeur, Sanitäts-Abteilung Chemnitz, "Arbeitsbehandlung in den Res. Lazaretten," March 6, 1943, Microcopy T78, roll 189, frames 613 1401–30, NA.

113. Gisela Bock, "'No Children at Any Cost': Perspectives on Compulsory Sterilization, Sexism and Racism in Nazi Germany," in *Women in Culture and Politics: A Century of Change*, ed. Judith Friedlander et al. (Bloomington: Indiana University Press, 1986), 288, 292.

114. *Meldungen aus dem Reich* (1984), 13:4811.

115. Omer Bartov, *Hitler's Army: Soldiers, Nazis, and War in the Third Reich* (New York: Oxford University Press, 1991); Daniel Jonah Goldhagen, *Hitler's Willing Executioners: Ordinary Germans and the Holocaust* (New York: Knopf, 1996).

116. Ian Kershaw, "The 'Hitler Myth': Image and Reality in the Third Reich," in Crew, *Nazism and German Society*, 197–215; Alexander Biddiscombe, *Werwolf! The History of the National Socialist Guerrilla Movement, 1944–1946* (Toronto: Toronto University Press, 1998), 279–81; Thomas Kühne, "From a War Culture to a Peace Culture? Changing Political Mentalities in Germany after 1945," *German History* 18 (2000): 232.

117. Detlev J. K. Peukert, *Inside Nazi Germany: Conformity, Opposition, and Racism in Everyday Life*, trans. Richard Deveson (New Haven: Yale University Press, 1987), 236–42, 247; John Bodnar, "*Saving Private Ryan* and Postwar Memory in America," *American Historical Review* 106 (2001): 807, 810.

118. Ridder, *Im Spiegel der Arznei*, 248–55; R. K. Schicke, "The Pharmaceutical Market and Prescription Drugs in the Federal Republic of Germany: Cross-National Comparisons," *International Journal of Health Services* 3 (1973): 223–36; Paul Betts, "The Twilight of the Idols: East German Memory and Material Culture," *Journal of Modern History* 72 (2000): 761. On postponement of a consumer society between 1933 and 1950, see Michael Wildt, *Am Beginn "der Konsumgesellschaft": Mangelerfahrung, Lebenshaltung, Wohlstandshoffnung in Westdeutschland in den fünfziger Jahren* (Hamburg: Ergebnisse, 1994).

119. Michael Geyer, "The Nazi State Reconsidered," in *Life in the Third Reich*, ed. Richard Bessel (Oxford: Oxford University Press, 1987), 59; Cocks, *Psychotherapy in the Third Reich*, 399–413.

120. Ga Mönchengladbach to Regierungspräsident Düsseldorf, March 30, 1950, Reg. Düsseldorf 54364 III, NWH; Cortez. F. Enloe, "Why There Were No Epidemics," in United States Strategic Bombing Survey, *The Effect of Bombing*, 82; McNeil, *Plagues and Peoples*, 286; "Low Health in Germany," *Times*, December 28, 1946; "Mild Winter Saves Berlin from Major Epidemics," *Observer*, February 10, 1946, PC 5, reel 106, Wiener Library; Michael L. Hughes, "'Through No Fault of Our Own': West Germans Remember Their War Losses," *German History* 18 (2000): 193–213.

CHAPTER 6

This essay was translated by Greg Eghigian and Paul Betts.

1. Jörg Fisch, "Zivilisation, Kultur," in *Geschichtliche Grundbegriffe: Historisches Lexikon zur politisch-sozialen Sprache in Deutschland*, vol. 7, ed. Otto Brunner, Werner Conze, and Reinhart Koselleck (Stuttgart: Klett-Cotta, 1992), 679–775.

2. Werner Sombart, *Händler und Helden: Patriotische Besinnungen* (Munich: Dunckler & Humblot, 1915); Klaus von See, *Barbar, Germane, Arier: Die Suche nach der Identität der Deutschen* (Heidelberg: Universitätsverlag C. Winter, 1994), 188, 304.

3. The first critical study on this theme provoked a lively controversy among historians in Germany. See Fritz Fischer, *Germany's Aims in the First World War* (1961; reprint, New York: W. W. Norton, 1967); as well as his "Twenty-Five Years Later: Looking Back at the 'Fischer Controversy' and its Consequences," *Central European History* 21 (1990): 207–23. More generally, see Georges-Henri Soutou, *L'Or et le Sang: Les buts de guerre économiques de la Première Guerre mondiale* (Paris: Fayard, 1989).

4. Michael Geyer, "The Stigma of Violence: Nationalism and War in Twentieth-Century Germany," *German Studies Review*, special issue (winter 1992): 75–110.

5. Ulrich Heinemann, *Die verdrängte Niederlage: Politische Öffentlichkeit und Kriegsschuldfrage in der Weimarer Republik* (Göttingen: Vanderhoeck & Ruprecht, 1983); Herfried Münkler and Wolfgang Storch, *Siegfrieden: Politik mit einem deutschen Mythos* (Berlin: Rotbuch-Verlag, 1988).

6. On transmoralistic conscience, see Heinz Dieter Kittsteiner, "Vom Nutzen und Nachteil des Vergessens für die Geschichte," in *Vom Nutzen des Vergessens*, ed. Gary Smith and Hinderk M. Emrich (Berlin: Akademie Verlag, 1996), 133–74.

7. Clifford Geertz, *The Interpretation of Culture* (New York: Basic Books, 1973), 100.

8. Gottfried Korff, "Rote Fahnen und geballte Faust: Zur Symbolik der Arbeiterbewegung in der Weimarer Republik," in *Fahnen, Fäuste, Körper: Symbolik und Kultur der Arbeiterbewegung*, ed. Dietmar Petzina (Essen: Klartext, 1986), 27–60; Victor Turner, *The Ritual Process: Structure and Anti-Structure* (1969; reprint, New York: Aldine, 1982).

9. Antonia Grunenberg, *Antifaschismus—ein deutscher Mythos* (Reinbeck: Rowohlt, 1993), 177ff.

10. For a critical reflection, see Hildegard Cancik-Lindemaier, "Opfer: Religionswissenschaftliche Bemerkungen zur Nutzbarkeit eines religiösen Ausdruck," in *Der Krieg in den Köpfen: Beiträge zum Tübinger Friedenskongress "Krieg-Kultur-Wissenschaft,"* ed. Hans-Joachim Althaus et al. (Tübingen: Tübinger Verein für Volkskunde, 1988), 109–20.

11. Paul Fussell, *The Great War and Modern Memory*, (New York: Oxford, 1975); Klaus Vondung, ed., *Kriegserlebnis: Der Erste Weltkrieg in der literarischen Gestaltung und symbolischen Deutung der Nationen* (Göttingen: Vandenhoek & Ruprecht, 1980); George L. Mosse, *Fallen Soldiers: Reshaping the Memory of the World Wars* (New York: Oxford University Press, 1990), 70ff.

12. On these efforts, see Vondung, *Kriegserlebnis*; Bernd Hüppauf, ed., *Ansichten vom Krieg: Vergleichende Studien zum Ersten Weltkrieg in Literatur und Gesellschaft* (Königstein: Forum Academicum, 1984); Sabine Behrenbeck, "Zwischen Trauer und Heroisierung: Vom Umgang mit Kriegstod und Niederlage nach 1918," in *Kriegsende 1918: Ereignis, Wirkung, Nachwirkung*, ed. Jörg Duppler and Gerhard P. Groß (Munich: Oldenbourg, 1999), 315–39.

13. Bruno Tobia, *L'Altare della Patria* (Bologna: In Mulino, 1998).

14. Der Stahlhelm, "Vorschlag für ein Reichsehrenmal vom Juli 1925," cited in *Der Reichskunstwart—Kunstpolitik in den Jahren, 1920–1933: Zu den Be-mühungen um eine offizielle Reichskunstpolitik in der Weimarer Republik*, ed. Annegret Heffen (Essen: Die Blaue Eule, 1986), 244.

15. On this, see Sabine Behrenbeck, *Der Kult um die toten Helden: National-sozialistische Mythen, Riten, und Symbole, 1923–1945* (Vierow bei Greifswald: SH-Verlag, 1996), 152ff.

16. Karl Prümm, *Die Literatur des Soldatischen Nationalismus der 20er Jahre (1918–1933): Gruppenideologie und Epochenproblematik* (Kronberg Taunus: Scriptor, 1974); Roger Woods, *Ernst Jünger and the Nature of Political Commit-ment* (Stuttgart: Heinz, 1982); Hans-Harald Müller, *Der Krieg und die Schrift-steller: Der Kriegsroman der Weimarer Republik* (Stuttgart: Metzler, 1986).

17. Franz Schauwecker, *Im Todesrachen: Die deutsche Seele im Weltkriege* (Halle: Dieckmann, 1919), 282.

18. Manfred Hettling and Michael Jeismann, "Der Weltkrieg als Epos: Philipp Witkops 'Kriegsbriefe gefallener Studenten'," in *"Keiner fühlt sich hier mehr als Mensch . . . ": Erlebnis und Wirkung des Ersten Weltkriegs*, ed. Gerhard Hirschfeld, Gerd Krumeich, and Irina Renz, (Frankfurt: Fischer, 1996), 216ff.

19. The absolutization of sacrifice continued a tradition that had already, since introduction of the military conscription in Germany, interpreted the dying of the soldier according to the scheme of Christian salvation through sacrifice. It was thought to be necessary for national unity or for saving the threatened community. A redeeming feature was ascribed to dying for the Fatherland. The sacrifice of the soldier was considered as a pledge for the victory and liberation of those surviv-ing. On this, see Reinhart Koselleck and Michael Jeismann, ed., *Der politische Totenkult: Kriegerdenkmäler in der Moderne* (Munich: Bild und Text, 1994).

20. Joseph P. Stern, *Hitler: Der Führer and das Volk* (Munich: Hanser, 1978), 28ff.

21. Certainly the war-wounded also claimed this special quality for them-selves, since their blood was also spilled for everyone. They, too, then relied on the image of Christ's death. See Christine Beil, "Zwischen Hoffnung und Verbit-terung: Selbstbild und Erfahrung von Kriegsbeschädigten in den ersten Jahren der Weimarer Republik," *Zeitschrift für Geschichte* 2 (1998): 139–57.

22. Sabine Behrenbeck, "Heldenkult oder Friedensmahnung? Kriegerdenkmale nach beiden Weltkriegen," in *Lernen aus dem Krieg? Deutsche Nachkriegszeiten 1918/1945*, ed. Gottfried Niedhart and Dieter Riesenberger (Munich: Beck, 1992), 344–64. See also Reinhart Koselleck, "Kriegerdenkmale als Identitäts-stiftungen der Überlebenden," in *Identität*, ed. Odo Marquard and Karlheinz Stierle (Munich: Fink, 1979), 255–76; Ulrich Linse, "'Saatfrüchte sollen nicht vermahlen werden!' Zur Resymbolisierung des Soldatentods," in Vondung, *Kriegserlebnis*, 262–74.

23. For an example of this thinking, see Ernst Bergmann, "Diese Toten sind ja nicht tot!" Foreword in Friedrich Wilhelm Ilgen, *Deutscher Ehrenhain für die Helden von 1914/18* (Leipzig: Dehain, 1931), 7f.

24. Friedrich Sieburg, *Abmarsch in die Barbarei: Gedanken über Deutschland,*

ed. Klaus Harpprecht (Stuttgart: Deutsche Verlags Anstalt, 1983), 65–67. Sieburg's vocabulary, punctuated by the central concepts of "pain, sacrifice, effort," is typical of many significant works of German and Austrian literature in the first three decades of the twentieth century. See Joseph Peter Stern, "'Der teure Kauf': Opferbereitschaft und Erlösungshoffnung. Die Übernahme religiöser Gedanken aus der deutschen Literatur in die nationalsozialistische Propaganda," in "*1937: Europa vor dem 2. Weltkrieg*" = Sonderheft *Journal für Ästhetik* (1987), 80.

25. On this, see Behrenbeck, *Der Kult um die toten Helden*, 299ff.

26. This information comes from Helmut Heiber, *Joseph Goebbels* (Munich: Deutscher Taschenbuch Verlag, 1988), 77ff; Jay W. Baird, *To Die for Germany: Heroes in the Nazi Pantheon* (Bloomington: Indiana University Press, 1999), 75ff.

27. Joseph Goebbels, "Bis zur Neige," *Der Angriff*, 6 March 1930.

28. This is how Baird formulates the basic message of the myth. See his *To Die for Germany*, 73.

29. On this, see Alfred Rosenberg's comments in *Völkischer Beobachter*, 1 March 1930.

30. "Die Fahne hoch," *Der Angriff*, 27 February 1930.

31. A commemorative article in *Der Angriff* (9 October 1930) on the occasion of Wessel's birthday ends with the vow, "Comrade Wessel, we will avenge you!"

32. Behrenbeck, *Der Kult um die toten Helden*, 335.

33. Klaus Vondung, *Die Apokalypse in Deutschland*, (Munich: Deutscher Taschenbuch Verlag, 1988), 150. Without a rational analysis of crisis and its causes, aggression easily grows into an unreflective affect. See Uwe-K. Ketelsen, *Literatur und Drittes Reich* (Vierow bei Greifswald: SH-Verlag, 1994), 346.

34. Rudolf Georg Binding et al., *Sechs Bekenntnisse zum neuen Deutschland* (Hamburg: Hanseatische Verlagsanstalt, 1933), 18.

35. Rolf Geissler, *Dekadenz und Heroismus: Zeitroman und völkisch-nationalsozialistische Literaturkritik* (Stuttgart: Deutsche Verlags Anstalt, 1964), 80f. On plans for an alternative world and the needs of Nazi supporters, see Ketelsen, *Literatur und Drittes Reich*, 300.

36. These were basic features of the so-called inner values of an SS man according to Himmler's notions. Joachim Fest, *Das Gesicht des Dritten Reiches: Profile einer totalitären Herrschaft* (Munich: Piper, 1963), 167.

37. Vondung, *Apokalypse*, 154; Mosse, *Fallen Soldiers*, 34ff. Also, see Jost Hermand, *Der alte Traum vom neuen Reich: Völkische Utopien und Nationalsozialismus*, (Frankfurt: Athenäum, 1985).

38. Vondung, *Apokalypse*, 206f.

39. Joseph Goebbels, *Michael: Ein deutsches Schicksal in Tagebuchblättern* (1930; reprint, Munich: Eher, 1934), 31.

40. Ernst Jünger, *Der Kampf als inneres Erlebnis*, (1921; reprint, Berlin: Mittler, 1933), 105. Hitler voiced a similar view: "Whoever believes in something false still stands taller than he who believes in nothing at all." Adolf Hitler, *Monologe im Führerhauptquartier, 1941–1944: Die Aufzeichnungen von Heinrich Heims*, ed. Werner Jochmann (Hamburg: Knaus, 1980), 105 (note of 24 October 1941).

41. On this, see Vondung, *Apokalypse*, 150ff.
42. See Behrenbeck, *Der Kult um die toten Helden*, 259ff.
43. Volker Ackermann, *Nationale Totenfeiern in Deutchland: Von Wilhelm I. bis Franz Josef Strauss. Eine Studie zur politischen Semiotik* (Stuttgart: Klett-Cotta, 1990), 150.
44. Ibid., 147–52.
45. On this theme, see Ulrich Linse, *Barfüßige Propheten: Erlöser der 20er Jahre* (Berlin: Siedler, 1983).
46. Linse, *Barfüßige Propheten*, 29. For the material that follows, see Ibid., 40.
47. Ibid., 34.
48. Ibid., 41f.
49. Adolf Hitler, *Mein Kampf*, 3. Auflage (1925; Munich: Eher, 1933), 395ff, 417, 516.
50. Linse, *Barfüßige Propheten*, 40f.
51. Ibid., 49f, 145.
52. In addition, the death of an innocent human being who must die because he does not want to give up or renounce his ideals or values is commonly termed a "sacrifice," although the more appropriate expression for this is "martyrdom."
53. Joseph Goebbels in *Der Angriff*, 15 May 1930.
54. Behrenbeck, *Der Kult um die toten Helden*, 197ff.
55. This is how Martin Loiperdinger interprets the party congress ritual of 1934 in *Rituale der Mobilmachung: Der Parteitagsfilm "Triumph des Willens" von Leni Riefenstahl* (Opladen: Leske und Budrich, 1987), 80f.
56. Herbert Böhme, Der Held, Poem reprinted in Hans-Joachim Gamm, *Der braune Kult: Das Dritte Reich und seine Ersatzreligion: Ein Beitrag zur politischen Bildung* (Hamburg: Rütten & Loening, 1962), 32.
57. Anna Teut, *Architektur im Dritten Reich, 1933–1945* (Berlin: Ullstein, 1967), 298ff.
58. Hansjoachim Henning, "Kraftzeugindustrie und Autobahnbau in der Wirtschaftspolitik des Nationalsozialismus 1933 bis 1936," *Vierteljahrsschrift für Sozial- und Wirtschaftsgeschichte* 65 (1978): 217–42.
59. *Reichsautobahn: Pyramiden des Dritten Reichs*, ed. Rainer Strommer (Marburg: Jonas, 1982).
60. In fact, the private savings accounts that were earmarked for the Volkswagen project were ultimately absorbed by the ever-demanding war economy.
61. On the subject of Hitler as symbol of Nazi propaganda, see Rudolf Herz, *Hoffmann und Hitler: Fotografie als Medium des Führer-Mythos* (Munich: Münchner Stadtmuseum, 1994), 260ff.
62. Rudolf Walther, "Fahrn, Fahrn, Fahrn . . . auf der Autobahn: Aus der Geschichte eines (deutschen) Mythos," *Die Zeit*, 16 September 1999, 104.
63. Wolfram Wette, "Ideologien, Propaganda und Innenpolitik als Voraussetzung der Kriegspolitik des Dritten Reiches," in Wilhelm Deist et al., *Ursachen und Voraussetzungen der deutschen Kriegspolitik* (= *Das Deutsche Reich und der Zweite Weltkrieg*, Bd. 19) (Stuttgart: Deutsche Verlags Anstalt, 1979), 113, 127.
64. Behrenbeck, *Der Kult um die toten Helden*, 474ff.

65. Hans Umbreit, "Plünderung und rationelle Ausnutzung," in Bernhard R. Koerner, Rolf-Dieter Müller, and Hans Umbreit, *Organisation und Mobilisierung des deutschen Machtbereichs*, vol. 1 of *Kriegsverwaltung, Wirtschaft und personelle Ressourcen 1939–1941* (Stuttgart: Deutsche Verlags Anstalt, 1988), 236.

66. On this issue, see Klaus Latzel, *Deutsche Soldaten—nationalsozialistischer Krieg? Kriegserlebnis-Kriegserfahrung, 1939–1945* (Paderborn: Schöningh, 1998), 133–45.

67. Rolf-Dieter Müller, "Das 'Unternehmen Barbarossa' als wirtschaftlicher Raubkrieg," in Gerd R. Ueberschär and Wolfram Wette, eds., *"Unternehmen Barbarossa". Der deutsche Überfall auf die Sowjetunion 1941: Berichte, Analysen, Dokumente* (Paderborn: Schöningh, 1984), 173–90; Rolf-Dieter Müller, "Die Konsequenzen der 'Volksgemeinschaft': Ernährung, Ausbeutung und Vernichtung," in *Der Zweite Weltkrieg: Analyse, Grundzüge, Forschungsbilanz* (Munich: Piper, 1989), 240–49.

68. Behrenbeck, *Kult um die toten Helden*, 533ff; as well as her "Über die Lesarten eines Menetekels," in. *Geschichtszeichen*, ed. Hein Dieter Kittsteiner (Cologne: Böhlau, 1999), 181–98.

69. Ian Kershaw, *Der Hitler-Mythos: Volksmeinung und Propaganda im Dritten Reich* (Stuttgart: Deutsche Verlags Anstalt, 1980), 193.

70. Heinz Boberach, ed., *Meldungen aus dem Reich 1938–1945: Die geheimen Lageberichte des Sicherheitsdienstes des SS*, vol. 17 (Herrsching: Pawlak Verlag, 1984), 6738.

71. The issue is addressed in Wolfgang Benz, "Verdrängen oder Erinnern? Der Krieg gegen die Sowjetunion im Bewusstsein der Deutschen," in *Erobern und Vernichten: Der Krieg gegen die Sowjetunion 1941–1945* ed. Peter Jahn and Reinhard Rürup (Berlin: Argon, 1991), 211–30.

72. Herfried Münkler, *Machtzerfall: Die letzten Tage des Dritten Reiches, dargestellt am Beispiel der hessischen Kreisstadt Friedberg* (Berlin: Siedler, 1985), 222.

73. Gudrun Kohn-Waechter, "Einleitung," in her edited *Schrift der Flammen: Opfermythen und Weiblichkeitsentwürfe im 20. Jahrhunderts* (Berlin: Orlanda-Frauenverlag, 1991), 12f.

74. Vera Neumann, *Nicht der Rede wert: Die Privatisierung der Kriegsfolgen in der frühen Bundesrepublik: Lebensgeschichtliche Erinnerungen* (Münster: Verlag Westfälisches Dampfboot, 1999).

75. Lutz Niethammer, "Heimat und Front: Versuch, zehn Kriegserinnerungen aus der Arbeiterklasse des Ruhrgebietes zu verstehen," in his edited *"Die Jahre weiss man nicht, wo man die heute hinsetzen soll": Faschismus-Erfahrungen im Ruhrgebiet*, Bd. 1 (Berlin: J. H. W. Dietz Nachf., 1986), 225.

76. Heinz-Dieter Kittsteiner, "Die in sich gebrochene Heroisierung: Ein geschichtstheoretischer Versuch zum Menschenbild in der Kunst der DDR," in *Historische Anthropologie* 2, no. 3 (1994): 457.

77. Ibid.

78. Sabine Behrenbeck, "Between Pain and Silence: Remembering the Victims of Violence in Germany," in *Life after Death: Violence, Normality and the Con-*

struction of Postwar Europe, ed. Richard Bessel and Dirk Schumann (Cambridge: Cambridge University Press, 2002).

79. Hermann Heimpel, *Über den Tod für das Vaterland* (Hannover: Buchdruckerwerkstätten, 1956), 7ff.

80. *Der Spiegel*, 15 June 1960; as well as *Frankfurter Rundschau*, 18 June 1960.

81. Eugen Kogon, *Frankfurter Neue Presse*, 7 September 1950. See also Edgar Wolfrum, *Geschichtspolitik in der Bundesrepublik Deutschland: Der Weg zur bundesrepublikanischen Erinnerung, 1948–1990* (Darmstadt: Wissenschaftliche Buchgesellschaft, 1999), 200–11.

82. Neumann, *Nicht der Rede wert*.

83. Michael Geyer, "Cold War Angst: The Case of West German Opposition to Rearmament and Nuclear Weapons," in *The Miracle Years*, ed. Hanna Schissler (Princeton: Princeton University Press, 2001.)

84. Geyer, "Cold War Angst."

85. Ian Kershaw, *Popular Opinion and Political Dissent in the Third Reich* (Oxford: Oxford University Press, 1983).

86. In West German collective consciousness, the day of the currency reform was a much stronger memory than the day that the new West German state was declared. See *Kölner Stadtanzeiger*, 7 September 1950.

87. Geyer, "Cold War Angst.".

88. Norbert Frei, *Vergangenheitspolitik: Die Anfänge der Bundesrepublik und die NS-Vergangenheit* (Munich: C. H. Beck, 1997), 15.

89. Presse- und Informationsamt der Bundesregierung, *Mitteilung an die Presse* Nr. 780/50; and Ernst Müller-Hermann in *Weser Kurier*, 7 September 1950. Similarly, Chancellor Adenauer made the following remarks during the National Day of Mourning, 16 November 1952: "Alle tragen ein Leid, das zur Einigkeit mahnt," in: *Süddeutsche Zeitung*, 17 Novmeber 1952. See on this also Wolfrum, *Geschichtspolitik in der Bundesrepublik Deutschland*, 60.

90. Sabine Behrenbeck, "Between Pain and Silence."

91. "Europa in einem Boot. Gedanken zum Volkstrauertag," *Rhein-Koblenz-Zeitung*, 14 November 1953. See also Frei, *Vergangenheitspolitik*, 133ff.

92. Frei, *Vergangenheitspolitik*, 23, 399.

93. See too the speech by German parliament president Hermann Ehlers on the occasion of the National Day of Mourning, 18 February 1951, in *Bulletin* des Presse- und Informationsamtes der Bundesregierung.

94. Frei, *Vergangenheitspolitik*, 22.

95. Ibid., 22, 400, 195ff.

96. Elisabeth Domansky, "A Lost War: World War II in Postwar German Memory," in *Thinking about the Holocaust: After a Half a Century*, ed. Alvin H. Rosenfeld (Bloomington: University of Indiana Press, 1997), 233–72.

97. Frei, *Vergangenheitspolitik*, 405.

98. Norbert Elias, *Studien über die Deutschen: Machtkämpfe und Habitusentwicklung im 19. und 20. Jahrhundert*, ed. Michael Schröter (Frankfurt: Suhrkamp, 1989), 429–32.

CHAPTER 7

I would like to thank the Social Science Research Council Berlin Program and the Friedrich Ebert Stiftung for support in funding the research for this project and I owe gratitude to Carolyn Steedman, Jonathan Zatlin, Samuel Temple, and Paul Lerner for useful consultation on this article.

1. Heide Fehrenbach, *Cinema in Democratizing Germany: Reconstructing National Identity after Hitler* (Chapel Hill: University of North Carolina Press, 1995), 56ff.

2. Ibid.

3. For a sample of literature on postwar rapes, see Annemarie Tröger, "Between Rape and Prostitution: Survival Strategies and Chances of Emancipation for Berlin Women after World War II," in *Women in Culture and Politics: A Century of Change*, ed. Judith Friedlander et al. (Bloomington: Indiana University Press, 1986); Erika M. Hoerning, "Frauen als Kriegsbeute. Der Zwei-Fronten Krieg. Beispiele aus Berlin," in *"Wir kriegen jetzt andere Zeiten" Auf der Suche nach der Erfahrung des Volkes in antifaschistischen Ländern. Lebensgeschichte und Sozialkultur im Ruhrgebiet 1930 bis 1960*, vol. 3, ed. Lutz Niethammer and Alexander von Plato (Berlin: J. H. W. Dietz Nachf., 1985), 327–46; Ingrid Schmidt-Harzbach, "Eine Woche in April. Berlin 1945. Vergewaltigung als Massenschicksal," *Feministische Studien* 5 (1984): 51–62; Gerhard Keiderling, " 'Als Befreier unsere Herzen zerbrachen,' Zu den Übergriffen der Sowjetarmee in Berlin 1945," *Deutschland Archiv* 3:28 (March 1995): 234–43. For a discussion of Helke Sanders's film on the subject of postwar rapes in Germany, see the special issue (72) of *October* (April 1995), particularly Atina Grossmann's article, "A Question of Silence: The Rape of German Women by Occupation Soldiers."

4. Ingrid Schmidt-Harzbach and Renate Genth, "Kriegsende und Nachkriegszeit in Berlin," in *Frauenpolitik und politisches Wirken von Frauen im Berlin der Nachkriegszeit, 1945–1949*, Renate Genth et al. (Berlin: Trafo Verlag Dr. Wolfgang Weist, 1996), 30.

5. German agriculture suffered from Hitler's attempts to assist rearmament. As part of this wartime economy, state regulators scrutinized agriculture to maximize efficiency and production. John Farquharson has suggested that this invasive state regulation actually led to counterproductive demands on farmers rather than improved efficiency. Allied bombings further exacerbated an agricultural economy struggling to keep up with demands in wartime. See John E. Farquharson, *The Western Allies and the Politics of Food: Agrarian Management in Postwar Germany* (Leamington Spa: Berg Publishers, 1985), 13ff. For a study of the effect of reparations on German industry, see Rainer Karlsch, "Die Reparationsleistungen der SBZ/DDR im Spiegel Deutscher und Russischer Quellen," in *Die Wirtschaft im geteilten und vereinten Deutschland*, ed. Karl Eckart and Jorg Roesler (Berlin: Duncker & Humblot, 1999), 9–30.

6. See Hans W. Schoenberg, *Germans from the East: A Study of their Migration, Resettlement, and Subsequent Group History since 1945* (The Hague: Martinus Nijhoff, 1970).

7. Landesarchiv Berlin Kalkreuthstr. (LAB-K) RG 260 OMGBS 4/8–3/2, Restricted U.S. Headquarters Berlin District, Office of Military Government (Berlin) Information Services Control Section, APO 755, U.S. Army, Survey Sub-Section, Public Opinion Survey Department, February 21, 1946, Survey No. 12.

8. From an interview with Anna Peters in Lutz Niethammer, "Privat-Wirschaft: Erinnerungsfragmente einer anderen Umerziehung," in *"Hinterher merkt man, daß es richtig war, daß er schiefgegangen ist" Nachkriegerfahrungen im Ruhrgebiet: Lebensgeschichte und Sozialkultur im Ruhrgebiet 1930 bis 1960.* Vol. 2, ed. Lutz Niethammer (Berlin: J. H. W. Dietz Nachf., 1983), 52–53, translated and reprinted in Robert Moeller, *Protecting Motherhood: Women and the Family in the Politics of Postwar West Germany* (Berkeley: University of California Press, 1993), 21.

9. The Soviet Military Administration (SMAD) set up rationing guidelines on November 1, 1945, for the whole Soviet Zone. The SED used the problems in provisions to its advantage in elections for socialist unity in March 1946 with the slogan "Die Sozialistische Einheitspartei Deutschlands—das ist Frieden, Freiheit, und Brot!" In the Soviet Occupation Zone (SBZ) the SMAD, headed by Oberst der Sowjetarmee Sergej I. Tjulpanow and Politischer Berater des Obesrten Chefs der SMAD Wladimir S. Semjonow, pursued a program of administration that was at first open and unplanned but increasingly concerned with exercising authority over all of Germany and with the reactions of the Western Allies and population to Soviet policies. See Rainer Gries, *Die Rationen-Gesellschaft. Versorgungskampf und Vergleichsmentalität: Leipzig, München und Köln nach dem Kriege* (Münster: Verlag Westfälisches Dampfboot, 1990), 48, 49, 57, 95.

10. Archiv der Deutschen Gewerkschaftsbund-Bundesvorstand (DGB) Gewerkschaftliches Zonenbeirat—Britische Besatzungszone (BBZ) 11/223.

11. On November 1, 1945, Category VI (or V in cities such as Leipzig) received a daily ration of 250 grams of bread, 20 grams of meat, 7 grams of fat, 15 grams of cereals, and 15 grams sugar. In comparison the recipients' "heavy laborer" card (Category I) received daily 450 grams of bread, 50 grams of meat, 31 grams of fat, 40 grams of cereals, and 25 grams of sugar. The rations were raised on August 1, 1946. See Gries, *Die Rationen-Gesellschaft*, 100–102.

12. Gries, *Die Rationen-Gesellschaft*, 94. Gries notes that a relative majority of citizens in Leipzig, the representative East German town, which he compares to Cologne and Munich in his book, existed on ration card Category VI. In August 1946, 210,000 Leipzig citizens (35 percent) had the "other" category (in Leipzig and Dresden this was Category V, elsewhere it was Category VI); ninety-eight thousand (16 percent) were in Category III for white-collar workers; the best categories of workers I and II had 183,000 (30 percent). See Ibid., 97–99.

13. There is considerable debate over when and how the hostilities of the Cold War transformed the agendas of the occupiers. Some crucial markers of this shift in 1947 were the formation of Bizonia, a combination of the British and American Zones into one administrative unit, the cessation of the American denazification program, and the declaration of the Truman Doctrine. However, earlier signs of heightened Cold War activity had already begun in 1946, including the joining of the communist KPD and the socialist Social Democratic Party (SPD) into one

ruling party, the SED, in the Soviet Zone, and Winston Churchill's "Iron Curtain" speech.

14. Günter J. Trittel, *Hunger und Politik: Die Ernährungskrise in der Bizone (1945–1949)* (Frankfurt: Campus Verlag, 1990), 53.

15. Andreas Malycha, "Die Illusion der Einheit—Kommunisten und Sozialdemokraten in den Landesvorständen der SED 1946–1951," in *Sowjetisierung und Eigenständigkeit in der SBZ/DDR (1945–1953)*, ed. Michael Lemke (Cologne: Böhlau Verlag, 1999), 98ff.

16. Harold Hurwitz, *Die Stalinisierung der SED: Zum Verlust von Freiräumen und sozialdemokratischer Identität in den Vorständen, 1946–1949* (Opladen: Westdeutscher Verlag, 1997), 326–27.

17. Niethammer, "Privat-Wirschaft," 28. Niethammer notes that the legend of the *"Stunde Null"* obscures the issue of how German history has led to the present day by denying the continuities from the Third Reich to the present; see his "Einleitung des Herausgebers," in *"Die Jahre weiß man nicht, wo man die heute hinsetzen soll" Faschismuserfahrungen in Ruhrgebiet: Lebensgeschichte und Sozialkultur im Ruhrgebiet 1930 bis 1960. Vol. 1*, ed. Lutz Niethammer (Berlin: J. H. W. Dietz Nachf., 1983), 8.

18. Alexander and Margarete Mitscherlich, *The Inability to Mourn*, trans. Beverly R. Placzek (New York: Grove Press, 1975).

19. Charles S. Maier, *The Unmasterable Past: History, Holocaust, and German National Identity* (Cambridge, Mass.: Harvard University Press, 1988).

20. Hermann Graml, "Die verdrängte Auseinandersetzung mit dem Nationalsozialismus," in *Zäsuren nach 1945: Essays zur Periodisierung der deutschen Nachkriegsgeschichte*, ed. Martin Broszat (Munich: Oldenbourg, 1990), 169–83.

21. Zygmunt Bauman, *Socialism: The Active Utopia* (London: George Allen & Unwin, 1976), 79.

22. Charles Maier, "The End of Longing? (Notes toward a History of Postwar German National Longing)," in *The Postwar Transformation of Germany: Democracy, Prosperity, and Nationhood*, ed. John S. Brade, Beverly Crawford, and Sarah Elise Wiliarty (Ann Arbor: University of Michigan Press, 1999), 271–85.

23. Zygmunt Bauman analyzed this as characteristic of the Stalinist system, which reconfigured the Protestant work ethic for the context of socialism; see Bauman, *Socialism*, 91.

24. *Der Deutsche Zweijahrplan für 1949–1950: Der Wirtschaftsplan für 1948 und der Zweijahrplan 1949–1950 zur Wiederherstellung und Entwicklung der Friedenswirtschaft in der sowjetischen Besatzungszone Deutschlands* (Berlin: Dietz Verlag, 1948).

25. Amt für Information der Regierung der Deutschen Demokratischen Republik, ed., *Unser Fünfjahrplan des friedlichen Aufbaus: Gesetz über den Fünfjahrplan zur Entwicklung der Volkswirtschaft der Deutschen Demokratischen Republik 1951–1955* (Berlin (East), 1952?), 4.

26. Jörg Roesler notes that the second half of the 1950s was characterized by consumption focused on new appliances, better quality goods, and a growing orientation toward fashion. See Jörg Roesler, "Privater Konsum in Ostdeutschland 1950–1960," in *Modernisierung im Wiederaufbau: Die Westdeutsche Gesellschaft*

der 50er Jahre, ed. Axel Schildt and Arnold Sywottek (Bonn: J. H. W. Dietz Nachf., 1993), 298.

27. Landesarchiv Berlin Breite Str. (LAB-B) Rep. 120 Nr. 226, Volksbildung 1953–1955, Entwurf, "Unser Berlin noch schneller voran im neuen Kurs."

28. Ibid.

29. Stiftung Archiv der Parteien und Massenorganisationen der DDR im Bundesarchiv (SAPMO-BA) Freie Deutsche Gewerkschaftsbund (FDGB) 15/158/1492, Ministerratsverordnung Dec. 10, 1953, Berichte der Zentr. Vorst. u. Bezirke, FDGB Bezirksvorstand Gross-Berlin Org.-Instrukteur-Abt. Berlin, Dec. 19, 1953, 7. Stimmungsbericht zur Verordnung des Ministerrates. IG TBL: Einige Betriebe sind zur Verordnung des Ministerrates Verpflichtungen eingegangen . . . IG Nahrung und Genuss.

30. LAB-B Rep. 120 Nr. 226, Volksbildung 1953–1955, Entwurf, "Unser Berlin noch schneller voran im neuen Kurs."

31. LAB-B Rep. 120 Nr. 226, Volksbildung 1953–1955, Material für Propagandisten, Lektion, "Wie wir leben, bestimmen wir selbst. Der neue Kurs zeigt uns den Weg in ein besseres Leben in Frieden" (Zum 1. Jahrestag der Verkündung des neuen Kurses) SED Bezirksllleitung Groß-Berlin Abt. Propaganda/Agitation.

32. Basic raw material industry and machine construction was to be raised 60 percent and worker productivity was to be raised 50 percent. See Hermann Weber, *Kleine Geschichte der DDR* (Cologne: Edition Deutschland Archiv, 1988), 89.

33. Walter Ulbricht, "Der Kampf um den Frieden, für die Sieg des Sozialismus, für die nationale Wiedergeburt Deutschlands als friedliebender, demokratischer Staat," *Protokoll der Verhandlungen des V. Parteitages der Sozialistischen Einheitspartei Deutschlands. 10. bis 16. Juli 1958 in der Werner-Seelenbinder-Halle zu Berlin* (Berlin: Dietz Verlag, 1959), 68.

34. Dietrich Staritz, *Geschichte der DDR 1949–1985* (Frankfurt: Suhrkamp, 1985), 125.

35. Bundesarchiv Potsdam (BAP) DL-1 Ministerium für Handel und Versorgung (Min. H.u.V.) 3902, 1/84 ZStA, File: Regierung der Deutschen Demokratischen Republik Staatliche Zentralverwaltung für Statistik beim Ministerrat, Vergleichende Darstellungen Deutschen Demokratischen Republik—Westdeutschland (Redaktionsschluß: 18 Juni 1959), Vertrauliche Dienstsache Nr. 1/493, 116. Ausfertigung 70 Blatt.

36. Silvia Rückert, "Spürbare Moderne—gehemmter Fortschritt: Plaste in der Waren- und Lebenswelt der DDR," in *Fortschritt, Norm und Eigensinn: Erkundungen im Alltag der DDR*, ed. Dokumentationszentrum Alltagskultur der DDR e.V. (Berlin: Ch. Links Verlag, 1999), 53–72.

37. Weber, *Kleine Geschichte*, 95.

38. SAPMO-BA FDGB Bundesvorstand (Buvo) 1548 Frauenabteilung, File: Stand der Gewerkschaftsarbeit mit den Frauen im Kreis Jena Brigadeeinsatz des Bundesvorstandes, Nov. 1959–Juli 1960, Document: "Vorschläge des Kreisvorstandes des FDGB an den Rat der Stadt und den Rat des Kreises Jena zur Erarbeitung des Kreisprogrammes für Dienstleistungen und Reparaturleistungen und die 1000 kleinen Dinge des täglichen Bedarfs."

39. Günter Pawelke et al., Kollektiv der Wirtschaftswissenschaftlichen

Fakultät der Karl-Marx-Universität Leipzig, *Mehr und bessere industrielle Konsumgüter: Eine Anleitung für die Praxis* (Berlin: Verlag die Wirtschaft, 1960), 75.

40. "Monat der Technik im HO-Warenhaus," *Neue Werbung* 3, no. 1 (January 1956): 23–25.

41. Amt für Information der Regierung der Deutschen Demokratischen Republik, ed., *Gesetz über den Fünfjahrplan zur Entwicklung der Volkswirtschaft der Deutschen Demokratischen Republik 1951–1955* (Berlin (East), 1951), 65.

42. These included ersatz coffee (May 1950); laundry detergent (August 1950); potatoes (September 1950); grains and legumes (January 1951); some textiles (February 1951); marmalade, synthetic honey, syrup, soap (October 1951); socks and stockings (March 1953); leather shoes (April 1953); and fish (July 1953). See Roesler, 'Privater Konsum,' in Schildt and Sywottek, *Modernisierung im Wiederaufbau*, 291.

43. In September 1950 the basic rationing card added 450 grams of meat and fat and the card for children added 300 to 450 grams. The per capita consumption of meat in 1936 was 46.8 kilograms and had only reached the level of 22.1 kilograms in 1950. See Peter Hübner, *Konsens, Konflikt und Kompromiß: Soziale Arbeiterinteressen und Sozialpolitik in der SBZ/DDR 1945–1970* (Berlin: Akademie, 1995), 146.

44. SAPMO-BA SED ZK Abt. Wirtschaftspolitik IV 2/603/76 October 5, 1948, Wo/Sch Besprechung bei der SMAD über die Errichtung von staatlichen Läden. Comment by Gen. Borowik.

45. "Über den weiteren Aufschwung der Industrie, des Verkehrswesens und des Handels in der Deutschen Demokratischen Republik: Aus dem Rechenschaftsbericht des ZK, den Diskussionsreden und dem Schlusswort des Genossen Walter Ulbricht auf dem IV. Partietag der Sozialistischen Einheitspartei Deutschlands. Berlin, 30. März bis 6. April 1954." (Berlin: Dietz Verlag, 1954), 11.

46. BAP DL-1 3205 MinHuV, HOZL, Hauptgeschäftsführer Hermann Streit, "Die Aufgaben und Ziele des 'Volkseigenen Handels'" *HO-Mitteilungen* no. 1 (April 20, 1949): 2.

47. This fact was often repeated as in a speech by Walter Ulbricht at an anniversary of the building of *Frauenausschüsse*. Cited in Sozialistische Einheitspartei Deutschlands, Zentralkomitee, *Frauen schaffen für das neue Leben. Ansprachen von Wilhelm Pieck und Walter Ulbricht und Diskussionsreden auf einer Beratung des Politbüros des ZK der SED mit Vertreterinnen der Frauenausschüsse aus Industrie und Landwirtschaft anläßlich des 3. Jahrestages der Gründung der Frauenausschüsse, Berlin 8. Januar 1955* (Berlin: Dietz Verlag, 1955).

48. Walter Ulbricht ushered in this idea in his comments. See *Protokoll der Verhandlungen des 2. Parteitages der Sozialistischen Einheitspartei Deutschlands, 20. Bis 24. September 1947* (Berlin: Dietz Verlag, 1947), 306.

49. SAPMO-BA FDGB Buvo 1548 Frauenabteilung. File: Stand der Gewerkschaftsarbeit mit den Frauen im Kreis Jena: Brigadeeinsatz des Bundesvorstandes. Nov. 1959–Juli 1960, Referat zum Frauenforum eingeladen durch den FDGB-Kreis vorstand Jena am 4. Februar 1960.

50. Pawelke, *Mehr und bessere industrielle Konsumgüter*, 31.

51. Ibid., 127.

52. Ibid., 31–32.

53. Ibid., 33.

54. Anne Hampele, "'Arbeite mit, plane mit, regiere mit'—Zur politischen Partizipation von Frauen in der DDR," in *Frauen in Deutschland 1945–1992*, ed. Gisela Helwig and Hildegard Maria Nickel (Bonn: Bundeszentrale für politische Bildung, 1993), 292–95; Ute Gerhard, "Die staatlich instiutionalisierte 'Lösung' der Frauenfrage. Zur Geschichte der Geschlechterverhältnisse in der DDR," in *Sozialgeschichte der DDR*, ed. Hartmut Kaelble, Jürgen Kocka, and Hartmut Zwahr (Stuttgart: Klett-Cotta, 1994), 389.

55. Petra Clemens recounts that one of her interviewees, Frau Behrmann, remembered a struggle against limited resources and uneven attention to "women's" problems from the textile factory management: "She had to "turn [nothing] into money" (*realisieren*) under the pressure of limited resources and distributed much despite shortages, thus she stood in permanent opposition to the fact that the women with daily emergencies always had to wait in line or were simply overlooked. For example, if the mill management paid undivided attention to construction of a factory store and the attainment and enlargement of its merchandise, things looked very different in other questions of provision, such as day care centers and kindergartens: 'Here the men didn't think that far.'" In Petra Clemens, "Die Kehrseite der Clara-Zetkin-Medaille: Die Betriebsfrauenausschüsse der 50er Jahre in lebensgeschichtlicher Sicht," *Feministische Studien* 1 (1990): 26.

56. While Lotte Ulbricht was vague about the concrete activities of the Frauenausschüsse in 1952, by 1959 social establishments and creation of kindergartens to relieve working women of housework was an integral part of the committees' agenda. See "Bedeutung und Aufgaben der Frauenausschüsse" from May 1952; and "Das sind die Aufgaben der Frauenausschüsse: Aus dem Diskussionsbeitrag auf der DDR-Bäuerinnenkonferenz in Erfurt am 28. und 29. Januar 1959," printed in *Der Freie Bauer* (February 8, 1959); reprinted in Lotte Ulbricht, *Reden und Aufsätze, 1943–1967* (Berlin: Dietz Verlag, 1968) 169–71.

57. Comment by Anneliese Kraft: Sachbearbeiterin für Sozialpolitik VEB Sachsenwerk Radeberg Bezirk Dresden in Sozialistische Einheitspartei Deutschlands, Zentralkomitee, *Frauen schaffen für das neue Leben*, 25.

58. In 1965 the women's committees were incorporated into the FDGB as "women's commissions" and therefore lost most of their already meager autonomy. See Clemens, "Die Kehrseite der Clara-Zetkin-Medaille," 20–34.

59. SAPMO-BA DFD Buvo 311, Büro des Sekretariats, Sitzungen des Sekretariats 80.-86. Sitzung, Jan. 4–Feb. 22, 1954, z. Prot. 81/IV Anlage 3, Vorlage an das Bundessekretariat, Betr: Bericht über die Arbeit auf dem Gebiet Konsum und HO, Berlin, den January 6, 1954.

60. In August 1954, the DFD's activity in the arena of consumption gained greater recognition when the minister for trade and supply, Curt Wach, championed a Minister's Council directive to promote advisory councils of DFD women to help retailing improve its practices. SAPMO-BA DFD 315, Buvo, Büro des Sekretariats, Sitzungen des Sekretariats 9.-14.Sitzung, Sept. 7–Oct. 25, 1954, Protokoll Nr. 14 v. Oct. 25, 1954, TO Punkt 10. Mitarbiet des DFD bei der Verbesserung des Handels, Anlage 7, Betr: Bildung von beratenden Ausschüssen

durch Frauen unserer Org. bei den VSTen des staatlichen Handels, Berlin, Oct. 22, 1954, Abt. Agitation.

61. Stores with HO-Councils:

District	Percentage of Stores/Restaurants with a HO-Council	Number
Neubrandenburg	21	178
Schwerin	15	134
Karl-Marx-Stadt	13	590
Cottbus	13	138
Magdeburg	10	—
Berlin	10	—
Frankfurt	10	—
Potsdam	4	—
Rostock	6	—
Suhl	7	—
Others	8–9	—

SAPMO-BA DFD Buvo 325 Büro des Sekretariats, File: Sitzungen des Sekretariats 93.-103. Sitzung, Nov. 19, 1956–May 6, 1957, Document: Zu Pkt 5 des Protokoll Nr. 104 v. March 12, 1957, Sekretariatsvorlage "Analyse über die Bildung und Arbeit der Beiräte in den Verkaufsstellen und Gaststätten der HO." Abteilungsleiter, Abt. Frau und Staat, Donth: Bundessekretärin, March 14, 1957.

62. Ibid.

63. SAPMO-BA DFD Buvo 296, Bundessekretariat, File: Sitzungen des Sekretariats des BV 18.–27. Sitzung, Jan. 8,–April 2, 1951, Protokoll Nr. 18/III, January 8, 1951, Anwesend: 1. Frau Elli Schmidt, 2. Frau Wilhelmine Schirmer-Pröscher, 3. Frau Elli Bergner, 4. Frau Louise Dornemann, 5. Frau Elfriede Marschall, TO: #6 Aufhebung der Lebensmittelkarten für Erzeugnisse von Getreide und Hülsenfrüchten., 1. Dem Schreiben an den Ministerrat der Regierung der DDR vom Dec. 23, 1950 wird nachträglich zugestimmt. Anlage 6 An den Ministerrat der Regierung der DDR, Berlin, Mit Bundesgruß DFD 1. Vorsitzende (Elli Schmidt) DFD Bundessekretariat.

64. In West Berlin this unemployment was especially severe. It rose in 1949 to peak in February 1950 at 309,000 unemployed or about 14.5 percent of the West Berlin population. See Rudolf Memberg, "Lage und Aussichten der Wirtschaft West-Berlins. Die wirtschaftliche Entwicklung seit 1948 und die Voraussetzungen für eine günstige Entwicklung," *Europa-Archiv* (Nov. 5, 1950): 3488; DGB, *DGB: Der Kampf der Gewerkschaften für die Freiheit Berlins. Berliner Gewerkschaftsgeschichte von 1945 bis 1950. FDGB/UGO/DGB* (Berlin: Rudolf Otto, 1971), 276.

65. The unemployment rate sank from its high point in 1950 to full employment from 1961 to 1966. See Werner Abelshauser, *Wirtschaftsgeschichte der Bundesrepublik Deutschland (1945–1980)* (Frankfurt: Suhrkamp, 1983), 110.

66. Michael Wildt, *Am Beginn der "Konsumgesellschaft": Mangelerfahrung, Lebenshaltung, Wohlstandshoffnung in Westdeutschland in den fünfzigen Jahren* (Hamburg: Ergebnisse Verlag, 1994), 74.

67. E. John et al., "A Comparative Study of the Structure and Development of Enlarged Consumption in Czechoslovakia, German Democratic Republic, Hungary, Poland and U.S.S.R.," in *Consumption Patterns in Eastern and Western Europe: An Economic Comparative Approach. A Collective Study*, ed. V. Cao-Pinna and S. S. Shatalin (Oxford: Pergamon Press, 1979), 68.

68. Ina Merkel, *Utopie und Bedurfnis: Die Geschichte der Konsumkultur in der DDR* (Cologne: Böhlau Verlag, 1999), 40.

69. Ibid., 159.

70. SAPMO-BA FDGB Buvo 1547 Part II, Industriegewerkschaft Metall Zentralvorstand, an das Frauensekretariat des Bundesvorstandes des FDGB, Feb. 8, 1958, Grothe Sekretariatsmitglied . . . , Abt. Arbeiterversorgung/Feriendienst, Berlin, Feb. 7, 1958, Gro/Ste., "Bericht über die Verwirklichung des Programms der Gewerkschaften zur weiteren Verbesseurng und allseitigen Erleichterung des Lebens der werktätigen Frauen und Mädchen."

71. André Steiner, "Zwischen Frustration und Verschwendung," in *Wunderwirtschaft: DDR-Konsumkultur in den 60er Jahren*, ed. Neue Gesellschaft für Bildende Kunst (Köln: Böhlau Verlag, 1996), 24.

72. Merkel, *Utopie und Bedurfnis*, 76ff.

73. Klaus Ewers, "Einführung der Leistungsentlohnung und verdeckter Lohnkampf in den volkseigenen Betrieben der SBZ (1947–1949)," *Deutschland Archiv* 13 (June 1980): 612–31; Norman Naimark, *The Russians in Germany: A History of the Soviet Zone of Occupation, 1945–1949* (Cambridge, Mass.: Harvard University Press, 1995), 195.

74. Silke Rothkirch, "'Moderne Menschen kaufen modern,'" in *Wunderwirtschaft*, 112–19.

75. BAP DL-1 2415 Min. HuV, Sektor Recht, File: Regelung der materiellen Verantwortlichkeit der Werktätigen im Handel, 1957–1959, Document: "Bestelldienst gut organisiert: Auszüge aus dem Diskussionsbeitrag des Kollegen Gerhard Reinelt, HO-Kreisbetrieb Brandenburg (Havel) auf der Leipziger Handelskonferenz," *Information für Funktionäre der Gewerkschaft Handel Nahrung Genuß*, nos. 18, 19 (September 1959): 10.

76. Andreas Ludwig, *Tempolinsen und P2: Begleitbuch zur Ausstellung "Tempolinsen und P2"* (Berlin-Brandenburg: be.bra verlag, 1996). See discussion in Paul Betts, "The Twilight of the Idols: East German Memory and Material Culture," *The Journal of Modern History* 72 (September 2000): 751.

77. For a contemporary British account of international developments in vending machines, see John L. Rogers, *Automatic Vending: Merchandising, Catering* (London: Food Trade Press Ltd., 1958).

78. Zentralkomitee der SED, *Durch sozialistische Gemeinschaftsarbeit*, 16.

79. Ibid., 94–95.

80. Ibid., 16.

81. SAPMO-BA, SED ZK Handel, Versorgung und Außenhandel IV 2/610/39, SED Hausmitteilung, an Abt. Handel, Versorgung, Außenh., von Abteilung Sicherheitsfragen, Diktatzeichen Gr/Np 546/292, March 22, 1960, Werter Genosse Lange!, Anliegend geben wir Dir einen Bericht betr. Ankauf von Westfernsehapparaten zur Kenntnis., Mit soz. gruß! Wansierski, Hauptabteilung -K-,—

Abteilung SE, Berlin, February 22, 1960, Betr: Westfernsehgeräte, Bezug: Huas-mitteilung 57/60, Aktenzeichen: Wei/Schu/2, v. January 20, 1960, Vogel Major d.VP.

82. C. Bradley Scharf, *Politics and Change in East Germany: An Evaluation of Socialist Democracy* (Boulder, Colo.: Westview Press, 1984), 182.

83. Michael Burawoy and Janos Lukacs, *The Radiant Past: Ideology and Reality in Hungary's Road to Capitalism* (Chicago: University of Chicago Press, 1992), 127–40.

84. For example, see the discussion of the high-priced intershops in Jonathan R. Zatlin, "Consuming Ideology: Socialist Consumerism and the Intershops, 1970–1989," in *Arbeiter in der SBZ-DDR*, ed. Peter Hübner and Klaus Tenfelde (Essen: Klartext Verlag, 1999), 555–72.

85. Merkel, *Utopie und Bedurfnis*; *Wunderwirtschaft*.

CHAPTER 8

1. Dennis L. Bark and David R. Gress, *A History of West Germany*, 2 vols. (Cambridge, Mass.: Blackwell, 1993), 1:30.

2. Theodore H. White, *Fire in the Ashes: Europe in Mid-Century* (New York: William Sloane Associates, 1953), 140.

3. National Archives, Plans and Operations Division Decimal File 1946–1948, Record Group 319 (P&O 430 section III case 30), "Report on Agricultural & Food Requirements," 1. Cited hereafter as NA.

4. "Alles in den Möhrenbach: Frau Wirthmueller hat auch Typhus," *Der Spiegel*, July 10, 1948, 8.

5. Wolf-Arno Kropat, *Hessen in der Stunde Null 1945/1947* (Wiesbaden: Selbstverlag der Historischen Kommission für Nassau, 1979), 209.

6. *Hamburger Freie Presse*, April 10, 1946, cited in *Das gespaltene Land: Leben in Deutschland 1945–1990: Texte und Dokumente zur Sozialgeschichte*, ed. Christoph Kleßmann and Georg Wagner (Munich: Verlag C. H. Beck, 1993), 73.

7. Thomas Berger and Karl-Heinz Müller, *Lebenssituationen 1945–1948: Materialien zum Alltagsleben in den westlichen Besatzungszonen 1945–1948* (Hannover: Niedersächsischen Landeszentrale für Politische Bildung, 1983), 57.

8. See NA/OMGUS: Information Services Division, Opinion Surveys Branch—Records Relating to Public Opinion/RG 260, "A Study of Food Consumption and Attitudes Toward Rationing and General Health of the German Population," Report 18 (August 14, 1946), results noted on p. 6.

9. Rainer Gries, *Die Rationen-Gesellschaft: Versorgungskampf und Vergleichsmentalität: Leipzig, München, und Köln nach dem Kriege* (Münster: Verlag Westfälisches Dampfboot, 1991), 94.

10. Edward N. Peterson, *Russian Commands and German Resistance: The Soviet Occupation, 1945–1949* (New York: Peter Lang, 1999), 36.

11. Mary Fulbrook, *The Divided Nation: A History of Germany 1918–1990* (New York: Oxford University Press, 1992), 165.

12. Martin Schnitzer, *East and West Germany: A Comparative Economic Analysis* (New York: Praeger Publishers, 1972), 309–10.

13. Bark and Gress, *A History of West Germany*, 1: 215.

14. Ingrid Schenk, *From Calories to Kidney-Shaped Tables: Consumerism and the Constitution of West German National Identity, 1945–65* (Ann Arbor: University of Michigan Microfilms, 1996), 40.

15. Berger and Müller, *Lebenssituationen 1945–1948*, 106–7.

16. This reconstruction of a conversation between Erhard and an angry U.S. army colonel according to Edwin Hartrich, *The Fourth and Richest Reich* (New York: Macmillan Publishing Co., Inc., 1980), 13.

17. " 'Frau Schäfer geht einkaufen,' " Der Bund/Gewerkschaftsstimme (July 31, 1948) cited in Kleßmann and Wagner, *Das gespaltene Land*, 177.

18. In the Soviet Zone, the state accumulated the gains from owning property, as did private individuals in the western zones.

19. "Das Leben ist mager in der Ostzone," *Süddeutsche Zeitung*, September 4, 1948, 3.

20. Ibid.

21. Ibid.

22. "Das gibt bei uns zu Hause nicht," *Quick*, January 9, 1949, 5.

23. Ibid., 7.

24. See "Käuferwünsche und Ladenhüter: Unverkäufliche Lebensmittel und Kleidungsstücke: Niemand will 'Jedermann,' " *Süddeutsche Zeitung*, August 18, 1949, 6.

25. "Das gibt bei uns zu Hause nicht," *Quick*, January 9, 1949, 6.

26. Ibid., 7.

27. " . . . davon haben wir alle den Vorteil," *Süddeutsche Zeitung*, July 18, 1953, 3.

28. Erhard lifted most ration and price controls on June 24, 1948, but a law designed to check excessively high pricing was passed on October 7, 1948. Prices were a key issue during the general strike on November 12, 1948, and discussion about price controls persisted into the 1950s.

29. " . . . davon haben wir alle den Vorteil," *Süddeutsche Zeitung*, July 18, 1953, 3.

30. Alan Kramer, *The West German Economy, 1945–1955* (New York: Berg Publishers, Ltd., 1991), 147.

31. Charles D. King and Mark van de Vall, *Models of Industrial Democracy: Consultation, Co-determination and Workers' Management* (New York: Mouton Publishers, 1978), 80.

32. Kramer, *West German Economy*, 217.

33. Marshall Dill, Jr., *Germany: A Modern History* (Ann Arbor: University of Michigan Press, 1970), 459.

34. "Mohrrüben sind in Leipzig eine Seltenheit," *Süddeutsche Zeitung*, May 8, 1953, 3.

35. "Gisela kann wieder lachen: Aber wer hilft den anderen Kindern?" *Stern*, March 22, 1953, 5.

36. Ibid., 4.

37. Ibid.

38. Ibid.

39. "Für die Kleinen:/Im Westen: zum Lachen/Im Osten: Zum Weinen" *Stern,* November 30, 1952, 18.

40. Ibid.

41. Ibid.

42. *Quick,* November 18, 1951, 1583.

43. For an extended discussion of the parameters of this debate, see Robert G. Moeller, *Protecting Motherhood: Women and the Family in the Politics of Postwar West Germany* (Berkeley: University of California Press, 1993).

44. For another example of the same theme, see "Mädchen ohne Uniform: Vier Volkspolizistinnen werden wieder frauen," *Stern,* August 26, 1951, 7. This feature listed the escape sagas of four former East German People's Policewomen, who were depicted both in their uniforms and, at the bottom left corner of the page, wearing dresses and drinking coffee at Berlin's Cafe Kranzler.

45. "Eine Büchse Schmalz ist eine Tagereise Wert," *Süddeutsche Zeitung,* July 28, 1953, 3.

46. Ibid.

47. "Schlaraffenland für Kauflustige: Massen-Andrang am ersten Tag des Sommerschluß-Verkaufs/Gefüllte Vororts-Züge," *Süddeutsche Zeitung,* July 28, 1953, 4.

48. Ibid.

49. Dill, *Germany: A Modern History,* 460.

50. "Des roten Ostens goldener Westen," *Stern,* November 24, 1963, 25.

51. Ibid.

52. Ibid.

53. See Elisabeth Pfeil, *Die Berufstätigkeit von Müttern: Eine empirisch-soziologische Erhebung an 900 Müttern aus vollständigen Familien* (Tübingen: J. C. B. Mohr, 1961), 113.

54. Ute Frevert, *Frauen-Geschichte Zwischen Bürgerlicher Verbesserung und Neuer Weiblichkeit* (Frankfurt: Suhrkamp, 1986), 256.

55. Pfeil, *Die Berufstätigkeit von Müttern,* 113.

56. Franz von Nesselrode, *Germany's other Half: A Journalist's Appraisal of East Germany* (New York: Abelard-Schuman, 1963), 59. Here Nesselrode seems to describe a phenomenon analogous to the West German "eating wave" that took place during the late 1940s.

CHAPTER 9

Portions of this essay were first published in my "The Twilight of the Idols: East German Memory and Material Culture," *Journal of Modern History* 72, no. 4 (2000): 731–65. Adapted by permission from The University of Chicago Press. © 2000 by The University of Chicago. All rights reserved. I thank Greg Eghigian, Dagmar Herzog, Peter Fritzsche, and Alon Confino for their constructive criticism.

1. Konrad Jarausch, "Normalization or Renationalization?" in *Rewriting the German Past: History and Identity in the New Germany,* ed. Reinhart Alter and

Peter Monteath (Atlantic Highlands, N.J.: Humanities Press, 1998), 23–39; and Stefan Berger, "Historians and Nation-Building in Germany after Reunification," *Past and Present* 148 (August 1995): 187–222.

2. Among the most important are Elizabeth A. Ten Dyke, "Tulips in December: Space, Time and Consumption before and after the End of German Socialism," *German History* 19, no. 2 (2001): 253–76; Daphne Berdahl, *Where the World Ended: Reunification and Identity in the German Borderland* (Berkeley: University of California Press, 1999); John Borneman, *Belonging in Two Berlins: Kin, State, Nation* (Cambridge: Cambridge University Press, 1992); Konrad Jarausch, ed., *Dictatorship as Experience: Toward a Socio-Cultural History of the GDR* (New York: Berghahn, 1999); and Lutz Niethammer et al., *Die eigene Volkerfahrung: Eine Archäologie des Lebens in der Industrieprovinz der DDR* (Berlin: Rowohlt, 1991).

3. A useful set of essays devoted to the theme is *History of Everyday Life: Reconstructing Historical Experiences and Ways of Life*, ed. Alf Lüdtke, trans. William Templer (Princeton: Princeton University Press, 1995).

4. George Rosen, "Nostalgia, a Forgotten Psychological Disorder," *Psychological Medicine* 5, no. 4 (1974): 340–54.

5. Volker Fischer, *Nostalgie: Geschichte und Kultur als Trödelmarkt* (Lucerne: C. J. Bucher, 1980), 9–15.

6. Peter Fritzsche, "How Nostalgia Narrates Modernity," in *The Work of Memory: New Directions in the Study of German Society and Culture*, ed. Alon Confino and Peter Fritzsche (Urbana: University of Illinois Press, 2002).

7. Heide Fehrenbach, *Cinema in Democratizing Germany: Reconstructing National Identity after Hitler* (Chapel Hill: University of North Carolina Press, 1993), ch. 3; Rudy Koshar, *Germany's Transient Pasts* (Chapel Hill: University of North Carolina Press, 1998), 209–88; and Dagmar Herzog, "'Pleasure, Sex and Politics Belong Together': Post-Holocaust Memory and the Sexual Revolution in West Germany," *Critical Inquiry* 24 (winter 1998): 393–444.

8. Fischer, *Nostalgie*, 15, 253.

9. Ulrich Herbert, "Good Times, Bad Times: Memories of the Third Reich," in *Life in the Third Reich*, ed. Richard Bessel (Oxford: Oxford University Press, 1987), 97–110.

10. Charles Maier, "The End of Longing? (Notes Toward a History of Postwar German National Longing)," in *The Postwar Transformation of Germany: Democracy, Prosperity and Nationhood*, ed. John Brady, Beverly Crawford, and Sarah Elise Wiliarty (Ann Arbor: University of Michigan Press, 1999), 276.

11. Winfried Schultze, *Deutsche Geschichtswissenschaft nach 1945* (Munich: Oldenburg, 1989).

12. Sylvia Tannenbaum and Diane Spielmann, *A Sense of Loss and Nostalgia: Encounters with the German-Jewish Past and Present* (Cincinnati: American Jewish Archives, 1992). The relationship between the exile and the "loathing and longing" toward the German past was particularly poignant in the legend of the "Golden 1920s." See Peter Gay, *Weimar Culture: The Outsider as Insider* (New York: Harper & Row, 1968), xiii–xiv.

13. Charles Maier, *The Unmasterable Past* (Cambridge, Mass.: Harvard

University Press, 1989); Richard Evans, *In Hitler's Shadow* (New York: Pantheon, 1989); Geoffrey Hartman, ed., *Bitburg in Moral and Political Perspective* (Bloomington: Indiana University Press, 1986); and Saul Friedländer, *Reflections on Nazism: An Essay on Kitsch and Death* (Bloomington: Indiana University Press, 1984).

14. Nikolaus Jungwirth and Gerhard Kromschröder, *Die Pubertät der Republik: Die 50er Jahre der Deutschen* (Frankfurt: Dieter Fricke, 1978).

15. "Heimweh nach den falschen Fünfzigern," *Der Spiegel* 32, no. 14, April 3, 1978, 90–114; and "Mit Pepita voll im Trend: Der neue Kult um die 50er Jahre," *Der Spiegel* 38, no. 14, April 3, 1984, 230–38. See also another piece on the revival of 1950s film and television, "Der Neger unterm Gummibaum," *Der Spiegel* 38, no. 2, January 9, 1984, 129–30. Perceptive comments can be found in Axel Schildt, *Moderne Zeiten: Freizeit, Massenmedien und 'Zeitgeist' der 50er Jahre* (Hamburg: Christians, 1995), introduction.

16. This was especially the case in the United States. See Richard Horn, *Fifties Style: Then and Now* (Bromley: Columbus Books, 1985); and Mark Burns and Louis DiBonnis, *Fifties Homestyle: Popular Ornament of the USA* (London: Thames & Hudson, 1988).

17. Rainer Gries, Volker Ilgen, and Dirk Schindelbeck, *Gestylte Geschichte: Vom alltäglichen Umgang mit Geschichtsbildern* (Muenster: Verlag Westfälisches Dampfboot, 1989), 132–35.

18. This is the subtitle of Fischer's wide-ranging book on nostalgia cited above.

19. Albrecht Bangert, *Die 50er Jahre: Möbel und Ambiente, Design und Kunsthandwerk* (Munich: Wilhelm Heyne, 1983).

20. Marianne Bernhard and Angela and Andreas Hopf, eds., *Unsere Fünfziger Jahre: Eine Bunte Chronik* (Munich: Wilhelm Heyne, 1984), 6; and Dieter Franck, ed., *Die fünfziger Jahre: Als das Leben wider anfing* (Munich: R. Piper, 1981), 28.

21. "Die Sehnsucht nach den 50er Jahre," *Quick* 44 (1983), quoted in Schildt, *Moderne Zeiten*, 18.

22. Useful corrective histories can be found in Arne Andersen, *Der Traum vom guten Leben: Alltags- und Konsumgeschichte vom Wirtschaftswunder bis heute* (Frankfurt: Campus, 1997); Michael Wildt, *Vom kleinen Wohlstand: Eine Konsumgeschichte der 50er Jahre* (Frankfurt: Fischer, 1996); Ilona Stölken-Fitschen, *Atombombe und Geistesgeschichte: Eine Studie der fünfziger Jahre aus deutscher Sicht* (Baden-Baden: Nomos-Verlagsgesellschaft, 1995); and Klaus Voy, Werner Polster, and Claus Thomasberger, *Gesellschaftliche Transformationenprozesse und materielle Lebensweise* (Marburg: Metropoli-Verlag, 1993).

23. Angela Delille et al., eds., *Perlonzeit: Wie die Frauen ihr Wirtschaftswunder erlebten,* (Berlin: Elefanten, 1985); Angela Delille and Andrea Grohn, *Blick zurück aufs Glück: Frauenleben und Familienpolitik in den 50er Jahren* (Berlin: Elefanten Press, 1985), introduction. Also, Anna-Elisabeth Freier and Annette Kuhn, eds., *Frauen in der Geschichte V: Das Schicksal Deutschlands liegt in der Hand seiner Frauen: Frauen in der Nachkriegsgeschichte* (Düsseldorf: Schwann, 1984).

24. Herzog, "'Pleasure, Sex and Politics,'" 398–99.

25. Hans-Peter Schwarz, *Die Ära Adenauer* (Stuttgart: Deutsche Verlagsanstalt, 1981–83), 383–88.

26. *Fifty-Fifty: Formen und Farben der 5oer Jahre* (Darmstadt: Arnold'sche Verlag, 1988), 12, 14–15.

27. Heinz Friedrich, ed., *Mein Kopfgeld: Die Währungsreform—Rückblick nach vier Jahrzehnten* (Munich: Deutscher Taschenbuch, 1988); and Martin Broszat et al., eds., *Von Stalingrad zur Währungsreform: Zur Sozialgeschichte des Umbruchs in Deutschland* (Munich: Oldenbourg, 1987).

28. Christian Borngräber, "Nierentisch und Schrippendale: Hinweise auf Architektur und Design," in *Die Fünfziger Jahre: Beiträge zu Politik und Kultur*, ed. Dieter Bänsch (Tübingen: Günther Narr, 1985), 210–41.

29. An excellent example is Inge Scholl, "Eine neue Gründerzeit und ihre Gebrauchskunst," in *Bestandsaufnahme*, ed. Hans Werner Richter (Munich: Kurt Desch, 1962), 421–27.

30. Christian Borngräber, *Stilnovo: Design in den 5oer Jahren* (Frankfurt: Fricke, 1979).

31. Schildt, *Moderne Zeiten*, 20.

32. Paul Betts, "The Nierentisch Nemesis: Organic Design as West German Pop Culture," *German History* 19, no. 2 (2001): 185–217.

33. Götz Eisenberg and Hans-Jürgen Linke, eds., *Die Fuffziger Jahre* (Giessen: Focus-Verlag, 1979), 7.

34. Michael Schneider, "Fathers and Sons, Retrospectively: The Damaged Relationship between Two Generations," *New German Critique* 31 (1984): 3–51.

35. Sigrid Wachenfeld, *Unsere wunderlichen fünfziger Jahre* (Düsseldorf: Droste, 1987); Horst Heidtmann, ed., *Das ist mein Land: 40 Jahre Bundesrepublik Deutschland*(Baden-Baden: Signal-Verlag, 1988).

36. Detlev Peukert, *Inside Nazi Germany*, trans. Richard Deveson (New Haven: Yale University Press, 1987), 242. The same point is made in Lutz Niethammer, '*Hinterher merkt man, daß es richtig war, daß es schiefgegangen ist*': *Nachkriegs-erinnerungen im Ruhrgebiet* (Berlin: J. H. W. Dietz Nachf., 1983), 17–106; and Simon Reich, *The Fruits of Fascism* (Ithaca: Cornell University Press, 1990).

37. Michael Wildt, "Changes in Consumption as Social Practice in West Germany during the 1950s," in *Getting and Spending: European and American Consumer Societies in the Twentieth Century*, ed. Susan Strasser et al. (Cambridge: Cambridge University Press, 1998), 301–16.

38. Michael Geyer, "Germany, or the Twentieth Century as History," *South Atlantic Quarterly* 96 (fall 1997): 663–702.

39. For example, Fritz Ringer, *The Decline of the German Mandarins* (Cambridge, Mass.: Harvard University Press, 1969).

40. Harold James, *A German Identity, 1770–1990* (New York: Routledge, 1989), 177–209.

41. Hermann Glaser, *Die Kulturgeschichte der Bundesrepublik Deutschland*, Bd. 2: *1949–67* (Frankfurt: Fischer, 1990), 162–77.

42. Sample titles include Arnold Gehlen, *Man in the Age of Technology*, trans.

Patricia Lipscomb (1957; reprinted, New York: Columbia University Press, 1980); Hans Freyer, *Theorie des gegenwärtigen Zeitalters* (Stuttgart: Deutsche Verlagsanstalt, 1955); Hans Sedlmayr, *Die Verlust der Mitte* (Salzburg: O. Müller, 1947); and Friedrich Sieburg, *Die Lust am Untergang* (Hamburg: Rowohlt, 1954).

43. Max Horkheimer and Theodor Adorno, *Dialectic of Enlightenment*, trans. John Cummings (1947; reprinted, New York: Seabury Press, 1972).

44. Jürgen Habermas, "Notizen zum Mißverständnis von Kultur und Konsum," *Merkur* 10, (March 1956): 212–28; and his *The Structural Transformation of the Public Sphere*, trans. Thomas Burger (1957; reprint, Cambridge, Mass.: MIT Press, 1989); Hans Magnus Enzensberger, *Einzelheiten I/II* (Frankfurt: Suhrkamp, 1962–64); as well as the essays collected in *Bestandsaufnahme*, ed. Hans Werner Richter (Munich: Kurt Desch, 1962).

45. Alexander and Margarete Mitscherlich, *Die Unfähigkeit zu trauern: Grundlagen kollektiven Verhaltens* (1967; reprint, Munich: R. Piper, 1977), 19.

46. See also Adorno's famous essay, "Was bedeutet: Aufarbeitung der Vergangenheit?" in his *Eingriffe: Neun kritische Modelle* (Frankfurt: Fischer, 1963), 141. The idea also colors some recent accounts of the postwar period. See also Hermann Glaser, *Kulturgeschichte der Bundesrepublik Deutschland, Bd. 1 1945–1948* (Frankfurt: Fischer, 1985), 20.

47. In any case, such "Coca-Colonization" literature is by no means extinct. See Reinhold Wagnleitner, *Coca-Colonization and the Cold War: The Cultural Mission of the United States in Austria after the Second World War* (Chapel Hill: University of North Carolina Press, 1994); Ralph Willett, *The Americanization of Germany, 1945–1949* (London: Routledge, 1989); and Jost Hermand, *Kultur im Wiederaufbau: Die Bundesrepublik Deutschland, 1945–1965* (Berlin: Ullstein, 1989). For a more balanced assessment, see Arnold Sywottek, "The Americanization of Everyday Life? Early Trends in Consumer and Leisure-Time Behavior," in *America and the Shaping of German Society, 1945–1955*, ed. Michael Ermarth (Oxford: Berg, 1993), 132–52.

48. Christian Zentner, *Illustrierte Geschichte der Ära Adenauer* (Munich: Südwest Verlag, 1984); Frank Grube and Gerhard Richter, *Das Wirtschaftswunder: Unser Weg in der Wohlstand* (Hamburg: Hoffmann und Campe, 1983); Eckhard Siepmann, ed., *Bikini: Die Fünfziger Jahre* (Reinbek bei Hamburg: Rowohlt, 1983); and Bernhard Schulz, ed., *Grauzonen Farbwelten: Kunst und Zeitbilder, 1945–1955* (Berlin: NGBK, 1983).

49. Wolfgang Benz, ed., *Die Geschichte der Bundesrepublik Deutschland, Bd. 4: Kultur* (Frankfurt: Fischer, 1989), 8–11. More generally, see Joan Campbell, *Joy in Work, German Work: The National Debate, 1800–1945* (Princeton: Princeton University Press, 1989); and Anson Rabinbach, *The Human Motor: Energy, Fatigue and the Origins of Modernity* (New York: Basic Books, 1990), conclusion.

50. Kaspar Maase, "Freizeit," in *Die Geschichte der Bundesrepublik Deutschland, Bd. 3: Gesellschaft*, ed. Wolfgang Benz (Frankfurt: Fischer, 1989), 345–83.

51. Werner Abelshauser, *Wirtschaftsgeschichte der Bundesrepublik Deutschland, 1945–1980* (Frankfurt: Suhrkamp, 1983), 6, 8.

52. Michael Wildt, *Am Beginn der Konsumgesellschaft* (Hamburg: Ergebnisse,

1994); Axel Schildt and Arnold Sywottek, eds., *Modernisierung im Wiederaufbau* (Bonn: J. H. W. Dietz Nachf., 1993); and Ursula Becher, *Geschichte des modernen Lebensstil* (Munich: CH Beck, 1990).

53. Friedrich Nietzsche, *On the Genealogy of Morals*, trans. Walter Kaufmann and R. J. Hollingdale (New York: Random House, 1967), 61.

54. The post-1989 success of East Germany's Reformed Communist Party, or PDS, has often been seen as its consummate expression. See Christian von Ditfurth, *Ostalgie, oder linke Alternative: Meine Reise durch die PDS* (Cologne: Kieperhauer & Witsch, 1998).

55. Marc Fischer, *After the Fall: Germany, the Germans and the Burdens of History* (New York: Simon & Schuster, 1995), 144.

56. Jonathan Osmond, "The End of the GDR: Revolution or Voluntary Annexation," in *German History since 1800*, ed. Mary Fulbrook (London: Arnold, 1997), 454–72.

57. Alan Nothnagle, "From Buchenwald to Bismarck: Historical Myth-Making in the German Democratic Republic, 1945–1989," *Central European History* 26, no. 1 (1993): 91–113.

58. Jürgen Habermas, "Der DM-Nationalismus," *Die Zeit*, March 30, 1990.

59. *Plötzlich war alles ganz anders*, ed. Olaf Georg Klein (Cologne: Kiepenhauer & Witsch, 1994); Dirk Philipsen, *We Were the People: Voices from East Germany's Revolutionary Autumn of 1989* (Durham: Duke University Press, 1993); Niethammer et al., *Die volkseigene Erfahrung*; and Hans Meyer, *Der Turm von Babel: Erinnerung an eine Deutsche Demokratische Republik* (Frankfurt: Suhrkamp, 1991).

60. Hermann Schäfer, "Alltagsgeschichte im geteilten Deutschland: Zur Konzeption und Darstellung um Haus der Geschichte der Bundesrepublik Deutschland," in *Probleme der Musealisierung der doppelten Nachkriegsgeschichte*, ed. Bernd Faulenbach and Franz-Josef Jelich (Essen: Klartext, 1993), 47–53.

61. Georg Bertsch and Ernst Hedler, *SED: Schönes Einheit Design* (Cologne: Taschen, 1994), 7, 27.

62. Gert Selle, "Die verlorene Unschuld der Armut: Über das Verschwinden einer Kulturdifferenz," in *Vom Bauhaus bis Bitterfeld: 41 Jahre DDR-Design*, ed. Regine Halter (Giessen: Anabas, 1991), 54–66.

63. Hans-Joachim Maaz, *Behind the Wall: The Inner Life of Communist Germany*, trans. Margot Bettauer Dembo (New York: Norton, 1995), 86. According to another observer, "West German empty shampoo bottles were lined up in [East German] bathrooms like icons for guests to see." See Ina Merkel, "Consumer Culture in the GDR, or How the Struggle for Antimodernity was Lost on the Battleground of Consumer Culture," in *Getting and Spending: European and American Consumer Societies in the Twentieth Century*, ed. Susan Strasser, Charles McGovern, and Matthias Judt (Cambridge: Cambridge University Press, 1998), 284.

64. *Der Spiegel* 50, December 11, 1989.

65. Marc Fischer, *After the Fall*, 146–48.

66. Ulrich Becker, Horst Becker, and Walter Ruhland, *Zwischen Angst und Aufbruch: Das Lebensgefühl der Deutschen in Ost und West nach der Wiedervereinigung* (Düsseldorf: Econ Verlag, 1992), 56.

67. Ralf Bartolomäus, "Gegenstand, mein Liebling," in *Von Bauhaus bis Bitterfeld: 41-Jahre DDR-Design*, ed. Regine Halter (Giessen: Anabas, 1991), 47.

68. Merkel, "Consumer Culture in the GDR," 297.

69. Rainer Gries, "Der Geschmack der Heimat: 'Hurra, ich lebe noch!' Bausteine zu einer Mentalitätsgeschichte der Ostprodukte nach der Wende," in *Ins Gehirn der Masse kriechen! Werbung und Mentalitätsgeschichte*, ed. Rainer Gries et al. (Darmstadt: Wissenschaftliche Buchgesellschaft, 1995), 193–214.

70. Andreas Kämper and Reinhard Ulbrich, *Wir und unser Trabant* (Berlin: Rowohlt, 1995); Gündrun Brandenburg, "Die Treue kommt oft zu spät: Was nach der Wende auf dem Sperrmüll landete, ist heute Objekt nostalgischer Begierden, *Berliner Morgenpost*, May 7, 1993; Anke Westphal, "Mein wunderbarer Plattenbau, Hoppla, Wir Leben Noch," *Die Tageszeitung*, August 25, 1995, 15–16; *Mit uns zieht die neue Zeit: 40 Jahre DDR-Medien*, ed. Heide Riedel (Berlin: Vistas Verlag, 1994); *DDR Souvenirs*, ed. Andreas Michaelis (Cologne: Taschen, 1994); and Gries, "Der Geschmack der Heimat," 193–214.

71. Anna Mulrine, "Icon Faces a Crossroads," *U.S. News and World Report*, February 2, 1998, 8.

72. Lutz Niethammer, "Erfahrungen und Strukturen: Prolegomena zu einer Geschichte der Gesellschaft der DDR," in *Sozialgeschichte der DDR*, ed. Hartmut Kaelble, Jürgen Kocka, and Hartmut Zwahr (Stuttgart: Klett-Cotta, 1994), 110.

73. *Wunderwirtschaft: DDR Konsumkultur in den 60er Jahren*, ed. Neue Gesellschaft für Bildende Kunst (Cologne: Boehlau, 1996).

74. Even so, rationing for meat, eggs, and butter was provisionally reintroduced in 1962. Jeffrey Kopstein, *The Politics of Economic Decline in East Germany, 1945–1989* (Chapel Hill: University of North Carolina Press, 1996), 48.

75. Ina Merkel, "Der aufhaltsame Aufbruch in die Konsumgesellschaft," *Wunderwirtschaft*, 8–20.

76. By 1967 35 percent of East Germans owned refrigerators, while 46 percent had washing machines.

77. Merkel, "Der aufhaltsame Aufbruch," 12.

78. Testimony resides in Lutz Niethammer's oral history of older workers in the GDR's industrial provinces, whose principal complaint was the poor supply of food and consumer durables. See Niethammer et al., *Die volkseigene Erfahrung*, 9–73.

79. Jonathan Zatlin, "The Vehicle of Desire: The Trabant, the Wartburg and the End of the GDR," *German History* 15, no. 3 (1997): 360–61, 380.

80. An excellent example is Andreas Ludwig, ed., *Tempolinsen und P2: Alltagskultur der DDR* (Berlin: Be-Bra, 1996).

81. Alf Lüdtke, " 'Helden der Arbeit'—Mühen beim Arbeit: Zur missmütigen Loyalität von Industriearbeitern in der DDR," in *Sozialgeschichte der DDR*, 188–213.

82. Iris Czak, "Spitzname Elvis: Interview mit Schorsch T.," in *Wunderwirtschaft*, 194. See also Jörg Engelhardt, *Schwalbe Duo Kultmobil: Vom Acker auf dem Boulevard* (Berlin: Be-Bra, 1995), 7ff.

83. Heinz Bude, "Schicksal," in his edited *Deutschland spricht: Schicksale der Neunziger* (Berlin: Berlin Verlag, 1995), 7–12.

84. Ina Merkel, . . . *Und Du, Frau an der Werkbank: Die DDR in den 50er Jahren* (Berlin: Elefanten Press, 1990); for a far-reaching discussion of changed power and status of women after 1989, see *Women and the Wende: Social Effects and Cultural Reflection of the German Reunification Process*, ed. Elizabeth Boa and Janet Wharton (Amsterdam: Rodopi, 1994).

85. Charles Maier, *Dissolution: The Crisis of Communism and End of the East Germany* (Princeton: Princeton University Press, 1997), 39.

86. Merkel, "Consumer Culture in the GDR," 296.

87. *Transatlantische   Unsicherheiten: Die   amerikanisch-europäischen Beziehungen im Umbruch*, ed. Bernd Kubbig (Frankfurt: Fischer, 1991); Jeffrey Herf, *War By Other Means: Soviet Power, West German Resistance and the Battle of the Euromissile* (New York: Free Press, 1991); Fritz Stern, *Dreams and Delusions: National Socialism in the Drama of the German Past* (New York: Vintage, 1987), 219–40; Charles Maier, *The Unmasterable Past: History, Holocaust and German National Identity* (Cambridge, Mass.: Harvard University Press, 1988), 121–59; and Michael Geyer, "Looking Back at the International Style: Some Reflections on the Current State of German History," *German Studies Review* 13, no. 1 (1990): 112–27.

88. Kaspar Maase, *Bravo Amerika* (Hamburg: Junius, 1992); Jennifer A. Loehlin, *From Rugs to Riches: Housework, Consumption and Modernity in Germany* (Oxford: Berg, 1999); and Uta Poiger, *Jazz, Rock and Rebels: Cold War Politics and American Culture in a Divided Germany* (Berkeley: University of California Press, 2000).

89. So much so that East Germans have even reclaimed the subversive pirating of West German and American consumer habits—especially for 1960s youth culture—as elements of a lost GDR idiom. See Gerlinde Irmscher, "Der Westen im Ost-Alltag: DDR-Jugendkultur in den sechziger Jahren," in *Wunderwirtschaft*, 185–93.

90. Quoted in Zatlin, "Vehicle of Desire," 358.

91. Nowhere was this prohibition more symbolically rendered than in the studied selection of "humility" (*Bescheidenheit*) as the central theme of the West German Pavilion at the 1958 World Exposition in Brussels, which was aimed to counter both former Nazi megalomania and postwar swagger about the country's enviable postwar economic development. See G. B. von Hartmann and Wend Fischer, eds., *Deutschland: Beitrag zur Weltausstellung Brussel 1958: Ein Bericht* (Düsseldorf: Nordwestdeutsche Ausstellungs-Gesellschaft, 1958), 9.

92. Gries et al., *Gestylte Geschichte*, 62.

93. Axel Eggebrecht, ed., *Die zornigen alten Männer: Gedanken über Deutschland seit 1945* (Reinbek bei Hamburg: Rowohlt, 1987), 18ff; quoted in Gries, *Gestylte Geschichte*, 76.

94. Andreas Huyssen, "After the Wall: The Failure of German Intellectuals," in his *Twilight Memories* (New York: Routledge, 1995), 38.

95. Most recently, *Das Kollektiv bin ich: Utopie und Alltag in der DDR*, ed. Franziska Becker, Ina Merkel, and Simone Tippach-Schneider (Cologne: Böhlau, 2000); and *Fortschritt, Norm und Eigensinn: Erkundungen im Alltag der DDR*,

ed. Dokumentationszentrum Alltagskultur der DDR, e.V. (Berlin: Ch. Links, 1999).

96. For very different views on the subject, See Eric Hobsbawm, *The Age of Extremes* (New York: Random House, 1994), 142–77; and Francois Furet, *The Passing of an Illusion*, trans. Deborah Furet (Chicago: University of Chicago Press, 1999), 209–315.

97. Tony Judt, "1989: The End of Which Europe?" *Daedalus* 123, no. 3 (1994): 5.

98. Michael Rutschky, "Wie erst jetzt die DDR entsteht," *Merkur* 9/10 (1995): 851–64.

99. Hans Aichinger, "Vom Ende der Nachkriegszeit," *Merkur* 21 (1967): 201–11.

100. Gert Schaefer and Carl Nedelmann, eds., *Der CDU-Staat* (Munich: Szczensy, 1967); and Karl Bracher, ed., *Nach 25 Jahren: Eine Deutschland-Bilanz* (Munich: Kindler, 1970).

101. Susan Sontag, "Fascinating Fascism," in her *Under the Sign of Saturn* (New York: Farrar, Straus & Giroux, 1980), 73–105; Rolf Steinberg, ed., *Nazi-Kitsch* (Darmstadt: Melzer, 1975); and Fischer, *Nostalgie*, 30ff, 214.

102. Friedländer, *On Kitsch and Death*; and Eric Rentschler, *Ministry of Illusion: Nazi Cinema and its Afterlife* (Cambridge: Harvard University Press, 1996), 1–24.

103. Alon Confino, "Edgar Reitz's *Heimat* and German Nationhood: Film, Memory and Understandings of the Past," *German History* 16, no. 2 (1998): 185–208.

104. At first glance the 1986 "historians' debate" may seem just another installment in the same revisionist story. After all, it too was motivated by historian Ernst Nolte's bold right-wing attempt to "relativize" the Holocaust by arguing that it was both defensive and hardly unique, having owed its roots and causes to Stalin's Gulag. The crucial difference, however, was that Nolte's scandalous thesis was summarily refuted by other historians and the public alike, thus representing in many ways the real swansong of the antifascist consensus.

105. Michael Geyer and Miriam Hansen, "German-Jewish Memory and National Consciousness," in *Holocaust Remembrance: Shapes of Memory*, ed. Geoffrey Hartman (Cambridge: Basil Blackwell, 1994), 175–90; and Siegfried Zielinski, "History as Entertainment and Provocation: The TV Series 'Holocaust' in West Germany," in *Germans and Jews Since the Holocaust*, ed. Anson Rabinbach and Jack Zipes (New York: Holmes & Meyer, 1986), 258–83.

Index